BEYOND THE MARKET

Jens Beckert

BEYOND THE MARKET

THE SOCIAL FOUNDATIONS OF ECONOMIC EFFICIENCY

Translated by Barbara Harshav

PRINCETON UNIVERSITY PRESS

PRINCETON AND OXFORD

ENGLISH TRANSLATION COPYRIGHT © 2002 BY PRINCETON UNIVERSITY PRESS

PUBLISHED BY PRINCETON UNIVERSITY PRESS, 41 WILLIAM STREET,

PRINCETON, NEW JERSEY 08540

IN THE UNITED KINGDOM: PRINCETON UNIVERSITY PRESS,

3 MARKET PLACE, WOODSTOCK, OXFORDSHIRE OX20 1SY

ORIGINALLY PUBLISHED IN GERMAN AS *GRENZEN DES MARKTES:*

DIE SOZIALEN GRUNDLAGEN WIRTSCHAFTLICHER EFFIZIENZ

© 1997 BY CAMPUS VERLAG

LIBRARY OF CONGRESS CATALOGING-IN-PUBLICATION DATA

BECKERT, JENS, 1967– [GRENZEN DES MARKTES. ENGLISH]

BEYOND THE MARKET: THE SOCIAL FOUNDATIONS OF ECONOMIC

EFFICIENCY / JENS BECKERT; TRANSLATED BY BARBARA HARSHAV.

P. CM.

ORIGINALLY PUBLISHED AS: GRENZEN DES MARKTES.

INCLUDES BIBLIOGRAPHICAL REFERENCES AND INDEX.

ISBN 0-691-04907-6

1. ECONOMICS—SOCIOLOGICAL ASPECTS. 2. DECISION MAKING—SOCIAL ASPECTS. I.

TITLE.

HM548.B43613 2002

306.3'4—DC21   2001058064

BRITISH LIBRARY CATALOGING-IN-PUBLICATION DATA IS AVAILABLE

THIS BOOK HAS BEEN COMPOSED IN BERKELEY BOOK MODIFIED TYPEFACE

PRINTED ON ACID-FREE PAPER. ∞

WWW.PUP.PRINCETON.EDU

PRINTED IN THE UNITED STATES OF AMERICA

1 3 5 7 9 10 8 6 4 2

CONTENTS

PREFACE

THIS BOOK began in a seminar given by Robert Heilbroner and Ross Thompson at the New School for Social Research in the autumn of 1990. Titled "The Autonomy of Economic Life," the seminar examined the relationship of the economy and society as well as that of economics and other social sciences. Ever since then, I have been interested in these subjects. I am grateful first to Hans Joas, who supervised the work, encouraging the clarification of conceptual issues. In many respects, my thinking has been deeply influenced by the work of Hans Joas and our many conversations. I would also like to thank Heiner Ganssmann, Wolfgang Knöbl, Claus Offe, Harald Wenzel, and Dietrich Winterhager, who read the entire book or individual chapters and made helpful remarks. My thanks to the Studienstiftung des deutschen Volkes for financial assistance. I wrote most of the dissertation in the academic year 1994–95 as a Visiting Research Fellow in the Department of Sociology of Princeton University, where the ideal working conditions were an essential advantage for the progress of the book. For making this stay both possible and intellectually stimulating I should like to thank the department, particularly Paul DiMaggio and Viviana Zelizer. I am grateful to the Gottlieb Daimler and Carl Benz Foundation for a stipend during my year in Princeton. Volker Bien, Karin Goihl, and Anne-Christin Muth helped with literature and preparation of the final manuscript. Last but not least, thanks to my wife Farzaneh Alizadeh for all her support during the not always easy phases of the writing process. The book is dedicated to the memory of my father.

Berlin, July 1997

Note: For the English translation, the chapter on Durkheim has been slightly abridged, while some new material has been added to the chapter on Giddens and to the conclusions. The other parts of the manuscript remain unchanged, except for some corrections in the interest of legibility. Permission from Kluwer Publishers for using material from my article "What is sociological about economic sociology? Uncertainty and the embeddedness of economic action" (Theory and Society 25: 803-840) is gratefully acknowledged.

Cambridge, Mass., February 2002

BEYOND THE MARKET

INTRODUCTION

ALTHOUGH sociology and economics have ignored one another for decades, developments in both disciplines during the past twenty years suggest that cautious rapprochements are beginning to crack the solid lines that have separated them. Catch phrases like those advanced by the American economist James Duesenberry (1960: 233)— that "economics is all about how people make choices; sociology is all about how they don't have any choices to make," are no more valid as a description of the relationship between the two fields today than they were when first pronounced.

Ever since the early 1970s, starting from criticism of the restrictive assumptions of the general equilibrium theory and developments in game theory, economics has clearly been opened to problems and subjects that had previously been ascribed essentially to the domain of sociology. These include developments in the economics of information, the transaction cost theory, principal-agent approaches, the new historical economy, and the incorporation of bounded rationality into game theory. No matter how varied these modeling strategies are, they all agree that more consideration should be given to psychological and social constraints, and that studies need to investigate how equilibrium models change when the heroic assumptions of information and structure of the standard models of economics are loosened.

Meanwhile, in the 1960s and 1970s, sociology moved away from functionalist and structuralist theoretical approaches and became increasingly devoted to approaches based on theories of action. Criticism of functionalism led especially to projects intended to make social structures and processes intelligible in reference to social action, without being tied to the rational-actor model for its behavioral typology. On this background, a renewed interest in socioeconomic problems has developed since the 1980s. In the 1950s and 1960s, economic sociology dealt with problems that were marginalized by economics. But the "new economic sociology" claims to be able to demonstrate on the ground of the substantial core areas of economic theory how economic functions can be understood better through sociological conceptualizations. Even though the objectives of the new economic sociology must be seen in the context of the repudiation of economic imperialism, it nevertheless reveals an opening to economics because sociology starts dealing with social phenomena that had long been considered the exclusive domain of economics.

In the mutual debate over the issues and approaches of each other's discipline, sociology and economics intersect. Thus, some of the modeling strategies, especially transaction cost theory and Douglass North's work in the field of economic history, were adopted with critical candor by economic sociology. In economic theory, those approaches also express at least a cautious opening to sociology. Historical data are included along with the possibility of "irrational" action on account of cognitive constraints, and the spread of inefficient equilibria on account of informational limitations, so that the field is partly dissociated from the assumption of universal efficiency of economic institutions.

While these developments in economics and the new economic sociology indicate an entente between the disciplines, they still remain separated from one another at the demarcation line of the rational-actor model. The central assumption of the maximization of utility has been both criticized and expanded by the theory of bounded rationality and by attempts to integrate altruistic behavioral motivations, yet the paradigmatic core of economics is defined by the action-theoretical notion of an individualized, universal maximizer of utility. Ever since the establishment of modern economics in the eighteenth century, the moral-philosophical justification for the behavioral model of *homo oeconomicus* has consisted of the expectation, expressed in the metaphor of the invisible hand, that action directed at self-interest leads to a desirable allocation of economic goods, both collectively and individually. Pursuit of private interest is the basis for the emergence of the common welfare. This link between behavioral expectations and institutional structure is also the basis of liberal economic policy: the demand for unlimited markets by removing trade barriers and restraining government regulation is justified normatively by the expected increase of wealth.

The new economic approaches developed as criticism of equilibrium theory with respect to its assumptions about market structures and the supply of information of market participants. They show that, often, under realistic premises, either no unequivocal equilibria exist or that stable equilibria with inefficient resource allocation develop. This results in market failure. But market failure calls into question the central link of economic theory between rational individual action, unlimited markets, and optimal distribution of economic goods; the claim of the superiority of rational individual action cannot be generally maintained under the more realistic assumptions. The close connection between self-interested action and economic efficiency becomes precarious.

In this book I try to explain how sociology can contribute to understanding the bases of economic efficiency. The decisive consideration here is that the discrepancy of the connection between rational action and efficient results asserted by economic theory forces the revision of the action theory that underlies the understanding of economic action. To substantiate this hypothesis, I shall demonstrate in the first part of the book why the emergence of efficient equilibria cannot be generally explained from the behavioral model of economic theory and, thus, that removing limits on markets does not per se lead to the increase of economic efficiency. Three central action situations can be identified for the functioning of the economy in which economically rational actors either achieve inefficient results or in which no rational strategy for the allocation of resources can be identified. These situations are cooperation, action under conditions of uncertainty, and innovation.

The critical discussion of the first part of the book raises two questions: how we can understand how actors in the three action situations arrive at efficient results, and how they make decisions when they cannot know what the optimal behavioral strategy is. The most important systematic starting point of a sociological concern with the economy is located in these two questions. They are central not only for determining the relationship between sociology and economics but also for the empirical understanding of economic structures and processes in market economies.

In the second part of the book, to get to an answer, I systematically examine conceptions of economic action in the tradition of sociological theory. Ever since sociology was founded, it has used both empirical and theoretical arguments against the economic theory of action and the notion of the emergence of social order from the behavior of actors pursuing their own self-interest. The discussions were linked both to the intensive debate with socioeconomic questions and often to the demand for the limitation of the market. Conceptions of economic sociology in sociological theory are particularly well suited for discovering designs for understanding the three action situations. They also fill a gap in the "new economic sociology," because the significance of considerations of economic sociology, especially in the classics of sociological thought, becomes more accessible in the field.

The choice and order of the concepts of economic sociology discussed are oriented toward the action situations in question. The projects of Émile Durkheim and Talcott Parsons prove to be especially fruitful for understanding cooperative relations but not for the problematics of uncertainty and innovation. On the other hand, Niklas Luhmann's systems theory is especially significant when acquiring the capacity to act under extremely contingent conditions. Yet understanding innovations demands a conception of creative action that can be derived from the new approaches of constitution theory; here works of Anthony Giddens are discussed as an example.

These studies represent debates with individual authors who all engage in the systematic debate of the assumptions of action theory for overcoming the specified limits of the economic model of action in explaining economic efficiency. Parallel to that, I pursue a second line of questioning:

how does consideration of the economy develop in the history of sociological theory? Whereas the debate with economics had a central significance for the founders of the discipline, in modern sociological theory it plays a much smaller role. This development also results in a shift between the four studies: in the investigations of Durkheim and Parsons, their conceptions of economic sociology are central; on the other hand, particularly in the last chapter on Giddens, the systematic aspect of action-theoretical considerations predominates.

Following the four studies, I shall compile the products of the analyses and discuss their significance for a theoretical underpinning of economic sociology, and also discuss the question of the social embeddedness of economic structures as a central condition of economic efficiency. A proper understanding of the significance of cultural, social, and cognitive structures for the efficiency of market economies can be achieved only when we go beyond the market as a universal institution for the allocation of economic goods and supersede the rational-actor model.

PART ONE
CRITIQUE

ONE

THE LIMITS OF THE RATIONAL-ACTOR
MODEL AS A MICROFOUNDATION OF
ECONOMIC EFFICIENCY

*The most intellectually exciting question on our subject
remains: Is it true that the pursuit of private interests
produces not chaos but coherence and if so,
how is it done?*
—*Frank Hahn*

WHEN modern economics was founded in the late eighteenth century, two axioms that still constitute the paradigmatic core of the discipline were established: the action-theoretical assumption that actors maximize their utility or their profit in their actions; and the idea that decentralized economic processes exist in, or at least strive for, an equilibrium in which the independently acting economic subjects can achieve an optimal realization of their economic plans. Ever since Adam Smith, the theoretical concept of order expressed in the notion of market equilibrium and the action-theoretical concept of choices of actors as oriented to the optimization of utility or profit have been considered together: the concept of order has its microeconomic base in the rational model of action; the "magic" connecting limb is the metaphor of the invisible hand.[1] Later on, the first theorem of welfare theory was formulated from this postulate, which says that, given a sufficient number of markets, the competitive action of all producers and consumers, and the existence of an equilibrium, the allocation of resources is Pareto-optimal in this equilibrium: none of the actors can enhance his utility by a change in the allocation of goods without impairing that of at least one other actor.

It can hardly be denied that a sturdy paradigmatic core for scholarly research is inherent in the two axioms and their connection: if the order of preferences is known, the normative premise of the maximization of utility on the basis of any set of preferences allows the anticipation of choices of the actors and their mathematical modeling; the concept of homeostasis refers to the socially desirable consequences of action oriented toward self-interest with the immense moral philosophical significance of the connection of a morally indifferent motive of action and a morally desirable result of action.[2] The optimality of the allocation situation in the equilibrium legitimates the market as the central economic institution with a capacity for universal approval.

The axioms of rationally acting actors and macroeconomic processes of equilibrium encountered both passionate critics and defenders. Ever since the action model of *homo oeconomicus* was introduced into economic theory, it has been subject to constant criticism. Its validity has been challenged not only by the Historical School in Germany, but also by the American institutionalists and now by an enormous literature from various disciplines that cannot be ignored.[3] The criticism argues both on an epistemological and an empirical level: an objective glance at the action of actors in economic situations demonstrates at once that they often do not follow the prescriptions of the model of the maximization of utility. As defined by the theory, "irrational" action is so prevalent in economic contexts that it does not seem admissible to exclude it simply as a deviation from the theoretical system for understanding economic processes. Actors do not maximize their utility but rather make allocation decisions at variance with the theoretical forecasts, by acting inconsistently or choosing suboptimal means to achieve stated goals. In the formulation of his first economic principle that every actor is guided only by self-interest, Edgeworth (1881:16) understood clearly that this was not a realistic description of action: "The concrete nineteenth century man is for the most part an impure egoist, a mixed utilitarian." The concept of forming macroeconomic equilibrium did not fare any better: the idea of an economic development evolving through the market, largely liberated from crises and social frictions, was soon rejected as an ideology by both Auguste Comte and Karl Marx; and the most highly respected alternative to orthodox economics of the twentieth century, Keynsian economics, has its core in the proof of a stable disequilibrium.[4] Finally, criticism of economic theory also turned against the postulate of the morally desirable consequences of action oriented purely toward self-interest. Durkheim (1984) saw economic relations oriented too much toward interest and too little toward morality as a definite cause of social anomie. Karl Polanyi (1944) analyzed the (necessarily abortive) attempt in the nineteenth century to establish a pure market society where exchange relations were no longer linked with principles of reciprocity or redistribution as a cause of the development of fascism in Europe. These lines of argument have been continued today, among others, by the American sociologist Amitai Etzioni (1988), who regards altruistic action orientations in economic contexts as a prerequisite for the market economy's ability to function.

The criticism of orthodox economic theory presented in this chapter does not proceed from the empirically observed discrepancy between theoretically deduced prescriptions of action and factually observed decision-making. For reasons that are explained later, the development of empirical weaknesses of economic theory is not regarded as a convincing starting point for a criticism. The strength of economic theory resides in the *normative* postulation of the connection between the action model of *homo oeconomicus* and a model of order derived from it in which efficient allocation equilibria prevail. Normative here means that recommendations for action can be derived from the theoretical models that imply how actors have to act if they want to optimize their individual utility, while the invisible hand of the market at the same time produces an equilibrium with optimal allocation of resources. A criticism of orthodox economic theories should begin with this strong point of the connection of models of action and order and should show why the normative claims of the theory are untenable. Considered systematically, there are exactly two action problems on which economic theory as a normative theory can founder: if, using the rational-actor model, strategies are recommended that lead to Pareto-inferior results; and if, because of the structure of the situation, it is not possible to identify an optimal manner of action. It can then be asked for the conditions under which actors can choose "irrational" strategies of action, which lead to *superior* results, and for the social mechanisms to steer action that are relevant for decision making under conditions in which an optimal strategy cannot be derived only from an ordering of preferences under the postulate of maximization of utility.

The three sections of this chapter are intended to examine these two limits of the economic paradigm as a prescriptive theory. Three action situations are discussed in which actors are confronted with the two systematic limits just mentioned: cooperation, action under conditions of uncertainty, and innovation. The discussion of the three action situations demonstrates that economic theory cannot *generally* derive efficient results from utility-maximizing action, but rather, under specific conditions, this theoretical model of action leads to Pareto-inferior equilibria or does not permit any derivation of an unambiguous strategy of action. According to the thesis that follows from this, we can imagine social order in the economy as defined by an efficient allocation of resources only if the actions of the actors are also integrated into nonmarket mechanisms of coordination. The achievement of efficient results of economic action requires the "social embeddedness" (Granovetter 1985) of actors, which either leads to deviation from the pursuit of rational individual strategies or actually enables actors to act in extremely complex or novel situations. These requirements are not consistent with the economic action model of universal maximization of utility, even though the line of criticism followed here does not call into question the at least intentional rationality of the actors as *homines oeconomici* but, rather, casts doubt solely on the efficiency of an action in line with the premises of the economic theory of action under specified conditions.[5]

In the first section of the chapter, using the cooperation problem in economic contexts, I examine the hypothesis of dispensing with rational action as a prerequisite for achieving efficient equilibria. The question of how rational actors can cooperate when noncooperation is the dominant strategy can be deduced from the prisoner's dilemma discussed in game theory. Empirically, it is easy to refer to examples of clearly irrational action of the actors, which can be seen in the cooperation that actually does take place (Marwall and Ames 1981). Instead of relying solely on these empirical observations, in this section I argue critically with such approaches in game theory that try to reconstruct cooperative action as rational strategy and thus solve the problem posed by the prisoner's dilemma within the theoretical premises of the economic theory of action. From this discussion I conclude only that cooperation cannot be explained comprehensively as the pursuit of a self-interested strategy of maximization.

In the second section, by means of the problem of uncertainty, I deal with the impossibility for actors to identify the optimal choice due to the complexity of the structure of the situation or due to cognitive limitations. The problem inserted into economic theory by uncertainty, unlike risk, consists of the fact that actors acting intentionally rational can no longer weigh the costs and benefits connected with various alternatives and thus *per definitionem* cannot make an optimal decision.[6] The theory founders again in its prescriptive function. Here, too, I argue with the modeling strategies developed in economic theory that claim to overcome the problem posed by uncertainty within the premises of the economic model of action.

The third and last section of the chapter concerns the aspects of innovation and learning. The neoclassical theory is designed as a static theory that starts from a fixed technology. Dynamic models regard technological change as an external shock, from which the economy moves back to an equilibrium. Innovative processes are understood very badly in orthodox economic theory as endogenous phenomena, and to this day Schumpeter's proposals for an economic theory of innovation are the starting point for modeling techniques that depart critically from neoclassical theory. From the perspective of the actor, investments in innovations cannot be derived rationally due to strategic uncertainty with respect to the action of other actors and the uncertainty of the utility of an innovation.

At the end of the chapter, we should be able to identify the three areas of cooperation, uncertainty, and innovation as central elements of economic processes at which the economic model of order as a normative theory encounters the limits cited. All three action situations refer to the limits of the economic theory of action and to the social embeddedness of economic action as a necessary presumption of the efficient allocation of resources. Cooperation, action under conditions of uncertainty, and innovation also represent increasingly important problems in economic contexts, which demand a better theoretical understanding. The tendencies toward decentralization in the organization of economic activities by constructing network structures, leveling hierarchies, cutting back on production by outsourcing, and the virtualization of organizations all reinforce the significance of cooperative relations that cannot be controlled by hierarchy. But how can the actions of the actors be integrated if there are possibilities of defection that can be used for one's own advantage? The curtailment of the life cycle of products and increasing market volatility emphasize problems of dealing with both uncertainty and innovation. Even if these empirical changes in the economy are not discussed explicitly in the following sections, they represent the background that lends practical significance to the discussion.

Before we begin our discussion, we must digress to consider the starting point of a sociological critique of the economic model of action.

Identifying a strategy of action that, under given preferences, enables the optimization of individual utility allows economic theory to make a clear distinction between rational and irrational action. This starting point for understanding economic action can be criticized both for the assumption of given preferences and for the presumption of rationality. While economic theory starts from existing preferences, it ignores questions about the emergence of preferences. In sociology, Talcott Parsons specified theoretically why the emergence of action goals cannot be explained within the rational-actor model. In *The Structure of Social Action* (1949a), Parsons, whose critical argument with economic theory is the subject of chapter 3, shows that, starting from the utilitarian theory of action, the problem of social order can be solved only if the assumption of action autonomy of actors is given up. According to Parsons, to understand why actors have certain preferences requires the introduction of normative action orientations, which adds to the economic theory of rational allocation of means and is the subject area of sociology. The emergence of preferences from the value attitudes of the actors can be called an important area of sociological investigation of economic life to which, for example, the sociology of consumption is devoted. Yet not making preferences the subject does not lead to a fundamental critique of the rational actor model but merely indicates that it is incomplete. An economic sociology that is developed around this issue completes the rational-actor model, without rejecting it for the explanation of the choice of action strategies.

If we want to develop a criticism of the economic model of action as a normative theory that is also a starting point for the establishment of economic sociology, we have to turn to the clear distinction between rational and irrational action in economic theory. On the one hand, the unambiguous differentiation is a prerequisite for the forecasting of the behavior of the actors given the postulate of maximization and for the mathematical modeling of the formation of market equilibrium through allocative decisions in exchange. On the other hand, it cannot be denied that actors follow the prescriptions of economic theory only unsatisfactorily and thus often act irrationally. Everyday observations show us the discrepancy between economic models of action and actual economic decision making. But why, it may be asked, can a theory, which so obviously does not hold up in the face of empirical observations, so successfully dominate a social science discipline whose task is to explain the functioning of a central social area of action? Clearly a discrepancy exists that requires explanation between the dominance of a scientific model of explanation, its extensive immunity against both internally and externally expressed objections, and the insignificance of approaches in economics that claim to analyze economic structures more realistically. If we want to explain this discrepancy, it seems practical to ask first of all to what extent empirical deviations from the theoretically deduced strategies actually affect the economic theory of action.

A distinction proposed by Robert Frank (1990) for the analysis of "irrational" action suggests an approach to the question. Frank's distinction asks about the attitude of the actor toward suboptimal action: if an actor is shown an alternative action superior to the one he has chosen, he can wish either to revise his previous decision or to stay with it in light of the new alternative. Frank calls the former "irrational behavior with regret" and the latter "irrational behavior without regret."

Regret for a decision made in the past after becoming aware of a better-defined action alternative is to be expected when a lack of information limited the alternatives considered, or when the utilities of the respective alternatives were incorrectly balanced against each other. Inefficient processing of information must be expected because of cognitive limitations. As a result, actors make systematic errors in judging alternatives, as indicated by cognitive psychology (see Kahneman, Knetsch, and Thaler 1986). Consideration of *sunk costs* or *framing* effects is also included here. In the world of the neoclassical model, such wrong decisions are excluded by use of the ceteris paribus clause, or the theory is immunized against them by the concept of *revealed preferences*. But if the task of economics as a social science is seen as understanding the actual decision making, irrational behavior with regret shows that the theory does not represent the empirical diversity of economic action. The empirical persuasiveness of the theory in the description of economic action depends on the actors actually following the strategies of action deduced from the theory. If this is not the case, at least the reduction of the claim can legitimately be demanded: even if many phenomena in the economic context can be understood as the results of rational-action, this does not apply unconditionally, and a comprehensive analysis of economic action must also deal with the deviations from the rational-actor model and their causes, assuming these are not merely rare and curious occurrences.

To understand why economic theory hardly appears to be affected by this empirical criticism, the status of economic theories in the self-conception of economics should be examined. Whether the action model of *homo oeconomicus* has empirical significance is indeed controversial among economists (Sen 1977; 1987), but it is hard to find representatives of the discipline who understand the action assumed in the model as a *full* description of the actual behavior of observed actors. Instead the prescriptive character is cited:

> Our theory is a *normative* (prescriptive) theory rather than a *positive* (descriptive) theory. At least formally and explicitly it deals with the question of how each player *should* act in order to promote his own interests most effectively in the game and not with the question of how he (or persons like him) will actually act in a game of this particular type. (Harsanyi 1977:16)

Determining the deviation of the actual behavior of the actors from the prescriptions of economic theory is an inadequate argument for its rejection if it does not claim to describe actual decision making in economic contexts. Only insofar as the postulates of the rational-actor model are understood as empirical statements about the actual behavior of actors do they have to confront empirical criticism.

But even on the basis of an understanding of economic theory that wants to investigate how the economy functions empirically and realistically, as a result of this criticism, the model of *homo oeconomicus* must not be rejected in advance. Going back to Max Weber, a defense of the economic theory of action for the purpose of empirical study consists of seeing it as a heuristic apparatus that provides a framework from which we can ask about the reasons that determined a specific decision (Frank 1990:85; Hollis 1991:91ff.; Weber 1988:146ff.). The "theory helps in studying actual given cases by providing a measuring rod with which the effect of a measurable deviation from the marginal case of zero can be calculated" (Hollis 1991:92). However, the concept of rationality within economic theory still needs justification in such a model. *Homo oeconomicus* can indeed be understood as a purely heuristic construct so that its concept of rationality itself contains no value judgment,[7] but such a position is always confronted with the obligation to justify why *precisely this* type of action is shifted into a privileged position, as opposed to which all other types of action orientations can constitute only a residual category.[8] Thus, a substantive decision that must be justified is linked with the choice of the economic concept of rationality as a theoretical starting point for the understanding of action.

At least three arguments can be advanced for such a justification. First, the competition in the market requires optimizing decisions from businesses that otherwise could not exist in competition. Second, efficient use of resources is one of the basic conditions of fulfillment of adaptive functions in all societies. Third, in modern market societies the orientation of action toward self-interest is socially legitimate in economic contexts. Consequently, the models of orthodox economics are oriented toward motives of action that are socially institutionalized for economic contexts of modern societies.[9] Against this background, actors in economic contexts have a strong basis of legitimation for action oriented toward the normative recommendations for action of economic theory, and there is no basis for a moral criticism of rational actors. Hence, there is a justification for placing purposeful rationality in a privileged position for the analysis of economic processes and pushing other action types off into the status of residual categories.

Yet it is crucial that irrational behavior with regret does not question the economic theory of action as a normative theory of recommendations of action: the superiority of the alternative deduced from the theory is recognized by the actor and, counterfactually argued, would have been chosen if the properties of the alternative had been known. As Jon Elster (1990:41) puts it: "We take little pride in our occasional or frequent irrationality." If it is correct that the individual and collective outcomes of economic action are optimized through rational action, then it follows normatively from the observation of empirical deviations only that the actors should be placed in a condition where they can act rationally. Better information and the awareness of cognitive "traps" that stand in the way of rational decision making would be the resulting demands. The function of economic theory, then, consists of informing actors about optimal strategies. Hence, irrational behavior with regret does not lead to the demand for the rejection of economic theory: the rational-actor model can be defended on an empirical plane as a heuristic apparatus and is not affected by it on a normative level. Consequently, irrational behavior with regret offers only an unsatisfactory base as a starting point for a sociological criticism of economic theory.

But in what respect does observation of irrational behavior without regret offer such a starting point? What characterizes this situation is that an action would be chosen again even if the actor learns of an alternative that demonstrates the chosen decision to be suboptimal. Examples of such action are paying a tip at a restaurant one will not come back to, or returning a lost wallet to its owner. If the normative concept of maximization of utility is followed, both actions are irrational as defined by the pursuit of self-interest, when a third person cannot retaliate.[10] Rational reinterpretations that explain the action as ultimately selfish are excluded here. Instead, the actions are to be understood as genuinely altruistic, and, even in confrontation with selfish action alternatives, the moral steadfastness of the actor shall be assumed. The preference is in sacrificing the maximization of utility, which negates the normative remuneration of the rational-actor model from the perspective of the actor. From the perspective of the participant, the optimization alternative is not recognized as such, and not necessarily because the actor rejects the action *goal* of increasing his financial assets but because certain *means* of reaching the goal are eliminated out of moral considerations. Out of a moral obligation, one gives a tip and does not profit from another's bad luck. But how can the observation of irrational behavior without regret become a sociological starting point for the criticism of the economic model of action?

The answer to this question depends on the possibility of integrating irrational behavior without regret into economic theory. One way to do that consists of expanding the concept of rationality so that altruistic action is seen as corresponding with the preferences of the actors. A utility is even ascribed to the morally good action. The actors can then still be understood as maximizing utility; however, the utility is not oriented exclusively to their own material self-interest but is obtained from honest action.[11] Thus, returning the wallet can be interpreted as a gain of utility from honest action which is above the utility of the money that is lost. By modeling preferences, all possible modes of action can be understood as maximizing action that contradicts the model based on selfishness in the narrow sense. The only remaining condition is that the preferences are consistent in themselves. Guilt, honesty, envy, sympathy, notions of fairness, or preservation of honor can acquire significance to guide action for the actors and transcend the orientation toward individual selfishness. Here, economists talk of tastes. And *de gustibus non est disputandum*. Such a reinterpretation of the economic model of action that clings to the concept of maximizing action but also allows arbitrary motivations of action can integrate into the model modes of action that are excluded by the model limited to selfishness. Donating blood, supporting charitable goals, and participating in a duel are no longer irrational modes of action but are now forms of maximizing.

If that is the case, then irrational action without regret does not represent a major limit for the economic model of action but simply requires the expansion of its concept of preferences. Yet, methodologically, it must be argued that such an expansion interpreting all modes of action as rational as long as they are consistent makes the concept of rationality a tautology and thus only defines the problem away. The concept of altruistic action itself becomes meaningless if such action, which is defined explicitly as renouncing the pursuit of strategies of action defined as selfish, suddenly appears as self-interested utility-maximizing. This important objection against expanding the concept of rationality leads to the conclusion that irrational behavior without regret represents a central limit for the rational model of action as a normative theory.[12]

Yet there remain two reasons why "irrational" action without regret is not a convincing starting point for a sociological consideration of economic action. (1) Theoretically, it must be noted that *business* decisions, even if these are not *determined* by the market, as assumed in the neoclassical production function, must be aimed at factor prices and anticipated market size. Businesses must observe systemic limitations that allow irrational behavior without regret only as a pathological form of action. A firm that institutionalizes motives of action other than economic profit has to expect that it will not be able to exist in the market.[13] Managers who deliberately act "irrationally" would probably be called insane.[14] Keep in mind here, too, that firms often do not make optimizing decisions. But they would justify all decisions with respect to the expected utility (profit) and would regret bad decisions *post festum*. Thus, a long- or short-term perspective in decision making can lead to radically different decisions, which, however, would not be characterized as intentionally irrational under the respective premises.

(2) Empirically, the statement can be warranted that actors in economic contexts seldom allow their action to be guided by altruistic motives even independent of systemically induced constraints; in the great majority of decisions they are oriented toward their own self-interest.[15] Examples of irrational action without regret cited in sociological criticism of the economic model of action remarkably relate either to a noneconomic area of action or to a marginal area of budget spending of households (Etzioni 1988; Frank 1992; Mansbridge 1990b). Among the noneconomic examples is voting or donating blood. Giving tips or monetary donations to charities usually affects only marginal parts of household budgets and therefore can hardly be cited for a general criticism of the assumption of a budget distribution oriented toward individual self-interest. Too many examples of intentionally rational allocation decisions preclude that: from daily shopping to the purchase of durable consumer goods to capital investments, actors consistently claim to be making optimizing decisions. That that is often not the case refers to irrational behavior with regret (thus an inefficient use of disposable resources) and not to altruistic motives of action. The preferences of the actors are oriented essentially to a

rational allocation of resources, so that a sociological criticism, whose understanding of action in economic contexts is based on altruistic preferences that deviate from those contexts, insists on marginal areas of economic action.[16]

These reflections lead to the conclusion that irrational behavior without regret represents a marginal phenomenon in economic contexts and, as such, does not indicate a systematic starting point for a sociological criticism of the normative premises of economic theory. An approach that assumes that actors in economic contexts in modern, differentiated societies normally strive for their own self-interest through their modes of action can explain much more than attempts to explain economic action from the assumption of a *deliberate* deviation from the principle of the maximization of utility. Cases of actors deliberately acting irrationally are rather deviations from a norm. To attempt to build a sociological criticism of the assumptions of economic theory on these exceptions would limit sociology to "deviant" cases and thus ironically acknowledge indirectly the validity of the theory of rational action for most decisions.

That is not necessarily to assume that economics has an adequate notion of economic action and that "irrational" action should not be taken into account. What is to be expounded are only the theoretical weaknesses of a sociological alternative to economic theory that first contrasts rational and irrational action and recognizes the justification of a sociological approach for the analysis of economic phenomena in the observation of action that contradicts the economic model of action, and then interprets these as a morally motivated deviation from the model. Thus, the existence and significance of morally and normatively guided action in economic contexts are not to be challenged, but attention will be paid solely to the question of *why* "irrational" action can acquire significance, even though an action oriented toward self-interest is firmly institutionalized. As long as we assume that actors can in fact derive their decisions from a preference order and thus achieve utility-maximizing decisions, a sociological criticism that refers to irrational behavior without regret must encounter the problematic assumption that actors deliberately transcended their interests to adapt their action to moral convictions.

Instead of that, I would like to propose seeking the starting point for economic sociology not in a criticism of the action model of *homo oeconomicus* per se but rather in the critical question behind both assumptions of economic theory—that, by action following the premises of the theory, actors can, in principle, achieve efficient equilibria; and that, even in extremely contingent action situations, actors can derive optimizing decisions from their preference order. This is where the sociological criticism of the economic model of action as a normative theory should start. The trouble spot is not the action motives of actors in economic contexts but rather the assumptions in the theoretical premises regarding the structures of the situation, which are the prerequisites for the deduction of efficient equilibria. If it can be shown that actors who follow the prescriptions of the model either achieve inefficient equilibria or that no strategy of action that guarantees an efficient allocation of resources can be deduced from the premises of the theory because of the specific structure of a situation, then the fundamental claim of the theory to explain the efficient allocation of resources from the rational actor model is rejected. On that basis, it can then be asked which action-theoretical prerequisites are required to explain the decision-making process and the emergence of efficient allocations of resources in extremely contingent situations. The task of economic sociology then does not consist of showing that actors deviate intentionally from their own selfish objectives but rather of developing theoretical concepts and carrying out empirical studies that explain, on the one hand, how intentionally rational actors make decisions when they do not know which is the optimal alternative and, on the other hand, to show how actors oriented toward their own self-interest can overcome inefficient equilibria that emerge from the pursuit of individually rational strategies. "Irrational" action is thus shifted to the center as an empirical phenomenon but retains a fundamentally different significance because it does not demand the transcendence of selfish objectives and does not have to be "regretted" either. "Irrational" action that turns out to be really rational action can be regarded as a *means of solving* the two systematic problems of action mentioned earlier. It points to the embeddedness of economic action as a foundation of economic efficiency.

Cooperation

Economic action can be reduced to the two basic forms of exchange and production. In exchange, two actors come together, one of whom has goods the other wants but does not possess himself.[17] The exchange of goods is in the interest of both actors because, by handing over their own goods, they can obtain commodities to which they ascribe a higher utility. At the same time, for both sides, the exchange involves risks that result from the false estimate of the quality of the goods and from the possibility that the other side will renege on the contract. Both sides are interested in realizing the exchange, but in the exchange relationship the possibility of obtaining an advantage by refusing commitments does apply. If actors are oriented toward maximizing their self-interest, it is rational for both actors to deceive the other about the qualities of the goods and, if possible, not to fulfill the contract. The possibility of reneging refers to the role of time in economic transactions. Either delivery of the goods takes place only after the advance payment by the exchange partner, or it requires an investment of resources for which a quid pro quo can be expected only later. Because both actors know the risk of the exchange relationship, the exchange can either be blocked or include high transaction costs. The risk is reduced through the legal means of a contract, but the possible contingencies that can enter into complex exchange relations are only partially predictable and thus cannot be considered fully when the contract is concluded.[18]

Production as the second basic form of economic action can be understood as an expedient treatment of nature, which does not initially demand the cooperation of several individuals. But as soon as the product is made by the division of labor, it requires the cooperation of at least two actors, who must come to an agreement about their respective input and the distribution of the product of their labor. Cooperation is advantageous for both actors because individually they either could not produce the product or could do it only at higher costs, and so the production would be less efficient. If there is no clear control and the product of the work is not credited to the individual actor, it is rational for each actor to contribute as little as possible to making the product and to claim the largest possible share for himself. A cooperation problem emerges with the same structural qualities as in market exchange. The expected behavior is described in the theory of public goods as "getting a free ride," whereas information economics speaks of "principal-agent problems" or of "moral hazard."[19] Here, too, it is to be expected that either the two parties do not cooperate advantageously or control mechanisms must be installed that entail costs and thus reduce the profit from cooperation.

Only since the 1970s has economic theory given the appropriate attention to problems arising from the cooperation of actors with antagonistic interests as central for understanding economic structures. The standard neoclassical model started from the assumption of complete information and neglected the possibility of reneging on contracts (Campbell 1995). On the background of the concept of complete markets, the general equilibrium theory also starts from the notion that exchange leads to the achievement of a Pareto-optimal equilibrium. But cooperation problems were not studied prominently in economic theory, which concentrated on studying market equilibrium processes. Instead, the basic model of neoclassical labor market theory, for example, stated dogmatically that the wages paid correspond to the marginal product of labor, thus systematically excluding principal-agent problems from consideration.

During the past thirty years, however, approaches have been developed in economics that deal with problems of the cooperation of antagonistic actors and attempt to analyze the structural consequences for market equilibria. Thus, information economics analyzes the problem of market failure due to an asymmetrical distribution of information (Akerlof

1970), which leads to Pareto-inferior states of equilibrium. Transaction cost economics (Williamson 1975; 1985) studies the existence of hierarchy (organization) as a function of market transaction costs, which emerge from the opportunistic action of selfish actors. Efficiency wage theory (Akerlof 1984) and more general principal-agent approaches of labor market economics move away from the assumption that the marginal wage corresponds to the value of marginal productivity and instead start from the notion that actors can behave opportunistically because of incomplete supervision of their activities. In general, these approaches can be characterized as renouncing the opinion represented in economic theory since the time of Adam Smith that the pursuit of individual self-interest would *in principle* lead to a Pareto-optimal situation of distribution. Instead it is now considered more prominently that the pursuit of individually rational strategies can lead to inferior conditions of equilibrium and to market failure.

An important exception to the marginalization of the problem of cooperation in exchange relations and in production organized by the division of labor in orthodox economics is game theory, which has been treating the problem of the cooperation of utility-maximizing actors analytically in the form of the discussion of noncooperative games since the 1940s.[20] Our starting point here is the conceptualization of the cooperation problem in game theory because it expresses the core problem succinctly and formally. Based on the models from game theory, the question is whether cooperative relations in economic contexts can be explained within the rational-actor model.

Game theory calls a strategic situation of two players in which mutual cooperation allows the best collective result, yet the dominant strategy consists of mutual noncooperation, the prisoners' dilemma. In terms of economic situations of cooperation, the problem can be described thus: actor A must decide if he should enter into a trade relation with actor B, in which he has to furnish an advance payment and B can or cannot fulfill the contract. A does not know if B will exploit the advance or cooperate by fulfilling the contract. If B does fulfill the contract, both actors receive a profit of ten dollars. But if B does not fulfill it, A loses five dollars and B gains fifteen dollars. So there is a material incentive for B to renege on the contract; on the premises of the economic theory of behavior, B will therefore not produce his work. Because actor A knows this, he will not make a deal with B, even if realizing the deal would be lucrative for both actors. The dominant strategy leads to the stable but inefficient equilibrium if A cannot force B to cooperative action, for instance, through sanctions. Because the sanctions themselves represent costs, the transaction will be realized only if these costs are less than the expected profit from cooperation for the two actors.

For an economic theory constructed on individual rationality, the prisoners' dilemma raises both a normative and an empirical problem. The empirical problem consists of the fact that we can observe cooperative strategies in economic contexts where noncooperative strategies had to be expected, given the premises of game theory. The question is whether, on closer examination, the strategies chosen by the actors can be reconstructed as rational and can thus be reconciled with the rational-actor model. If not, then the normative problem emerges that rational actors, contrary to the assumption incorporated in the first theorem of welfare theory, achieve only a Pareto-inferior equilibrium under certain conditions. But then the behavioral model of economic theory cannot make the general claim of explaining an efficient distribution of goods with the behavior model of *homo oeconomicus*. Conversely, superior results can possibly be achieved with nonrational strategies. Thus there is an interest in developing a theory that studies such strategies and their assumptions beyond the rational-actor model.

Cooperation in a prisoners' dilemma situation can also be understood as irrational behavior without regret.[21] Yet, at the same time, this characterization is misleading because it does not express the difference between the cooperation problem and the examples of irrational action mentioned previously. The examples of altruistic action, which indicate the willingness of actors to renounce utility, are not consequentialist in the sense that the orientation of behavior would aim at maximizing utility. The actors have preferences that are not included in the action model oriented to material self-interest. But this does not apply to the prisoners' dilemma. As long as the other players also cooperate, the actors can achieve the increase of their individual utility through cooperation. Merely the expectation of a noncooperative strategy choice by the interacting partner makes it rational for every individual not to cooperate. The observation of cooperation—or of trust in view of risk—can therefore be identified as a central starting point for a criticism of the economic model of action. This applies to the empirical level, because we can observe cooperative action, and to the normative level, because only a deviation from what is presented as a rational individual strategy allows an efficient allocation of resources. Unlike the altruistic action discussed previously, cooperation in a noncooperative game increases market survival; moreover, without cooperative action, an economy based on the division of labor is inconceivable. On the other hand, cooperation does not lead to Pareto-efficient equilibria under all circumstances.[22]

The range of rational-choice explanations of social action raises a metatheoretical question: whether cooperative behavior must be understood as "irrational" (which thus seriously affects the theory of the rational choice), or whether, in light of the specific conditions of the behavioral situation and the expectations of the actors, it can be reconstructed as rational. If the latter is the case, then the prisoners' dilemma can be overcome within the theoretical premises of the rational-actor model. If this is not possible, economic theory must refrain from the central postulate that rational individual action leads in principle to stable equilibria, which also fulfill the condition of Pareto optimality. This in turn would justify asking about the presumptions under which actors disregard individual rational strategies, and precisely because of that, are moved into a position to achieve superior results.

In the search for the solution of the prisoners' dilemma within the paradigm of the economic model of action, two strategies can be distinguished, which Michael Taylor (1990:224) labeled the internal and the external solution. "*Internal* solutions neither involve nor presuppose changes in the 'game,' that is, the possibilities open to the individuals . . . , together with the individuals' *preferences* (or more generally attitudes) and their *beliefs* (including expectations). *External* solutions, on the other hand, work by changing the game, i.e., by changing people's possibilities, attitudes, or beliefs." The internal solution assumes a reformulation of the situation in which cooperation proves to be a *rational* strategy for the individual. The best-known internal solution of the prisoners' dilemma is the expectation of repeated games, in which cooperation (if one assumes a profit from additional games) becomes the rational strategy. By embedding the paradox of cooperation in the "supergame," the dilemma is overcome. In this section, I first examine the solution of the prisoners' dilemma by repeated games. External solutions of the prisoners' dilemma assume that positive or negative sanctions by a force that can impose sanctions (state, community) change the strategies of the actors and can thus induce cooperation.[23] The problem here is that the realization and maintenance of sanctions themselves must be explained as rational. A second-order free-rider problem emerges that has to be solved within the framework of the rational-actor model. Only against the background of the critical discussion of these defenses of economic theory can it be decided whether cooperation in noncooperative games represents a limit for economic theory that makes it necessary to go beyond the behavioral theory at its foundation.

The Internal Solution

The theory of repeated games is based on the realistic intuition that two actors would not necessarily view a possibility of cooperation as a unique situation but would expect to cooperate again in the future with the same players. Such a game is called a supergame, which, under certain assumptions, leads to conditional cooperation as a dominant strategy (Axelrod

1984). Conditional cooperation is understood as a strategy in which player A makes his own cooperation dependent on the strategies pursued by player B. In case of player B's noncooperation, player A will not cooperate either. In the tit-for-tat strategy developed by Rapoport, player A does not cooperate after the defection of B until player B makes a cooperative move and then A cooperates again until B again reneges. So the game begins with a cooperative move from A, and, in all additional moves, A always chooses the strategy played before by B. In the trigger strategy, player A also begins with a cooperative move, but reacts to a single noncooperation from B with a perpetual withdrawal of cooperation.

Whereas a Nash equilibrium[24] is achieved by mutual noncooperation in the single prisoner's dilemma game, in the supergame of the repeated prisoners' dilemma, neither of the two players has an incentive to defect because the foregone opportunities for profit from further rounds of the game prevent them from achieving a greater utility through noncooperation. The rational individual strategy is cooperation, which leads to efficient equilibria, as long as the prospect of future gains of cooperation in the next rounds of the game has a higher valence than the direct gain from defecting. Cooperation becomes a self-enforcing strategy through which transaction costs stemming from the external solution can be completely avoided. In game theory, this is called the Folk Theorem,[25] which says "that any cooperatively feasible point of the game can be achieved in equilibrium in the supergame" (Mertens 1989:239). In experimental tests, the cooperative behavior of players of repeated games changes in the supergame; first the frequency of the cooperative strategy decreases, yet in a sufficiently long period of play cooperation clearly increases. The interpretation is that the decrease of cooperation at the start of the sequence of play represents a reaction to the initially fruitless attempt at cooperation, yet in the course of the game cooperation is accepted as a dominant strategy (Rapoport 1989:201). In a computer simulation carried out by Axelrod (1984), tit-for-tat achieved the most efficient cooperation results.

Among advocates of game theory, the internal solution of the prisoners' dilemma by supergames is considered an elegant way that allows cooperation in ostensibly noncooperative games to be explained within the premises of the rational-choice theory. The structure of the solution consists of a reinterpretation of the game, not a change of the rules of the game. The elegance is that, unlike external solutions, what has to be considered is not the change of preferences through sanctions, which involves the difficulty of explaining the sanctions themselves from the rational behavioral calculation of the actors. But can repeated games in fact satisfactorily explain the paradox of cooperation? I discuss this question by asking about the presumptions under which cooperation in a supergame proves to be a stable equilibrium.

The first presumption consists of the expectation of an unlimited continuation of the game. If a rational actor knows that game n will be the last game, the pay off matrix of the normal prisoners' dilemma applies to this game with defection as a dominant strategy because there is no longer a possibility of retaliation in case of player B's noncooperation. So it is rational for A not to cooperate in the last game. Because B knows that A will not cooperate in the last game, it is rational for B not to cooperate in the penultimate game. This principle of backward induction continues back to the first game, which correspondingly does not achieve cooperation either.[26] In actual situations, actors are unlikely to maintain an unlimited relationship of cooperation. Because all the players know this about each other, backward induction must be expected to set in, and thus a cooperative equilibrium will not be achieved.

The theory of repeated games can be defended against this objection by relaxing the assumption of the endless continuation of the game. It is sufficient, if the end of the game is unknown to the actors or if the players assign a high probability to the possibility of continuation. Under these assumptions, the logic of backward induction can be broken through. The higher the calculated probability of the continuation of the game, the more a cooperative strategy can be expected. Instead of starting from the strong assumption of the infinite continuation of the game, an expectation value can be shaped that considers the decision of the player for additional cooperation as a function of the expected value of all future gains. The realistic assumption is that future yields have a lower value for actors than present ones, from which the algorithm of a discount parameter can be developed. Then, whether players decide for cooperation depends decisively on the level of the discounting of future expected gains of cooperation (Hechter 1990a:242ff.; Hegselmann 1992:185). The discounting must be small enough to evaluate the yield of future cooperation higher than the payoff that could be obtained directly through noncooperation. The higher the discounting, the lower the value of the expected future cooperation and the more likely is noncooperation. Hence, the choice of strategy can be described as a function of the discounting parameters, which results, however, in the possibility of multiple equilibria, not all of which fulfill the condition of Pareto optimality and thus lead to the indeterminacy of the model. Efficient solutions to the prisoners' dilemma can emerge from repetition, but this is not necessarily the case (Hechter 1990a:242). Taylor (1990:228ff.) argues that, with a sufficiently small discounting of future yields of cooperation by the actors, conditional cooperation represents a unique equilibrium. But then, it can be asked how we know about the discounting rates for the supergame that allow us the Pareto-optimal equilibrium. Because this can clearly only be introduced ad hoc, the indeterminacy of repeated games cannot be overcome. It cannot be known which equilibrium will in fact result (Kreps 1990:103).

The second central presumption for the achievement of the cooperative equilibrium in the supergame is the assumption of perfect information of the players. By perfect information, the knowledge of all previous strategies of all players and the resulting equilibria is understood (Hechter 1990a). The assumption of perfect information in supergames increases the probability that actors achieve Pareto-optimal equilibria. Mirman (1989:196) even claims that in a noncooperative game with two actors "common knowledge" is required. Common knowledge contains perfect information, in addition to information about the environment (preferences and equipment) and the mutual knowledge of the players that each of them has access to complete information. Only given the presumption of common knowledge can one's own strategy be chosen dependent on the strategy of the other player, and vice versa, so a rational game structure can be developed. If player A plays a tit-for-tat strategy but cannot know unambiguously on the basis of incomplete information whether player B is cooperating or playing a defection strategy, he cannot retaliate as defined by the strategy professedly played. If he never retaliates, he can be exploited by player B; if he retaliates too often, he has to put up with high opportunity costs for noncooperation. Hechter (1990a:243) points out that the assumption of perfect information implies that "real-world participants in collective action dilemmas would have *zero monitoring costs.*" In fact, a rational presumption exists for conditional cooperation in the most precise assessment of the behavioral intentions of the other players. But, in a sufficiently large group, this knowledge realistically involves high information costs or it turns out that only an incomplete surveillance of the behavior of the other actors is possible. Even in a two-person game with incomplete surveillance (i.e., principal-agent situations), inefficient market equilibria can be observed (Akerlof 1984). Starting from a situation with incomplete information, the problem of multiple equilibra, which are at least partially inefficient, reemerges. Thus, the conclusion may be drawn that the force of conviction of the internal solution of the prisoners' dilemma by supergames decreases the more realistically the conditions of the actors in the model are conceived.

This general conclusion can also be confirmed by the third presumption for the solution of the cooperation problem by repeated games. Only by starting with the idea that the transaction will always be carried out with the same person can cooperation develop as a dominant strategy. It can easily be recognized that B's possibility of completing the transaction with different exchange partners will lead to the exploitation of A. B will always disappoint the trust A placed in him through a cooperative move because, in the next round, he can always cooperate with another actor.

Thus, A loses the possibility of retaliating and, as a rational player, he will not even enter the cooperative relationship. Axelrod's consideration of repeated games (1984:100) also starts with stable relations of couples as a presumption for cooperation: "An individual must not be able to get away with defecting without the other individuals being able to retaliate effectively. The response requires that the defecting individual not be lost in a sea of anonymous others." This point is very important because it refers to the significance of social structures as a presumption for the solution of the cooperation problem through repeated games. Within the rational-choice paradigm, the significance of social structures for the realization of cooperation has been worked out most clearly by James Coleman (1990a; 1990b; 1990c). Using the modeling of a several-person prisoners' dilemma, Coleman can show that cooperation decreases as the size of the group increases, and thus he concludes: "The results of an iterated prisoners' dilemma (with the same two persons interacting over a large number of interactions) cannot be extended to a population of freely interacting individuals" (Coleman 1990a:272). Instead, the possibility of cooperative relationships, as Coleman explains in another essay (1990c:137ff.), must be regarded as a function of the length of the relationship between the actors and the possibility of communication within the group.

But these presumptions lead us to a possibility of stabilizing cooperative relations through repetition, even if they do not deal with a pure couple relationship. If player B has a future interest in cooperation with other players, then he can signal to these players with his present cooperative action with others that he will not exploit their trust by defecting. The *reputation* that B achieves through present cooperation is a basis for his future possibilities of cooperation. This idea is central for understanding business relationships founded on trust. Coleman (1990c) cites both New York diamond dealers and London business banks as examples of cooperation founded on reputation. A diamond dealer in Manhattan turns over several hundred thousand dollars worth of diamonds to another diamond dealer for an expert appraisal without even getting a receipt. Credit contracts of business banks are transacted by telephone on the basis of oral promises with the obvious expectation that both partners will fulfill the contract.[27]

Reputation as a condition of a rational decision for cooperation in the prisoners' dilemma is critically dependent on two points. On the one hand, all players must be able to observe the past behavior of B and thus to know if B is in fact cooperating.[28] On the other hand, there must be a mechanism that links B's future behavior to his action in the past (Kreps 1990:106ff.). The need to observe the actual action of the actors was cited earlier. Even in the case of the cooperation of one player with many others, distinct equilibria can be obtained, dependent on the strategy pursued by B. Player B need not always cooperate, but he can, for example, pursue a strategy in which he decides in a quarter of all transactions to defect and thus pocket a higher gain. A stable and self-reinforcing equilibrium takes shape as long as the payoffs for A are higher for cooperation than for perpetual defecting. Yet, which equilibrium this will be cannot be determined by the rational-actor model.

However, A must be able to observe the strategy played by B if efficient equilibria are to be possible. Starting from a competitive structure, it is possible for player A to cooperate with various Bs and to decide on cooperation with the B who has the best reputation. Yet, once again, a presumption is the possibility of observing the reputation of the various Bs. Including reputation in the repeated prisoners' dilemma allows at least a partial separation of cooperative relations from established player couples. But at the same time, the information presumptions in the model increase: it is impossible for player A to retaliate against B if B defects because A will come in contact with B only once. Thus, there must be a sufficient probability that B will hold the next round of the game. Moreover, B's transactions must be sufficiently transparent to all potential cooperation partners so that B must assume that retaliation can be carried out against his strategy of defection. Reputation can be an issue only under the presumption of transparency. The fulfillment of this condition is complicated by the fact that B has an interest in the strategic use of reputation effects. Player B can achieve an optimal result if he often pockets additional profits from defecting and, at the same time, can fool potential cooperation partners into believing he will not exploit the trust placed in him. The different interest in correct information refers to the informational difficulties of the reputation model as a rational foundation for cooperation decisions. It can be expected that this model can solve the cooperation problem only under the social-structural presumption of relatively closed social groups because the flow of information becomes less correct as the group expands. Coleman (1990c:139) talks of firmly established communities as the social structure enabling cooperative relationships based on trust.

These objections and specifications resulting from the presumptions of modeling supergames can lead to the conclusion that supergames can solve the cooperation paradox only under specific assumptions that are remote from the real conditions that confront actors in economic contexts of modern market societies. This conclusion does not mean that the expectation of a long-term cooperation relationship beyond a single game has no influence on the probability of cooperation. This outcome is well known from experimental studies, and the examples of socioeconomic case studies also underscore the significance of reputation and long-term exchange relations for the formation of cooperative rela-tions.[29] But the argumentation should support the thesis that supergames cannot be considered a complete solution of the cooperation problem. On the other hand, this naturally does not mean that the cooperation problem cannot be overcome within the theories that start with the as-sumption of selfishly oriented actors. That is, if rational actors can be led to refrain from the dominant strategy of noncooperation by sanction mechanisms and if the emergence and maintenance of the sanction mech-anisms themselves can be explained rationally, cooperation in noncoop-erative games cannot be interpreted as irrational action. This approach is called the external solution.

The External Solution

External solutions of the prisoners' dilemma change the expectations of the actors with regard to the behavior of the other actors—hence the ex-pected utility of the choice of a specific behavioral alternative changes. Through the threat of sanctions, there is a higher probability that player B will cooperate in the prisoner's dilemma, and thus, with his own cooper-ation strategy, player A can expect a utility greater than from noncoopera-tion.[30] The classical example of the external solution of the prisoner's dilemma is Thomas Hobbes's *Leviathan*. The state of nature, which is destructive for all actors, is overcome by giving part of the right of sover-eignty to the central governmental power, which in exchange protects the individuals against violent attacks. Social peace through the Leviathan is advantageous for all individuals. In other words, the noncooperative strategy of the struggle of all against all is transformed into a cooperative strategy involving increased utility by raising the costs for the defection strategy. The expectation of cooperative behavior of the other actors is rational if the sanctions by the Leviathan in case of noncooperative behav-ior are greater than the expected gain from defecting. Hobbes's contract theory represents the core of the argumentation of external solutions of the cooperation paradox. Instead of the Leviathan, social norms (Cole-man 1990a, 1990b, 1990c), institutions (Hechter 1990a), emotions (Frank 1992), or political entrepreneurs (Barry 1970) can be cited that influence expectations in the action of the third party. Norms and institu-tions are thus understood as specifications that define what action is al-lowed or not in specific situations. These specifications of action are sanc-tioned by positive stimuli or negative consequences with contempt. Norms and institutions that are to lead to overcoming the Pareto-inferior but stable equilibrium of the defecting strategy must therefore fulfill two conditions: first, they must first align the behavior normatively with coop-erative behavior; second, they must be covered by sanctions that make observing the norm the superior, self-interested strategy of behavior. Under these conditions, players can mutually start with the notion that their own willingness to cooperate will not be exploited by the defection of the other players.[31]

While turning over the rights of sovereignty in exchange for protection undeniably produces a collectively rational result, one objection to Hobbes's argumentation is that this cannot show how rational actors come together and achieve accord on the surrender of the rights of sovereignty. That is, while it is rational for everyone to institutionalize the Leviathan, it is rational for every individual not to take part in it. The Leviathan can be understood as a public good whose production is affected by the classical problem of free riders. So, an explanation of the overcoming of the prisoners' dilemma through the external solution within the economic model of behavior does not depend only on referring to sanctions but rather on explaining the establishment and maintenance of the force of sanctions themselves from the rational behavioral motivations of the actors. James Coleman (1990b:52) aptly elucidates this problem with Æsop's fable of "The Council of the Mice": the mouse council is summoned to discuss how the cat, who is slowly decimating the mouse population, can be stopped. The second-order free-rider problem is clear from the suggestion of the wise mouse, who would hang a bell around the cat to warn the mice in advance when the cat is approaching. This suggestion is applauded by the mouse council, but then the question of which mouse is to hang the bell around the cat arises. For the mouse who is entrusted with this heroic mission, the costs of the "sanction" are higher than the utility achieved from it.

To solve the second-order free-rider problem, Coleman (1990b) refers to the social relations between actors. Thus, in a three-person prisoners' dilemma, players B and C together can move player A to a strategy of cooperation if their common payoff for the cooperation is greater than the cost of the sanctions necessary to make cooperation a rational strategy for A. While B and C alone cannot credibly threaten A, because the cost of sanctions is beyond the individual gain from cooperation, the social relation between B and C can overcome this situation. Players B and C must agree on a bilateral exchange that B carries out the sanction against A and C assumes part of the costs of sanctions in exchange. But instead of one individual "heroic sanctioner," it can also be imagined that incremental sanctions, which are decentralized and accumulate, can lead to a credible threat and make a cooperation strategy rational for the renegade actor. Coleman argues that sanctions along with the existence of norms are dependent in principle on the fact that it is advantageous for the individual actors to participate in the costs of sanctions—the free-rider problem is solved either by subdividing sanctions into smaller units or by "taking over" part of the costs of sanctions by the actors who do not carry out the sanctions. But the last solution is conceivable only in a game with three actors, in which two actors can agree through a bilateral exchange on the sanctioning of the renegade actor. By putting Coleman's argument into practice, it turns out that, even in a small number of players, the calculation of rational strategies becomes extremely complex and it is thus empirically improbable that actors can calculate which sanction contribution is rational for them. Naturally, a further demand is that it must be possible within the group to identify a free rider, which presumes a high visibility of the actors and their behavior. This is also confirmed by Hechter, who considers the emergence of cooperative institutions with positive externalities possible only under the presumption of the transparency of individual contributions and individual utility:

> For a joint good to be maximally excludable, both individual production and distribution must be highly visible. In the absence of visibility, neither free-riding (a production problem), nor overconsumption (a distribution problem) can be precluded. Production visibility is at a maximum when individual effort can be well-measured by output assessment. Distribution visibility, however is at a maximum when individuals must draw measurable shares of the joint good from some central store or repository. (Hechter 1990b:18)

An interest in the control of the use of resources exists for every individual actor if his own contribution is endangered through its use by other actors. Hechter formulates the second-order free-rider problem so that the control of the use of the public good by others is not a sufficient protection for the individual investment, and therefore *every* actor must have his own interest in participating in the sanctioning of noncooperative actors. Making the individual contributions and the utility of the public good visible enables the exclusion of free riders and thus transforms the public good into a private good. Hechter's example of rotating credit associations shows that such a solution of the second-order free-rider problem is to be expected in small groups, at any rate, where individual action can be identified.

The problem of the necessary visibility of the action of actors represents a central limitation of solutions of the prisoners' dilemma that want to explain sanctions with the rational behavior of the actors. We cannot assume that Pareto-efficient strategies dominate because the presumptions for the solution of the second-order free-rider problem are not given. In too many situations, actors can act unobserved, and if the norm is covered only by sanctions, the socially desirable behavior in many cases is not obtained (Hollis 1992). This result is also confirmed by computer simulations that Axelrod (1986) carried out. In the model, raising the costs of sanctioners for punishing the renegade actors leads to a rapid removal of sanctions. Punishment itself can be supported by a metanorm but will then enter an infinite regression, which intensifies the free-rider problem in every round: who punishes the one who did not punish the renegade actor, who did not punish the renegade actor, and so on?

Another possibility of the external solution of the prisoners' dilemma consists of defining the term norm differently. Instead of expecting socially desirable behavior from external sanctions, we can imagine norms as internalized modes of behavior that exist independent of sanctions or at least cannot be reduced to them. If norms are followed, even though the actor thinks he is not observed and therefore does not expect external sanctions we can speak of internalized norms. Action that conforms to norms does not occur out of fear or the expectation of positive sanctions but rather from an *internal conviction*. In the sociological understanding of norms, processes of internalization play a prominent role.[32] In the hypothetical borderline case of a complete control of behavior by internalized norms, the second-order problem of free riders is resolved because no external sanction is required to maintain social norms. But to what extent is such an understanding of norms compatible with the theory of rational action? James Coleman (1990b; 1990c) has dealt most comprehensively with this question from the perspective of the theory of rational choice. Coleman asks about the rational presumptions for the internalization of norms from two points of view—from the perspective of the actor, who is eager to internalize norms in the other actors, and from the perspective of the person who is the object of the internalization—and establishes the following definition: "Internalization of a norm [means] that an individual comes to have an internal sanctioning system which provides punishment when he carries out an action proscribed by the norm or fails to carry out an action prescribed by the norm" (Coleman 1990c:293).

The problematics of this definition are discussed later. For Coleman, the rationality of internalizing a norm in other actors results from a cost-utility calculation that compares the costs of internalization with the costs of sanctions. Attempts at internalization must be expected if the control of action achieved this way involves lower costs as the functional equivalent of external sanctions. With regard to the principal-agent problem in economic contexts, this means, for example, that a business firm will invest in getting its employees to identify with the goals of the firm if this costs less than controlling behavior through explicit control mechanisms. This argumentation seems conclusive, even if, on an empirical level, such cost-utility analyses confront considerable difficulties. How should an entrepreneur (principal) know if the desired norms are in fact internalized and the employee (agent) is not only feigning internalization to behave strategically for his own advantage in unobserved moments?

This points to the second question of why actors should let their action be influenced by processes of internalization. Obviously, this means an infringement of the maximizing assumption of the theory of rational choice. The principal-agent problem appears only because the actors have different interests, whose individual pursuit always entails negative externalities for the other actors. Coleman (1990c:252ff.) explicitly emphasizes this difficulty and proposes as a solution the development of a theory of mental change, which is to explain why observance of internalized norms is compatible with the interests of the actors. The paradox to be solved is "to account for *changes* in utilities (or goals) on the basis of the principle of *maximization* of utility" (516). Processes of internalization and identification should bring this about since redefining one's own interest reduces the distance between needs and their fulfillment: the actor himself changes (and not the world!) and is thus satisfied with the world.[33] This opportunistic solution, however, is both substantively and methodologically unsatisfactory. It is to be rejected substantively because it legitimates affirmative attitudes toward bondage as maximizing action. The satisfied slave is no longer a paradox but appears as a rational actor who increases his utility by losing his interest in freedom.[34] Methodologically, Coleman cannot demonstrate convincingly that the desired theory of mental change is not simply a superficial attempt to save the theory. This shall be shown based on both conceptions introduced by Coleman to explain internalized norms.

The first conception is contained in Coleman's definition of the internalization of norms cited earlier, which assumes a kind of intrapsychic struggle between the preferences of the actors and social norms. In this conception, the preference of the actors is adhered to. On the level of observed action, it can be ascertained that actors have not adapted their action to the maximization alternative on the basis of given preferences, which can be explained by the fact that they have also followed the social norm without the threat of external sanctions. But such an interpretation is not compatible with the rational-actor model because it requires the notion of *internal sanctions* that allow such action to be still understood as maximizing behavior. Yet, it cannot be seen so much as a solution of the cooperation problem within the rational-choice paradigm as rather an immunization strategy of the economic term of rationality that is aimed at understanding arbitrary action based on a theory of self-interested preferences. Action that deviates from the selfish strategies of action is always then perceived on the basis of a disposition of behavior assumed to be universally applicable, which cannot be refuted even by contrary observations. Rather, cooperative action is an expression of self-sanctioning. But, it must be asked, can an actor adopt an instrumental attitude toward *internalized* norms?

The conception of the theory of mental change pursues another strategy of argumentation, which leads, however, to the same result. Here, the notion of internal sanctions, which is problematic because it is not externally accessible, is given up, but the change of preference is claimed instead. This is also an immunization strategy because, in the final analysis, every action can be interpreted as a change of preference, without leaving a systematic space for the possibility of irrational action. Such an argumentation is tautological. By assuming the change of preferences of the actors, it negates the prisoner's dilemma as a starting problem. The strategy of cooperation is declared the dominant strategy and the prisoner's dilemma can be represented as a cooperative game with a stable and efficient equilibrium. Harsanyi objects to such a "solution strategy" from the perspective of game theory:[35]

> As a practical matter, social situations not permitting enforceable agreements often have a socially very undesirable incentive structure, and may give rise to many very painful human problems. But these problems cannot be solved by arguing that people should act as if agreements were enforceable, even though they are not; or that people should trust each other, even though they have very good reason to withhold this trust. (Harsanyi 1986:95)

Thus, it can be maintained that the preference for a cooperation strategy in the prisoners' dilemma can be explained not within the limits of the rational-actor model by reference to internalized norms but rather if the concept of rationality is expanded so that it only satisfies the criterion of consistency. But this expansion relinquishes the normative content of the rational-actor model to a large extent and is therefore not to be pursued any further. This rejection naturally does not say anything about the actual role of internalized norms in social situations of behavior. It simply indicates that this concept of norms is outside the behavior model whose persuasive power is studied here. The concept of internalized norms cannot be cited to defend the economic model of behavior but can only criticize it. It refers to the autonomy of norms—that is, their at least limited independence from calculating considerations (Elster 1989:131).

Functionalist Solutions

If one assumes that norms cannot be reduced to sanctions, the opposite may be argued: The existence of a norm is the proof of its rationality. This functionalist argument would explicitly admit that norms cannot be understood as an expression of the costs of sanctions, but that norms and institutions would be explained by their collectively desirable result. The norm of cooperating in a situation characterized by the prisoner's dilemma would be understood by its contribution to the achievement of the efficient distribution situation. Examples of a norm-oriented action that is considered irrational but that can contribute to rational results are cited by Robert Frank (1992). If an actor can make it appear credible that he is acting irrationally, he can possibly obtain results that are in his interest. Frank calls this a "strategy of emotions," and cites this situation among others to illustrate it:

> Jones has a $200 leather briefcase that Smith covets. If Smith steals it, Jones must decide whether to press charges. If he does, he will have to go to court. He will get his briefcase back, and Smith will spend 60 days in jail, but the day in court will cost him $300 in lost earnings. Since this is more than the briefcase is worth, it would clearly not be in his material interest to press charges. . . . Thus, if Smith knows Jones is a purely rational, self-interested person, he is free to steal the briefcase with impunity. Jones may threaten to press charges, but this threat would be empty. But now suppose that Jones is *not* a pure rationalist; that if Smith steals his briefcase, he will become outraged, and think nothing of losing a day's earnings, or even a week's to see justice done. If Smith knows this, he will let the briefcase be. If people expect us to respond irrationally to the theft of our property, we will seldom need to, because it will not be in their interests to steal it. Being predisposed to respond irrationally serves much better than being guided only by material self-interest. (Frank 1990:57)

This example demonstrates the reverse of the paradox of the irrationality of rationality, which is essential for the prisoners' dilemma. Smith's action oriented to the social norm of honesty brings him a better behavioral result than a purely self-interested behavior. Obviously, norm-oriented behavior allows credible threats or promises to be made which would be noncredible on the basis of a purely self-interested behavior. But how can the *emergence* of norms be explained by the rational result of social optimization through norms? Four arguments can be presented against the possibility of a genetic explanation of norms from their function.[36] First, on an epistemological level, such an attempt at an explanation gets into the problem known as a functionalist fallacy, that is, that the function of a norm cannot explain its emergence.[37] Second, it can be argued from an evolutionary perspective that an efficient social norm has greater chances of survival than an inefficient one. But this would not be a genetic explanation either. Third, the norm can be interpreted as inauthentic: although (or because!) a person is a rationally acting actor, he pretends to act irrationally because he knows that this leads to a better result of behavior. This approach, however, is connected with the paradox that a person cannot rationally decide to act irrationally; it is difficult to fake irrationality (Elster 1989:136; Frank 1990:59). Moreover, such a strategy of behavior in continuous cooperation would be useless because of the negative effects of reputation.[38] But, fourth, a counterfactual argument is also against an explanation of norms by their contribution to collective desirable results, as emphasized by Jon Elster.[39] If norms could be explained by their efficiency, one could legitimately expect that *all* efficient norms exist and *no* inefficient norms. But, in fact, social norms can easily be cited that do not enhance the efficiency of the distribution equilibrium, and we can also think of norms that would be desirable from the perspective of an increase of utility of the actors, yet do not exist.

The critical consideration of the external solution of the cooperation paradox appealing to sanctions was to indicate that we cannot reduce social norms to economic acts of maximization but rather must grant them an autonomous status, which excludes the explanation of norms within the economic model of behavior. This exclusion does not claim that sanctions have no significance for maintaining norms but only denies the possibility of reducing norms to sanctions. Moreover, the discussion of the external solution of the paradox of cooperation has shown clearly that a purely self-interested behavioral motivation is connected with high transaction costs for the achievement of cooperative actions. The contributions of the actors for the provision of the collective good in production, as well as the share of the collective good every actor claims for himself, must be precisely observable. But high information expenses are also caused by the necessary observation of uncooperative behavior, which must be identified if sanctions are to be imposed on the renegade actor. The costs of information are added to the costs of sanctions for the actual punishment or the positive incentive. In the discussion of the internal solution of the prisoners' dilemma, the necessary costs of supervision are also emphasized. Only if the players can observe the strategies of the other players can they adjust their strategy rationally to the action of the other players. Perfect information or the complete transparency of the behavior of the actors is a prerequisite for the solution of the cooperation problem through supergames. Moreover, the need to supervise the actions of other actors called attention to the social structure as a variable to explain the willingness of actors to cooperate in economic contexts. The groups actors integrate into must be small enough so that a sufficient flow of information can be realized as a prerequisite for the willingness of rational actors to cooperate. The internal solution presumes the high visibility of the actions of the actors as well as the expectation of long-term cooperative relations, which can be expected in relatively closed communities.

The exacting conditions for the solution of the prisoners' dilemma within the economic model of action indicate that cooperative relations cannot be realized if they are based solely on the calculating considerations of the actors. Overcoming the state of nature cannot be explained by relying solely on the economic model of action. Cooperation can be expected only in cases of long-term relations of cooperation with a sufficiently large payoff from future transactions and in clearly defined communities, where the action of a third party can be relatively easily observed and sanctions against renegade actors can be provided with low costs. Cooperation based on calculation consequently entails high transaction costs and, in an economy based increasingly on cooperation, rising transaction costs must be expected (Sabel 1993; Piore 1995). This impediment to a process of structural transformation in the economy would be decisive, and it can be argued that trust can bring relevant competitive advantages.

Yet it is not enough to engage in wishful thinking that reciprocal trust is desired by actors—with the rational goal of increasing economic efficiency. That would simply ignore the starting problem of the paradox of cooperation and hence would not get anywhere. But if we face the situation of observing more cooperative relations in economic contexts than we can explain on the basis of the economic model of action, then the question of alternative explanations arises.

Uncertainty

The discussion of cooperation referred to the difficulties of overcoming the prisoners' dilemma using the premises of the economic theory of action. The actors achieve a Pareto-efficient equilibrium only when defection is not the dominant strategy of the game. Attempts are made to overcome this problem through repetition and sanctions. Yet the internal and the external solutions presume a great deal about the supply of information of the actors who have to supervise the moves of other actors. But even under these conditions, multiple equilibria have to be expected, but which specific equilibrium will be achieved in the game cannot be deduced theoretically. In actual cooperation relationships, incomplete information and an asymmetrical distribution of information have to be expected, which lead to principal-agent problems and thus rule out overcoming the paradox of cooperation under the assumptions of the economic theory of action. Long-term relations and the expectation of sanctions can be interpreted as structural elements of the stabilization of cooperation, but such an interpretation does not mean a solution of the prisoners' dilemma. If this conclusion is justified, then the problem of cooperation represents the first central limit of the rational-actor model as a normative theory. This limit can be formulated thus: under specific conditions action aimed at maximizing individual utility leads to Pareto-inferior equilibria, whose overcoming can be explained only by integrating the possibility of "irrational" action. It can be rational to act nonrationally.

This section is devoted to a second limit of the economic model of action, which can be attributed to the problem of uncertainty. The problem is not that an individually rational strategy of behavior impedes the achievement of efficient results, as in the problem of cooperation, but rather that an optimal strategy cannot be discerned. We want to maximize our utility, but we do not know which strategy of behavior we should choose for that because we do not know the causal relations from which we can deduce an optimizing decision. It is not *irrational* to act rationally but rather *impossible* to act rationally.

The problem of uncertainty entered modern economic discourse with the marginal utility revolution, but only since the 1960s has the discipline of economics shifted to focus fully on the implications of uncertainty—often studied alongside the problem of asymmetrical distribution of information—and the resulting consequences for equilibrium theory. Moreover, there is a fundamental break between these two phases of the study of uncertainty. The early considerations of uncertainty in economic theory were to be bases for developing alternative theories in economics, which are free of the assumption of perfect markets and the concomitant expectation of designing optimal allocation equilibria. This approach, which can expound the implications of uncertainty for the economic model of behavior, is discussed in this section first by representing the consideration of the problem of uncertainty in the works of Carl Menger—and the Austrian School of Economics—and in Frank Knight, John Maynard Keynes, and Herbert Simon. These four authors see uncertainty as the central limitation of the economic model of order and use the problem as a starting point for their projected theories that deviate from orthodox economics. On the other hand, the approach discussed in connection with the economic modelings of action under uncertainty, which have been developed in the tradition of the general equilibrium theory as well as in game theory, is quite different. These are attempts to interpret situations with uncertainty so that they are compatible with the assumptions of optimizing decisions. Hence, models of decision making are used that are based on stochastic modeling techniques, especially the Bayesian decision theory. In the discussion of these approaches, two groups of problems are to be worked out. First, the unrealistic starting point of unlimited cognitive capacity of the actors so that no discrepancy exists between complicated mathematical modeling and the actual action is an empirical problem that justifies critiques from the perspective of behavioral science. At any rate, the solution strategies are not yet doubted on a theoretical level, and at least the possibility of maximizing decisions under uncertainty remains open. Second, theoretical limits for assuming optimizing action do, however, arise under conditions of uncertainty if we start from an asymmetrical distribution of information.

Uncertainty as a Starting Point of Intraeconomic
Criticism of the Equilibrium Theory

Uncertainty represents a prominent problem in the economic discourse of the twentieth century.[40] The significance for economic theory can be inferred from the fact that four of the most relevant intraeconomic criticisms of the orthodox model of the creation of efficient market equilibria on the basis of optimizing action are based on the problem of uncertainty: the Austrian School, the explanation of profit by Frank Knight, the assertion of stable disequilibria in John Maynard Keynes, and Herbert Simon's theory of satisfycing.

Carl Menger (1871)—and following him, the Austrian School of Economics—considered the knowledge of actors about the causal relation between an object and its capacity to fill human needs as one of four qualities that made an object an economic good. Unlike Walras's equilibrium theory this causal knowledge is not assumed in the premises of the theory. Instead, the Austrian School considers the limits of human cognitive capacity as sources of uncertainty in the production process. Economic relations are characterized by the uncertainty of outcomes and unintended results of action. Including uncertainty establishes the indeterminate character of economic decisions because actors cannot fully anticipate the consequences of their actions, and thus it emphasizes that the future is open in principle. The indeterminacy of decisions makes economic situations contingent and thus opens room for creative behavior or entrepreneurial activity (O'Driscoll and Rizzo 1985; Steele 1993). The entrepreneur takes the role of a venturesome actor who has superior knowledge. Actors orient themselves in contingent situations by rules that can be crystallized socially as institutions and reduce the contingency of the world (Buchanan 1989; Vanberg 1994). Yet the assumption of limited knowledge about future conditions of the economy is most significant for the rejection of all government planning: considering uncertainty, even a government planning authority cannot have the knowledge necessary for a rational political determination of the production process (Hayek 1948). The conclusion is: based on the dispersion of knowledge among several actors, prices are the rational mechanism for the coordination of decentralized economic decisions.

The most important conceptual contribution to the problem of uncertainty is Frank Knight's distinction between risk and uncertainty. In *Risk, Uncertainty, and Profit* (1921), Knight tried to provide an explanation for the existence of profit in market economies. Assuming the existence of perfect markets with complete knowledge, a polypolistic market structure, and the absence of time, economic theory cannot explain profit because a market will attract new bidders until the price of the item corresponds to the marginal cost of production. For Knight (1921:197), this market model is based on the assumption "of practical omniscience on the part of every member of the competitive system," which is why Knight considers it unrealistic. Actors are confronted with uncertainty about the future conditions of the economy, and therefore, in a dynamic economy, they can make no decisions that lead to efficient equilibria results. He distinguishes between changes of the economy whose probabilities can be foreseen and those about which the actors can have no information that will allow them to calculate probabilities. Knight calls the first situation risk, the second uncertainty:

> The practical difference between the two categories, risk and uncertainty, is that in the former the distribution of the outcome in a group of instances is known (either through calculation *a priori* or from statistics of past experience), while in the case of uncertainty this is not true, the reason being in general that it is impossible to form a group of instances, because the situation dealt with is in a high degree unique. (229)

Economic change per se cannot explain profits either, because under the condition of the foreseeability of change in the economy, no disequilibrium emerges. Situations with risk can be transformed into situations with certainty, when actors insure themselves against risks. The costs of insurance are then part of the costs of production of all products, and thus there can be neither gain nor loss. From this, it follows for Knight that situations characterized by uncertainty are central to explain profit.[41] Uncertainty brings the question of "what to do and how to do it" (268) into the foreground of economic analysis, and makes the actual execution of decisions a secondary problem. For their action, actors must rely on "mechanisms" that emerge from the situational conditions of uncertainty and help them make decisions under conditions of informational limitations. Knight especially refers here to the specialization of functions in businesses through hierarchical structures and professional role differentiation.

In the same year that Knight's theory of profit appeared, Keynes published his *Treatise on Probability* (1921), in which he tried to understand the epistemological aspects of the problem of probability and uncertainty.[42] He defined uncertainty in a clear parallel with Knight as a situation in which the probability of the incidence of a certain event "is unknown to us through our lack of skill in arguing from given evidence. The evidence justifies a certain degree of knowledge, but the weakness of our reasoning power prevents our knowing what the degree is."[43] Keynes's notion of uncertainty (1973b:112) is aimed at the assumption of complete knowledge in orthodox economics and is still relevant in the discussion of investment behavior. Capital investments are characterized by a high degree of uncertainty, hence the question of how investors make an investment decision. In the *General Theory* (1936), Keynes emphasized the significance of conventions, especially the expectation of investors "that the business situation will last forever." Moreover, he stressed the relevance of mimesis (1973b:114), advice, style, and custom (117) for maintaining the ability to act in situations with uncertainty. Every one of these "mechanisms" enables a behavior "which saves our faces as rational, economic men" (114), but at the same time all of them are molded by sudden and drastic changes. The uncertainty of the yield of capital investments influences the level of investments in an irrational and unpredictable way because the liquidity preference curve is unstable and elastic. Thus uncertainty lets investors' expectations become a central variable for determining the interest rate in Keynes's theory. At the same time, this enables the emergence of underemployment equilibria. The introduction of uncertainty is central for Keynes in order to find an understanding for economic processes:

> If . . . our knowledge in the future was calculable and not subject to sudden changes . . . a small decline in money income would lead to a large fall in the rate of interest, probably sufficient to raise output and employment to the full. In these conditions we might reasonably suppose that the whole of the available resources would normally be employed; and the conditions required by the orthodox theory would be satisfied. (119)

In the economic theory of the postwar period, Herbert Simon and, with him, the Carnegie School regarded uncertainty as a central problem for the development of a theory of decision making. Unlike the formulation of the problem in the Austrian School, in Frank Knight, and in Keynes, Simon does not doubt the possibility of optimizing action in principle and thus the theory of rational choice as a normative theory of decision making. According to Simon's theory, it is not the *situational structure* of uncertainty that prevents maximizing decisions but rather the *cognitive limitations* of the actors. A discrepancy emerges between the complexity of the causal structure of the situation and the cognitive capacities of the actors:

> The limits of rationality have been seen to derive from the inability of the human mind to bring to bear upon a single decision all the aspects of value, knowledge and behavior that would be relevant. The pattern of human choice is often more nearly a stimulus-response pattern than a choice among alternatives. Human rationality operates, then, within the limits of a psychological environment. (Simon 1945:108)

In principle, however, the discrepancy between cognitive capacities and situational complexity can be overcome in Simon's notion, if the capacities of the actors to process information are enhanced. This conviction is expressed in Simon's interest in computer technology as an instrument of optimizing decision-making processes (Simon 1992). Nevertheless, the main focus of Simon's work resides in the development of a theory of behavior that explains decision making under conditions of an incomplete mastery of the causal structure of the situation. The notion of bounded rationality is introduced for decision making in which the actor chooses not the optimal alternative but rather an alternative that satisfies his level of aspiration. The level of aspiration is determined by the actor's ambitions, his perceived needs, and future plans. The theory of bounded rationality also calls on the problem of uncertainty with respect to the optimizing alternative in decision making situations to support giving up the assumption of optimal decision-making. The *satisficer* is not a maximizer. But, unlike the previous approaches presented, Simon is not interested primarily in problems of market failure or in the possibility of changing the structure of the situation but rather in understanding real action under given conditions. If it is valid, the theory of bounded rationality refutes the economic maximizing assumption as an empirical claim but not as a normative theory. Yet, although the theory of bounded rationality cannot operationalize at what point actors stop seeking further alternatives, a reinterpretation as optimizing behavior also seems to be possible. That is, if the search costs connected with arriving at a decision are considered, breaking off the search for a better alternative can be understood as a maximizing decision in view of the costs of further acquisition of information (Riker and Ordeshook 1973). Yet it can be objected that this argumentation misjudges the problem of uncertainty: on account of uncertainty, the utility of the investments in further search activities is ex ante unknown, and thus the investment cannot be represented as optimizing behavior.

From this brief description of various theoretical developments considered as alternatives to the tradition of the general equilibrium theory within economics, it should be clear that the problem of uncertainty within the discipline is considered significant enough to use it as a starting point for alternative modelings of economic processes that give up the optimization postulate of the orthodox theory. The various theoretical approaches, by introducing uncertainty, agree to explain economic phenomena that are excluded by the orthodox standard model, but which can be observed nonetheless as empirical phenomena: the existence of institutions (Austrian School), profit (Knight), stable disequilibrium (Keynes), and suboptimal decision making (Simon). In situations where the assumption of perfect markets cannot be maintained empirically because of prevailing situational conditions or cognitive limitations on the side of the actors, market failure must be expected and the conception of order based on the "invisible hand" must be questioned.

If uncertainty is understood as a situation in which it is not possible to deduce decisions from preferences because the consequences of various alternatives cannot be seen unambiguously or are at least probabilistic, then the microfoundation of the economic theory of order is affected. There is no position from which a particular alternative can be described as superior ex ante. Thus, the core of orthodox economics as a normative theory of decision making is called into question. The significance of this point can be read from the comments of two rational-choice theorists who regard uncertainty as the Achilles heel of economic theory: "Assuming that we are facing a choice under uncertainty, does rational-choice tell us anything about what we ought to do? The answer is: very little" (Elster 1986:6). The economist Charles Schultze also refers to the central status of the possibility of rational action for the theory: "When you dig deep down, economists are scared to death of being sociologists. The one great thing we have going for us is the premise that individuals act rationally in trying to satisfy their preferences. That is an incredibly powerful tool, because you can model it" (quoted in Kuttner 1985:76).

At the same time, the question arises of how actors can reduce uncertainty and stabilize extremely contingent situations of interaction. In other words, the question is, What do we do when we don't know how we can make a maximizing decision? This question cannot be posed within the orthodox economic models because the theory states axiomatically that actors make decisions that maximize utility or profit and only under this condition can the theoretical concept of order as a collective result of individual optimizing action be maintained. Thus, uncertainty represents a limit of the combination of the rational-actor model and a Pareto-efficient macro result that brings the Hobbesian problem of regulation back into economics: At least some actors will not achieve Pareto-optimal exchange results, and no stable Pareto equilibria are developed. This limit of the economic model of order can be approached from two sides. On the one hand, the problem of uncertainty can be enlisted for an explanation of empirical observations of market failure. This is the procedure of Keynes, Knight, and the transaction costs approach discussed later. On the other hand, it can be approached from the sociological side with the study of the cognitive, social, and cultural mechanisms actors resort to when they act under conditions of uncertainty. This approach starts explicitly from the notion that actors are provided with decision-making mechanisms through which they reduce the contingency of the situation. These decision-making mechanisms cannot be understood as altruistic motives of action but rather transcend the simple dichotomy of rational and irrational action. This process can be termed *intentional rationality*, which does not suspect the goals of the actors in economic contexts but rather attacks the simplified consideration of goal-means relations in economic theory.

Intentionally rational actors want to maximize their utility, but because of the complexity of the situation and/or the limited cognitive capacities of information processing, they do not know unambiguously which means they can use to achieve this goal. The dichotomy of rational versus irrational action logically presumes knowledge of the relationship between means and ends, because otherwise it is impossible to distinguish these two categories without operating with the tautological notion of revealed preferences. For a prescriptive economic theory that is interested in explaining the emergence of efficient equilibria, studying the decision-making mechanisms under uncertainty is interesting because it can turn out at least ex post that these are responsible for the *prevention* of market failure. This would imply that, in certain information structures of a situation, we achieve efficient equilibria not on the basis of the action model of economic theory but through action oriented to social norms or tradition. Naturally, this leaves open the opposite possibility that social or cultural mechanisms relevant for transactions also have destructive economic consequences.

Uncertainty in the General Equilibrium Theory

The economists discussed earlier, who used the problem of uncertainty as a central starting point for their projected theories by explicitly moving away from the idea of a social and individual optimization through the invisible hand, are all characterized by the willingness to give up the concept of Pareto-efficient equilibria. At the same time, assessment of their position within economic discourse suggests that, while they produced important and respected contributions to economic research in the twentieth century, they were outside the core of the discipline, which developed along the general equilibrium theory that goes back to Walras, and maintained the postulate of market optimization.

Unlike the modeling discussed earlier, uncertainty is not recognized in the general equilibrium theory as a limit of the concept of economic order and thus is also not readily enlisted as a systematic justification of the inclusion of institutional or cognitive mechanisms for understanding economic action. Instead, uncertainty is considered simply as a complication of the decision making of actors, which demands the integration of more mathematical operations for the identification of optimal strategies of action. Thus, the proceeding of the general equilibrium theory is fundamentally different from the modeling of uncertainty cited earlier: the focus is the attempt to eliminate the category of uncertainty in Frank Knight's distinction. An example of that is the argumentation of Hirshleifer and Riley

(1992:10), who reject Knight's distinction between uncertainty and risk and announce the deduction of optimal strategies of action under uncertainty on the basis of subjective probabilities. Thus, the term uncertainty, as Knight used it, is given up. The reinterpretation of situations as risky, which were described as uncertain by the authors discussed earlier, is important for the argumentation of this section for two reasons. On the one hand, the strongest defenses of the market model can be seen in it. Only if it can be shown that these models related to uncertainty do not allow any satisfying solution of the problem can uncertainty be cited as a limit of the economic model of order. On the other hand, the significance of the problem of uncertainty is indirectly acknowledged in this approach: it only requires the efforts to reinterpret all situations with incomplete information as simply risky because uncertainty—as defined by Frank Knight—has such far-reaching consequences for the economic model of order.

The general equilibrium theory, whose most important developments originated with Léon Walras (1874) and in the twentieth century with the work of Kenneth Arrow and Gerald Debreu (1954), saw its task as proving the possibility of the existence of a general competitive equilibrium in the economy and the proof that such an equilibrium fulfills the condition of Pareto optimality.[44] Arrow and Debreu were able to honor both claims mathematically. They can also insert a modeling of uncertainty, which is, however, based on extremely demanding premises. For this model, they use so-called dated contingent commodities, which are "made possible" by the assumption of complete future markets. Goods are defined by four attributes: the physical qualities, the place, the time of delivery, and the external conditions at the time of availability. For every good thus defined, a special market exists. Thus there is a price for umbrellas that are supplied in Princeton on March 24, 2010, when it is raining. Given the existence of all future markets, firms and households can "determine their entire production and consumption plans, for they know the prices of all goods in all future periods, and they can insure themselves against all eventualities" (Backhouse 1985:290). In the Arrow-Debreu model, all exchange processes can take place at one point in time because uncertainty about the condition of the world in future periods can be allowed for by contingent contracts at time t_0. The economy is reduced to a static equilibrium in which time and uncertainty cannot appear as problems. Even at period t_0 all markets exist for periods t_1 to t_n, and the uncertain future is brought into the present by contingent contracts. If markets are specified for all possible characteristics of future situations, uncertainty is modeled in a way that allows the same market mechanisms as under conditions of certainty, and accordingly a Pareto-optimal equilibrium is expected (Arrow 1983:142).

This modeling of uncertainty, however, demands the assumption of the existence of complete markets for contingent contracts, which can be expected only under the assumptions of the theoretical model, not in an actually existing economy. The theoretical analysis of the presumptions for an economy with a stable, market-clearing equilibrium is not to be confused with the description of a concrete, existing economy. The modeling of uncertainty known as the state-of-the-world approach presumes that all possible contingencies are known, that these are mutually exclusive, and that the actors have no influence on the actual incidence of a situation. Moreover, the actors must always be able to see which state of the world actually exists, and they have to be able to allocate at least the subjective probabilities of the occurrence of every possible state (Gravelle and Rees 1992). Naturally, every one of these assumptions can be challenged, but the significance of the Arrow-Debreu model resides in the far-reaching defense of the possibility of the formation of Pareto-optimal equilibria even under the condition of uncertainty, along with precisely working out presumptions on which the theory *can fail*. If the presumption for an optimal allocation of resources through the "invisible hand" of the market is inherent in the existence of complete markets, then the question arises, Under which conditions do incomplete markets have to be expected? This question refers to the assumptions made in the state-of-the-world approach.

In the economic discussion about the modeling of uncertainty in Arrow-Debreu, the assumption that has proved to be especially problematic is that the partners to the contract know at the point of executing the contract which specific contingency has really occurred. In 1968 Radner indicated that contingent contracts for future situations are not concluded if one of the parties at time t_n does not know which state of the world actually exists. Market failure because of asymmetrical distribution of information has been discussed in economics as a central subject ever since, and Arrow has also turned his attention to the limitation of the general equilibrium theory in view of an asymmetrical distribution of information. An asymmetrical distribution of information leads to the problems of moral hazard, adverse selection, as well as agency problems, and strategic action. These problems, which are spelled out more precisely later, indicate that, under certain conditions, markets cannot materialize and market equilibria can be shaped that do not fulfill the condition of Pareto optimality.

Criticism of the assumptions of the Arrow-Debreu model established a new plan of research that abandons the assumption of a symmetrical distribution of information. The problem of uncertainty under the condition of an incomplete but symmetrical distribution of information is regarded as well understood through the use of stochastic methods. The theory of rational expectations can find a use for the explanation of choice of optimizing decisions on the basis of probabilities and through the introduction of random parameters.[45] The model is not fundamentally changed by the inclusion of subjective probabilities, if we assume that the actors share the same information and the same subjective probabilities. "Bayesian rationality" (Harsanyi 1978) can be integrated into a static economic analysis (Hammond 1987). We do not go into the technical device of stochastic modeling of uncertainty here. The Bayesian approach to the modeling of optimizing action under uncertainty is thoroughly controversial (Gul 1991), but objections can be formulated independent of the question of the soundness of the Bayesian theory of decision making. Yet, first, we present a behavioral criticism of the attempt to develop stochastic methods that aim at eliminating the category of uncertainty.

The complexity of decision making under the use of elaborated stochastic rules increases considerably, and it becomes increasingly unlikely that actors correctly understand all relevant variables of the model. Heiner (1983) especially developed a theory of action under uncertainty against the background of such a behavioristic criticism of economic modelings of uncertainty. Heiner argues that, as the situational uncertainty increases, the chance of discovering the right situation for the choice of an alternative decreases, and the chance of discovering the wrong situation for the choice of this alternative increases. Such a behavior-oriented approach, which is compatible with Simon's theory of bounded rationality, is important to show that actors in very complex situations are overtaxed in the use of probabilistic decision making. Empirically, it can be derived from this approach that actors, in their actual behavior, do not follow the stochastic rules of decision making because these are not completely understood. Heiner's conclusion is that, under conditions of uncertainty, contrary to the assumptions of the economic theory of action, actors could achieve superior results of action if they limit the contingency of the action situation through rigid structures. However, the argumentation cannot be cited against the theoretical validity of economic models of decision making as long as these can show that, even under conditions of uncertainty, Pareto-optimal market equilibria can be achieved if the actors only follow the prescriptions that are theoretically deduced.

If we had to leave the argumentation here and could not also engage in theoretical criticism, we would have to label the empirical action of actors that deviates from the prescriptions of the theory simply as irrational action with regret, and the task would consist of attempting to support actors to optimize their decision making. But with the further development of information economics that grew out of the criticism of the Arrow-Debreu model, a second line of criticism can be deployed, one that shows that the probabilistic manipulation of the problem of uncertainty under the condition of an asymmetrical distribution of information encounters *theoretical* difficulties that no longer guarantee a Pareto-efficient distribution of goods (Postlewaite 1987:133). The discussion of asymmetrical distribution of information in the economy yields insights of how market failures emerge and whether market interventions can lead to an increase in welfare. But, at the same time, they show clearly that the means of the economic theory of action are inadequate to understand the overcoming of market failure. On the economic side, this is indicated especially by Arrow, who in the pathbreaking article "The Organization of Economic Activity" (1983 [1969]) emphasized the significance of social norms for overcoming market failure on the basis of an unequal distribution of information. A few examples of the market failure caused by an asymmetrical distribution of information are cited to illustrate the problems arising from it.

A classic example of a Pareto-inferior market equilibrium on the basis of an asymmetrical distribution of information is Akerlof's (1970) model of the used-car market, which illustrates adverse selection. This model shows that an unequal knowledge of buyer and seller about the quality of the used car to be sold prevents the existence of a positive equilibrium price in this market. If used cars each have a different quality and the potential buyer does not know the quality of the specific auto, the buyer is only willing to pay an average price for the car. This leads the sellers of cars of above-average quality to take their offer off the market, and thus the average quality of the offered cars drops. This circle continues so that no car can be sold for a positive price.[46] The basis for the market failure in the example is the asymmetrical distribution of information between potential buyer and the seller, which gives rise to strategic considerations on both sides. Because sellers generally, aside from those with better-than-average-quality cars, have an interest in not informing buyers of the actual quality of the cars, the buyer does not get reliable information. The buyer knows this, and the seller knows that the buyer knows it. The equilibrium that is formed is not Pareto-efficient because of a cessation of market transactions in which the buyer and the seller would have enhanced their utility. Adverse selection refers to the significance of the structure of information for the efficiency of equilibria and, conversely, gives an explanation for market failure.

Another form of market failure because of an asymmetrical distribution of information is discussed in economics under the rubric of moral hazard.

Moral hazard may be defined as actions of economic agents in maximizing their own utility to the detriment of others, in situations where they do not bear the full consequences or, equivalently, do not enjoy the full benefits of their actions *due to uncertainty and incomplete or restricted contracts* which prevent the assignment of *full* damages (benefits) to the agent responsible. (Kotowitz 1987:207)

Moral hazard can be represented most clearly with problems of insurance. The purchase of insurance can change the risk behavior of the buyer in a way that was not seen by the insurance company. Fire insurance can have an influence on the policyholder's concern about fire prevention or can even motivate him to commit arson. Because the insurance company does not know how the concrete policyholder behaves, the possibility of such behavior represents a special gamble for which, however, no special market can be created because actors at high risk will not voluntarily reveal themselves. The result is a relatively high insurance premium which, conversely, deters people from taking out insurance if their risk of the event insured against is low.

The problem of moral hazard leads to the closely connected principal-agent problems, which were discussed in the previous section. When acts cannot be directly observed (hidden action) or actors know relevant data that the principal does not know (hidden information),[47] the result of the action on the behavior of the actors cannot be directly concluded. Uncertainty about the actual state of the world exists. The principal-agent problem can give important insights especially for the explanation of labor market inefficiency. If it is assumed that the demand curve of a business is known by management but not by labor, and an optimal labor contract would imply that wages vary with demand, but the number of employees remains constant, then the asymmetrical structure of information allows the exploitation of labor, but this cannot be proved. Independent of the actual situation of demand, management would explain that demand is low in order to lower earnings. Because labor knows this, the optimal structure of contracts will not be materialized (Rosen 1985).

The problem with regard to uncertainty that arises from an asymmetrical distribution of information is that it cannot be said unequivocally whether all participants achieve the same or a higher level of welfare when the allocation of goods changes through further exchange, or whether the exchange enhances the Pareto efficiency of the distribution situation. This problem is not posed under conditions of certainty or uncertainty that affect all actors equally. That is, all actors know whether further exchange will enhance Pareto efficiency, and the exchange is contingent on the fulfillment of this condition.

> When each agent has different information the problem becomes more complicated. Some agents may know that certain events cannot happen while others might not know this. What probabilities should be used to calculate an agent's expected utility—his own beliefs, those of the best informed agent, the totality of the information held by all agents or some entirely different probability? (Postlewaite 1987:134)

Clearly, the question concerning the explanation of market failure is how the asymmetrical structure of information can be overcome and the actors thus achieve efficient equilibria. Here, a plethora of suggestions for solutions can be cited. Insurance companies can hire detectives or offer different groups of customers various policies, and by their choice the policyholders reveal their risk. Principals can supervise the action of the agents, and adverse selection can be overcome by sending signals of quality like warrantees or recall campaigns. But, these measures, which in principle are always linked with transaction costs, are only an inadequate solution to the problem: "But procuring information through inquiries or the spread of signaling information by suppliers can be connected with enhanced costs and risks, so that the asymmetry of information is only evenly reduced, but not eliminated" (Schumann 1992:417).

Investments in procuring information or concluding complicated contractual rules that specify the action of the agents represent transaction costs that can even cause market failure. This is to be expected if the transaction costs of overcoming the uncertainty evoked by an asymmetrical distribution of information are higher than the advantages of transaction: "Market failure is the particular case where transaction costs are so high that the existence of the market is no longer worthwhile" (Arrow 1983:149). The transaction costs emerging in markets are designated as the second cause for incomplete markets. In conclusion, I examine the transaction cost economics that analyzes market failure as a function of uncertainty with regard to incomplete contracts.

Naturally, transaction costs do not emerge only because of asymmetrical distribution of information but can be understood generally as costs of information and communication. In market transactions, these include the costs of preparing, concluding, executing, and overseeing contracts. Transaction cost economics studies alternative "governance structures" as a function of specific transaction costs.[48] "Governance structures" were first conceived in the bipolar confrontation of market and business (Coase 1990; Williamson 1975), and later network structures were included by Williamson as an additional structural possibility for transactions (Williamson 1991). The existence of businesses (hierarchy) is explained by Coase as an expression of market failure because of market transaction costs. The combination of transaction cost analysis with the problem of uncertainty is established by Williamson (who is a student of Herbert Simon) by starting with the possibility of opportunistic action of the actors because of incomplete information with regard to the actual intentions of the other actors. In concluding complex contracts, future events relevant to the contract cannot yet be designated and thus cannot be considered in the text of the contract. Hence, contracts are always incomplete (Williamson 1985). Uncertainty in transactions opens the possibility of opportunistic behavior, which burdens market transactions with enhanced risks. With merchandise that has a high asset specificity, the risk of the incompleteness of the contract increases, and other parts of the value chain can be expected to be integrated into the firm through vertical integration. Consequently, it is the incompleteness of contracts necessarily resulting from the uncertainty of future contingencies that allows the opportunistic behavior of transaction partners and causes market failure.

The discussion of market failure due to an asymmetrical distribution of information and because of transaction costs, which starts from the general equilibrium theory, is to show that uncertainty can be a cause for the formation of Pareto-inferior equilibria. The information structure of the situation refers to the limits for the formation of complete markets and can be called on to explain inefficient equilibria. Attempts to change the structure of information can lead to prohibitively high transaction costs, which also prevent the emergence of desirable markets. The characteristic of the situation of uncertainty is that actors do not know which is the optimal alternative because they cannot identify the state of the world unambiguously or at least probabilistically. But if, under the assumption of rationally acting actors, we must expect market failure, the question then is how these inefficiencies can be prevented. What mechanisms can overcome market failure due to uncertainty? Empirically, informational structures resulting from an asymmetrical distribution of information and incomplete contracts do not necessarily always lead to market failure. But if we cannot explain how actors solve this problem within the economic theory of action, this justifies an opening of the theoretical perspective to the cognitive, structural, and cultural mechanisms on the basis of which actors make decisions when they do not know how the maximizing decision looks.

Innovation

Unlike any other organizational form of economic activity, capitalistic social formations are distinguished by their dynamic. From the development of the steam engine and the railroad to microelectronics and gene technology, economic history since the beginning of industrialization in the eighteenth century can be understood as a process of steady technological-progress. Technologies that often remained constant for decades or even centuries in precapitalist social formations, which can be described as technologically stagnant, change in short intervals with the advent of capitalistic economic structures and dramatically accelerate the internal dynamic of development. An explanation of the functioning of economic processes is impossible without an understanding of technological dynamics.

Through technical innovations, marginal costs in production processes are lowered or new markets are opened through product innovations. Technological change represents the main source of economic growth in capitalist societies and is thus of central significance for welfare considerations. Technological change has a profound influence on market equilibria, and the value of an economic theory must also be measured by its possibility to provide an explanation of endogenous innovative processes.

Innovations and technological change for the economic process have not always been considered central to economic theory. This claim holds true, although the interconnection of scientific research, technological dynamics, and the market was initially very significant for political economy. Back in the eighteenth century, Adam Smith considered the increasing specialization of scientific research and the connection between science and the progress of the machine-building industry as well as the possibility of learning curve effects. Karl Marx's economic theory saw technological innovations as the dynamic driving force of economic and social development. Marx (1967) distinguished between social formations according to the development of productive forces and saw the reproduction of capitalist modes of production as critically dependent on the perpetual revolution of the production process. Yet the significance of innovative processes in theory declined with the development of neoclassical economic theory. Kirzner indicates that right after the marginal utility revolution until about 1920, economic theory was still interested in the role of the entrepreneur. This interest arose from the question of what connection there was between innovation and profit (Kirzner 1985:2ff.). Pure profit was regarded as a residual quantity requiring explanation that remained after all production factors had obtained the price for their marginal product. The phenomenon of profits that cannot be explained within the framework of neoclassical theory provoked the study of entrepreneurial activities. The works of Frank Knight (1921) and Joseph Schumpeter (1961 [1911]), investigating the significance of innovative activities and the problem of uncertainty, are to be understood in this context. Schumpeter understood innovation as the real seed of capitalism, and his theory of economic development placed the entrepreneur, as a creative, innovative actor, in the center of the analysis of capitalist development. However, Schumpeter did not design his theory of the entrepreneur within the static neoclassical equilibrium theory but rather justified from the significance of innovative processes that this theory has to be supplemented.[49]

Yet Schumpeter's merely partial recognition of equilibrium theory for the understanding of economic processes was a minority position. Instead, consideration of allocative processes of the market on the premise of the formation of efficient equilibria moved into the foreground of economic discourse at the beginning of the twentieth century. Neoclassical theory started, ceteris paribus, from a constant technology, so that dynamic processes of change in the equilibrium models were not considered. Under the assumptions of the model, all income could be attributed to the marginal product of the production factors so that no residual category of profit appeared from which the significance of innovative processes could be analyzed. Even Walras's system does not foresee the entrepreneur making a gain or loss. The basis for this development must be seen mainly in the endeavor for a mathematical formulation of economic theory (Kirzner 1985; Nelson and Winter 1982:195).

Interestingly, the works of Knight and Schumpeter are not formalized. But since the 1920s, the dominant trend within economic theory has consisted of a mathematically precise expression of theoretically developed concepts of economic relations. In this process, the significance of the consideration of innovative process has constantly declined because it resists an endogenous explanation on the basis of the assumptions of the general equilibrium theory (Nelson and Winter 1982:195). Starting from a market equilibrium with efficient resource allocation, the effects of technological change on markets can be studied as a change of the production function, but endogenous causes of technological change cannot be designated. A new technology will lead to a changed allocation equilibrium and to price changes, and can be described as a process of adaptation from one equilibrium to another. However, neoclassical theory starts from a timeless adaptation and the possibility of the complete forecast of equilibrium prices (24).

Innovations are studied here as a third situation of action not only because they are central for understanding economic development but because innovative activities, as has to be proved, are confronted at the same time with *both* systematic problems that are identified as the limits of the rational-actor model. On the one hand, because of the uncertain results of innovative activities,[50] innovations are encumbered by the problem that an optimal investment in innovations cannot be determined ex ante; and on the other hand, the positive externalities of innovations refer to the problem of cooperation. By representing the consideration of technological change in the neoclassical theory of production, this section first illustrates that this theory is concerned in any case with equilibrium effects, but does not provide an explanation of the endogenous causes of technological changes.

Technological Change in the Neoclassical Theory

Interest in integrating questions of technological change into the model of production and growth in the general equilibrium theory first developed in the 1950s under the pressure of the residual debate. Various authors had shown empirically that the growth of the American economy can be explained only to a small extent by the increase of the use of resources and for the most part has to be attributed to the more efficient use of input factors (Abramovitz 1956; Solow 1957). This empirical result of research refutes the neoclassical theory that sees the source of economic growth in the increase of production factors and, based on that, describes equilibrium processes of adjustment that presuppose constant graduations of outputs. The economy is interpreted as being in a moving equilibrium in which successive increases in production factors lead to an increase of demand, through which market equilibrium is maintained. Empirical studies, however, have shown that the neoclassical explanation of economic growth through rising quantities of factors leaves a large part of actual economic growth unexplained as a residuum. Clearly, the growth of production could be explained only by including technological process.

In his *Theory of Economic Development*, Schumpeter (1961:103) had already protested against the neoclassical theory of growth with the argument that growth in factors of production was of negligible importance for the explanation of long-term growth. Schumpeter's intuition was picked up again in the 1950s. The task consisted of integrating technological progress into the neoclassical theory of production and growth. One possible way of doing that had been shown by Hicks (1932) and Schumpeter (1961), who indicated that technological change could be represented as a shift of the production function. Hence, the neoclassical consideration of innovative processes concentrated on the mathematical analysis of the *result* of technological change for the production function, with the goal of modeling technological change within the concept of the production function, which would allow it to be integrated into the static theory. Technical progress is defined as an increase of the global factor productivity, which leads to a shift of the production function. This change can be based on new production methods, the creation of new goods, or the development and utilization of new ways and means to satisfy human needs. Technical progress shifts the isoquant of the national product toward the origin, through which the decreased use of production factors is represented geometrically. Hence, the increase of labor productivity is no longer explained as movement along the isoquant of the production function that assumes steady graduations of outputs, but instead describes growth as a function of higher labor productivity. But, at the same time, the endogenous causes of technical progress are not analyzed but rather only their *effects* within the equilibrium model; how the shift of the production function is induced remains open.

Neoclassical theory endeavors to fit technical progress into other economic contexts and to formulate conditions under which these contexts are not disturbed by technical progress. At the center of this procedure are various conditions of neutrality for technical progress.[51] The neutrality classifications represent conceptual constructs that have only a slight explanation value for the effects of technical progress that occur in reality. It is extremely improbable that technical progress, as assumed in Harrod-neutral changes, has no influence on the employment structure and relative price of goods (Metcalfe 1987:619). Thus, the significance of the concepts of neutrality resides less in a description of the effects of empirically observed technical progress than in the formulation of the conditions under which technical progress can be integrated into the neoclassical theory of production and growth. The distribution constant of the concepts of neutrality corresponds with the Cobb-Douglas production function in which the income distribution does not change even in an altered factor input ratio because of the elasticity of substitution of one. This can be shown based on an example with the production factors of capital and labor as well as the price factors of interest and wages: when the factor price ratio of wages to interest rises by 1 percent, a substitution of labor by capital is achieved. With an elasticity of substitution of one, the substitution amounts to precisely 1 percent of the labor; thus the total income of the labor factor remains constant. Therefore, income neutral progress fills the conditions of a Cobb-Douglas production function because it starts from constant distribution (Cezanne 1994:117).

The Cobb-Douglas production function, however, is suited only for the representation of neutral technical progress, because nonneutral progress leads to a change in distribution and thus does not fill the condition of the substitution elasticity of one. Therefore, the integration of technical progress into the theory of production demands a production function that allows the variable distribution of income. The problem here is that there is an unlimited number of such functions and hence the effect of technical progress cannot be determined unambiguously within the theory of production. Depending on what production function is taken as a basis, the portion of the productivity increase changes, which has to be ascribed to a greater capital intensity and to technological progress. Posing the problem this way led Arrow et al. (1961) to develop an approach in which the elasticity of substitution is still assumed as a constant but does not have to correspond to the value one. The so-called CES function (constant elasticity of substitution) allows the consideration of nonneutral progress in production theory. If the restriction of the constant elasticity of substitution is allowed to fall, however, unlimited production functions are conceivable. Thus, the models presume constant scales of returns for a determined description of the effect of technical progress. Moreover, along with the problem of the indeterminacy of the consideration of technical progress in the theory of production with nonconstant scales of returns is the additional problem that the CES functions give no evidence about the effects of technical progress in reality but are purely theoretical, formalized model considerations.

This consideration of the microeconomic analysis of technical progress is to show that, if necessary, the models can deduce the effect of technological progress under extremely rigid conditions. Because these conditions do not exist in reality, the indeterminacy of the models has to be assumed. However, there are approaches within neoclassical equilibrium analysis that try to understand why technological progress usually takes a labor-saving *direction*, and they thus consider endogenous causes of the course of technological progress at least to some extent. Hicks (1932) starts with the trend of increasing wages and argues that entrepreneurs substitute relatively expensive labor with relatively cheap material capital and thus introduce technically better production methods. This argument is not methodologically convincing, however, because the substitution of labor on the basis of the increased price of this factor is not necessarily linked to technical progress. In other words, the entrepreneur is not interested in the reduction of *specific* costs but rather in cost reduction as such. The increased price of a factor may lead to a search for possibilities of cost reduction, but it makes no difference whether this happens through a saving of labor or capital (Salter 1960). But Hicks's suggestion of an explanation of the direction of technical progress from factor incomes was picked up again later. Kennedy (1964), Samuelson (1965), and von Weizsäcker (1966) argued that it is not the increased cost of labor that gives a labor-saving direction to technical progress but rather the significance of the share of wages in the production costs. Because the wage quota is larger than the capital quota, it is more lucrative to seek possibilities for labor savings. Kennedy assumes that firms at any given time are confronted with "innovation possibility frontiers" that form boundaries for technically possible innovations. The limit sets the proportion of a factor that can be saved in a ratio to the proportion of the other factors to be saved. Jon Elster (1983a:105) objects to this argument that limits to the possibility of innovations can be relevant to behavior only if they have a psychological reality for the entrepreneur: "There may well be, at any given point in time, objective limits to the innovations that can be made on the basis of existing technical knowledge, but these limits can make no difference for behaviour and have no explanatory power unless they manifest themselves somehow to the agents."

The discussion of neoclassical explanations of the direction of technical progress makes it clear that this cannot be explained convincingly. This conclusion also applies to neoclassical attempts to establish the *causes* of technological progress (Kaldor 1957; Arrow 1985b). One concept for this is in the model of investment-induced progress, which starts with the notion that an investment in new equipment always contains a progress or learning effect. Because of learning effects, with every new generation of production equipment more efficient methods of production are introduced, and these lead to an increase of labor productivity. Arrow's model of learning-by-doing starts with the assumption that new equipment investments increase the present production capacity and at the same time also produce new technological knowledge, which increases future productivity.

The approach of investment-induced learning is to be judged as a further development of the economic consideration of technological progress because such progress is no longer assumed to be purely exogenous, and thus as coming from out of the blue, but is now a result of the production process. "Technical change in general can be ascribed to experience, that is the very activity of production that gives rise to problems for which favorable responses are selected over time" (Arrow 1985b:159). Through new equipment, new knowledge is produced, which in turn brings investments. Thus, the shift of the production function (technological progress) is linked inseparably with a movement along the production function (substitution of the production factors). Because the instrument of the production function can no longer be used here, Kaldor and Mirlees (1962) developed the "technical progress function," which allows social aspects—like motivational structures and the spirit of invention—to be integrated into the model. A historical dimension introduced into Arrow's learning model regards the present production capacity as a function of past learning success, which keeps materializing in more efficient forms of operations. In the model of investment-induced progress, however, social conditions and the learning effect are simply taken into account formally. In Kaldor's model, the motivational aspects were not even explained; and in Arrow's model, the effect of technological progress is understood as an automatic function of investments. It requires no special motivation or activities aimed at producing more efficient methods of production and interfering in the equilibrium process. Models of investment-induced learning axiomatically start from a rate of progress without explaining endogenously how it came about.

But if we consider processes of innovation empirically, they are the result of specific activities aimed at changing the production process or at the introduction of new products; they cannot be understood as routines, whose results can be forecast in detail. Models of induced innovation omit the whole problematic of the unpredictability of the success of innovative attempts and the resulting problem of a discontinuous change, which refers to the study of concrete innovative changes and the significance of the individual perception of the behavioral context by the actors. Schumpeter recognized the creative function of the entrepreneur in his activities for the composition of new combinations of factors and rejected the static equilibrium analysis of neoclassical economics for understanding economic development because of the discontinuity of the changes evoked by technological innovation (Schumpeter 1961:93ff.). Starting from a constant rate of progress, as in the model of induced innovation, this complex of problems is omitted, without showing that technological change corresponds empirically in some way to the assumptions made in the model. The assumption that technological change does not emerge in large part from deliberate actions, with which entrepreneurs react to market stimuli, is especially unrealistic. This procedure reflects the possible insignificance of discontinuous innovative processes for understanding economic development less than the inability of a theory aimed at static adaptation processes to integrate dynamic disequilibrium processes into the structures of the theory (see Freeman 1987:859).

In the 1980s, however, building on Arrow's work, Paul Romer (1986; 1990) developed a theoretical approach with the endogenous growth theory, which explains innovations as a result of the internal dynamic of businesses. Unlike Arrow, Romer did not regard innovations as public goods but as partially privately appropriated, through which private investments in innovation activities and thus technological change can be integrated endogenously into the model. In Romer's model, this assumption is based on the inclusion of market power through which businesses that invest in technological innovations can achieve prices above the marginal production costs. Thus the costs of innovation can be amortized. With the assumption of market power, referring explicitly to Schumpeter, Romer frees himself from neoclassical theory where power plays no role in equilibrium. Because the marginal value of human capital occupied with research and development can be appropriated only partially because of the positive external effects of innovative activities, according to the theory, investments in innovative activities are expected to remain suboptimal. The endogenous theory of technological change thus shows, on the one hand, that investments in innovative activities are premised on incomplete competition and, on the other, that an optimal rate of investment cannot be expected solely through market stimuli. Hence, innovations prove to be another limit to the efficient market allocation of economic goods.

In sum, it can be maintained that neoclassical theory is concerned primarily with the *effect* of technological progress within the framework professed by production and growth theory. The various concepts of neutrality indicate the rigid conditions under which innovations can be integrated into the static consideration. These conditions are not given empirically. Production functions neither exist with the qualities assumed by the theory nor is technological progress income-neutral. In explaining the *direction* of innovative changes, neoclassical theory can give no convincing answer to the question of why this generally has a labor-saving effect. The idea of an orientation to objectively given limits to the possibilities of innovation presumes a knowledge of these limits by the actors; but, in light of the complexity of innovation decisions, this assumption is heroic. As for an endogenous explanation of the *causes* of technological progress, neoclassical theory can only refer to the rigid concept of investment-induced progress. Because the rate of progress is linked to material capital investments, an automatic behavior of technological change is assumed; this is not given empirically and does not make the microproblematic of innovative activities disappear completely. But the endogenous theory of technological change developed by Romer shows that imperfect markets can be a presumption for more efficient equilibria and thus refers to Schumpeter's critique of the 1930s.

Institutionalist and Evolutionary Approaches

Nelson and Winter (1982:204) have indicated the stubborn bifurcation of the consideration of innovations and technological change within economics. On one side are the previously described models of production and growth theory, as well as considerations from welfare theory, which, however, do not refer to the empirical practice of technological changes. On the other side, since the 1960s, a research literature has emerged in economics that deals with the empirical development of technological change from a microperspective and pays attention to historical and sociological aspects.[52] This literature joins the tradition of Schumpeter in the broadest sense by recognizing limits for neoclassical equilibrium theory in the consideration of innovative processes and technological change. Central assumptions of the neoclassical theory, like the use of a unified technology, the timeless learning of new technologies, and the possibility of optimizing decision making in situations with uncertainty, are abandoned, and, instead, empirical observations of innovative processes and the diffusion of new technologies are used to explain economic phenomena like different rates of profit, the perpetuation of inefficient technologies, and disequilibria. On the microeconomic level, the rediscovery of the significance of the entrepreneur to explain economic processes of change, which began in the late 1960s (Kirzner 1985), is also part of these economic considerations. The circuitous way the theory dealt with phenomena of technological change was considered by some economists of the neoclassical tradition as problematic,[53] but only a few approaches can be perceived that open neoclassical analysis to empirical insights.

Economists interested in the microeconomic aspects of technological change refer particularly to the significance of genuine uncertainty of the results of innovative activities as a central variable to explain the significance of structuring and order-generating elements in the innovation process. If it is not possible to make optimizing decisions for investments in innovations because it cannot be determined ex ante what output is achieved with a given input, actors orient themselves by institutionalized rules of decision making that allow a reduction of complexity. Thus, institutionalized rules are created that explicitly break with the maximizing assumptions of neoclassical theory whose rational actors are provided with complete information, and a transition is made to the consideration of world views, embodied in "beliefs" and social practices. Unlike the expectation of neoclassical theory, empirical studies show that the reaction of firms to technological innovations is "sticky," and there is no question of a constant flexible optimization. Giovanni Dosi, who has tried in various works to distill theoretical substrata from empirical studies of technological change (Dosi 1988; Dosi and Orsengio 1988), sees the structuring of change based particularly in the nature of the learning process: "Technologies develop along relatively ordered paths shaped by the technical properties, the problem-solving heuristics and the cumulative expertise embodied in *technological paradigms*" (Dosi and Orsengio 1988:16).

Instead of starting from the complete flexibility of actors in innovation decisions, which is guided solely by the optimization postulate, technological paradigms refer to change along determined paths, which, once taken, can be hard to leave because of actual and cognitive sunk costs. The paradigms lead both to "lock-in" effects, which makes adjustment to market changes more difficult, and to the reduction of uncertainty, which makes purposeful behavior in complex environments possible. Thus, technological change is regarded as relatively independent of market signals and linked rather with endogenous historical developments. Rosenberg (1976:110) has shown that market stimuli for the reduction of costs can explain so little "of the particular sequence and timing of innovative activity" because they always exist. Therefore, it requires *specific* endogenous stimuli that can be explained from technological paradigms and specific structural indicators like the size of the enterprise, scale effects, and the different capacity for innovation of enterprises. The selection mechanisms within technological paradigms refer to the control of economic processes of change and the generation of structures of order in the economy through an "evolutionary hand" and less through the "invisible hand" of the market.

Knowledge of the dynamics of technological change based on empirical studies contradicts the neoclassical claim of utility-maximizing action of rational actors in dynamic environments. Existing technologies are used differently, enterprises have different profit margins, and, in view of the complexity of innovative processes, an optimal rate of innovation cannot be expected. This leads to the observation of an extremely variable "fitness" of firms in their market environment and can be used as a starting point for modeling an evolutionary theory of technological change.[54] Here, the selection procedures that develop in the course of history are considered on the basis of the different adjustment capacities of organizations and organization populations. This approach is not examined more closely here, because this chapter is concerned simply with a critique of orthodox economics, whose premise consists of the efficient allocation of resources through the market, assuming rationally acting actors. The evolutionary theory relinquishes the equilibrium and rationality concept of neoclassical economics and is hence not to be criticized from the same perspective. However, I do hint at the danger in evolutionary theory of assuming, with the structural dependence of action, an overdetermination of technological development in the economy, and thus neglecting the significance of voluntary, creative aspects of action in innovation and learning processes.

The Problem of the Optimal Rate of Innovation

The empirical findings of technological change described in the preceding paragraphs which were to show the problematic of neoclassical theories of induced innovation, cannot be taken as a theoretical rejection of the normative superiority of a theory that derives social optima from individual maximizing decisions in decentralized market structures. The essential limitation of the conception of induced innovation is that technological progress is considered not as an independent economic function but as an inherent part of the production activities. Consideration of technological change as a by-product of other economic activities is to be discarded, and innovation should be understood as a result of purposeful investments in research and development. If it can be shown that competitive markets are capable of generating an optimal rate of innovation, we can then explain theoretically why a market organization structure of innovative activities in the economy reaches a normative primacy from the point of view of economic welfare. The expectation of efficiency of economic theory would thus not yet be fulfilled empirically, but it would be shown theoretically that market structures and rational action lead to an optimal rate of innovative activities.

It should be anticipated that such an optimal rate of innovative activities cannot be deduced under the condition of competitive markets. This is connected, on the one hand, with the informational structure of uncertainty in innovative processes, which was discussed earlier. "What markets cannot do is to deliver information about or discount the possibility of future states-of-the-world whose occurrence is, to different degrees, the unintentional result of present decisions taken by heterogeneous agents characterized by different competences, beliefs, and expectations" (Dosi and Orsenigo 1988:18). On the other hand, the reasons for a suboptimal allocation of resources for innovative activities have to be seen in the special qualities of innovations as economic goods. These qualities are to be discussed here.

Kenneth Arrow (1985a) was concerned with the efficiency of competitive markets for generating optimal levels of innovative activity. An optimal use of resources for research and development exists when the marginal utility of these activities corresponds exactly to the marginal utility for alternative possibilities of the use of the resources. In the article "Economic Welfare and the Allocation of Resources for Invention" (1985a [1962]), which had a substantial influence on subsequent economic research on the relationship of market structure and innovation activities, Arrow cites three reasons why market failure can occur in case of innovations: uncertainty, the possible indivisibility of goods, and the impossibility of private acquisition of goods. These conditions for market failure represent only the negation of the assumptions under which the general equilibrium theory can deduce an optimal resource allocation. Because of the specifics of innovations, however, these assumptions are fulfilled only very conditionally in research and development, and therefore a suboptimal allocation of resources must be expected.

Arrow first emphasizes the risky nature of innovative activities. The result of investments in research and development cannot be predicted and it must therefore be expected that the goals of developing markets through product innovation or cost reduction through changes of the production process are not achieved. Because this risk cannot be taken by all enterprises, underinvestment in innovation results. However, this inefficient result can be met by shifting risks by taking out insurance. Businesses can transfer the financial risk of a failure or a higher expenditure on their research to a third party by taking out insurance, which bears these costs in case of a loss. In reality, this takes place in contracts on a basis of full cost compensation, which is used especially in military research. Development and construction costs are paid by the state as a party to the contract, along with additional profits. But another insurance mechanism against the risks of investment in innovation is also financing by issuing stock to distribute the risk of failure and make it acceptable for the individual actors. Finally, the organization of research and development in big businesses is a form of insurance. Here, the business acts as its own insurer, which can survive the failure of individual research projects. However, the possibility of insurance does not lead to an efficient allocation of resources for innovation either: that is, shifting risk generates the problems of moral hazard and adverse selection, described in the previous section, because the stimulus for efficient use of resources is weakened: "The shifting of risks is again accompanied by a weakening of incentives to efficiency. Substitute motivations—whether pecuniary, such as executive compensation and profit sharing, or nonpecuniary, such as prestige—may be found, but the dilemma of the moral factor can never be completely resolved" (Arrow 1985a:109).

Another aspect of the inefficiency of markets for the allocation of resources for innovation can be deduced from the specific qualities of innovations as economic goods. Innovations have characteristics that make them comparable to information and limit them in competitive markets. An optimal market allocation presumes that information is available without cost to all actors, assuming there are no transaction costs in the transmission. This is the only way that information (innovation) can be used optimally under the criteria of welfare economics and that monopoly capital annuities can be prevented. In the neoclassical standard model, this condition is always filled. Yet, in filling the condition, there is no stimulus to invest in innovations. Instead the stimulus for innovation consists precisely of creating property rights (patents or at least a first-mover advantage), but this leads in principle to the suboptimal use of innovation from the perspective of welfare economics. Thus, the existing paradox is "that in a free-enterprise economy the profitability of invention requires a nonoptimal allocation of resources" (Arrow 1985a:112). In slightly different words, a distinction can be made between private and social yields of innovations. Social yields result from the utility of the innovation for the increase of efficiency of production processes or the development of new products.[55] But a stimulus for the allocation of private resources in innovation exists only if at least as much can be appropriated privately so that investment is profitable, taking opportunity costs into account. But how can the yield of an innovation be appropriated privately? As soon as the knowledge exists, it is difficult for the innovator to keep other entrepreneurs from using it. But if others are kept from it, then the social utility is determined only from the usage of the information by the innovator, which is in principle suboptimal.[56]

It is well known from the discussion of the protection of intellectual property that the information character of innovations creates enormous problems for a private appropriation. Patents can never be so complete as to make all information available from the innovation accessible only by purchase, and they also have a limited validity, after which the information is freely available. In the process of research, information on the procurement of more information is constantly used without having to pay for it. Only under this condition is the system of patents socially tolerable at all, but, at the same time, the stimulus to invest in innovations is weakened. The limitation of property rights in innovations also helps explain why this problem arises most strongly in the area of basic research. On the one hand, this research is characterized by high risks, and on the other, the "scatter effect" of positive externalities, from which other actors derive utility, is doubtless greatest. But private property rights to information are also curtailed by enticing labor to leave its employer and by use of the information itself,[57] which at least shifts the thinking of other actors in view of the new limits of possibility.[58]

Along with the possibility of introducing patent systems, keeping innovations secret,[59] or appropriating a large part of the social yield through monopoly formation, there is another option—as with other public goods—of organizing research and development by the state. Through state intervention in research, the private risk inherent in investments in research and development can be absorbed, and innovation can be removed from the presumption of the possibility of private appropriation. Aside from the adjunct problems of moral hazard and adverse selection mentioned earlier—which can be met partially by designing payment systems or nonpecuniary behavioral guidance, and by norms specific to professions—the government organization of research naturally means separating it from competitive markets, which acknowledges that an optimal level of investment in innovation in a competitive economy cannot be explained exclusively by market stimuli.

This result is also acknowledged by the more exacting models of the general equilibrium theory, which study questions of competitive structure and innovation based on game theory. Here we shall describe only the model sketched in the early 1980s by Dasgupta and Stiglitz (1980a), which shows that in, "F + E games," there must be no solution.[60] In the model, the market structure is considered not as given exogenously but rather as a set of several interacting enterprises whose activities let a specific market structure emerge. The model assumes that investments in innovations are profitable; uncertainty is neglected. If we start from an equilibrium, then two businesses investing in innovations have to invest the same sum. But this cannot be an equilibrium because then one firm could raise its investments marginally, and thus increase its chance of profit from the investment from 50 to 100 percent. If, in an equilibrium, only one enterprise would invest, the expected profit had to be zero because otherwise competitors would appear. If we assume a Nash equilibrium, the behavior of the investing firm has to be optimal relative to the action of the other players. However, this cannot be the case if the investing firm expects no profit, because it could then increase its profit by reducing its investments. Thus, it is shown that in an equilibrium, only one firm can invest, but that at the same time, this assumption is inconsistent, and therefore there is no solution to the game.

The discussion of the difficulties of explaining innovation in equilibrium models raises the question of how actors decide on innovation. There is no doubt that actors try to maximize their profit through innovation. But, if no optimal investments in innovations can be deduced because the output cannot be anticipated for sure from the input, or because no equilibrated solution can be represented, actors cannot possibly make their decisions on the basis of considerations of optimization or achieve a socially efficient allocation of resources. The "invisible hand" of the market does not lead to socially desirable results. There is a fundamental ambiguity between alternatives of innovation. How this ambiguity is assimilated into actions and contributes to the social order of the economy requires explanation. Which assumptions are required to make actors invest in research and development under conditions of uncertainty and the difficulties of the private appropriation of products of innovation also demands explanation.

In *The Theory of Economic Development*, Schumpeter (1961) argued that entrepreneurs are indeed interested in profit, but innovation cannot be understood from the motive of goal-oriented utility-maximizing. "Such economic subjects [entrepreneurs] do indeed live luxuriously. But they live luxuriously because they have the means to do that, they do not acquire to live luxuriously" (1961:136). What Schumpeter (134) saw as an irrational striving for changes by introducing new combinations of factors required a motivational structure that was not oriented primarily toward pecuniary intentions. Instead, Schumpeter cited "the dream and the will to found a private kingdom" (93) the will to win, and the joy in appearances as three motivational prerequisites of entrepreneurship. The innovative achievement of entrepreneurs is understood as creative action that is contrasted with the static-hedonistic action of economic theory.[61] "The typical entrepreneur does not ask himself if every effort he undertakes also promises a sufficient 'enjoyment margin.' He does not bother with the hedonistic fruits of his labor. He is restless because he can do nothing else, he does not live to enjoy what is acquired" (137).

Even without agreeing with Schumpeter's list of concrete motives, on the background of the difficulties of the neoclassical explanation of innovations developed here, we can grant the argument that "irrational" motives for this process as defined by economic theory can be relevant because the discontinuous change through innovation does not allow any predictable cost-utility calculations. If such calculations were possible, it would in fact require no entrepreneurial function, but solely that of management, and the "simple joy in doing" (138) would be a meaningless motivation for action at best. But under the conditions of uncertainty, the deduction of optimal strategies is not possible. If we simply do not want to assume that actors act arbitrarily, we need a positive theory of decision-making behavior under given conditions. But such a theory exceeds the theoretical bases of the economic model of action.

The critique developed in this chapter casts doubt on the rational-actor model as a conclusive theory of decision making in economic action contexts. The concomitant question is what theories of action can help us understand how actors achieve efficient results of action. There is an obvious empirical interest in this question because, despite the difficulties indicated, actors cooperate with one another and also act in situations with uncertainty; and there is a normative interest as well. Under which conditions do actors manage to develop trust and thus achieve superior results of action? How can actors deduce strategies under conditions of uncertainty? What assumptions are required for investments in innovations despite uncertainty and limited possibilities of private appropriation? To answer these questions, we need a theoretical conception of action that is detached from the typological commitment to rational optimizing, which also considers the embeddedness of economic action into an institutional and normative order as well as the social structure of the actors.

In the four studies presented in Part II, I try to obtain elements of a sociological conceptualization of the three action situations from the theoretical conceptions and formulations of Émile Durkheim, Talcott Parsons, Niklas Luhmann, and Anthony Giddens that are relevant for economic sociology.[62] This procedure was selected because sociology, in its founding stage (1890–1920), also developed as a critique of economic theory. In this formative phase of the field, most of the theories taking shape agree that social order cannot be based on the economic theory of action.[63] But, at the same time, sociology accepts the problem of social order itself as the central question of social theory. So it can be expected that in the tense relationship with economic theory, approaches evolved that can indicate starting points to overcome the indicated limits. "Overcoming" does not mean locating theoretical positions that must be commensurable with the postulates of economic theory. Economic theory is not likely to be reformed by an external impetus. This would require an alternative theory that could be formulated mathematically and produce unambiguous results. There is nothing of the sort in sociological theory. Hence, "overcoming" also implies consideration of explanatory models for understanding the problem, which do not submit unconditionally to the formal and theoretical demands of orthodox economics. The limits of the theory are interpreted here as limits of the understanding of action based on a teleological interpretation of action, which is also a precondition for the mathematical formalization of economic theory.

While the primary goal of discussing the works of these sociological theorists is to find indications for an action theory that allows for a superior understanding of the developed systematic problems in economic decision making, it has at the same time an additional aim. It is also intended to give a systematic assessment of the authors' contribution to economic sociology.

PART TWO
CONCEPTS

PART TWO

TWO

ÉMILE DURKHEIM: THE ECONOMY

AS MORAL ORDER

> It is not possible for a social function to exist without any
> moral discipline. Otherwise, there is nothing left except
> individual cravings, which cannot regulate themselves because
> of their essential limitlessness and insatiability, but must
> be controlled from outside.
> —*Émile Durkheim*

É MILE DURKHEIM belongs to that generation of sociologists of the nineteenth and early twentieth centuries who found the subject matter of sociological study in the process of social transformation and the conflictual transition from traditional agrarian societies to modern industrial societies that was caused by industrialization. The question of the possible social cohesion of societies that are marked by increasing individual freedom and the concomitant dissolution of relationships based on tradition had concerned political philosophy since the seventeenth century. Both contract theories and the theory of order of political economy sketched an optimistic scenario for the problem of social order in modern societies. The pacification of social relations is expected by giving up individual rights of sovereignty to the Leviathan or by market coordination, even if the members of society no longer belong to a moral community. This optimism was obviously counteracted by socioeconomic crises, which affected all industrializing societies in the nineteenth century. The misery of the proletarian masses documented in countless contemporary studies and literary descriptions and in the political conflicts—not only between capital and labor, but also between the middleclass, the clergy, and the nobility, or forces of restoration, reform, and revolution (Müller 1983)—make the incipient social structures seem profoundly anomistic.

The development of Durkheim's sociology and the significance of the economy in it must be understood from Durkheim's double awareness of crises, which refers on the one hand to the economic, social, and political situation of France after the defeat in the war of 1870–71, and on the other to the failure of the humanities (*sciences morales*) to contribute to overcoming social anomie.[1] The Third Republic was marked by political instability, which not only caused "elementary democratic rights [to be] institutionalized only hesitantly and comparatively late, but also prevented the strict formulation of a farsighted policy that could have confronted the nascent socioeconomic problems" (Müller 1983:17). Durkheim saw the economic and political anomie of French society as an expression of a moral crisis, which was closely linked with the changes in economic structure. The development of the market as a dominant mechanism of economic coordination was read as social disembedding of the economy, which disconnects it from the moral order of society.

If political instability and economic anomie in France represented elements of the objective social crisis, Durkheim saw the disparate state of the humanities as another aspect of the crisis, because they prevented a scientific contribution to overcoming the anomic conditions of society.[2] As for the liberal economic theory, the problem was that no reform initiatives could be derived from it because it expected markets to be self-regulating. Durkheim was convinced that only social reforms guided by scientific insight into the laws of society—and not revolutionary abolition or restoration[3]—could overcome the social crises and contribute to the goal of a just social order. For Durkheim, following the tradition of thought of Saint-Simon, Comte, and Espinas, the task of sociology as the *science of morality* consisted of scientifically discovering social (moral) conditions and their institutional presumptions, which enable social integration and overcoming anomic states. For this, sociology must develop as a science that deals empirically with the bases of social integration. Thus, beyond the political and socioeconomic crises, Durkheim perceived an intellectual crisis in the transition from traditional to modern society, which is also responsible for the anomie in the Third Republic; and he saw reviving the moral sciences as a prerequisite to solving the crisis. Durkheim's concern with the economy occurs against this sociopolitical background from the specific perspective of a theory that asks for the preconditions of social order in modern societies. The starting point for investigating economic relations is not the conditions of the efficient functioning of the economy, but rather its contribution to the reproduction of social order or, respectively, its potentially destructive effect on social integration.

These general considerations show the three levels on which the debate with economics occupied a central place for Durkheim. First, Durkheim sees that, in the process of the development of modern industrial societies, the economy develops into the structurally most important social realm.[4] At the same time, the penchant toward functional differentiation of the economy in industrial society represents a central cause of economic and social anomie. The development of the economy is read as an increasing deregulation of economic relations, which disconnects their moral links. Contractual relations that are felt by society as unjust become possible and thus contradict the goal of a just social order. The anomie of economic relations is an expression of a lack of social regulation and can be overcome only by restoring a moral rule to the economy. Durkheim's first reference to economics consists, therefore, of localizing the economy as a central cause of the social crisis in the transition from a traditional to a modern society, and labeling this crisis as moral.

The second reference to economics is methodological. Durkheim develops his outline of sociology as a science of morality in a debate with utilitarian approaches in social theory.[5] Starting from the primacy of society, Durkheim's social theory breaks away from both the contract theory of political philosophy and the explanation of social order in political economy based on the harmony of interests of competing participants in the market; and here the critical debate with Herbert Spencer plays a prominent role. Durkheim sees the establishment of his program of sociology as a science of morality in clear opposition to concepts of order that start from the individual.

Third, closely related to this methodological level is an institutional level, where Durkheim argues with economics. Durkheim sees himself facing the task of legitimating sociology as a new scientific discipline vis-à-vis the other social sciences and humanities, and so he had to demarcate its proper subject area and define its methodological approach. Economics assumed a special significance for Durkheim because it claimed to have outlined a theory of social order of modern societies in the model of the market, and because it could resort to a well-developed theory. Nevertheless, Durkheim's rejection of the economic model of order goes along with the rejection of classical economics. In Durkheim's view, the economy must also be analyzed from the perspective of a social order preceding individual behavior; hence, Durkheim's sociology asserts imperialist claims over economics.

From the explanation of the centrality of economics—as a social, methodological, and institutional domain—the debate with the functioning of the capitalist economy can be expected to assume a central value in Durkheim's work. That is, however, only conditionally the case. The title of Durkheim's best known monograph, *The Division of Labor in Society* (1984[1893]), does hint at the investigation of the structures and institutions of an economic order based on the division of labor. In opposition to this expectation, however, neither in *The Division of Labor in Society* nor in other writings is Durkheim concerned in detail with the structures of the market economy. Durkheim's debate with economics is directed essentially at the consideration of economic institutions, which are, however, not studied empirically but are considered in the normative perspective of the function they should assume for regulating economic relations.

The structure of economic relations in industrial society appears mainly as a pathological deviation from a normative model.

Concern with the significance of economic institutions for the social cohesion of society occurs essentially in the two works, *The Division of Labor in Society* and *Professional Ethics and Civic Morals* (1992[1896–1900]). In the former, Durkheim raises the question of how modern societies that are characterized by increasing functional differentiation, can develop the necessary requirements for social cohesion. The analysis of economic institutions is embedded in the critique of Spencer's utilitarian social theory, and only in the third book of *The Division of Labor in Society* are some aspects of the empirical structure of economic relations in the process of industrialization described. In the lectures, *Professional Ethics and Civic Morals*, the historical and anthropological reconstruction of the development of the institutions of property and contract are in the foreground along with the justification of the establishment of professional guilds for regulating economic relations in industrial societies. In addition, there are remarks on economics in the lectures published posthumously by Marcel Mauss, *Le Socialisme* (1971), and in *Suicide* (1951 [1897]), *Rules of Sociological Method* (1966 [1895]), and various programmatic writings, articles, and reviews (Durkheim 1885; 1900; 1908; 1978a; 1978b).

The incongruity between the causal significance Durkheim ascribes to the economy for the contemporary social crisis and the negligible analytical attempt to understand the functioning of modern economic structures can be explained with reference to Durkheim's sociological program itself, on the one hand, and with the division of labor within the Durkheim school, on the other. If it is understood as a premise of Durkheim's sociology that, even under the conditions of modern social development, social order depends on the moral integration of the actors, and institutions are both an expression and a guarantee of this morality, then the perspective of the economy and its institutions almost necessarily results: economic institutions and economic action must also be bound up morally in modern contexts. In this programmatic nexus of meaning, the analysis of such economic structures, which are regarded as anomic—because they lack the moral bond—loses centrality because it can depict only the data of the pathological condition, which is proved sufficiently in any event by the obvious socioeconomic crisis. It is enough to indicate the anomic condition of the economy and to interpret anomie as a deficit of regulation.[6] A detailed analysis is worthwhile only for economic institutions like contracts and property, which can be interpreted as moral entities. So, the causality Durkheim ascribed to the economy for the social crisis does not contradict the negligible analytical attention to the *existing* anomic economic structures, because few additional clues for the necessary reform of the economy would result from the analysis. Attention must be directed instead to the structural characteristics of functioning economic formations. Their anatomy gives information about the necessary institutional reforms that can transform the *pathological* condition of the economy to a *normal* one and thus allow a socially acceptable organization of the economy.[7]

But also keep in mind that, even during his lifetime, more than other sociologists in the early stages of the profession, Durkheim was able to form a school with his program of sociology. Important empirical studies in economic sociology, which refer explicitly to Durkheim's program of sociology, were produced especially by François Simiand and Maurice Halbwachs.[8] In the debate with Durkheim's concept of the economy, this would suggest resorting to these studies from the Durkheim School. But because, in the context of systematic inquiry, this book is concerned with general concepts, it is precisely Durkheim's theoretical and conceptual articles that are expected to yield the most information. What stands in the foreground is Durkheim's premise that stable economic relations cannot be developed if the social bonds between actors are based solely on their selfish interests.

In this chapter, I am concerned with Durkheim's conceptualization of the economy from the interpretive angle of the establishment of sociology as a science of morality, directed practically to the socioeconomic and intellectual crisis of France at the end of the nineteenth century. Initially, we focus on Durkheim's methodological starting point, which creates the sociological perspective by criticizing various contract theories and political economy as starting points for explanations of social order. But the chapter centers on Durkheim's argument with the institutions of contract, price, property, and technology, and the incipient attempt to understand these as part of a moral order. This concept is dealt with most concisely in *The Division of Labor in Society* and in *Professional Ethics and Civic Morals*. The emphasis on the institutional embeddedness of action is the central demarcation line of Durkheim's economic sociology. Based on Durkheim's critique of the market as a coordination mechanism of economic exchange, I shall try to deal with the tension between individuality and the moral bond, which is central for Durkheim's argument with economics. On the one hand, Durkheim welcomed the individuality taking shape in modern societies and, on the other hand, he saw that it had to be bound morally and institutionally so that a just social order could develop. Yet, in the discussion of the institutions of contract and price, Durkheim clearly bound the action of the actors in market contexts of modern economics so strongly into a moral order that the market function of coordinating antagonistic cooperation relations is almost abolished. However, Durkheim's support of institutionalizing professional groups to regulate economic relations (discussed in the last section of the chapter) suggests possible solutions of the cooperation problem.

Sociology as the Science of Morality

In the Opening Lecture of 1887 (Durkheim 1978a), Durkheim expressed the conviction that sociology could be established as a science only if it presented a clearly outlined program of research that delineated it from other sciences and developed its own method of research, which would allow it to study the laws of society as well as to substantiate the practical use of sociology. Like no other sociologist at the inception of the profession, at the beginning of his career Durkheim developed a program in which he defined the subject matter, the methodology, and the delineation of sociology as opposed to other disciplines. A debate with Durkheim's understanding of economics and his criticism of outlines of economic theory should start from this conceptual definition of sociology because Durkheim's view of economics develops on the background of the program of establishing sociology. Durkheim does not use the empirical analysis of economic processes or institutions to outline his concept of economics but almost derives it deductively from the program of sociology as the science of morality.

In *The Rules of Sociological Method* (1966[1895]), Durkheim provides a twofold definition of sociology. On the one hand, he defines "social facts" as the subject matter of the profession, and on the other, in the foreword to the second edition of the book, he defines sociology as a science of institutions.[9] Social facts, according to Durkheim, are "every way of acting, fixed or not, capable of exercising on the individual an external constraint; or again, every way of acting which is general throughout a given society, while at the same time, existing in its own right, independent of its individual manifestations" (Durkheim 1966:13). Three qualities that characterize this definition of the social fact can be distinguished: it is external to the individual, it is general, and it exercises a restraint on action. Durkheim's concept of society is marked by seeing it as an entity preceding social actors, which serves to regulate action. Durkheim (1971) considers this concept as the "socialist" one, which starts from the premise that society cannot be understood as the sum of its parts but rather exhibits an independence. "Society is not merely a sum of individuals. Rather, the system formed by their association represents a specific reality which has its own characteristics" (Durkheim 1966:103). Ontological precedence resides not in the individual but in society as a supraindividual entity, which exists sui generis and regulates social action. Hence Durkheim dissociates himself from individualistic social theories and also understands his sociological program in stark contract to economic theory. As a science of morality, sociology is concerned with the regulative influence on the behavior of members of society and on the integration of social groups; at the same time, this social influence cannot be understood as the deliberate result of a contrast between the actors.

According to Hans-Peter Müller's (1983:42ff.) interpretation, Durkheim develops a position of sociological realism that integrates three elements: the naturalness of society, the restraint of the social, and the discontinuity of individual and society. The naturalness of society means that the domain of the social is also subject to an objective law that can be studied precisely, just as nature and its laws are already studied by the natural sciences. This position, which is adopted especially from Saint-Simon and Comte, shall establish sociology as a positive science. The dualistic interpretation postulating that only physical nature is subject to objective laws whereas the social world can be shaped contingently by human will is rejected. The possibility of the contingent shaping of social relations would prevent the establishment of sociology as a positive science because no laws of society that could not be reduced to the individual could be discovered. The positive version of sociology developed in *The Rules of Sociological Method* can also explain why Durkheim demands "considering social facts as things" (Durkheim 1966:14). Social rules have an objectivity that transcends the subjective will and therefore can be studied as independent entities of society. The goal of sociology consists of discovering the laws of society, the only means that allows them to be influential and that makes reformist interventions in society conceivable: "It is sociology which, by discovering the laws of social reality, will permit us to direct historical evolution with greater reflection than in the past; for we can change nature, whether moral or physical, only by conforming to its laws" (Durkheim 1978b:75).

The second element of Durkheim's sociological realism asserts the restraint of society, that is, the existence of social constraints that begin with society and exercise a regulating influence on social action. These constraints cannot be understood as the deliberate result of a compact between the members of society because society is a force transcending the individuals, which always exists independently from them. In the third aspect of sociological realism, the idea of the discontinuity of individual and society, Durkheim turns against both the harmonious ideas of economic theory, which hold that social order emerges from the pursuit of individual interests, and against extreme versions of organizational theories, which see individual action as merely the execution of a higher will, and thus exclude all freedom of action.

In developing the notion of sociological fact, Durkheim cites several examples to explicate social facts as sociological objects of research. These examples give first clues to the consideration of economics. They include law and customs, as well as religious dogmas, styles, clothing fashions, language, coinage, and procedures of industrial production. Apart from the problematic heterogeneity of the use of the term (Müller 1983), this list shows clearly that Durkheim subsumes economic structures and institutions under social facts. This is also confirmed by the foreword to the second issue of *L'Année Sociologique* (1960a:348), where Durkheim states explicitly that economic facts are also social facts.

Durkheim's Critique of Economics

With the program of sociology as the science of morality, Durkheim had the means to delineate sociology from the other social sciences and relate it to them. Durkheim's critique of the situation of the humanities in France objected strongly to philosophy and its speculative nature. But he was mostly concerned with contrasting sociology to two types of theories of social order: contract theories of political philosophy that understand the emergence of society from the deliberate decision of the members of society and view the restraint emanating from society as the result of individual agreement; and the type of social theory of economics that understands society as a natural result of the aggregation of individual pursuit of interests in exchange. From the perspective of Durkheim's sociological program, both types of social theories are unsuitable starting points for a sociological theory of order because they locate ontological primacy in the individual and do not understand society as an entity that precedes the individual (Durkheim 1978a:44).

Contract theories of political philosophy regard society and the restraint on the individual emanating from society as the deliberate result of a contractual agreement in which individuals give up the rights of sovereignty to a governmental authority, expecting pacification of their social relations. In contrast, Durkheim's concept of the social fact asserts the reverse connection of a sociality that precedes the individual. Society is a fact that confronts actors with the same objectivity as natural laws and, like any natural law, it cannot be viewed as a deliberate product of human action.[10] Durkheim's critique also objected to the paradox of a *deliberate restraint* within contract theory and thus advances directly to the cooperation problem: why should free and independent individuals come together for the purpose of limiting their own freedom by establishing an apparatus of restraint?

In contrast, for economic theory "social life is essentially spontaneous and society is a natural phenomenon (Durkheim 1966:122). In this perspective, society is indeed also an entity that can be reduced ontologically to individual actors, but society does not materialize through a deliberate act of creation but rather as an unintended result of economic exchange. Thus, Durkheim sees the nature of the economic theory as an at least limited model for shaping the social sciences. For him, economics is the first science that understood that social life is also subject to a set of laws (Durkheim 1978a). This can be explained with two examples from the French context: for Durkheim, the physiocratic tradition is the first school of thought that proceeds from the assumption of economic laws that regulate economic relations. According to the physiocratic view, the function of the economists consists of discovering these laws and thus creating the necessary knowledge for government intervention. Therefore, the parallel to Durkheim's sociological program consists not only in the acknowledgment of the existence of social laws and ascribing the task of discovering them to the social sciences, but also in the view shared with the economists that the social sciences can intervene in social processes. One important difference between the physiocrats and Durkheim is that Durkheim did not consider the state as the central authority of intervention.

In the Opening Lecture of 1887, Durkheim himself explained the ability of economics to provide a model to analyze sociological facts by referring to economic price theory. The price of a good is determined by the aggregate of supply and demand. At the same time, the price is experienced by the individual actor as a datum he cannot escape. Price thus contains the elements Durkheim uses to describe social facts.[11] This analysis of price is surprisingly similar to the description of the French economist Léon Walras, who explained the model of the price taker independent of Durkheim, at about the same time: "Wheat is worth 24 francs a hectolitre. We observe, first of all, that this fact partakes of the character of a *natural* phenomenon. This particular value of wheat in terms of money, that is to say, this price of wheat, does not result either from the will of the buyer or from the will of the seller or from any arrangement between the two" (Walras 1954:69). The externality of the price, which cannot be changed by a deliberate act of the individual, can be understood as analogous to the naturalness of social laws. This is where Durkheim saw the progress of the economic concepts of order compared with contract theory (Durkheim 1978a:46).

Yet, in the introductory lecture in Bordeaux, Durkheim is conciliatory toward economics. Later he uses the example of price formation variously to emphasize the inadequacy of the economic understanding of economic processes. Prices are still regarded as sociological data, but Durkheim objects to the idea that prices can be understood as the result of individual budget distributions in the perspective of utility maximization and could therefore vary arbitrarily according to supply and demand. Instead, Durkheim emphasizes the social character of price formation. I return to that in detail later. Yet the rejection of the view that prices can be understood as the result of the aggregate of individual economic exchanges reveals the first aspect of Durkheim's critique of economic social theory. Unlike contract theories, economic theory sees society and individual as standing in continuity with one another, which is expressed in the harmony of individual interests and social requirements. This materializes from the compatibility of self-interest of actors in exchange, which makes social restraint for regulating behavior superfluous. Durkheim's critique of economic theory is directed against the idea of the emergence of society from the exchanges of presocial individuals, in which the notion of the restraining character of society gets lost. Economics must "absolutely distort social phenomena" (Durkheim 1966:101) because it misjudges their social character, which consists of the external and independent pressure they exercise on the individual.

Durkheim's second critique of economic theory is directed against the a priori assumption of rational action, which takes actors out of their specific, historically concrete social milieu. According to economic theory, man "is naturally inclined to the political, domestic, and religious life, to commerce, etc.; and it is from these natural drives that social organization is derived" (Durkheim 1966:122). The normative and analytical method of economics contradicts Durkheim's program of an inductive social science that draws up laws on the basis of empirical observations. The subject matter of the social sciences is not analytical abstraction but the real discoverable complexity of social life in its concrete features—thus the actual functioning of the economy and the decision-making process of actors. The laws of economics are criticized because of their deductive character, which conceals the rules empirically governing the economy. "Economic and, more broadly social laws are not, then, very general facts which the scholar induces from the observation of societies, but logical consequences deduced from the definition of the individual" (Durkheim 1978a:49).

In *The Rules of Sociological Method*, Durkheim's critique is that economics does not investigate inductively whether economic relations are in fact formed according to the law of supply and demand. The laws of economics are rejected as "maxims of practical wisdom" (Durkheim 1966:27) and are contrasted to the type of laws of the natural sciences that are discovered inductively. The inductive method is to guarantee that the social regulations valid in a specific milieu can be discerned. But this is precisely what economics does not achieve, according to Durkheim:[12] "The laws of political economy are of so general a nature that they are disconnected from any collective form; exchange, production, value, and so on, are seen as products of very simple forces common to all mankind" (1960a:348).[13]

From both critiques of economic theory—starting from the individual and renouncing an empirical and inductive method of research—Durkheim concludes that economics, even though it is concerned with social laws, cannot serve as a basis for the social sciences. Only when economics adopts Durkheim's sociological method does it follow the principle of determinism and can it perceive economic phenomena as entities separated ontologically from the individual (Durkheim 1978b:82). Durkheim's judgment of economics is ultimately as negative as his judgment of the contract theory: "When one sees in society only the individual and reduces the concept of that individual to a simple idea which admittedly is clear, but also dry and empty, a concept from which everything living and complex has been extracted, it is natural that nothing very complex can be deduced from it and that one ends up with simplistic and radical theories" (1978a:52).

Durkheim's critique of economics suggests that the determination of the subject matter of sociology aims not at a systematization of the social sciences that would place sociology *alongside* the other sciences. Instead, Durkheim's definition considers sociology the only legitimate social science, whose programmatic development delegitimates competing research methods in the social sciences.[14] Sociology is contrasted with the existing social science approaches and seen as an evolutionary advancement in scientific investigation of social relations (Durkheim 1978b:72). This applies especially in comparison to methodological individualism in economics, but also vis-à-vis the speculative methodology of philosophy.

The imperialistic gesture of Durkheim's programmatic works can be seen from his repeated classification of economics as a "branch of sociology" (1978b:81),[15] thus making it a special field of sociology. The caliber of the subject matter and methodology of the envisioned type of economics also result from this *subordination* of economics under the sociological program of a science of morality. The study of economic phenomena must start from the premises of Durkheim's sociological program; economic structures and institutions cannot be understood as an expression of individual maximization of utility or of striving for wealth but must be analyzed as sociological facts (Aimard 1962). Economics is accused of explaining "all economic life . . . [as] definitely dependent on a purely individual factor, the desire for wealth" (Durkheim 1966:101). In contrast, Durkheim repeatedly emphasizes that economic functions are social functions. The preface to the second issue of *L'Année Sociologique*, says: "The principle of this method is that religious, legal, moral, and economic

facts must all be treated according to their nature, that is, as social facts"
(Durkheim 1960a:348).[16]

The programmatic subsuming of economics under the program of sociology also explains why Durkheim keeps referring positively to works of
the circle of the Historical School in Germany in his early writings. In fact,
information can be inferred about Durkheim's own idea of a sociological
conception of the economy from his reconstructive comments emphasizing the kinship of the Historical School to his own theory. And it can be
argued that the Historical School gave Durkheim an essential impulse for
the form he suggested of including economics in his historic and inductive
plan of research. This is especially plausible because, after spending the
academic year 1885–86 in Germany, Durkheim could describe himself as
an expert in the discussion of the humanities in Germany and expressed
a great appreciation for them (Lukes 1985:86ff.). This was reflected in
the Opening Lecture of 1887, in which Durkheim (1978a:60) cited the
Historical School as illustrative for the study of the economy. A few years
later, in *The Rules of Sociological Methods*, Durkheim (1966:17ff.)
adopted the methodological program of the Historical School in his own
outline of the subject matter and method of sociology. Even before the
introductory lecture in Bordeaux, Durkheim had been extremely positive
about the economic works of the Historical School in a report on the
situation of the social sciences and humanities in Germany, titled "La
science positive de la morale en Allemagne" (1887), which originated in
connection with his sojourn in Germany. In the report, Durkheim sympa-
thized especially with the view of Schmoller and Wagner, that economic
action did not occur apart from concrete social configurations, but rather
that the concrete historical and social milieu was a constituent element in
economic exchange.

This view corresponds with Durkheim's critique of economic social theory. The casual transition from individual action and socially desirable
results is also challenged by the Historical School: "For the German economists, on the other hand, this harmony between the two disciplines and
fields of activity, desirable as it may be, is only a dream of the theory, an
hypothesis that is hardly confirmed by the facts. The progress of industry
and morality do not necessarily agree" (Durkheim 1975:270). Durkheim
sympathizes with Schmoller's definition of economic action. Forms of economic production are determined by the conditions the actors confront
and, by custom, they become "a form that urgently intrudes on our will"
(275). But this is not to deny the significance of economic forces, as Durkheim explains in another part of the report: "The maxims of morality with
regard to property, contracts, and labor cannot be understand if the basic
economic factors from which they are inferred are not known; on the

other hand, one would have a completely wrong idea of economic development if one ignored the moral forces that are operative in it" (276).

This reciprocal influence of social action in economic contexts through
economic interests *and* social pressure does accord with Durkheim's position of the incomplete determination of the individual by an omnipotent
sociality. Despite this consequence, Durkheim disagrees with regard to
the role granted to the state by the Historical School in the process of
social change and the regulation of the economy. Durkheim objects to the
centrality of the state, which asserts the legislative creation and change of
moral phenomena, and he argues that the social connections are "almost
always much too complex to be grasped completely by human understanding that is not yet so far advanced" (28).

Economic Institutions as Social Facts

Durkheim's "imperialistic" program, which subsumes economics under
sociology, also assumes the burden of proof of having to show that economic structures and processes are an expression of socially legitimated
rules and cannot be understood as a result of individual maximization of
utility. Durkheim has a culturally and socially shaped understanding of
individual utility and the way to pursue it. Economic institutions must
possess the features he uses to determine social facts and that make them
obligatory for social action: externality, generality, and social compul-
sion. Economic theory conversely explains the normative deregulation of
the economy as a presumption of its efficient and socially advantageous
functioning.

To a large extent, Durkheim's sociological program avoids the burden
of proof by dispensing with an empirical study of the functioning of economic institutions. Instead, he proceeds almost deductively by starting
from the premise of the functional necessity of the social regulation of
economic relations and analyzes economic institutions accordingly as an
expression of this normative order (Durkheim 1984:164). This procedure
is inherent in the methodological program: in *The Rules of Sociological
Method*, Durkheim demands that sociology must first study social phenomena in their normal state and then turn to the pathological forms.[17]
Normality does not mean an extant empirical reality—at least for the
transformation process of industrialization, this frequently corresponds
to pathology—but rather the "most frequent forms" (Durkheim 1966:56)
of a phenomenon. The criterion of normality refers to the general conditions of social life in a specific social formation, so that this changes with
the process of social evolution (1966:64). Yet the need for social regulation of individual action remains constant, even if the form of social pres-

sure and solidarity changes in the course of history. For a *normal* development of economic relations, Durkheim (1984:301ff.) assumes that actions are institutionally and morally embedded and therefore transcend the selfish interests of the exchange partners. If the moral bond of the actors is too weak, he expects economic anomie, which is an expression of a *pathological* development in society. Through this procedure, which immunizes the premises of the analysis, Durkheim's perspective on the capitalist economic order that evolved in the transformation process of the nineteenth century is definitely preformed. Durkheim's view of the economy is always determined by the condition of a *normal* economic order, on the background of which empirical observations of the economy are analyzed as deviations.

The possibility that an alternative to previous economic formations would appear in the market economy, which integrates economic relations without recourse to a previous solidarity of individuals, is a priori ruled out. The normality of society cannot be imagined without moral integration of economic processes and structures, too, and conversely, economic crises are interpreted almost automatically as deficient regulation, to be mended only by a moral reintegration of the economy. This is not to criticize Durkheim's emphasis on the functionality of moral regulation for integrating economic relations but only to indicate a method that does not even consider the possibility of a completely changed type of integration of economic relations in modern market economies. The market cannot be viewed as a problematic but efficient institution of economic coordination of modern society. Instead, Durkheim "dogmatically" (Rüschemeyer 1982:585) sees the moral order of society, conveyed through the institutions of contract and price, as guiding and coordinating economic relations. Durkheim does not consider that the market mechanism could prove to be a superior mechanism of allocation *because* it is morally unpretentious, which relieves the actors of the moral reflection of their acts and makes it possible to do without the difficult collective determination of standards of justice because the acknowledgment of the justice of the market mechanism is itself enough, for which simple general conditions like sufficient size and free access must be satisfied.

Yet this critique of Durkheim's methodological procedure in considering the emerging market order must also be modified historically against the background of the critical debate with economic theory in chapter 1: Durkheim's sociology and his critique of methodological individualism develop precisely from the experience of the *failure* of the market as a mechanism of social integration and the *absence* of the development of a modern, market-guided, *and* just social order. From today's point of view, it is only an experience to be reconstructed historically that Durkheim brought to the reflection on the moral bases of contractual relations as the starting problem of *The Division of Labor in Society*. In view of the economic and social crises of the nineteenth and early twentieth centuries, it is much easier to see why he perceived the empirically observed moral deregulation of social relations as the tragedy of the modern age:

> Losing increasingly the transcendency that placed it, as it were, above human interests, the social organization no longer has the same power to resist. Yet at the same time it is more strongly under attack. As the work of wholly human hands, it can no longer so effectively oppose human demands. At the very moment when the flood tide grows more violent, the dyke that contained it is breached. Thus the situation becomes much more dangerous. (Durkheim 1984:315)

In the next four sections, I deal with the four economic institutions in the center of Durkheim's debate with economics: contract, price, property, and the production technology.[18] I try to show that Durkheim's conceptualization of economic institutions is conveyed by the intention of a *link* between individual autonomy and moral regulation but that, ultimately, Durkheim did not succeed in outlining a theoretical conception that does justice to this intention. Instead, in Durkheim, the institution of contract is applied so that exchange relations always transcend the individual interests of the exchange partners. In Durkheim, the social anchoring of the institution of contract not only has the function of mutually insuring the exchange partners that obligations entered into will be fulfilled but also the function of adjusting exchange to the goal of social justice. Consequently, the institution of contract is overtaxed because it demands that the exchange partners transcend their individual advantages. In the subsequent section on price theory, I examine Durkheim's resistance to a market regulation of the economy. Here, it turns out that Durkheim's price theory is quite close to Thorstein Veblen's institutional value theory. Finally, by contrasting Durkheim's price theory with neoclassical theory, the problem of the excessive strain on the institution is indicated again, when prices are to be oriented to socially legitimate ideas of justice instead of developing in market exchange. The obligation of the individual for just prices leverages the market mechanism. This critique of Durkheim's view of the function of contracts and prices does not mean that the claim of admitting socially legitimate notions of justice into economic contexts is not valid. At the conclusion of the section, I specify the conditions under which moral standards can be admitted into processes of market distribution, examining Durkheim's institutional view of the economy for the possibilities of its use for economic sociology. The two concluding sections complete the two preceding ones, using two other institutions—property and production methods—to demonstrate Durkheim's idea of the institutional regulation of the economy.

The Contractual Embedding of Exchange

Durkheim saw contracts as the most important economic institution in modern society. Because he considered the significance of contract relations as going far beyond the economic framework, he analyzes them not in a study of economic sociology but develops them in connection with a theory of social integration. The increasing functional differentiation of modern society leads to the extension of contractually regulated exchange relationships, which become the dominant mode of social interaction and act as a functional substitute for the social cohesion of a "solidarity from similarity," which tends to disintegrate in the process of modernization. In *The Division of Labor in Society*, Durkheim uses the relative loss of significance of the socially cohesive penal law to the advantage of restitutory law regulating individual relations, including public law and private law, to describe the waning significance of generally binding and authoritative convictions for society in terms of legal history (1984:101–2). The increasing significance of private law in modern society reflects the expansion of contractually regulated private exchange relations, which are themselves considered the result of an increasing division of labor in modern societies and are thus an expression of functional differentiation.[19] The central question for Durkheim is how a society that relies increasingly on private contracts and is shaped by voluntaristic exchange relations can guarantee its social cohesion. The discussion of contracts as an economic institution must be considered in the context of this question which puts the goal of explanation far beyond the economic area in the narrow sense, and aims at a theory of society.

With the question about the connection of differentiation through division of labor and social integration, Durkheim addressed one of the most significant problems of social theory of the eighteenth and nineteenth centuries, which had previously been considered by such figures as Adam Ferguson, Adam Smith, Karl Marx, Gustav Schmoller, and Herbert Spencer (Joas 1996; Rüschemeyer 1985). Also in terms of social theory, the liberal tradition of economics, dating back particularly to Adam Smith, had described the connection between the division of labor, the gain in economic welfare, and social integration in the pursuit of individual interest. Social integration guided only by the self-interest of actors, who exchange goods on the market on the basis of private contracts, succeeds—under conditions of competition—through the invisible hand of the market, without requiring the actors to act for the common good (Heilbroner 1986). This theoretical basis of political economy is important for understanding Durkheim's notion of contracts because he uses the liberal tradition as a background that he disavows.

However, Durkheim refers not so much to Adam Smith as to the sociology of Herbert Spencer. Like Durkheim, Spencer was also interested in the transition of traditional to modern society, and Durkheim's contrast of mechanical and organic solidarity was paralleled by Spencer's distinction between military and industrial types of societies. For Spencer, industrial societies are shaped by an increase of the division of labor, which is caused by increasing population density and, following Charles Darwin's biological model, demands functional differentiation in niches as a strategy of survival. Contractually regulated relations become the dominant type of social interaction, and Spencer understands society as an aggregate of these instrumental relationships. In many respects, Durkheim's consideration of the division of labor develops in agreement and in direct debate with Spencer's model (Corning 1982; Rüschemeyer 1985). Durkheim also sees organic solidarity as characterized by the growth of contract relations, and the causes of the division of labor are adopted extensively from Spencer. The essential differences consist of three points. First, Durkheim does not see the advantage of the division of labor in a gain of economic wealth, but rather in the formation of a changed form of social integration, which serves as a functional equivalent for "solidarity out of similarity." Second, for Durkheim, society is not formed of individual exchange relations, but rather precedes them and is a precondition for them. Third, Durkheim does not consider contracts, on which the exchange of goods depends, as a private matter of the exchange partners involved but rather as an institutionally embedded social fact. Even though Durkheim's *The Division of Labor in Society* is thematically and partially even substantively close to Spencer's sociology, these three distinctions express Durkheim's difference with the individualistic starting point, which is so significant that *The Division of Labor in Society* can be understood as a polemic against the utilitarian theory of society (Parsons 1949a:343).

In connection with Durkheim's understanding of contracts as an economic institution, the third difference cited between Durkheim and Spencer should be discussed here. Durkheim shares Spencer's view that societies of the organic type (or industrial type, in Spencer) are characterized by the increase of contractually regulated relations. Yet, at the same time, he does object to the idea that exchange relations could be understood as purely individual matters between two private subjects, so that the sociality of modern societies tends to be reduced to short-term, instrumental relations of interested partners and society exists merely as a result of these relations.

Durkheim's previously cited reasons for rejecting such a view are linked clearly with the considerations in economic theory discussed in chapter 1 by means of the cooperation problem. If contractual relations were based only on interest, one would have to count on a great instability and conflicting nature of social relations because "self-interest is, in fact, the least consistent thing in the world" (Durkheim 1984:152). The pursuit of individual interests cannot solve the Hobbsian problem of order. Durkheim gives two reasons for the necessity of a social bond as a precondition for contractual interactions: on the one hand, he shows that contracts do not in principle regulate all possible contingencies *expressis verbis*. Even if this were theoretically possible, it would also be prohibited for economic reasons because of the emerging transaction costs. Without a joint social basis of the exchange partners, exchange would be extremely risky for the parties if the conditions of contract are incompletely specified. That is, there is no reason to assume that actors adjusted purely to their instrumental advantage ever maintain an agreement made if this no longer corresponds to their own interests. Durkheim fictitiously anticipates the prevention of exchange relations themselves as a result of the absence of social obligations: "If, therefore, we had each time to launch ourselves afresh into these conflicts and negotiations necessary to establish clearly all the conditions of the agreement, for the present and the future, our actions would be paralysed" (161). Thus, the cooperation problem is in the center of Durkheim's concept of economic sociology.

Durkheim's second reason cited for the necessity of social bonds as preconditions for exchange is connected with the kind of social relations he expects between exchange partners when their bond is limited to market relations. Exchange creates an unsatisfactory social bond for the stablity of social relations and thus of society: "In the fact of the exchange, the various agents involved remain apart from one another and once the operation is over, each one finds himself again 'resuming' his self in its entirety. The different consciousnesses are only superficially in touch: they neither interpenetrate nor do they cleave closely to one another" (152).

But, for Durkheim, the stability of social relations is also a precondition for the nonpathological development of the economy. As Durkheim illustrates in book 3 of *The Division of Labor in Society*, economic anomie, which is a form of the abnormal division of labor, is caused by inadequate contact of the actors. Stabilizing this requires the formation of clearly defined modes of action, customs, rules of behavior, and mores in economic relations. This contrasts with the assumptions of microeconomic theory, in which the efficiency of the market depends on the willingness of the actors for constant change of relations and on the anonymity of the market participants. In contrast, in an act that varies "with every fluctuation in stimulatory impressions" (Durkheim 1984:164), Durkheim sees only the threatening disorganization of social order. In this sense, Durkheim is "no theoretician of the market" (Schmid 1989:633) but sees the perfection of the market as a threatening anomie. From this perspective, the dilemma of Spencer's conception of society is that exchange relations cannot create the type of social relations they themselves depend upon: "For men to acknowledge and mutually guarantee the rights of one another, they must first have mutual liking and have some reason that makes them cling to one another and to the single society of which they form a part" (Durkheim 1984:77). Durkheim's premise of economic sociology contrasts with Spencer's explanation of the emergence of society *from* these relationships.

The constitutive interdependence of exchange and contract, expressed in that "all exchange is a contract explicit or implicit" (Durkheim 1992:174), suggests studying this institution to understand the relationship of exchange relations and social regulation. The pursued thesis states that the concept of the contract Durkheim introduced is pervaded so strongly with moral demands on the contract partners that the market price determination is nullified and the market as a guiding instrument of economic exchange is effectively eliminated. Two interpretations of the conceptualization of the social embedding of trade relations presented by Durkheim are to be rejected. On the one hand, is the view represented by Lukes (1985) that Durkheim's concept of organic solidarity is aimed simply at the effects of solidarity emerging from actors who are separated from each other but are at the same time dependent on each other. This interpretation underestimates the significance Durkheim ascribes to social regulations that enter into exchange relations through the institution of contract.[20] On the other hand, it should be noted that, for Durkheim, the function of "non-contractual elements of contract" is not exhausted in the production of orderly exchange relations.[21] Instead, the concept of contract in Durkheim is much stronger because the contract has the function of linking the sphere of the market with the socially established notions of a just social order. As a result, I would stress that Durkheim overtaxed the institution of contract by allocating the function of social regulation of exchange relations as defined by a just social order. That is, it cannot be shown how notions of social justice can permeate decentralized organized exchange relations if these contradict individual interests. Only through the introduction of intermediary organizations in the form of professional groups does Durkheim propose an institutional dimension that can show how contractual relations and prices can be connected back to socially negotiated concepts of justice.[22] I discuss the professional groups in the last section of the chapter.

To get to Durkheim's concept of the contract, I first discuss his historical and anthropological reconstruction of the evolution of the private or consensual contract, which explains its moral character.[23] This shows clearly how closely Durkheim links contracts with the moral integration of society and how the notion of the interests of the exchange partners has no systematic place in it. Durkheim follows the development of contract

relations over four general stages, the first two representing only pre-
forms. His problem consists of explaining how harmonious declarations
of intent of two individuals can achieve a binding force for them, and
how the parties to the contract feel obligated to fulfill their declarations
of intent (Durkheim 1992:178). This problem results directly from Durkheim's critique of Spencer's utilitarian theory of society, with the argument that interests represent an unsatisfactory basis for the stabilization
of a society relying increasingly on exchange relations.

Durkheim begins his reconstruction with the institutions of the *blood
covenant* and the *real contract*, which creates an obligation toward the
conveyor through a one-sided advance concession. Both institutions,
however, are not really contracts, because the obligations do not rely on
declarations of intent that precede exchange. The blood covenant, however, contains a factor whose entry into the contract has a central significance for Durkheim, that is, the joint reference of ego and alter ego to a
sacred force external to them. Obligations within the clan are not primarily obligations vis-à-vis the person but rather vis-à-vis the deity, whose
moral authority exercises a behavioral restraint on the individual. The
force of the deity, as Durkheim explains in the *Elementary Forms of Religious Life* (1965[1912]), is society itself.

The first of the conditions of declarations of intent sufficient for a form
of contract is the *ritual contract* in which the declarations of intent are
expressed verbally. Yet they contain their binding force only in the ritual
utterance of the agreement through which they enter into connection with
the sacred power, which is also a guarantee for the fulfillment of the contract: "The declaration is made by words. There is something in words
that is real, natural and living and they can be endowed with a sacred
force, to be pronounced in ritual form and in ritual conditions. They take
on a sacred quality by that very act" (Durkheim 1992:182). Because of
its origin, the contract has a sacred character and, to that extent, is external to the individuals. The binding force of the contract thus refers beyond
the parties to the contract to society. Through the ritual utterance of the
obligations entered into, these obtain a moral authority. Durkheim sees
residues of the ritual forms of the conclusion of contracts in modern law
in the demands on forms for the legal validity of contracts (187).

The transition from the ritual contract to the *consensual contract*, as
Durkheim characterized the contractual bond of two private subjects, is
indicated by the decline of ritual forms, through which society as the guar-
antor of the contract apparently moves to the background. Contacts still
rely on verbal agreement, but the words lose their sacred character (202).
The increase of contract relations through the expansion of trade made
extravagant ceremonial demands for the conclusion of contracts impracti-
cal (191, 197). But the functional demand of the consensual contract to

bind the parties to their declaration of intent without requiring a ritual reference to the sacred could only be carried out because of changed social conditions. The problem of the consensual contract is that the transcendence of the individual contained in the ritual contract tends to disappear, and the obligation is entered into only toward the person of the contract partner. So it must be guaranteed that the contract partner feels obligated to his declaration of intent, in a way that is functionally equivalent to the obligation entered into in the real contract and the ritual contract. Durkheim sees the possibility of consensual contracts in the decline of ritually created bonds and the simultaneous development of individual rights, which *sanctify the individual himself*. The contract, then, contains its commitment from individual rights, whose violation by the nonfulfillment of one of the contract partners means an offense against a sacred principle expressing the moral authority of society. Even if the consensual contract can no longer resort to external force on the individual, the apparently pure individual relations are themselves raised to the status of a moral authority, whose violation provokes social sanctions. Durkheim's sociology of law is thus based not so much on the deterrent effect of punishment as on the attracting force of the moral authority of the principle of individuality.

The consensual contract does not represent the final stage of the evolution of the development of contract. Instead, Durkheim asks about the conditions under which consensual contracts can claim moral validity. Durkheim's answer to this question entails a central point for my hypothesis that Durkheim tends to eliminate the market as a coordination mechanism of decentrally organized economic allocation decisions. The basic principle, which is also firmly established in the legal system is that a contract is valid only if the declaration of intent is not made under duress or threat, is not immoral, and corresponds to formal requirements. But Durkheim (1984:162) expands this criterion beyond these legal conditions by declaring invalid those contracts whose consequences are disadvantageous to one of the parties to the contract. Contracts can be made on the basis of an unequal distribution of power of the parties to the contract and lead, despite formal consent, to the exploitation of one of the parties. As a result, they are felt to be unjust by "society" and thus do not have the moral authority that contracts are granted only by society. This does not mean that unjust contracts are not supported by the legal system, but for Durkheim (1992:207, 211, 216), this is an inconsistency of the legal system and he expects that, in the future, it will insist more strongly on just contracts. Independent of the legal system, unjust contracts at least lose their moral authority because contracts rely not only on consensual agreement but also on their fairness.[24] Thus, the significance of the justice of contracts ascribed by "society" increases along with the reevaluation of individual rights, because unjust contracts represent an offense to the moral principle expressed in these rights. Therefore, Durkheim sees contracts under the condition of nonpathological social development as always just contracts, and they acquire their moral value only under this condition. But this also means a control of exchange relations through socially established ideas of justice.

In *The Division of Labor in Society*, Durkheim sees the social regulation of contracts as much stronger than in the later *Professional Ethics* as guaranteed by the legislative form of contract law. This includes formal requirements, the ban on usury, or the ban on making immoral contracts (Durkheim 1984:158ff.). Thus, contract law and the legal system also acquire the function of clarifying litigation from the contract relation: if all contingencies of possible developments cannot be established contractually, an authority is needed to avoid or decide conflicts between the parties to the contract. This function is exercised by the law, "and this regulation is mandatory upon us, although it is not our handiwork but that of society and tradition" (161). Therefore, the obligatory character of contracts goes beyond the decisions agreed upon by the parties to the contract and comprises all the legal norms of contract law, in which the moral authority of the society is institutionalized. The decreasing significance Durkheim assigns to the legal system for regulating exchange relations indicates an increasingly pessimistic attitude toward the role of the state for the regulation of economic relations.

Jeffrey Alexander (1982:144) sees the emphasis on contract law in *The Division of Labor in Society* as an expression of an instrumental concept of order in this work. Shifting the regulative function into the moral integrity of the individual in the later writings can be understood, *pace* Alexander, as an expression of Durkheim's idealistic turn. At any rate, even in *Division of Labor in Society*, along with the rights of the individual and contract law, Durkheim cites a third factor of the social integration of contractual regulations. The rules of mores, which consist of rules of custom, conventions of trade, and professional duties, that are "purely moral" (Durkheim 1984:162) because they cannot be pursued judicially but nevertheless exercise a regulative influence on the shaping of the contract.

The previous remarks should have indicated that Durkheim views contracts as always subject to regulation that cannot be transcended by the parties to the contract. Therefore, contracts never start from the individual, not even if, as in the consensual contract, no metaphysical force is ostensibly involved in concluding the contract. The rights of the individual, contract law, and mores oblige the parties to the contract to fulfillment and exercise a regulative function on the content of the contract. The social regulation of exchange relations by the institution of contract leads Durkheim to express the catchy formula: "In a contract, not everything is contractual" (Durkheim 1984:158).[25] In somewhat different words, one can speak of the social embeddedness of exchange relations. By being embedded in the rules of society, contracts transcend the individually negotiated contractual decisions, exceed the privacy of the parties to the contract, and thus become an economic *institution*, whose external constraint cannot be evaded by individuals. Consequently, Durkheim also objects to the designation of "private rights"; instead, "all law is public law, because all law is social" (81).[26] Thus, in functionally differentiated societies, exchange relations as a dominant type of social interaction are not expelled from social morality but are instead regulated by it.

Durkheim sees the social embeddedness of exchange relations as the necessary guarantee for the stabilization of a solidarity characterized by the increase of functional differentiation and the resulting growth of individual autonomy, whose unity is therefore no longer produced by a collective consciousness. Durkheim's central ambiguity about the tendency of the collective consciousness to dissolve in modern society can be seen here. On the one hand, while Durkheim sees the extension of individuality and voluntary social relations as a central element of the development of modernity, and even welcomes it, he also sees this tendency linked with the threatening disintegration of society if it is not informed by a social morality suited to individualized social relations, which subjects these relations to a changed social control. What Durkheim saw as central to the crisis of his time, a deficit of socially obligatory action, appeared along with the need for the moral bonding of individuals. The thesis pursued in *The Division of Labor in Society*—in the central element of the development of modernity (i.e., the functional differentiation of society), this regulation develops as organic solidarity out of the relation of mutual dependence of the actors—builds on the close association of exchange and contract, which makes it seem initially as if even the conditions for the emergence of the new solidarity reside in the functional interdependence of relations characterized by the division of labor. In fact, with organic solidarity, Durkheim is primarily concerned not with the shaping of a moral infrastructure out of exchange relations themselves but with the emergence of solidary relations on the basis of the connection of exchange with the *institution* of contract.

For Durkheim, the theoretical stimulus in the argumentation against Spencer was sharing the premise of functional differentiation with Spencer and, at the same time, giving this phenomenon a completely different interpretation, by not deriving the need for an individualistic social theory from it but, instead, interpreting the contractual regulation of exchange as a continuity of the power of society over the individual. The need for the moral regulation of relations between individuals is also maintained for the stage of organic solidarity, but this is less visible. The decisive theoretical handle in Durkheim's interpretation of the division of labor resides not in the sociological reinterpretation of functional interdependence but in the characterization of the contract as the institution regulating exchange relations. It is the normative expectation of the development of *fair contracts* that Durkheim systematically links with the consecration of the individual in modernity, through which relations that appear at first glance to be purely spontaneous remain subject to moral regulation. However, a closer consideration of the role Durkheim assigns to contract in *The Division of Labor in Society* shows that he overtaxes the institution, and in the last resort his theory cannot integrate the ambivalence between the individuality of market exchange and the moral integration of the market participants.

Market relations are characterized by the simultaneous appearance of antagonistic and cooperative interests. The actors have an interest in entering a relation with another in order to get to goods or services not otherwise available to them; at the same time, there is a latent conflict over the conditions of the exchange. In the general equilibrium theory, no problem of political order emerges from the antagonistic interests of the actors because, under the assumed conditions of perfect competition, sufficient magnitude of the market, and the like, every good is exchanged at its equilibrium price, which is at the same time a definition of social justice. The problem of an unjust price has no place in the theory. The actors are interested in exchange and in maintaining the market because they can thus enhance their utility, and they submit to the equilibrium price because they find no exchange partner who would pay them a higher price. In the context of these theoretical premises, the contract and contract law have the function of guaranteeing the legal security of the market participants and thus excluding opportunistic behavior, deceit, and violence. In the context of economic theory, stable exchange relations can be explained on the basis of a weak normative integration of the actors. The mutual "insinuation of integrity" (Berger 1992) of the exchange partners, protected by enforced property laws, is enough.

If the function of contract and contract law in liberal economic theory is compared with Durkheim's concept of contract, it becomes obvious that, for Durkheim, the institution of contract must assume a much more extensive function. Durkheim's critique of economic theory claims that the unregulated market mechanism, contrary to the promises of economic theory, does produce unfair prices and hence economic anomie. The price formed in the market is based on different starting positions[27] and reflects socially unauthorized power differences of the market participants, which leads to unfair contracts. This possibility, which is excluded a priori in neoclassical price theory, refers to a potential difference between a market price and the price of the good felt as socially fair,[28] which Durkheim also

considered pathological: contracts that are unfair have no moral authority and would not exist under the conditions of a *normal* social development based on mutual moral responsibility of the parties to the contract
for the individual rights of the other. Therefore, it is not freedom of contract and legal security that stand in the foreground of Durkheim's contract theory but the function of the contract for regulating the exchange
relation of goods. Expressed more subtly, the institution of contract *substitutes* for the market as an allocation mechanism. As the actors in economic theory are price takers on the basis of the market mechanism, for
Durkheim they are price takers on the basis of the moral authority of the
institution of contract.

One problem of Durkheim's contract theory derives from the possible
discrepancy between the market price and the price determined by the
demand for the reproduction of a just social order. The behavioral expectation of economic theory is that actors seek to maximize their utility in
exchange. But if the exchange is regulated not by self-interest but by possibly divergent social notions of justice, then the exchange partners must
transcend their individual interests because only thus can the exchange
be adjusted to achieve the collectively shared ideas of justice. As long as
this behavior is voluntary, it can be characterized as irrational behavior
without regret, *pace* Robert Frank (1990). The contract would then be
the institution that transforms the antagonistic nature of market exchange into a venture aimed at society's notion of justice. To achieve this
result, the institution of contract must connect the actors closely enough
so that exchange partners agree to prices as defined by a just social order,
which means a Pareto-inferior exchange of goods for at least one of the
parties involved. This overstrains the institution of contract. On the one
hand, the exchange relations of goods had to be sufficiently specified, in
contract law and the moral norms operative in exchange, thus in line
with the socially established notions of justice. Durkheim explains that
Spencer assigned to contracts the purpose "of ensuring for the workman
expenditure on his behalf equivalent to what his labor has caused him.
If this really is the role of the contract, it can never fulfill it unless it is
being regulated much more meticulously than it is today" (Durkheim
1984:163). On the other hand, the normative bonds or the legal sanctions
had to be *sufficiently strong* to bind the actors effectively to behavior
oriented to social justice. Only if all actors allow their action to be controlled by socially established notions of justice can the possibility of individual actors achieving advantages as free riders and thus contributing
to the erosion of moral action be excluded. Because Durkheim's concept
of social constraint is based not only on negative sanctions in case of
deviant behavior but also on a positive attraction originating in institu-

tionalized rules, the socially just price must be a guideline for the action of all actors in the market.[29]

The regulation of contract relations, Durkheim assumed, would lead to just contracts. Only under this condition can contractual relations serve as a functional replacement for the collective consciousness and transform antagonistic exchange relations into cooperative relations. Paradoxically, the legal institution takes over the function of *preventing* the market mechanism as defined by economic theory and not *enabling* it, as assumed by liberal legal theory. Moreover, the type of solidarity claimed in *The Division of Labor in Society* is considerably modified: the antagonistic market exchange as the typical form of economic relation in functionally differentiated societies can produce a new morality only if the actors are so strongly integrated morally that they still feel obligated to commutative justice, even if this means a suboptimal exchange result for them individually. Instead of a new type of solidarity, we should speak of a shift in levels of social control: in the type of society of organic solidarity, the institution of contract must regulate exchange to correspond with the notions of social justice established in society. The solidarity of the members of society is produced not by the functional interdependence based on the development of the division of labor but by the generally binding and authoritative convictions operative in moral individualism, contract law, and mores. But in the process, as opposed to the assumptions of Hans-Peter Müller (1983:147), Durkheim's concept of contractual solidarity is not welded to that of industrial solidarity in Spencer, but, on the contrary, the notion of contract is so strongly burdened normatively that it approximates Durkheim's own concept of mechanical solidarity.[30]

The normative strain on the contract indicates the problematic nature of the solution Durkheim finds for the dilemma that forms the starting point of his reflections; that is, on one side, social relations based on individual interests expand, which Durkheim welcomes in principle as a gain of freedom; yet, on the other hand, these do not produce a collective optimization, the promised result of economic theory, but rather, on the contrary, cause social anomie. Therefore, as early as *The Division of Labor in Society*, and not only in the later writings about education, a concept of solidarity becomes apparent that is not concerned with the autonomous moral development emerging from the interactions between actors as defined by Piaget. Durkheim tends to embed the pursuit of individual interest in such a strong sociality that the individual freedom of action of economic actors threatens to disappear.[31] To prevent free riders, he assumes a social cohesion that effectively binds all participants and thus elevates the socially determined conditions of market exchange to a standard of action for all actors equally. The phrase coined to assess the educational sociology, that Durkheim "threatens to suffocate the element of autonomy" (Müller 1986:91), can also be applied to *The Division of Labor in Society*. The question of whether a moral structure that can transcend the actors' short-term striving for advantage can be developed out of exchange relations themselves ultimately remains open in Durkheim because of the disciplining function of contract and the systematic association of contract and exchange.

Whereas the social order is based on moral individualism in the later writings, in *The Division of Labor in Society* the regulative function of the state is included more forcefully. In view of the references to mores and conventions, however, it seems doubtful whether Durkheim did in fact strive for an external solution to the problem of order, as Jeffrey Alexander (1982:141ff.) claims. We can only agree with Alexander's conclusion that Durkheim forced the voluntarism of the actors into the background. Yet this happens not only by external factors of order but also in the conception of the moral obligation of the actors for just exchange.

The significance of moral structures in Durkheim's economic sociology led Peter Corning (1982:366) to reproach Durkheim for confusing the terms division of labor, cooperation, and exchange, and to consider these terms incorrectly as isomorphic. For Durkheim, a "normal" social development—as distinct from a pathological one—demanded that the antagonistic division of labor of the market be transformed by mechanisms of social regulation into a form of division of labor that can rather be called cooperation. The critique of the deficient differentiation of the notion of division of labor was continued by Schmid (1989), who interprets Durkheim's *The Division of Labor in Society* as "a theory about the communal production of collective goods."[32] No matter how problematic Durkheim's relation to market regulations of economic relations may be, it is not correct to interpret Durkheim's concept of the division of labor as if the antagonistic nature of exchange relations disappeared completely in it. On the contrary: it can be shown in the problematic normative overload of the institution of contract that Durkheim derives his views from the problem of antagonistic competitive relations in the market and thus had in mind the problems of action discussed in the section on cooperation in chapter 1. If Durkheim had not considered market exchange, it would be incomprehensible why he devoted so much attention to the institution of contract. Without the dominance of the market, there could be no gain of significance for private contracts. The division of labor in organizations is not primarily dependent on contracts for the integration of the differentiated tasks but operates with hierarchies.[33] If Durkheim had wanted to focus on internal cooperative relationships, he would have grappled more strongly with questions of power and control.[34]

Reading *The Division of Labor in Society* as a theory of the moral basis of cooperation for the production of collective goods (Schmid 1989) salvages what I consider an interpretative obliqueness and imprecision. The interpretative obliqueness is that only if the central tension between the market and the need for a moral regulation of exchange, which expresses the liberal *intention* of Durkheim's sociology, is seen in Durkheim's social theory can justice be done to that theory. Peter Wagner (1990a:229) formulated this tension for the founding fathers of sociology: "Unable to stick to the idea of quasi-automatic regulation of interest conflicts, but similarly unwilling to move completely away from the tenets of bourgeois liberalism, they [i.e., classical sociologists] devoted their analytical efforts to the search of phenomena which might provide for a workable development of society."

The confirmation of this general description in Durkheim is that he does not demand the socialization of the economy and the abolition of the market but solely its regulation. "The role of solidarity is not to abolish competition, but to moderate it" (Durkheim 1984:302). At least programmatically, Durkheim stresses that, because of the restless dissatisfaction with the status quo, an element of anomie is always to be expected in modern societies.[35] But if Durkheim's notion of division of labor is seen purely as dealing with cooperative relations aimed at the provision of a collective good, then individual action is linked to a specific contribution to the collective good, which makes the tension between the individual and social regulation drop out of the theory in favor of a collectivist interpretation.[36] There is the danger of interpreting Durkheim too collectively. A more appropriate interpretation seems to be understanding Durkheim as a theoretician of the market, whose contemporary historical experiences and specific intellectual background involved him in the attempt both to defend interest-oriented market relations and to embed them in a sociality that keeps transcending their antagonistic nature. This attempt can correctly be rejected as not convincing, but this happens against the background of recognizing the tension between individuality and the moral integration of sociality that was central for Durkheim and does not resolve this in either direction.[37] This statement does not contradict my earlier interpretation, because I merely claimed that Durkheim did not succeed in outlining a concept of economic theory that would do justice to the tension that is built into the theoretical orientation.

In support of this argumentation, it can be cited that an interpretation that implies that Durkheim did not see the antagonistic nature of market relations and therefore that the division of labor must be understood as a morality of cooperation for the production of collective goods contains the imprecision that Durkheim was not concerned explicitly with the production of collective goods. The supposition that Durkheim could have assumed the emergence of a new form of solidarity from the division of labor because he understood exchange processes as a common consolidation of resources for the increase of wealth in society (Schmid 1989:633ff.) cannot be supported by linking Durkheim's theory with the problematic of the theory of public goods. Schmid's suggested analogy with the cooperation problem must be challenged because the conflict of the contractual determination of a "just price" as Durkheim defined it goes far beyond the problematic of collective goods.

In economic theory third parties cannot be excluded from using collective goods, not even if they contributed nothing to producing the goods. This led Olson (1965) to conclude that—aside from special conditions— collective goods are not produced in sufficiently large groups, even though every individual could increase his utility from the optimal provision of collective goods. Although the production of collective goods would bring a higher utility for everyone, it is rational for each individual not to participate in the costs of production. One example involves price agreements that founder because every individual actor raises his market share by undercutting the price above the equilibrium price in order to drive the other bidders out of the market and finally achieve a monopoly. But Olson's considerations are based on the assumption that *all* actors profit from collective goods as soon as they are produced. Yet this premise is violated in Durkheim's notion of a just price, which can be shown by the example of the price for labor. If the just price for labor is above the market equilibrium price, then production costs are raised, and this cannot be in the interest of the entrepreneur, completely independent from every problem of contribution. The individual entrepreneur will not only not make any contribution to it but will instead introduce resources to prevent enforcing a higher price for labor. The higher price for labor is not a collective good but a "collective bad" for every entrepreneur. It is not plausible to assume that Durkheim did not perceive the conflict-laden nature of price fixing, which goes far beyond a problem of contribution. Although in the collective good problematic in sociology, as distinct from economic argumentation, it can be imagined that actors develop contexts of trust in situations of cooperation that stabilize the action situation and enable the production of collective goods, this is hardly conceivable with the introduction of a just price, whose realization signifies a deterioration of the situation for one party. That is, it is a fundamentally different problem: in collective goods, the problem consists of generating individually "irrational" behavior as a prerequisite for an efficient equilibrium. Even though actors try to get around their own contribution for the collective good, they still have an interest in ultimately getting it produced. Thus, the question is simply how actors in the situation can be moved not to act on the basis of their individually rational strategies but rather to choose such a course of action that will enable collective *and* individually advantageous results. On the other hand, to fix a just price, an *altruistic motive* is assumed in those actors who have to bear the costs for it one-sidedly. But how should a solidarity take shape from a situation that has an unambiguous win-lose calculation?

The problematic of Durkheim's consideration of market relations consists, therefore, of considering these as relations between individuated actors, on the one hand, and, on the other, of constricting the radius of action of market participants so strongly by sociality that individuality almost disappears in it. The problematic of regulating contracts and thus exchange relations of private actors based on their morality is how actors should agree on what a just price should look like. If these standards are not produced by the division of labor itself, they will have to be determined as a reflexive self-commitment, which encounters two complexes of problems. On the one hand, in modern societies, competing notions of justice are institutionalized, and thus the idea of justice itself is hotly contested. Starting with these conditions, a normative system can be maintained only if it offers sufficient stimuli and does not burden the actors with overly high costs of cooperation. On the other hand, the complexity of causal relationships increases rapidly in modern societies so that the means for enforcing shared ideas of justice often cannot be stated unambiguously. This refers to the problem of uncertainty. Against this background, it is not surprising that modern societies do not form the social cohesion Durkheim expects, and he is confronted empirically with "pathological" market relations.

Durkheim's Normative Price Theory

Durkheim's ambivalence about economic theories of value has already been cited in the discussion of the concept of contract. Durkheim did recognize the objective nature of prices, which the actors experience as a fact, but he denied the view that prices are realized through the aggregation of individual demand functions. This critique results from two premises in Durkheim's work: the rejection of individualistic theories of order; and the question of the assumption of a *just* social order, on which the integration of society depends.

Even though Durkheim's explanations of the issue of price and economic value are fragmentary, they reveal a theory of social value that shows certain parallels to the value theory of American institutionalism. I would like to call Durkheim's theory a *normative price theory*, because for him, as distinct from the classical value theory of labor and neoclassical price theory, the issue is not explaining the realization of actual *market* exchange relations of goods but of understanding price as the reflection of socially anchored ideas of just exchange relations. In essence, Durkheim tries to show how price materializes neither through supply and demand on the basis of individual preferences nor through the labor output that went into the commodity, but is influenced through the social order at the time: "The value of things, in fact, depends not only on their objective properties, but also on the opinion of them" (Durkheim 1908:114).

In a discussion with economists of the Société d'économie politique, Durkheim uses examples of influencing prices by religious doctrines to explain this statement. "If religious opinion bans some beverage, wine, for example, some meat (pork), wine and pork lose their exchange value, on the whole or in part" (ibid.). The economic opinion expressed in the price is dependent on moral, religious, and aesthetic views in society.[38] This central dimension of value is missed with the explanation of value from labor input: "In reducing property [i.e. value] to terms of labor, we admit that the value of things derives from objective and impersonal causes, not subject of any appraisal. But nothing of the kind. The value depends on opinion and is a matter of opinion" (Durkheim 1992:125).

As a counterargument to the labor theory of value of political economy, Durkheim cites the fluctuation of prices of already produced goods whose value obviously changes although the labor output that went into it remains unchanged.[39]

But when considering social value, Durkheim is concerned mainly with the price for labor and not so much with the price for consumer and investment goods. Durkheim saw the malaise of the laborer in the social transformation process of industrialization as a central component of the anomie of French society.[40] Only if the worker's pay improves can the social conflicts in society be expected to diminish. The significance of the price for labor within Durkheim's normative price theory is also clear since Durkheim almost always uses examples from this area when he speaks of value. He goes into detail in the discussion with members of the Société d'économie politique:

> The wage rate depends on a fundamental standard that corresponds to the minimum of resources necessary to allow a man to live. But, in each period, this standard is set by public opinion. What was considered a sufficient minimum yesterday no longer satisfies the demands of the moral conscience today simply because we are more sensitive to certain feelings of humanity than in the past. (Durkheim 1908:114)[41]

Durkheim interprets the anomie expressed in the conflict between capital and labor as a result of an unjust, low pay of the worker.

There is no support for this argumentation either in classical labor theory of value or in neoclassical price theory: the former sees wages as equivalent to the value of labor, and the latter as the price of the produced marginal product. Neither theory offers any room to focus on the question of the justice of the wage level. Within nineteenth-century economic theory, however, Durkheim could have adhered to Marx's distinction between the market value of the labor force and the worth created by the worker in the labor process. Marx's theory of surplus value uses the structure of the ownership of property to explain why a part of the value created in the process of labor is not contained in the wage but is withheld from the worker. Yet nowhere does Durkheim refer to Marx's theory. Instead, he interprets the low pay of the worker as a result of the breach of the socially existing norms of a just wage, which expresses the deficient regulation of the economy. Unlike Marx, therefore, Durkheim did not see specific structural elements of the capitalist economic order per se as causing social conflicts or anomie and justifying the structural change of the ownership of property, but rather deficiencies in the moral integration of society, which simply indicate the need of moral reintegration for a normal—nonpathological—development. This is despite Durkheim's recognition, in clear parallel to Marx, that the labor market exhibits structural peculiarities that allow pure market coordination only at the price of social friction: "[A] whole section of the population cannot abandon their function in this way, since no other is available to them. Even those possessing more freedom of mobility cannot immediately take advantage of it" (Durkheim 1984:163).[42]

But, for Durkheim, such a structural disequilibrium merely shows that the economy cannot be coordinated by the market alone but requires control by a moral regulation which neutralizes the structural disequilibria. The anomie of the economy refers to the need for regulation and the actual deficiency of control of the economy. The basis for the normative determination of the wage level is therefore not an empirical observation of the development of wages but a social interest in just prices. Durkheim's normative price theory cannot be understood as that every empirical price that can be found reflects the moral demands of society; instead, he starts from the existence of the idea of a just price, which is expressed by public opinion and at the same time can actually be violated.

What is the relation of Durkheim's normative price theory to the contemporary value theories of economics? Although the classical labor theory of value has an objective standard of value in the exhaustion of the labor force necessary for the supply of products and the subjective neoclassical theory of value sees value as expressed in the price, value manifested in public opinion is analytically much harder to grasp. In one place in *The Division of Labor in Society*, Durkheim tries to determine social value more precisely:

> It represents the amount of useful work intrinsic to it. By this must be understood not the total labour that it may have cost, but the part of that effort capable of producing socially useful effects, that is, effects that correspond

to normal needs. Although such a quantum cannot be calculated mathematically, it is none the less real. The principal conditions as a function of which it varies can even be grasped without difficulty. These are, especially, the sum total of effort needed for the production of the object, the intensity of the needs that it satisfies and finally the extent of the satisfaction that it affords. Moreover, in fact, it is around this level that the average value fluctuates. It only diverges from it under the influence of abnormal factors. In that case, the public consciousness generally more or less vividly perceives this deviation. That consciousness finds unfair any exchange where the price of the article bears no relationship to the effort expended and the services it renders. (Durkheim 1984:317)

The first sentence of this definition hints that, in his notion of value, Durkheim depends on the classical labor theory of value by relating the value with the amount of labor put into the product. Hence it can be understood why Durkheim (1908) speaks of a partially objective determination of value that is only influenced by public opinion. Under systematic points of view, however, this objective element of the theory of value recedes into the background completely when Durkheim acknowledges as value creating only that labor that corresponds with the criterion of social utility.[43] This has nothing to do with Marx's formulation of the "socially useful labor time" (Marx 1967:53), which aims at the use of production methods available in society as a measuring rod for the creation of value in the labor process. Instead, Durkheim is concerned with the social recognition of the product, which is what transforms energy into value in the production process. It "is not the amount of labor put into a thing which makes its value; it is the way in which the value of the thing is assessed by society, and this valuation depends, not so much on the amount of energy expended, as on the useful results it produces, such at least as they are felt to be by the collectivity" (Durkheim 1992:216). The objectivity of value means its independence and externality as a sociological fact, which is measured by the prevailing ideas of usefulness and not by the labor that goes into the product.

The classical labor theory of value is concerned with explaining why qualitatively different products are exchanged for one another in specific exchange relations. The representation of one commodity in another could thus function as a measure of value of the commodity. Both in the classical theory of value and in neoclassical price theory, the market represents an objective and anonymous mechanism of price shaping. Durkheim's normative price theory, however, rejects the market as a mechanism for determining value. The social utility expressed in the price obviously cannot be determined by the actual market demand because, in any case, it would reflect the individual utility that Durkheim rejects as a basis.

Durkheim sees the functional equivalent of the market in public opinion, which is assigned the task of determining the social value of commodities. If the value and thus the price of a product is determined according to its social utility, then criteria are required for this utility. Because Durkheim admits that the social value cannot be determined mathematically, it clearly concerns an implicit, socially obligatory background knowledge or a social idea of justice that defines "socially useful effects" and "normal needs." In this sense, the (just) price is a social fact: it is external, general, and exercises a restraint. Durkheim begins with the notion that a sufficiently concrete understanding of the just price exists in society:

> We know of course that in every society and in all ages, there exists a vague but lively sense of the value of the various services used in society, and of the values, too, of the things that are the subject of exchange. Although neither of these factors is regulated by tariff, there is, however, in every social group a state of opinion that fixes its normal value at least roughly. There is an average figure that is considered as the true price, as the one that expresses the true value of a thing at a given moment. (Durkheim 1992:209)[44]

Durkheim's normative price theory systematically gets away from both concepts of value of economic theory: from the classical labor theory of value by limiting the value-creating labor to socially useful labor, and from neoclassical theory by rejecting the market formation of prices. There is a much stronger substantive affinity to the institutionalist value theory of Durkheim's contemporary, Thorstein Veblen.[45] Veblen distinguishes between the value and the price of a good, calculating the value of the good by its contribution to the general wealth of society. The individual action is judged by how much it contributes to the collective wealth. Veblen defines the collective wealth as a maximum output of goods and services. This handicap is turned critically as a normative standard against the reality of the result of American economic life that he observed at the end of the nineteenth century. He rejected businesses using resources to produce goods that do not serve *social* wealth or that serve it only inadequately. The obvious parallel of this concept of value with Durkheim's consists of the use of a social criterion for the determination of value. Both theories thus confront the problem of specifying a criterion for value. Whereas Durkheim locates the measuring rod of value in ideas of social justice, Veblen (1921) demands the installation of a board of technicians to oversee the social efficiency of production.[46] For Durkheim, such a body designed to regulate the behavior of actors was linked to the same paradox as the introduction of the Leviathan in Hobbes's political philosophy. How are antagonistic actors, who are each interested in their own utility, to agree on the establishment of an institution that is to constrain their behavior? Aside from the problem of the control of an organ to supervise production, Veblen's proposal did have the advantage of being morally less exacting because the behavior of economic actors would always be directly controlled and the objective of a just social order would not have to be reflected upon in relations of exchange themselves.[47]

The question that results from Durkheim's normative price theory is, How can the social idea of a just price, articulated in public opinion, be made obligatory for the action of the exchange partners? Durkheim does admit that the just price can be violated by the actual price agreed upon between two parties to a contract. Labor contracts in particular are notoriously characterized by unjust prices (Durkheim 1984:163). Durkheim seems to blame two different causes for this pathology; one of them— the existence of different social power—is considered a justification for political reforms. The other cause—the deficient moral regulation of economic relations—does not refer directly to institutional reforms. Instead, here Durkheim expects an increase of moral influence by slowing the pace of social change.[48] The demand raised in the later writings for a reestablishment of professional groups aims at an institutional contribution to the stabilization of economic relations, which Durkheim expected to produce a stronger effect of public opinion on exchange relations. The significance of social power for maintaining unjust prices is to be considered here first and then the problem of the moral regulation of market relations.

Unjust prices are caused by the different power of the parties to the contract, which is based on the unequal distribution of wealth in society. Thus social reforms are required to remedy the pathological situation. For this, Durkheim relies on legal measures, particularly government regulation of labor relations and a reform of inheritance law. The introduction of the minimum wage and social security are seen as measures of social legislation.[49] Durkheim ascribed much more significance to the creation of material equality of starting conditions, which was to be achieved by limiting the possibility of transmitting wealth by a reform of inheritance law. The institution of inheritance establishes social stratification, which allows unjust contracts and thus contributes to the pathology of society: "A privileged contracting party could make use of the advantage he holds to impose his will on the other side and oblige him to give the thing or service being exchanged at a price below its true value" (Durkheim 1992:213). Durkheim sees a reform of inheritance law as justified because, under the conditions of moral individualism, the institution of inheritance is delegitimatized: "Such a limitation to the right of disposal is in no way an attack on the individual concept of property—on the contrary. For individual property is property that begins and ends with the individual" (216ff.). The goal Durkheim pursued with the idea of a reform of the right of inheritance is the complete abolition of status privileges, which are to be replaced by meritocratic principles—a person's wealth should strictly reflect the achievements the individual has produced for society.[50] The connection of social power and personal wealth shows that Durkheim had little idea of the structural inequality of power. Thus Durkheim's reformist attention was directed at attempts to level monetary differences in society but not at the economic structure that reproduced the unequal distribution.[51] Here a clear reliance on Saint-Simon's normative rejection of income that is not earned by the activity of the producer can be seen. But only in a "society of producers" could equal material starting conditions overcome structurally inherent inequalities of power between buyers and sellers of labor.

Beyond political and institutional reforms, Durkheim relies especially on the development of the moral consciousness of the members of society. Under conditions of moral individualism, this is expected to profess stronger loyalty to egalitarian principles and thus increase the pressure on status privileges. Unjust prices that are based on privileges that actors did not obtain through their own service to society are increasingly delegitimated, and contracts that are realized on the basis of unequal power lose their moral legitimation for Durkheim (1992:212, 213). The breach of the just price is a violation against society that transcends the parties to the contract because the consensual contract is based in the socially mediated rights of the individual, whose respect thus represents the basis of the moral obligation of contracts (266). If the contract "is not fair, then, since it lacks social value, it must be stripped of all authority" (Durkheim 1984:162). The function of the institutionalization of professional groups also suggested by Durkheim is less the external regulation of economic relations than the stabilization of these relations by regular contact and the formation of moral standards specific to professions; they also represent support for the morality of the actors.

The suggestions for institutional reforms and the expectation of the development of moral awareness still leaves the question open of how, under the conditions of the market distribution of goods, the exchange partners can be constrained to accept the just price. Durkheim ultimately cannot answer this question satisfactorily because of an unsolved ambiguity of his price theory, which ultimately refers again to the unresolved question of the relationship of moral regulation and individual autonomy. By contrasting Durkheim's normative price theory with neoclassical microeconomics, I intend to show that the close connection between the social regulation expressed by public opinion and the actual price revolving around it, which is considered the normal case in Durkheim's price theory, represents the central unsolved problem of the theory. This holds because the social value can become the actual exchange relation between commodities only if either the market price formation is eliminated or a social cohesion develops, which would then revoke the process of individualization of modern society. The latter is not to be expected in modern societies, and is also rejected by Durkheim for empirical and normative reasons.

From the perspective of microeconomics, Durkheim's normative price theory can be understood as that the marginal utility or marginal productivity of a good is determined not by individual preferences or by the production function but socially. This is at least as a result compatible with economic theory in the area of consumer demand: how preferences are formed does not matter for microeconomic theory. What is required is simply the stability of preferences. Thus far, we can agree with Durkheim from the perspective of economic theory that, for example, the religious ban on the consumption of pork affects the price of this commodity. Yet, note that the price is not determined socially, but rather the demand for the item is influenced socially, and consequently the price changes.

However, this compatibility of economic value theory and Durkheim's normative price theory does not apply to the production function. If we start from two substitutable production factors (capital and labor) and the efficiency principle, the demand for a production factor is determined only by its contribution to the marginal product.[52] Here—at least if economic theory is followed—demand is not socially determined but is purely economic. So Durkheim had to show that the demand for labor is determined by moral principles established in society, even if it violates the principle of efficient factor allocation.

This assumption is extremely demanding in two respects. On the one hand, the deliberate violation of the economic principle—that is, "irrational" behavior without regret (Frank 1990)—would assume the social willingness to give up part of the possible social wealth because production factors are not used efficiently. On the other, the excessive use of labor would demand cooperation from *all* employers because otherwise individual employers would achieve market advantages through noncooperation and, under the conditions of perfect competition, would drive those willing to cooperate out of the market. Some employers would demand less labor and thus achieve a factor combination that would bring them market advantages. Social cohesion would have to be strong enough to prevent deviant behavior, which could claim to be rational individually, for the employer, *and* collectively.

A somewhat different scenario, even if with an equally demanding result morally, is obtained if we start from the premise that the price itself is regulated by moral principles. This seems to be closer to Durkheim's intention precisely because it challenges the market realization of price through supply and demand functions. In this scenario, the price for labor above the equilibrium wage rate would lead to the substitution of labor by capital; thus, unemployment would deliberately be tolerated.

Moreover, the price for labor above the equilibrium wage rate would be maintained only if there was an effective control of the price for labor either by a central control power (government or law) or by a social restraint expressed as moral obligation. Starting from Durkheim's notion of the *fait social*, which implies not only constraint but also free acknowledgment of moral principles by the actors, enormous moral demands are set here, too, because it again requires the cooperation of all employers and/or all suppliers to be able to stabilize the desired result. But this assumes a moral bonding that cannot be expected in modern societies, which is confirmed by the fact that Durkheim is confronted empirically with "unjust" prices. The assumption Durkheim expressed in *The Division of Labor in Society*, that these are temporary phenomena in a fundamental process of social transformation, is hardly convincing. It seems more correct that prices in modern societies are not deliberately oriented to moral criteria.

These critical remarks, however, do not mean that Durkheim's normative price theory had to be completely rejected. So far it has only been shown that, given the existence of markets and the erosion of social cohesion in modern societies, a socially determined "just price" is unlikely to be realized when attended by an intentional violation of efficient factor allocation. This neither denies the existence of social conceptions of fair prices nor their potential relevance to market allocation. In relation to economic sociology, Durkheim's normative price theory may be productively applied in two respects: normatively entrenched notions of just prices could be employed by both collective actors and the state in order to legitimize action and mobilize solidarity necessary for influencing prices; and the effects of normative orientations on the allocation of factors may be assumed whenever the actors lack information for optimizing decisions.

An example of the first area involves wage disputes between collective actors. Demands for higher wages appeal to an unspecified standard of fair remuneration. The reference to a socially legitimized wage rate aims at delegitimizing the action of the employers. A parallel appeal to a normatively entrenched standard of justice may be found in the remarks by employers that higher wages would lead to a decrease in the number of jobs available. This suggests that employees would be violating normatively anchored standards of justice—that is, the notion of full employment—when calling for a pay raise. By pointing to socially sanctioned standards, the collective actors could increase their negotiating power and, at the same time, change the price of labor in their favor. In contrast to the Durkheimian theory of price, the notions of just prices legitimated within groups would not enjoy universal recognition. Instead they would merely increase the interested parties' chances of success by attaining significance as moral authority in a conflict of interests.

The second area to which Durkheim's contractual theory may be applied to economic sociology is based on the consideration that the social evaluation of goods and services is always mirrored in the individual calculation of utility, intentionally oriented to the criterion of economic efficiency. According to the argument leveled against the assumptions of microeconomic theory, the combination of factors is concomitantly shaped by society, even though this ostensibly concerns purely economic decisions of allocation. This thesis rests on an argument of complexity that states that the uncertainty of economic relations is so great in modern economic systems that it is often impossible for actors to reach maximizing decisions. This assumption represents the starting point of the theory of bounded rationality, in which the cognitive limitations of the actors interested in maximizing decisions are consulted to explain suboptimal decisions (Simon 1957). Moreover, the institutional organization theory shows how, in an organizational field, institutionalized ideas of efficient organizational structure are perpetuated through processes of imitation and routine, even if these represent suboptimal solutions from market points of view (Powell 1991). This argument may serve to verify Durkheim's claim about the importance of extraeconomic criteria for economic processes of allocation. Unlike Durkheim's approach, the concern here, however, is not the suboptimal allocation of production factors based on normative grounds of social justice; the point, rather, is simply to show that, in reality, social and cultural norms enter into complex economic decisions.

The Development of Property

Along with contract and price, Durkheim analyzes the development of property rights as another economic institution. Unlike the two institutions discussed in the preceding sections, he was hardly concerned in *The Division of Labor in Society* with the significance of property but focused on this subject in detail only in the lecture course, *Professional Ethics and Civic Morals*. While the question in *Professional Ethics and Civic Morals*, too, remains directed at the assumptions of the integration of modern societies on the background of existing social anomie, the argument of the social (moral) character of institutions is made in terms of the sociology of religion through the reconstruction of their origins in the sacred: religious systems of classification represent the origin of the development of economic institutions. This bifurcation between the current reference and an argument that deals especially with the early forms of human social organization can be seen most clearly in the first part of the lectures, where

Durkheim discusses the social relevance of professional groups. In the first lecture, Durkheim emphasizes the current significance of a revitalization of professional groups for overcoming the lack of moral regulation in the economy, and the next two lectures deal with the significance of professional groups in ancient Rome and the Middle Ages. The moral nature of contracts is also studied in the *Professional Ethics and Civic Morals* through the development of contract law in archaic societies. As for contracts, we know from *The Division of Labor in Society* that Durkheim was interested in knowing under what conditions contracts lose their moral respect, which leads to the demand for just contracts.

In the discussion of property as a moral fact in the *Professional Ethics and Civic Morals*, the reconstruction of the derivation of property law from religious classifications in archaic societies predominates so strongly that the impression might emerge that Durkheim was interested solely in a theory of the origin of property that tries to contrast with the theoretical systems of Mill, Kant, and Rousseau, by focusing on the *moral* respect for property rights. Although this is obviously part of Durkheim's concern, the discussion of property is ultimately motivated by the critique of existing property relations, which Durkheim regards as contributing to the contemporary socioeconomic crisis. Durkheim's demand for a reform of inheritance law is derived from the discrepancy asserted between the order of moral individualism in modern society and the legally codified institution of obtaining property by inheritance. Therefore, in the discussion of property rights, the contrast between normal and pathological can also be found, but with a decisive difference in terms of economic sociology: the pathology that emerges from unjust contracts is mediated by the *market mechanism* and is caused by the unsatisfactory moral regulation of the behavior of the partners to the contract; the pathology that emerges from the acquisition of property rights through inheritance, on the other hand, is mediated by the *legal system* and is caused by the discrepancy between moral order and legal regulations. Both forms of pathology, therefore, refer to different measures of reform. While unjust contracts point to the need for the moral reintegration of the individual, the "normality" of the moral nature of property demands legal reform.

Durkheim attaches to the discussion of the moral foundations of property rights a sociophilosophical argument that can be traced back to ancient philosophy and was a central object of reflection for political philosophy of the eighteenth and nineteenth centuries. The ancient tradition focused on the problem of the blend of private and public interest through private property, hence on the danger of political corruption by private property. Plato demanded that the rulers of the Republic should possess no property (Ryan 1987). Yet Durkheim argues with a tradition of political philosophy that was concerned with the moral justification for claims of private property. This question occupied Locke, Hume, and Mill in England, Rousseau in France, and Kant and Hegel in Germany, among others. The argument in the background, on the one hand, is about showing that the existing order of property, characterized by the dominance of the church and the nobility and based on status privileges, cannot be justified in terms of moral philosophy. A concept of property was developed that deduces the right of property from labor and stipulates it as a central institution of the evolving bourgeois social order. For Durkheim, the confrontation is once again one between individualistic social theories and a type of theory that gives priority to the social.

Yet, in terms of the historical development of ideas of Durkheim's works, the reference to the discussion of property and the demand for a reform of the order of property must be seen especially in connection with Saint-Simon. Even before *Professional Ethics and Civic Morals*, where Durkheim outlines his own theory of the emergence of private property, in the lectures delivered in Bordeaux in 1895–96 entitled *Socialism*, he examined the discussion of property in Saint-Simon. Saint-Simon had considered the reform of existing property rights as the most urgent reform measure for a rational organization of production. The existing order of property privileged the landowner over the agricultural producer and precluded an efficient organization of economic activities. Durkheim (1958:157) does criticize Saint-Simon's reform proposal for not being radical enough—Saint-Simon was aiming especially at changing the allocation of credit to farmers—but he does agree with him that property reform is the central lever for increasing economic productivity and for integrating society.

In *Professional Ethics and Civic Morals*, Durkheim no longer refers to Saint-Simon but outlines his theory of the development of private property in an argument with the property theories of Locke and Mill. The reason for not mentioning Saint-Simon was that Durkheim was interested not especially in the question of the efficient organization of production but rather in the question of the moral justification of the acquisition of property. Locke and Mill see the moral foundation of private property rights as embodied in one's own output—thus in the right of appropriation of the product of one's own activity. Durkheim's objection to this individualistic starting point is that it was neither obvious that the product of labor does not belong to society nor explainable why property can be acquired through gift or inheritance—hence with no effort. Both these arguments pushed aside theories that explain the institution of property from an ontological starting point of the individual. Finally, Durkheim also rejects Kant's (1996) theory of property, which analyzes private property rights as an appropriation through an act of will of what was initially the property of the collective (of mankind), but acknowledging property rights is considered enforceable only by force. Thus, Kant's moral theoretical considerations are overshadowed by an ultimately individualistic theory of the enforcement of property rights. This cannot explain how private property can assume a moral character, and thus be *respected* by a third party and not only be *asserted* by power and the threat of force.

Using an analogy to the historical derivation of the evolution of contract, Durkheim develops the theory of property from the religious principle of the distinction between the sacred and the profane. For this, property rights are interpreted so that their core consists of the possibility of excluding a third party from the use of the property. Other characteristics of property rights—such as the right of use, the right to the fruits of the property, and the right to further disposal of the property—were systematically subordinated to the primary defining characteristic of exclusion. The justification for that is that the *jus utendi, jus fruendi*, and *jus abutendi* are parts of property rights, but these rights can also be bestowed without the person having to have title to the property. Except for the possibility of government intervention in property rights, this does not apply to the right of excluding other persons. Thus, Durkheim (1992:142) concludes: "The right of property consists in essence in the right to withdraw a thing from common usage."

Durkheim's central observation is that the exemption of a thing from general use is found in principle in the distinction between the sacred and the profane: "The thing appropriated is a thing distinct from common property. Now this feature is also shared by all religious and sacred things" (143). The sacred is taboo and a symbolic boundary exists that demands distance and respect and is transgressed by contact. Injury or appropriation of the sacred object or the sacred person is punished by the community. In the theory of property, Durkheim extends the principle of the sacred beyond isolating religious symbols to the appropriation of real estate in general. The emergence of private real estate and the respect for this institution are explained by religious belief in the sacred character of the land. In this, Durkheim is supported by contemporary anthropological studies showing that in archaic societies the canonization of land and resources was used to exclude the "profane population" from the otherwise general accessibility: the sacred character of a piece of land excludes third parties from using it and thus constitutes property rights. Crossing the boundary to sacred property is also an offense against the sacred and is sanctioned.

As the lectures continue (Lecture 13), Durkheim pursues an argument for the relation between property and sacredness which seems to invert the described origin of the isolation of land by making the ground taboo. "From a certain point in evolution, the whole of nature takes on a sacred character [. . .] gods crowd in everywhere" (154). The problem no longer consists of excluding a third party *from* the land—this is assumed—but rather of admitting the property owner *to* the land. "The husbandman cannot enter the field without trespassing on their [i.e., the sacred essence] domain; he cannot till or shift the soil without disturbing them in their possession. Thus, he is exposing himself to their anger, which is always redoubtable, if he does not take the right precautions" (155).

Access to the sacred can only be possible through sacrifice, including especially the sacrifice of the first fruits of the field. Only by offering a sacrifice is the remaining part of the harvest sufficiently profane to be consumed or sold. But only the person (family) who has produced the sacrifice has access to the field and its fruits; thus property rights are also established by the sacrifice. At the same time, it is the sacred character of the ground—hence neither labor (Locke) nor the possibility of the forceful defense of the property claim (Kant)—that creates respect for the property.

Analogous to the elaborate deciphering of the sacred as society itself in the sociology of religion, Durkheim interprets the sacred character of the ground as an expression of the original appropriation of the land by society. Individuals take property rights from society, and the sacrifice, which makes the private appropriation possible, can be read as an impost paid to society. Durkheim sees a residue of the connection between sacrifice and appropriation in the institution of taxes: "These sacrifices, these first-fruits of all kinds, are the earliest form of taxes. First, they are debts that are paid to the gods; they can become tithes paid to the priests, and this tithe is already a regular tax that later on is to pass into the hands of the lay authorities. These rites of atonement and propitiation finally become what amounts to tax, although unsuspected" (163).

The original private appropriation of real estate also represents only an explanation for the *origins* of private property, whose character has changed in the course of history. First, real estate is alienable through the change of family structures themselves and thus becomes a commodity. The family is no longer organized around a property, but, vice-versa, property is defined in reference to the person of the property owner. Second, Durkheim sees the sacred origin of property only for real estate and not for movable property, which is profane. Therefore, the historical genesis produces a radical change in the relation of property and property owner, and, in the course of it, property increasingly loses its collective character and assumes the private character that Locke regarded as the origin of property (165ff.).

The result of Durkheim's reconstruction of the historical development of property rights is that they originate in society, but this establishment in society tends to be dissolved in the process of social evolution. Locke and Mill were wrong about the historical explanation, but they adequately described the nature of property rights in the evolving modern bourgeois society. Confirmation of this agreement is that, like Durkheim, Mill was also extremely critical of the institution of inheritance. The justification of private property based on labor cannot legitimate property acquired with no effort. For Durkheim, only property resulting from socially useful activity is justified.

Nevertheless, it would be surprising if Durkheim explained an economic institution by the acts of individuals. A closer examination of Durkheim's justification of private property also clarifies its moral content in modern societies: that is, unlike Locke, private property is legitimized not in terms of natural right from labor output but from the developing moral order that focuses on the individual. Moral individualism is the social presumption for the justification of the acquisition of private property by individuals on the basis of labor output. The perspective directed critically at the hereditary transmission of property arises only on the historical background of moral development: in previous social formations private property was not based on labor, and the hereditary transmission of property was in complete accord with morality. It is only the discrepancy between a legally codified order of property and the development of moral individualism that necessitates a reform of inheritance law. Yet it can be explained from the moral basis of modern society why property acquired through labor is *socially* respected and its acknowledgment is not based solely on relations of force.

The Institutional Character of Production Technology

In *The Rules of Sociological Method* (1966:3), one of the examples Durkheim cites to explain the term *social fact* is production technology. The social constraint emanating from the methods of production is explained by the inevitably negative economic consequences of refusing to keep up with technological progress: "As an industrialist, I am free to apply the technical methods of former centuries; but by doing so, I should invite certain ruin" (Durkheim 1966:3). This shows that Durkheim sees methods of production as an objective technological and economic criterion; violating it produces no moral protest but does lead to an economic punishment that exercises an objective pressure. An "indirect constraint" (1966:10) is exercised by the market.

The heterogeneity of social facts indicated by including technological standards under social facts has led to the criticism that Durkheim used the term to denote such disparate phenomena that it is not precise. In Durkheim's examples of social facts, Müller (1983:73) sees extremely different ways in which these assume a compulsory character for individual action: as the most important types, Durkheim cites legal norms, moral commandments, and conventions, whose violation is punished with social sanctions. As distinct from this type were examples of language, currency, and production methods that reflect not social norms but rather "technological and economic conditions of the possibility of goal attainment" (ibid.); violating them entails economic but not social sanctions.

In fact, the problematic heterogeneity of Durkheim's understanding of social facts can be correctly referred to, but the example of the methods of production shows that Durkheim did not formulate the separation between moral rules and technological constraint so sharply. In the programmatic article, "Sociology and Its Scientific Field" (1960b), Durkheim describes the violation of economic rules as the violation of a morally established mode of action:

> Economic organization, too, imposes itself on us with imperative necessity. When we try to rebel against it, we are certainly not blamed for our rebellion alone; such innovations often awaken resistances of a moral character. However, we must keep in mind not only the impossibility of not conforming almost completely with the rules of the *technical consacrata* but also the fact that "consecrated" is not a vain word. In industrial society as well as in everyday relations, traditional practices that are respected in our milieu cannot help but exert an authority on us that is sufficient to contain our divergencies; an authority, however, which being minor, controls them less efficiently than does moral discipline. Still, between the two, there is only a difference in degree. (Durkheim 1960b:366f.)

By regarding technology itself as consecrated, Durkheim takes it out of the purely objective and material status and grants it a moral authority that elevates it to the realm of the sacred. Therefore, it seems as if Durkheim sees the obligatory nature of certain methods of production not only in the economic punishment following violation of them, but also grants this at least a limited moral status, which is established in the social milieu. At one place in Durkheim's discussion with economists of the Société d'économie politique concerning production methods and organizational structure, he also refers to this social status of technology: "There are even forms of production that tend to generalize, not only because of their objective productivity, but because of certain moral virtues attributed to them by public opinion: such as cooperation" (Durkheim 1908:114). Even more direct is the link between technology and society in *Elementary Forms of Religious Life*, where technology is brought in direct contact with religion: "That is how the most diverse methods and practices, both those that make possible the continuation of the moral life (law, morals, beaux-arts) and those serving the material life (the natural, technical, and practical sciences), are either directly or indirectly derived from religion" (Durkheim 1965:255).

Durkheim refers to the cultural embedding of production methods, which makes these into moral entities, and violation of them has consequences not only for the market position of the enterprise but also evokes moral protest. This emphasizes the institutional nature of the technological side of production. Both forms of external constraints found in the mode of production can be interpreted as progressive and conservative forces effectively operating parallel to one another. While the constraint exercised by the market causes a constant pressure to revolutionize methods of production, the cultural establishment of the mode of production resists these changes or influences their direction. This insight can be fruitful in terms of industrial and organizational sociology explaining why organizations resist change and why it is so difficult for labor organizations to break with routines (inter alia, Argyris and Schön 1978). Resistance to organizational change can then be understood not only economically as an expression of feared losses or in terms of cognitive psychology, but also as an expression of the *social* establishment of methods of production. While economic theory and sociology in the tradition of Weber's theory of bureaucracy views organizational structures and production methods determined by criteria of efficiency, Durkheim's institutional approach can describe the cultural embedding of structural arrangements and show that these satisfy not only criteria of efficiency but also correspond with criteria of social adequacy (inter alia, Meyer and Rowen 1977; DiMaggio and Powell 1983). Durkheim does not elaborate a program to describe the cultural embedding of production methods and technology, but a few remarks do provide clues for that.

Anomie and Forced Division of Labor

Durkheim's view of economic institutions refers to their social establishment and their character as *social facts*. Economic institutions are general, external, and exercise a regulating constraint on action in economic contexts. Thus Durkheim objects to the individualistic theories of institutions of political philosophy and orthodox economics, which assign ontological primacy to the individual. Private exchange relations in industrial societies are also viewed as morally regulated. The "cult of the individual" taking shape in the modern age demands mutual respect for the rights of the individual and fair exchange relations, in which the rights of others are not violated. Yet the representation of economic relations advanced by Durkheim does not represent any description of the empirically discovered economic situation. Instead, Durkheim sees the industrial conflicts of the nineteenth century as an expression of the violation of the socially sanctioned idea of a just economic order, which indicates the lack of institutional and moral control.

In its most general form, Durkheim's diagnosis of the contemporary crisis consists of the observation of the inadequate regulative influence of society on economic relations, which promotes economic anomie. In the context of Durkheim's principle of the confrontation of the normal and pathological state, the historical and anthropological reconstruction of economic institutions from their origin in the sacred serves the discovery of that normality which allows forms that deviate from the normal state to be identified as pathological. In view of the social embedding of economic relations found universally in history, the deficient social regulation of the economy expressed in the socioeconomic crisis is a pathological state that acts destructively from the perspective of society.[53] For Durkheim, the limit of the market was inherent in this. The abnormality of economic structures that Durkheim observed in contemporary industrial society refers to the need for their moral reintegration. Before I go into Durkheim's institutional reform proposal to establish professional groups in the next section, I first discuss the causes of abnormal forms of economic relations because it can show what social structural preconditions Durkheim saw as linked to social integration and thus the "normal" functioning of economic processes.

Durkheim is concerned with pathological deviations from the morally integrated functioning of the economy both in book 3 of *The Division of Labor in Society*, where he grappled with abnormal forms of the division of labor, and in the study of *Suicide*, where the problem of economic anomie is the focus. In *The Division of Labor in Society*, anomie is still complemented by two other abnormal forms, the forced division of labor and an imprecisely described "another abnormal form" (Durkheim 1984:323). The three abnormal forms of the division of labor best represent an empirical description of the economic relations Durkheim confronted in his time. Anomie and the forced division of labor, which are to be the focus here, are significant for Durkheim's understanding of the integration of the economy into the moral order of modern societies.

Durkheim expects anomie of economic relations when the coordination of various functions in society is disturbed. A normal social development appears only when the social structural changes of the economy in the course of industrialization develop in harmony with the change of the moral integration of society, and thus form a solidarity that corresponds with the integrative demands of the new type of economy. Durkheim (1984:153, 195) sees this harmony deeply disturbed in French society because the formation of the new morality did not keep pace with economic changes due to the *speed* of economic change.

Durkheim expresses the connection between sudden social change and anomie most clearly in *Suicide* (1951). For the unprepared individual in question, change represents a crisis that destroys social relations and customs, because social models of orientation are devalued. According to Durkheim, a crisis of moral regulation must thus be expected not only in an economic recession and its resulting impoverishment but also in every rapid economic growth. The reason for that is in the repeal of valid moral measures of orientation and the resulting loss of social orientation. The establishment of new standards of justice that allow actors to find a support for their otherwise unrestrained passion is a slow process (Durkheim 1951:252ff.). Thus, Durkheim's diagnosis of crisis can be used to show that he considers the normatively regulated control of behavior of actors in economic contexts indispensable, if massive social friction was not to result. Yet, in *The Division of Labor in Society*, the evidence of anomie is also set as a kind of "temporal hypothesis of crisis" (Müller 1983:132). According to Durkheim, what is to be expected is that the moral development slowly adapts to the new social structural conditions and thus social anomie is overcome. The mechanism Durkheim assumes for this consists essentially of processes of habituation: "Since a body of rules is the definite form taken over time by the relationships established spontaneously between the social functions, we may say *a priori* that a state of *anomie* is impossible wherever organs solidly linked to one another are in sufficient contact, and in sufficient lengthy contact" (Durkheim 1984:304).

Durkheim expands this idea in the preface to the second edition of *The Division of Labor in Society*, elevating the formation of customs itself to a source of moral rules:

> It is impossible for men to live together and be in regular contact with one another without their acquiring some feeling for the group which they constitute through having united together without their becoming attached to it, concerning themselves with its interests and taking it into account in their behavior. And this attachment to something that transcends the individual, this subordination of the particular to the general interest, is the very wellspring of all moral activity. Let this sentiment only crystallize and grow more determinate, let it be translated into well-defined formulas by being applied to the most common circumstances of life, and we see gradually being constituted a corpus of moral rules. (Durkheim 1984:xliii)

Emphasizing the stabilization of social relations in economic contexts by processes of habituation—even if it is completely inadequate to explain the social conflicts of industrialization—is one of Durkheim's central insights in economic sociology. Shaping routines and consolidating them as institutions in processes of habituation is significant for structuring highly complex decision-making situations and for forming expectations in view of the action of a third party. This produces stabilizing effects in market relations. The idea of shaping solidary relations in processes of interaction also adds an essential element to the idea of regulating economic relations by orienting contracts toward socially determined, just prices, as examined in the previous sections. That is, under certain social structural conditions, for example, the deceleration of economic change, the indication is that ideas of justice can be formed in the interactions of the actors. This idea of the emergence of solidary relations in action will be discussed again in the last chapter.

Here, I would like to point only to the significance of the concept of custom and emergence of stable social structures to explain social cooperation in sociological theory and in economic sociology. Weber also saw habituation as an important aspect of stabilizing economic relations.[54] An example of current sociological theory in which habit plays a significant role is the term "ontological security," introduced by Anthony Giddens with reference to the phenomenological tradition.[55] The concept of habit also plays an important role for cognitive psychology and theoretical considerations in game theory. Kahneman's experiments refer to the significance of habit formation for accepting exchange relations between goods: "Psychological studies of adaptation suggest that any stable state of affairs tends to become accepted eventually, at least in the sense that alternatives to it no longer readily come to mind. Terms of exchange that are initially seen as unfair may in time acquire the status of a reference transaction" (Kahneman et al.1986:730ff.).[56]

In the discussion of the cooperation problem in chapter 1, the significance of solid group structures for the possibility of overcoming the cooperation problem was emphasized. Coleman (1990a) and Axelrod (1984) both see the possibility of supergames dependent on the limitation of the cooperation partners involved in the game, thus on stable social relations. The difference with Durkheim is that Durkheim expects a change in the perception of the other actors from stable social structures, and hence he sees an action emerge that reflects the *interests of the group*. Game theory, on the other hand, does not dissociate from the postulate of the pursuit of selfish goals; by introducing iterative games it is only that the payoff matrix changes.

The second form of abnormal division of labor cited by Durkheim, "the forced division of labor," can be analyzed as a mirror-image complement to anomie (Müller and Schmid 1988:504). But, unlike anomie, its remedy cannot be entrusted to processes of self-organization. Durkheim sees the forced division of labor caused by existing status differentiations in society, which assign social positions, but which do not conform to the developing individualistic type of morality. The existing status privileges concern institutionalized residues of a previous social order, which has been delegitimated by the process of moral change and therefore can be maintained only by force (Durkheim 1984:310ff.). The forced division of labor exists when "the distribution of social functions . . . no longer corresponds to the distribution of natural talents" (311). Durkheim regards individuals as bearers of social functions, who have to fill a specific role for which they are predisposed, analogous to the relationship of cell and organism. The social organism is disturbed when people are pressed into an unsuitable role. But this is precisely what happens when roles are assigned socially by status privileges. Durkheim calls for the establishment of equal opportunity that would enable the occupation of social positions under meritocratic principles, which represent the only legitimate criteria under the conditions of moral individualism that can justify social stratification. The abolition of the unequal distribution of power on the basis of status privileges is also, as shown earlier, a precondition for shaping contract solidarity, which is based on making *just* contracts (316). Unequal social power leads to contracts that bring the underprivileged classes only a part of the value they produce for society.

The parallel of the forced division of labor and anomie is that, in both cases, there is a disproportion between moral order and the economic structure. The difference is that, in the case of anomie, a *lagging morality* adapts over time to the new structure and thus reproduces the unity of the organism, whereas, in the forced division of labor, the residue of a *previous morality* has to be cleared away by institutional reform. This also indicates that Durkheim's consideration of the relationship of legally codified institutions and moral rules implicitly contains a theory of institutional change: new institutions are formed on the basis of altered structural demands in processes of habituation and are consolidated into legally codified structures, which, in the normal development of society, conform to the corpus of moral rules of society. One example of this is inheritance law. In prebourgeois society, the hereditary transmission of property conforms completely with moral considerations. Yet, in the case of extensive moral change, legal institutions can lead a conflicting afterlife and have to be abolished deliberately by institutional reforms. The existing inheritance law loses its legitimacy in the moral rules of society when these rules require the establishment of meritocratic principles as an expression of moral individualism (Durkheim 1992:216). A political reform for the radical limitation of the possibility of hereditary transmissions of wealth is needed to reestablish the congruency between law and morality, and to overcome the forced division of labor as an expression of the discrepancy between the two structural elements.

Stabilizing Economic Relations with Professional Groups

The theory of institutional change indicated in Durkheim's discussion of the abnormal forms of the division of labor refers both to the elements Durkheim sees as the causes of the contemporary economic crisis and to possible therapies. Durkheim sees the cause in the deficient moral bonding of economic relations, and also in the discrepancy between the moral order and the existing statutory law. This is expressed in unjust contracts and in acquiring unearned income through inheritance. Both these causal attributions result, on the one hand, in the demand for the creation of structural conditions to develop a moral order appropriate to industrial society and, on the other, in the demand to remove such legal institutions that clash with the morality of the developing social order. Viewed systematically, it is not clear which of those two changes is more important to Durkheim. By locating the cause of unjust contracts in differences of wealth based on unearned income, it can be concluded that Durkheim sees the reform of inheritance law as the decisive lever to remedy the socioeconomic crisis. As opposed to this, however, Durkheim also considers the limits of such a reform. Durkheim's self-critical objection is that even the creation of complete equality of opportunity is no guarantee for the establishment of just contractual relations. Only the determination of the rights and duties of the actors in a professional field, both between each other and with regard to the community, could allow justice to emerge in economic relations. Moreover, Durkheim (1984:lvi) sees the institution of the family endangered by a reform in inheritance law.

Durkheim avoids this alternative by proposing another variant of reform that both includes the idea of the moral regulation of the economy and contains institutional demands. In industry, professional groups are to be formed on the model of organizations in the professions as well as ancient corporations and medieval guilds. Establishing professional groups is to promote morality, which is the prerequisite for making just contracts.[57] This is no longer based on processes of self-organization, as in the discussion of anomie in *The Division of Labor in Society;* instead there is a demand for the establishment of an intermediary institution in which the economic parties determine the regulation of economic relations.

The idea that economic relations could be reregulated by the establishment of intermediary institutions can be traced back to Durkheim's first publication of 1885, but this idea only gradually takes shape and, in a few texts, forms the kernel of Durkheim's reform proposals for overcoming the socioeconomic crisis. In *The Division of Labor in Society*, the concept of professional groups is still relatively insignificant. Yet, two years later, in *Suicide*, Durkheim announced a special study of the function of the professional group. This project was not carried out, but in the second edition of *The Division of Labor in Society* in 1902, he added a detailed foreword (1984) dealing with the idea of the professional groups.[58] In this essay, Durkheim (lff.) describes the revival of professional groups as the most urgent public task. The anomie of the economy indicates that "professional ethics only exist in a very rudimentary state" (xxxii) because in the economic sphere a moral force that could connect economic relations that currently exist in a Hobbesian state of nature is lacking. Thus, in the works preceding the foreword to the second edition, a shift of emphasis can be seen: the demand for a reform of inheritance law tends to retreat and the professional groups acquire a greater significance. The demand for the establishment of intermediary institutions to regulate economic relations can be interpreted as an increasing pessimism with regard to the position taken in *The Division of Labor in Society* that economic anomie is a temporary phenomenon that can be expected to be overcome in time. It is also an expression of Durkheim's lack of trust in government regulation of economic relations.

Unlike interpretations that view Durkheim's demand for the reestablishment of professional groups as proof of the conservatism of his sociology, I see this concept as Durkheim's most important institutional proposal in regard to the solution of the cooperation problem. Durkheim did not elaborate the concept very much, and the strong reference to ancient corporations and medieval guilds might appear at first glance to justify the rebuke of restoration, but this institutional proposal does contain elements that can combine the market, the moral demands of cooperation, and voluntarism together in the organization of the economy. In this corporatist solution, actions are determined neither by previous moral demands on the actors as social facts nor by government regulation. Instead, Durkheim seems to view the professional groups as involving a system of rules drafted autonomously by the actors, whose cohesive force comes from belonging to a community. In the intermediary professional groups, the possibility of *negotiating* the validity of the standard of justice demanded in economic relations is institutionalized. Here it shall be argued that it is precisely the *process* of negotiation that can produce a cohesive force of social regulation. This probably applies best to relatively small and stable groups and thus is especially relevant for organizations or economic regions and only to a lesser degree for the guidance of national or global market processes. This argument is developed only in the last chapter of the book incorporating further considerations of social theory. Here, I first examine the concept of the professional groups and discuss Durkheim's critical position with regard to government regulation of economic relations in that connection.

Durkheim also uses his method of historical reconstruction to justify the reinstitutionalization of professional groups; this method allows him to view the regulation of economic relations as normal because it is historically predominant. The most recent development, considered historically, in which professional groups have receded, seems like a pathological exception. The long historical tradition of professional groups is used as proof of their functional necessity. Both in *Professional Ethics* and in the foreword to the second edition of *The Division of Labor in Society*, Durkheim devotes most of his attention to describing the significance and function of professional corporations in ancient Rome and the Middle Ages. He shows that the professional groups not only had a direct reference to religious life but also observed a plethora of social functions, which granted the corporation a moral significance in society comparable to that of the family (1984:xlv). Durkheim explicitly denies the impression that his proposal to reinstitutionalize corporative relations in economic life was intended to pursue restorative political goals. Instead, in the context of the analysis of the causes of the decline of guilds, he indicates that these "had finally become an obstacle to the most urgent progress" (Durkheim 1951). So the revival of professional groups can be meant only in the sense of a functional equivalent whose concrete forms cannot be deduced from historical models of professional groups.

Even if Durkheim presents no elaborated blueprint for the organizational form of the professional groups, it is clear from his specifications that he sees them as democratic groups organized on a national or even international plane. The professional groups are to consist of a bicameral elected assembly of employees and employers from all branches of industry. Subordinate groups are established on regional and local levels. The task of the professional federations consists of determining labor conditions, negotiating wages, and establishing conditions of competition (Durkheim 1984:lii). In this institutional form, the system of professional groups adapts to the changed economic structure of industrial states but maintains its function of moral integration of economic relations. In the professional group, a group structure is to emerge that forms the context in which a system of rules can develop that assumes an obligatory character as a social fact for the members. The rules developed from the professional groups have the function of counteracting selfish forms of behavior rewarded by the market (xxxiv). At the same time, over and above the function of the emergence of a moral milieu, Durkheim also grants them the function of stabilizing economic relations through habituation, which is to be expected through the regular contact of the group members.[59]

With the demand for the institutionalization of professional groups to regulate economic relations in industrial society, Durkheim takes a position between the two extremes of a purely market-regulated economy and the direct government control of economic relations. According to Durkheim, the goal of the moral regulation of economic relations can be achieved neither by the state nor by the market, but rather demands the establishment of intermediary institutions that set "the structural presumptions for the creation of moral individualism" (Müller 1983:152). Durkheim conceives of the professional groups as institutions that stand between the individual and the state and thus introduce an additional institutional-structural plane that serves as a buffer between state and individual and, at the same time, generates a moral fabric that is proper for the milieu of the economy.

In the remarks on Durkheim's relation to the Historical School in Germany, it was already shown that Durkheim rejects the proximity of the Historical School to the state as the crucial intervening force in economic relations. Durkheim sees this as the central point where his view of economic progress diverges from that of Schmoller and Wagner. Yet Durkheim's critical position with regard to the role of the state developed essentially in the debate with the sociology of Auguste Comte, who reified the state into the central institution for the social integration of functionally differentiated societies in the immediate aftermath of the French Revolution. Durkheim sees that, as segmental social structures lose significance, the spheres of government action expand,[60] but he repeatedly criticizes this development with the example of the regulation of economic relations as erroneous: "It is not the government that can at every moment regulate the conditions of the different economic markets, fix the prices of goods and services, regulate production to the needs of consumption, etc." (Durkheim 1984:297). The state lacks knowledge of the environment of the economic groups or individual industries that would be the prerequisite for regulatory interventions.

Cooperation and Morality

In Durkheim's view of economic institutions and his reform proposals for overcoming the contemporary socioeconomic crisis, the critical debate with the expectation of economic theory that exchange relations of selfish actors are integrated by the market into a stable social order plays a dominant role. The basis of the argumentation that distinguishes Durkheim from economic theory is that relations between private subjects are always guided by social values and institutional regulations, and therefore cannot be understood starting from the rational actor model. Durkheim's sociological contribution to the solution of the cooperation problem therefore is the thesis that it is the social embeddedness of action that enables actors to pursue strategies that are irrational from the perspective of the rational actor model but might nevertheless yield superior results.

While Durkheim's reference to moral regulations of individual behavior is to be granted a high rank for understanding the cooperation problem, the concept does not explain how control of economic relations by values is compatible with the market mechanism. If exchange relations are determined by "public opinion," what is the role of the market in arriving at a price? This question is not answered satisfactorily by Durkheim's theory. But if, with Durkheim, we start with the idea that the market mechanism should not be abolished, but is retained in the functionally differentiated economy, another question arises: how can the morally controlled integration of action be protected against exploitation by free riders? While the influence of social values on the demand for consumer goods can plausibly be explained, it is not possible for the production function of enterprises to be intentionally directed by values other than the efficiency criterion. Because of competition, enterprises are systematically forced to orient their market decisions toward factor prices. But if exchange is to be oriented to socially mediated criteria of justice, Durkheim must then assume the transcendence of individually advantageous acts through moral commitment.

Although this problem is not satisfactorily resolved, there are three suggestions in Durkheim's discussion of economic regulation that seem especially promising for answering the question of why actors do not regularly follow opportunistic strategies. The first suggestion is the notion of habitual action, which distances the understanding of action from the idea of a relentless calculation of best options. The second suggestion is the notion of moral individualism. For Durkheim, the process of individualization does not entail the detachment of the individual from society. Instead, modernity itself includes a moral learning process through which respect for the rights of the individual gains an important role in the decision for specific action strategies. Far from being ruthless optimizers of their selfish interests, actors do develop moral respect for the consequences of their decisions for others. Although these rights might be disregarded in pathological cases, we normally do not deceive the partner to a contract, even if we could do so without risking harm to ourselves. The third suggestion is the concept of professional groups, which can be seen as the most important institutional proposal Durkheim advanced. One objection to the rules of economic relations negotiated in professional groups can be that they can be exploited by free riders. But Durkheim is concerned here with the *emergence* of social norms, and the process of emergence itself can be seen as having significance for the binding nature of social ideas of value in action. Even though Durkheim was not so explicit about this, it can be argued that in the discursive process of negotiating social regulations in the professional groups, a cohesive force emerges that can at least tend to restrict opportunistic behavior. But it can also be cited that not only are behavioral strategies negotiated among the functional groups represented in the professional group but that the *definition* of interests is also involved.

Although economic theory dogmatically assumes that actors are always provided with a preference order and have information that allows the recognition of optimizing strategies, the problematic of uncertainty refers to the idea that actors in complex situations cannot derive any unambiguous strategies. The function of intervening even in the process of defining the interest of the market participants and shaping strategies to pursue goals can then be granted, at least in part, to the professional group. The context in which this takes place, that is, in the presence of representatives of various interest groups, can be assumed to exercise a substantial influence on the results of this process. In view of the political and social background of a severe crisis that motivates Durkheim's writing, this argumentation is quite plausible. The regulative determinations made by the professional groups reduce the complexity of the highly contingent situation by introducing rules and thus enabling the stabilization of expectations of action, which is the prerequisite for integrating economic relations. Such an argumentation can be supported by Durkheim's emphasis of the processes of habituation and by the connection of regulation and freedom formulated in the preface to the second edition of *The Division of Labor in Society*:

> In vain one may claim to justify this absence of rules by asserting that it is conducive to the individual exercising his liberty freely. Yet nothing is more false than the antimony that people have too often wished to establish between the authority of rules and the freedom of the individual. On the contrary, liberty (by which we mean a just liberty, one for which society is duty bound to enforce respect) is itself the product of a set of rules. (Durkheim 1984: xxxiii).

This interpretation of the social embedding of economic relations by regulative activity puts the emphasis not on conscious transcendence of economic interests, but is based instead on the notion that superior alternatives of action are not known to actors or that the uncertainty of the action situation prevents the recognition of an efficient insertion of means. Against this background, Durkheim's emphasis on custom and the programming of acts by social regulations assumes a theoretical significance for explaining the stabilization of economic relations. If we consider the cooperation problem, in which deviation from individually rational strategies enables the achievement of a superior goal of action, morally motivated ways of acting can enter into behavior without damaging the efficiency criterion of the market because utility is increased for all players.

In this situation, morality and market are not rival mechanisms, and the solidarity effect Durkheim expected in these situations from regular relations between the actors, can in fact be expected to exercise stabilizing functions by supporting the emergence of contexts of trust.

APPENDIX

Systematizing the View of the Economy in Sociological Theory: From Durkheim through Weber to Parsons

The centrality of economics for Durkheim, both in distinguishing sociology from utilitarian social theories, and as a field of social problems, can be generalized for the founding stage of sociology in the late nineteenth and early twentieth centuries. For Tönnies, Simmel, and Weber in Europe, and for Veblen, Commons, and Mitchell in America, the socioeconomic conflicts generated during the process of industrialization *and* the debate with orthodox economics represent landmarks for the respective development of their work. The emergence of sociology as an independent academic discipline parallels crucial processes of development in economic theory, particularly the marginal utility revolution, beginning around 1870. Marginalist economics, developed at about the same time by Walras in Switzerland, Jevons in Great Britain, and Menger in Austria, produces two crucial changes in the theoretical structure of economics. On the one hand, the notion of value is reformulated subjectively, so that the unsolved problem of the relation of value and price in classical theory can be overcome by dispensing completely with theoretical considerations of labor value. On the other hand, economic theory is immunized against practical socioeconomic questions by examining problems of distributive justice only within the market model. Prices are studied along with the formation of market equilibrium, in which the original distribution of goods as a political and moral problem is externalized. The paradigm change in neoclassical economics strengthens economics by generating a research program whose models are based on a few fundamental assumptions. Economic relations can be formulated mathematically, and the claim of the lawlike nature of economic relations moves it from all the social sciences most closely to the scholarly ideal of the natural sciences. In the center of neoclassical economics is a core of abstract and deductively acquired theory, analogous to the laws of movement in physics.[61]

If the classical economics of Adam Smith and David Ricardo can still be understood as social theory concerned with the question of the social order of societies increasingly characterized by market relations, the nucleus of neoclassical economics focuses on the question of forming market equilibrium. That does not mean that Jevons, Walras, or Menger were not interested in the contemporary social situation in their countries and wanted merely to grant legitimation for a laissez-faire policy. Nothing would be farther from the truth. In his later work, Jevons demanded government intervention to provide public goods and supported the nationalization of various industries (Backhouse 1985:75). Even more interesting is the connection (or, more precisely, separation) of equilibrium analysis and social reform in Léon Walras. Along with his classical work in the development of economic theory, *Elements of Pure Economics, or The Theory of Social Wealth* (1874), Walras was also concerned with socioeconomic problems in two books that attract less attention today, *Études d'économie politique appliqué* (1896) and *Études d'économie sociale* (1898). In the tradition of natural rights, Walras distinguishes between fairness of distribution and exchange. The analysis of economic equilibrium is concerned with conditions for fair exchange. These conditions are that a good has the same price in all places and that the price of an article corresponds to the cost of production. Free competition, therefore, has the function of producing fair exchange. Maintaining free competition demands government intervention, among other things, by regulating prices and providing public goods. But, in addition, equality of opportunity also demands fairness of distribution. Walras argues that property rights consist only of the product of one's own labor. Hence, Walras deduces that real estate cannot be appropriated privately, but belongs to the community, and his reform proposal demands "expropriating" profits from real estate by taxation. Far from promoting a laissez-faire economic policy, Walras can be characterized as a "social reformer, a socialist in the nineteenth century sense of being someone who believed in the rational reform of society. He accepted neither the individualism of the orthodox French school of economists, nor the collectivism of the Marxists, but he argued for a synthesis of collectivism and individualism" (Backhouse 1985:82). While this sentence can be applied word for word to Walras's contemporary, Durkheim, the decisive distinction consists of Walras's differentiation between a market-controlled sphere of the economy, and an area of social structural assumptions, where the presuppositions for free competition are located, which is defined only negatively against the sphere of the market.

In the theories of Jevons and Walras, the tendency to a center-periphery distinction that cannot be found in classical economics can be seen. Here, social reform measures are designed to approach the utopia of a perfect market. Indeed, even in the 1930s, economists were still concerned with social fields conceived outside economics,[62] but the conceptual separation referred to a differentiation process within economics, which ultimately removed it from a science of society.[63] Economics demarcates a "structuring boundary" (Stölting 1986), which determines what belongs to the subject matter of the field and what questions are located outside of economics. Walras's reform proposals had no influence either in his own time or for the history of economic dogma (Backhouse 1985:83). Questions external to the core of pure economics preserve their systematic connection with the equilibrium analysis in the center only because they are directed toward the institutional presumptions for the efficiency of the allocation processes of the market. Analyses of allocation efficiency of the market direct the view of ascribing cause for the socioeconomic crisis and social reform toward the production of preconditions for distributive justice. In neoclassical theory, economics per se does not turn its back on contemporary socioeconomic problems but simply uses proof of market efficiency to reject such reform proposals that want to substitute or limit this allocation mechanism. At any rate, neoclassical theory excludes all considerations of the distribution of economic goods; it liberates its analyses from questions of the initial distribution of wealth and power as well as the class structure in society, and thus frees itself from the questions that increasingly determine the political agenda.

On the one hand, this development consolidates the position of economics as a positive science; and on the other, it restricts the subject matter treated by the discipline to the functioning of market processes under utopian conditions. In two respects, this is central for the further development of sociology, which, as a "science of society," takes over the social theoretical legacy of economics.

On the one hand, scientific theoretical standards from the natural sciences are introduced into the social sciences, which subjects the often speculative and metaphysical nature of the *sciences morales* or the cultural sciences to an intense pressure for legitimation. Especially in the subject matter of economics treated by orthodox economics did competing views have to examine the claim of a positive science of economics on the model of the natural sciences. This is expressed in the German-language context in the quarrel between Menger and Schmoller over methods (*Methodenstreit*). But in the Opening Lecture (1978a) and *The Rules of Sociological Method* (1966), Durkheim also explained the programmatic conceptualization of sociology in relation to economics and its use of the notion of laws. The debate with the claims of economics reflects the pressure for legitimation.[64] On the other hand, it is more difficult for sociology to become established as a holistic "science of society" because it thus gets into direct debate with economics, which is already institutionalized in the university. The Historical School and somewhat later American institutionalism, which pursued a holistic concept of social theory and investigated economic structures, were right in the middle of this conflict, which they ultimately could not withstand.[65] The development within economics drew the structuring boundary which can no longer easily be crossed.

At the same time, as Simon Clarke (1991), among others, has indicated, the process of specialization in economics and the insistence of economics on the type of rational action and deductively obtained economic laws create a space for theories that turn to noneconomic institutions and other rationalities of action. The specialization of economics also represents a self-limitation that "releases" externalized noneconomic areas of action from economic theory as subject matter for other social sciences. This is especially clear in Vilfredo Pareto's (1980) distinction between logical and nonlogical acts, assigning the former to economics and the latter to sociology.[66] This "remnant field" is indeed amorphous and had to be structured by a theoretical program. As a science of society that asks about the preconditions of social order, sociology can be established only if it develops a metatheoretical framework in which neoclassical economic theory is *acknowledged* and complemented. Acknowledgment of neoclassical economics circumvents the controversy with economics and also constitutes a complementary relationship to it. The *complement* is possible because of the self-limitation of the economic approach. In retrospect, it can be stated that sociology pursued an institutional strategy "which would minimize confrontation with other, well-established academic fields" (Wagner 1990a:225).[67]

This rough representation of the situation of sociology in its founding phase allows us to systematize the observation of economics in sociological theory, which understands its development in the complementary relation to the evolution of economics. The previous chapter explained that Durkheim conceptualized sociology as a comprehensive social science that tried to delegitimate orthodox economics and applied the program of a science of morality to economic structures as well. Although some economists did protest this approach, the really surprising fact is that Durkheim succeeded in institutionalizing sociology with this program in France. From a systematic perspective, Durkheim's sociological imperialism can be understood as the earliest definition of the relationship of sociology and economics: the legitimacy of a science that starts from the postulate of rational individual action and rejects the idea of moral or political regulation of economic relations is challenged with epistemological and political considerations. In the context of the situation of economics and the socioeconomic and political situation in France, sociology can still claim the field of economics for itself. Economics in France does not have the institutional advantage characteristic of other European countries and the United States, which presses, in these countries, the concept of a holistic social science, whose program is the moral regulation of social relations into a politically defensive position (Weisz 1983).

Seen from the systematic perspective of a history of the differentiation of the social sciences, Durkheim's sociology (in the aspect of its integration of economics) is coterminous with the Historical School in Germany and institutionalism in the United States. Those schools that emerged in different intellectual milieus agree that a normative force of order that has a regulating influence on market relations must prevail in the economy. This is different from the neoclassical approach, which does not challenge the need for a normative order in society, but locates it outside the sphere of the market and assigns it the function of guaranteeing the structural preconditions for the functioning of the market allocation model, which is itself justified morally with the efficient allocation of goods. What is special about Durkheim's sociology consists not of rejecting the separation between market relations free of morality and morally integrated social relations beyond the market, but rather of the *time* when Durkheim formulates such a program and carries it out institutionally.

This can be illustrated clearly by a comparison with Max Weber's position, which emerged at the same time as Durkheim's. The argument with questions of socioeconomic development in Germany in the transition to the modern age and possible social reforms represents the background for Weber's economic historical studies, too. Particularly the early study titled *Die Verhältnisse der Landarbeiter im ostelbischen Deutschland* (1892) and the inferences Weber drew from that and formulated in the *Freiburger Antrittsvorlesung* ([1895]1992) on the political regulation of economic relations can be compared *systematically* with Durkheim's demand for a moral regulation of market relations. They show the significance of the socioeconomic crisis of the process of industrialization in Weber's thought, too. Weber does see the economic efficiency of the newly emerging agrarian structure in the East Elbian region, but this development is nonetheless rejected for nationalistic arguments, hence on a normative basis. To summarize Weber's position, criteria of economic efficiency cannot be solely decisive for economic policy, but national and social values must be taken into account. Weber called for state intervention to guarantee these goals even against the operational logic of the market. Weber's position can be compared with Durkheim's in that neither wants to let the market have the last word in controlling socioeconomic development. Weber's empirical and inductive procedure in *Die Verhältnisse der Landarbeiter im ostelbischen Deutschland* (1892) also corresponds to the methodological demands on sociology formulated in Durkheim's sociological program. The difference is Weber's much stronger concentration on the state, expressing the link to the tradition of the Historical School.

Yet Weber's further development affected by the epistemological debate between Menger and Schmoller in the *Methodenstreit* is interesting for the systematic conceptualization of the development of the relationship between sociology and economics. Agreeing with Menger, Weber saw that economics and the social sciences in general should have a more solid epistemological foundation than that of the Historical School in the historical and philosophical notions of "national spirit" or "the will of the state," and he also saw the danger of empirical and historical studies that lacked theoretical guidance. Weber recognized the need for an abstract and deductive theoretical basis of the social sciences for historical and empirical studies.[68] In *Principles of Economics* (1871), Carl Menger had explained that the center of economics consists of a body of ahistorically valid laws that assert themselves like natural laws, independent of the intentions of economic actors. The a priori principles on which economics should be based could not be generated by observation of concrete configurations, but only on the basis of intuition and imagination. The task of economics consisted of discovering these laws, which had to be isolated from the factors mixing in concrete historical reality. In his methodological writings, Weber accepted the action theory of marginalistic economics for the analysis of the modern market order and, agreeing with Menger, he considered the emergence of capitalist economic institutions as a social crystallization of individual rationality. For Weber, however, the deductively obtained laws of the social sciences could not achieve empirical validity in the sense that empirical reality could be deduced from them. They are only a heuristic instrument to facilitate forming hypotheses for the study of historical events (Weber 1988:188ff.). Weber accuses the theory of marginal utility of having "misunderstood the meaning of this theoretical thought" (188) by imitating the model of the natural sciences. "The abstract theory intended to be able to rely on psychological axioms and the result was that the historians called on an empirical psychology to be able to prove the invalidity of those axioms and to deviate psychologically from the course of economic processes" (188ff.).

Even if the reductionist theoretical assumptions of action of neoclassical economics could serve as a cornerstone of the foundations of the social sciences for Weber, he also wanted to understand them solely as "ideal types" and thus not be sealed off against historical and empirical data. Economic rationality therefore has no universal a priori validity but merely indicates a dominant value orientation for economic relations in modern capitalism; but this is definitely not the only possible value orientation and thus cannot claim any universal validity either. The historical location of economic rationality makes understanding the historical origins of the dominance of this particular value orientation in modern capitalist societies one of the central tasks of the social sciences. Ideal types are in the context of a research program that is interested in comparative historical studies but also places a methodological emphasis on the need to use theory to deal with historical events against the research tradition of the old Historical School.

> What interests us about the emotional attitude of man in his social relations is in every case specifically emphasized according to the specific cultural significance of the relationship in question. Thus, it concerns extremely heterogeneous and extremely concretely combined mutual emotional motives and influences. Social and psychological research means a scrutiny of various *individuals*, mutually disparate kinds of cultural elements and their capacity to be interpreted for our subsequent understanding. Starting from the knowledge of individual institutions, whose cultural limitation and cultural meaning, we will learn to *understand* intellectually in increasing proportion, but we will not deduce the institutions from psychological laws nor will we want to *explain* them from elementary psychological symptoms. (Weber 1988:189)

This compromise proposed by Weber in the *Methodenstreit* "reconceptualized epistemologically" (Wagner 1990a) Menger's theory program and represents the central systematic advance of the relation between sociology and economics from Durkheim to Weber. In the confrontation between the empirical research program pursued by Schmoller—but also in another form by Durkheim in France—and the abstract and deductive foundation of economics demanded by Menger, Weber came down on the side of an analytical foundation of the social sciences. Weber's compromise did take the objections of the Historical School against such a program seriously, which was expressed in the reformulation as ideal types of what Menger assumed were universal laws of the economy; but Weber's position is on Menger's side. This also applies to Weber's rejection of a holistic understanding of sociology as a general social science whose task was seen as contributing to overcoming the crisis of the "moral" integration of society:

> The belief that it is the task of scientific work to cure the "one-sidedness" of the economic approach by broadening it into a *general* social science suffers primarily from the weakness that the "social" criterion (i.e., the relationships between persons) acquires the specificity necessary for the delimitation of scientific problems only when it is accompanied by some substantive predicate. (Weber 1949:67)

But if economic rationality is only *one* historically shaped and contingent value orientation and not a psychologically based universal law of human action, the question then arises of what other value orientations can also be differentiated as "ideal types" and why the specific action orientation of economic rationality could achieve a dominant role in the modernization process of Western capitalist countries. Weber's (1978:12ff.) action typology, as we know, distinguishes four orientations on the basis of which actors choose means to achieve goals. For Weber, rational economic action is characterized by orientation toward purposive rationality. Along with purposively rational action, Weber also distinguishes between value rational, affectual, and traditional action, concepts that are all introduced as deficit residual categories—following the interpretation of Wolfgang Schluchter (1979).[69] The typology of action allows Weber to integrate economic types of action into a larger analytic framework, and this classification can be seen as Weber's most important systematic contribution: "The distinctiveness of Weber's contribution lay not in his 'economic sociology,' but in his situating the formal abstraction of marginalist economics within a broader analytical framework, thereby creating the possibility of developing sociology not in opposition to economics, but as an autonomous and complementary discipline" (Clarke 1991:265).

Thus, viewed systematically, Weber's contribution in conceptualizing the relationship of sociology and economics can be seen in reconciling sociology with marginalist economics, by establishing a sociological theory of society based on the recognition of economic theory. Weber's sociology develops as a critique of neoclassical theory by challenging the universal validity of economic laws postulated by Menger and as an attempt to situate neoclassical economics in a more broadly applied cultural theory that recognizes marginalist economics under specific conditions (Clarke 1991; Stölting 1986).

THREE

TALCOTT PARSONS: THE ECONOMY

AS A SUBSYSTEM OF SOCIETY

An economy cannot be "purely economic"
because it is a social system.
—*Talcott Parsons*

TALCOTT Parsons can be considered the last sociological theorist whose work is formed by the debate with economics. Parsons's theory shares the central significance of the economy with both Durkheim and Weber. If the two meanings of the economy as a social field and the discipline of economics are distinguished, the development from Durkheim through Weber to Parsons shows that socioeconomic problems tend to lose importance and that there is a stronger emphasis on the institutional and methodological debate with economics. In the chapter on Durkheim, it was noted that the development of his work had to be understood against the background of the crisis of social integration of French society. For Durkheim, the methodological debate with the individualist concept of order in economics also played a significant role, but he was not concerned with an epistemological critique per se but rather with formulating a practical role of the social sciences for overcoming the crisis of French society. The emphasis shifts with Weber's methodological writings. Although his early study of *Die Verhältnisse der Landarbeiter im ostelbischen Deutschland* (1892), an important socioeconomic problem and thus an aspect of the "social question," was in the foreground, the debates with the Austrian School and the development of the typology of action have the function of contributing to the clarification of the epistemological status of sociology. Programmatically and in Weber's sociohistorical studies, the socioeconomic aspect remained in the center, but it concerned the *understanding* of socioeconomic relations and not a directly practical contribution of sociology to contemporary social problems.

The reference function of economics for the development of Parsons's theory is based unequivocally in the theoretical interest of determining the relationship of sociology and economics (Parsons 1977). Parsons's biography can help explain why he was personally sensitive to the socioeconomic problems of the time, and this could have been a reason for Parsons's turn to institutional economics and sociology as a student at

Amherst;[1] but behind this interest is primarily neither the experience of crisis of the generation of the European founders of sociology, nor the effort to achieve a contribution to change the socioeconomic situation. Instead, Parsons's preoccupation with economics can be understood in the continuity of the methodological debates that had crystallized in the *Methodenstreit* between Menger and Schmoller and had attracted the attention of Weber and, a bit later, of Alfred Schütz (1932). Parsons found himself in his own time confronting a debate, systematically similar to the *Methodenstreit*, between institutional and neoclassical economics, a debate that split American economists into two camps in the early twentieth century (Ross 1991). Parsons's attempt to determine the relationship of sociology and economics, however, was maintained more firmly than Weber's by institutional motives for the establishment of sociology as an independent field in the university (Camic 1991).

In terms of theory development, Parsons's concepts of economic sociology represent the continuation of the systematic advance of the relationship between sociology and economics begun by Weber; sociology no longer endeavors to *replace* economic theory but rather defines questions of economic sociology supplementing and acknowledging economic theory. The significance of the debate with economic questions can be demonstrated by biographical references and the development of Parsons's work: Parsons's studies in Amherst, London, Heidelberg, and Harvard focused on economics. Parsons's first position as an instructor at Amherst and Harvard was in the department of economics, and his publications began with several articles in professional economics journals, in which he critically examined controversies within economics.[2] In his early work, *The Structure of Social Action*, he was concerned not only with the sociological theories of Durkheim and Weber but also with the economic theory of Marshall and the work of Pareto. The subsequent early study of professions, in Parsons's own words, grew "logically out of the combination of my concern with the nature of modern industrial society and the conceptual framework in which I had approached it" (Parsons 1977:33). The clear reference of Parsons's outline of sociological theory to economic theory can also be seen in the later structural-functional phase: the elements of a theory of exchange in the general theory of social systems and the media theory elaborated in the 1960s clearly point to the reference function of economic theory even where Parsons was not concerned with questions of economics or economic sociology (Chazel 1989; Johnson 1973; Saurwein 1988).

Two phases can be clearly distinguished in Parsons's works in economic sociology: the early work associated with *The Structure of Social Action*, first published in 1937; and the resumption of the concern almost twenty years later with the problem of defining the relationship between sociology and economics in *Economy and Society* (1956), which he wrote with Neil Smelser. Whereas, in *The Structure of Social Action* Parsons separates economics and sociology analytically within the general action scheme, in *Economy and Society* he distinguishes the economy analytically as a subsystem within the AGIL scheme (defined later in this chapter) and elucidates the boundary interchanges between the economic subsystem and the other social subsystems. This development implies a theoretical reconceptualization in Parsons's work, and thus both periods are considered separately here. In *Economy and Society* another stage can be seen for the aspect of the historical development of the conceptualization of economics in the history of sociological theory: the metatheoretical concept in which economics is located no longer develops in debate with outlines of economic theories, but rather an outline of sociological theory is *used* to conceptualize economic problems (Parsons and Smelser 1956:6).

This chapter focuses on the study of the boundary interchanges of the economy with other subsystems as they are conceptualized by Parsons and Smelser in *Economy and Society*. The theoretical scheme of mutual boundary interchanges between the subsystems offers an instrument to analyze the anchoring of economic action in the functional needs of social reproduction. In the process, Parsons makes it clear that economic functions can never be understood isolated from institutionalized patterns of value and societal goals, and that it is precisely this bond of the economy that is a prerequisite for its ability to function. According to Parsons, the market finds its prerequisites in the necessary bond with the institutionalized system of values of society. In recent years, Parsons's early writings have received considerable attention in economic sociology, whereas the conception presented in *Economy and Society* has hardly been discussed from 1956, when the book appeared, to now.[3] By reversing the focus in this chapter and centering on *Economy and Society*, I am also trying to counter this one-sided history of reception.

Economic and Sociological Theory in Parsons's Early Work

The voluntarist theory outlined in *The Structure of Social Action* (1937) was to indicate a way out of the limitation of the utilitarian model of action and its immanent contradictions. In sociology since Durkheim, this limitation has been seen as the inability of the utilitarian model of action to explain how a stable social order is formed. In *The Structure of Social Action*, Parsons starts from the existence of social order and asks about the assumptions in the tradition of utilitarian theory that do not allow it to explain the stability of social order.[4] Parsons ascribes the theoretical instability of the utilitarian model to the *utilitarian dilemma*. This emerges from the link of the postulate of individual autonomy of action with the assumption of the arbitrariness of the goals of action. The individual determination of the action goals does indeed guarantee the autonomy of the actor, but the utilitarian model cannot show how actors select their goals and coordinate with one another. According to Parsons, this "normative chaos," which does not allow any stable personal or social order, can be overcome within the utilitarian theory of action only if the goals of action of the actors and their coordination are assumed to be externally defined, which, at the same time, evades the assumption of the autonomy of the actors. Thus, according to Parsons's interpretation, the tradition of utilitarian theory does not succeed in showing how the autonomy of action and a stable social order are combined with one another.

Like Durkheim, Parsons also rejects as possible solutions of the problem of social order the proposals offered by contract theory of political philosophy and of political economy (Ricardo, Smith), directed toward a convergence of interest. In the voluntaristic theory of action, Parsons proposes that a theoretically satisfying solution of the problem of order depends on integrating normative elements into the action frame of reference and starting, on the empirical level, from functioning normative structures that are considered integral components of the actor's value system. Moral restrictions of individual autonomy of action and the formation of normative obligations represent the final basis of social integration, but not physical sanctions or calculation, even if both are not empirically absent (Parsons 1949a:404).

Parsons's critique of the utilitarian theory of action and the intuition derived from it of the need for a normative consensus for the integration of society are well known.[5] And we are not concerned here with another interpretation of Parsons's critique of utilitarianism. Instead, what is to be explained is that the action theory developed in *The Structure of Social Action* can be understood only against the background of the significance of economic theory for Parsons. The proposed analytical delineation of sociology in *The Structure of Social Action* represents the metatheoretical solution that Parsons finds to define the relations of sociology and economics that emerge from a ten-year concern with this problem. The starting point was the conflict in American economics that split neoclassicism from the Institutional School, which had been formative for Parsons's early intellectual development. A systematic correspondence with Durkheim's debate with economic theory can be seen in the problem of demarcating sociology from economics. Emphasizing the need for normative integration in the sphere of economics is also clearly close to Durkheim. Nevertheless, through the epistemological critique of empiricist theories, which Parsons saw especially represented in American institutionalism, he succeeded in a completely different demarcation of sociology from orthodox economics, which complied much more with it. Parsons's position can be interpreted as a radicalization of Weber's proposed compromise in the *Methodenstreit* in which the critique of the a priori status of economic laws dropped out (Burger 1977).

In this section, the development of the action frame of reference is to be pursued first from the debate with both competing schools of economics. This is not intended as a comprehensive presentation of Parsons's theory development or the reconstructions of sociological and economic theories in his early work.[6] The argumentation here is to explain the systematic establishment of the central significance of economic theory for Parsons's early theoretical development, and to work out the conception of the action frame of reference as a theoretical and methodological solution. Moreover, what is interesting in this context of Parsons's early work is the question of the significance of the "higher synthesis," which emerges from the debate with the relationship of sociology and economics, for a theoretical understanding of the incorporation of normative elements into the theory of action and its significance for the problematic of cooperation.

As a student, Parsons was confronted with two schools of economic theory that fought for hegemony in economics in the United States at least until the 1920s (Backhouse 1985:221ff.). On the one hand, Parsons was involved with American institutionalism, which he had encountered as an undergraduate at Amherst in the seminars of Walton Hamilton and Clarence Ayres (Camic 1991:XV). At that time, Hamilton was the most prominent representative of institutional economics; and Ayres, who was originally a philosopher, was to be the most important representative of the Institutional School in the 1950s and 1960s (Reuter 1994:52ff.). Although the historical roots of American institutionalism, founded primarily by Thorstein Veblen, were in the tradition of the German Historical School, it was especially grounded in American pragmatism and the populist movement.[7] In Parsons's (1934–35:435ff.) own view, institutionalism can be characterized by its radical rejection of the rational-actor model of classical and neoclassical economics. Veblen sees orthodox economics as logically dependent on a hedonistic psychology, but this cannot be confirmed positively. According to Veblen, the optional latitude of actions is limited by institutional complexes that are consolidated as customs and produce relatively stable patterns of action. For Veblen, the task of economics consists not of constructing taxonomies—for which he reproaches neoclassical theory—but rather of explaining the origins of institutions and their evolutionary change. In this respect, institutionalism intends a positive comprehension of economic processes and rejects the nomological type of theory of orthodox economics. Yet Parsons sees the development of orthodox economic theory and the later controversy with historically oriented theories in economics not as an ideological debate but rather as an expression of real economic changes. Orthodox economics, oriented to the individual and starting with free competition, reflects "the actual economic order of their time [which] was one in which individual competitive enterprise played a very prominent part" (658). The institutional critique arose, on the other hand, because of more precise empirical studies, but also because of "changes in concrete economic life itself" (ibid.).

Chronologically, Parsons first encountered institutional economics and neoclassical economics only through the point of view of the institutionalist critique. Parsons spent one year at the London School of Economics (1924–25) and a subsequent academic year in Heidelberg; that academic ambience warrants the conclusion that, in any case, he debated with neoclassical economics from the perspective of institutionalism, the Historical School, or Political Economy (Camic 1991:XVIIff.). At the same time, the critical reference of the institutionalists to orthodox economics and the encounter with the writings of Weber in Heidelberg must have contributed to crystallizing the definition of the relation of sociology and economics as the subject that was to dominate Parsons's work for over a decade, until *The Structure of Social Action*. In retrospect, Parsons (1977:23) dated his interest "to go thoroughly into the relations between economic and sociological theory" from the summer of 1926, when he returned to Amherst, where he was an instructor for a year. A year later, at Harvard, Parsons begins an intense debate with orthodox economics.

The articles Parsons published between 1932 and 1937, mainly in the *Quarterly Journal of Economics*, were concerned with the problem of determining the relation between sociology and economics by reconstructing sociological and economic theories. They can be understood as independent preliminary work for *The Structure of Social Action* and show Parsons's critical relation to the traditions of both institutionalism and orthodox theory. In view of the significance of the institutional school for Parsons during his student years, it must be surprising that he seeks the theoretical frame of reference in orthodox theory and clearly rejects institutionalism, mainly from epistemological points of view.

Parsons develops a position in the debate between institutionalists and neoclassical theory in which, on the one hand, he shares the empirically oriented critique of institutional economics of the reductionist assumptions of neoclassicism and, on the other hand, he does not consider the empirical methodology of American institutionalism and the Historical School in Germany a theoretically suitable alternative to orthodox economic theory. Parsons presents this position primarily in the two articles published in 1934 and 1935 in the *Quarterly Journal of Economics*, "Sociological Elements in Economic Thought" (1934–35) and "Some Reflections on the 'Nature and Significance of Economics'" (1935). In these works, Parsons distinguishes between two ways of viewing economics, which roughly represent the two poles of the economic controversy. He characterizes the institutional approach as claiming that the task of economics was to give a "full and explanatory account of a given sector of concrete reality" (Parsons 1934–35:420). The position taken by the representatives of the neoclassical theory is presented as a theory "which isolates economic activities 'artificially' from the rest of human action" (647).

In "Some Reflections on 'The Nature and Significance of Economics,'" clearly influenced by Durkheim and his concept of the noncontractual conditions of contract, Parsons shows the significance of cultural factors for the coordination of economic activities. It is inconceivable to Parsons that an economy can manage without the coordinating function of these elements. The factors of social influence appear as a "set of normative rules, obligatory on the participants" (Parsons 1991a:170), and are designated as economic institutions. These institutions have the minimal function of linking economic action to mutually advantageous rules that would otherwise be evaded by actors oriented toward self-interest: "It should be clear that 'economic action' cannot be conceived as taking place in a social vacuum, but that since it involves the exclusion of certain highly useful . . . means of acquisition, there must at the very least be some system of control over activities which eliminates or keeps within bounds the use of such means as force, fraud, and strategic position" (ibid.). The basis of economic institutions is not in the economic system itself but in the values of the community, and thus, for Parsons, they are a noneconomic factor, which is, however, of central significance for the economy's ability to function.

In the controversy between institutionalists and the representatives of neoclassical economics, Parsons's emphasis on the significance of social factors for the economic system's functioning ostensibly places him on the side of the institutionalists. Their essential critique of the orthodox theory of economics refers to the exclusion of all culturally and historically defined elements, whose influence on processes of economic allocation is empirically so obvious.

Parsons formulates his support for the institutional position from another perspective, too, which he develops primarily in the article, "Sociological Elements in Economic Thought." Here he reconstructs theories from the orthodox and institutional traditions from the perspective of what significance is granted to cultural, social, and historical aspects to explain the functioning of the economy. It appears that the tradition of orthodox theory, at least as a theory of order, also always cites normative elements that are intended to lend plausibility to the assumption of socially harmonious results of individual utility maximizing. Parsons (1934–35:425ff.) includes here the notion of "moral feeling" in Adam

Smith, the significance of customs and mores in David Ricardo, and the emphasis on social power in the process of economic reproduction in the economic theory of Karl Marx. Less surprising, the subsequent discussion of "empirical" economic theoreticians (e.g., Veblen, Marshall, and Sombart) shows the plethora of social factors of influence that are significant for understanding the way economic processes function in these theories. Parsons's conclusion from the reconstruction of theory is analogous to the one in the article, "Some Reflections": orthodox economic theory operates on the basis of concepts that are defined too narrowly to include the empirical diversity of the concrete economic facts. This position represents a fundamental critique of neoclassical economics, at least when the latter understands the postulate of individual utility-maximizing as an *empirical* description of economic processes.

Yet Parsons does not intend to strengthen the institutionalist position within the debate of American economics from the side of sociology. Instead, as Bruce Wearne (1989:64) has summarized, he stood "above the battle." As a sociologist,[8] he was concerned with a "higher synthesis" that avoids the dilemma of empirical integrity and lack of theory, on the one hand, and theoretical abstraction and empirical meaninglessness, on the other.[9] Parsons tries to do this with a consideration that objects to the implicit epistemological program of the institutionalists. The result of establishing the empirical significance of normative elements that can be found in the center of economic processes is definitely not that they also had to enter into shaping theories. Only if the inclusion of concrete economic phenomena is demanded from economic theory does the gamut of noneconomic elements have to be taken into account in the design of the theory. Yet the consequence of this would be that "economics is then a branch of applied sociology" (Parsons 1934–35:452). A central concern of Parsons in the articles of the 1930s and in *The Structure of Social Action* is demonstrably to speak out against such a holistic understanding of sociology as an "encyclopedic science" whose task would be the "photographic reception of concrete phenomena" (661) and to develop a methodological concept that would overcome this idea. Clearly, this is the central contrast to Durkheim's theory.

Parsons seeks the solution to the dilemma in an *analytical* separation of the sociological and economic subject matter, which would define separate areas of research for both social sciences, areas that no longer indicate any difference in the empirical field of investigation. Economics and sociology are each to study an analytically separate element of concrete human action. His suggestion, which can be traced back to Pareto's separation of logical and nonlogical action, was "to abandon the empiricist basis altogether, admitting frankly that economics should not and cannot be concerned with a full explanation of concrete facts, whether they be those of 'economic activities' or any others, but must reconcile itself to be limited to the analytical abstraction of one of the fundamental factors in human action and its study for the purposes of the systematic formulation of theory in 'artificial' isolation from the rest" (646ff.). Parsons pleads for a plurality of specialized social science disciplines that are to be considered according to the model of orthodox economics as analytical theories and would also find their subject unilaterally in one "aspect" of social action. Concrete social phenomena in their totality contain elements of all these theories. The goal is not a critique of economic theory but rather an elaboration of "a sociological supplement to an avowedly abstract economics" (421). The background for this step is Parsons's epistemological conviction that the task of science does not consist of the holistic account of empirical observations. Instead, the sciences that deal with human action, among which Parsons included both economics and sociology, must *understand* reality, which is possible only by developing a theory whose essence consisted of analytical abstraction (661). As Parsons explains with a reference to the philosopher Alfred Whitehead (which was later cited again), an empirical understanding of theory was a "fallacy of misplaced concreteness" (Whitehead 1925:74), whose error consisted of taking the abstract for the concrete. With the reference to Whitehead, Parsons challenges the possibility that an analytically demarcated social science discipline could exhaustively describe an area of social action; in this sense, both economics and sociology are necessarily abstract.

But to determine the analytical subject areas of sociology and economics, Parsons also needs a metatheoretical framework that brings the various empirical spheres of influence into a consistent analytical system, which can theoretically guide the analytical differentiation of sociology and economics.[10] Parsons developed this theoretical framework with his action frame of reference, whose task is to reproduce both the *unity* of the sciences of action as well as the *difference* of the contribution specific to each field.[11]

Parsons (1949a:44) describes the action frame of reference, whose smallest analytical unit consists of the "unit act," in the categories of an actor, ends, means, external conditions, and norms as standards of selection. These categories specify the elements of action sequences in which the paradigmatic starting point of the *voluntaristic* theory of action is in assuming actors who are deliberate but who act under restrictions. By emphasizing the dimension of the actor, Parsons dissociates himself axiomatically from behavioristic theories.[12] The elements of the "unit act" result from this foundation of action theory: an action must have a goal; to achieve the goal a means must be used that can be manipulated by the actor; the action takes place in a situation that imposes restrictions on the actor and it requires a normative orientation enabling the actor to decide between alternative goals; and the action represents foundations for the interpretative performance of the acting person. The normative element constitutes a social context in which priorities of the actors are anchored between individual and collective goals.

The metatheoretical framework drafted within the action frame of reference seeks the "higher synthesis" to solve the controversy between institutionalists and orthodox economics on the orthodox side. Parsons's program starts from the epistemological self-description of orthodox economics to determine the relationship between sociology and economics, and he criticizes it only for being incomplete. In 1932, in a methodological manifesto of neoclassical theory titled *On the Nature and Significance of Economics as a Science* (1969:24), the English economist Lionel Robbins had defined the subject matter of economics as "that aspect of behaviour which arises from the scarcity of means to achieve given ends." Parsons's critique of orthodox economics formulated on the basis of the utilitarian dilemma implied that this understanding of action could not explain the formation of a stable social order because the materialization of action goals is not explained. By assuming the goals of the actors as a given, Robbins locates the determination of the objective of the use of economic means outside the field of economics. The "unit act" then completes the neoclassical theory with the element of the normative orientation for the selection of action goals. Thus Parsons has a theoretical frame that allows him positively to join the orthodox economic tradition, which is flatly rejected by the institutionalists, and at the same time to admit the normative element of social action a systematic place in this analytical system. The determination of action goals does not drop out of the systematic of the social sciences, but rather belongs to the analysis as an integral part of the "unit act." Economics studies an analytically separate component of the general system of action—that is, the relation between ends and means, in which rationality is defined by an efficient choice of means. Accordingly, agreeing almost word for word with Robbins, Parsons defines the subject matter of economics as "the science which studies the processes of rational acquisition of scarce means to the actor's ends by production and exchange, and of their rational allocation as between alternative means" (Parsons 1949a:266). In the debate between institutionalists and orthodox economics, on the background of the action frame of reference, Parsons can occupy a position that agrees with the former in an empirical respect, without necessarily ending in a critique of the latter.

Yet Parsons rejects a positivistic understanding of economics. The starting point of Parsons's *sociological* view of the economy was the observation that economic, social, political, and cultural factors are combined in the economic sphere of action. Thus far, Parsons remains firmly in the tradition of the institutionalist view of the economy. If the propositions of neoclassical economics were indeed a description of economic reality, a sociological view of economic relations would be redundant. But this is not the case. Therefore, orthodox economics understood as a positive science perpetrates the fallacy of misplaced concreteness just like institutional economics. Neoclassical economics may not misunderstand its own propositions as empirical but must acknowledge their analytical nature. One result of Parsons's debate with economic theory is that it needs a *nonempirical methodology* that must be based on analytical abstraction (Wenzel 1990:99). The empirical relevance of the maximizing postulate depends on how far "men do in fact *try* (not merely 'tend') to 'economize,' to 'exploit' the conditions of their lives rationally in order to satisfy their wants" (Parsons 1991a:160). The analytical demarcation of the social sciences also objects to a positivistic understanding of orthodox economics, which thinks it can find abstract laws unqualified in empirical reality. Parsons uses this argument against Robbins. Although Robbins (1969:16) also sees his description of the economy as analytic, he makes no distinction between the norm of utility maximizing and the actual actions of economic subjects. For Robbins, utility-maximizing action is "imposed by the influence of scarcity" (17). Robbins thus gets around what Parsons (1991a:160) considers the central distinction between the natural sciences and the social sciences, which consists of the voluntaristic element of action.

Parsons establishes the place of economics even more concretely. Economics is concerned with the intermediate sector in the means-ends chain in which Parsons counts all action elements, except for the externally given restraints of action (ultimate means) and the aspect of the normative integration of action (ultimate ends). In this intermediate sector, he distinguishes between technological, economic, and political means-ends relations, in which economics deals only with economic relations. These are determined by the fact that in a situation with several actors, scarce means must be allocated between several alternative uses. Economic rationality is distinguished from technological rationality by the fact that the latter starts from *one* actor and *one* clear end and thus contains essentially less complex means-ends relations.[13] But Parsons also distinguishes a political element from the economic means-ends relations. Although economics starts from an appropriation of goods through production or exchange based on respect for property rights, Parsons sees a possibility of the forceful appropriation of goods in the political means-ends relations, which is not considered by economic theory. One rational means of reaching ends can consist of the exercise of force. Parsons sees this "political factor" as the subject of political science (Parsons 1991a:164ff.; 1949a:739ff.). The dividing lines drawn by Parsons show how strongly the analytic differentiation of the scientific disciplines is constructed by means of orthodox economics. The definition of neoclassical economics is acknowledged and the other behavioral sciences are positioned around this core. Thus, on an analytical level, not only is the exclusion of normative elements as components of economic theory sanctioned but so is the abstraction of economic theory from power relations.

The "solution" of the controversy between institutionalists and orthodox economics in the "unit act" gives Parsons the theoretical instrument to take a significant step forward—that is, to determine a systematically defined place for sociology as a science of action. This plan is prepared by an interpretation of the history of sociological theory, which integrates it into the binary system of the debate between analytical orthodox economics and empirical institutional economics. In "Sociological Elements in Economic Thought" (1934–35), in the category of empirical theorists, which is contrasted with abstract economic theory, Parsons cites not only Veblen and the Historical School, but also Durkheim and Weber. The significance of these two sociologists is thus reconstructed in the framework of the internal economic conflict that originally interested Parsons. Despite the refinement of Parsons's analysis of the various theoretical approaches in the article and later in *The Structure of Social Action*, they all fall into the residual category of encyclopedic science defined negatively against orthodox economics. Only the action frame of reference allows the empirical significance of the "sociological factor" to be brought into a theoretical framework that fulfills the epistemological standards professed by economic theory, and is thus able to lead sociology out of its diffuse status. The development of the general system of action and the positioning of economics as that science which studies the relation of means to ends open an analytical space that can be occupied by sociology. As Parsons elucidates theoretically, using the utilitarian dilemma mentioned earlier, and explains empirically with the discussion of sociological elements in the means-end relationship studied by economics, ends cannot be considered accidental and determined purely individually. Instead, it requires a coherent system of ends that synchronizes the ends of the individual to one another and links the ends of members of society with one another. "Action can only be understood as in some way dependent upon and related to such a socially integrated system of ultimate ends" (Parsons 1991a:163). The analytically demarcated subject matter of sociology consists of the study of this system of ultimate ends, the "value factor." Accordingly, Parsons defines sociology as "the science of the role of ultimate common ends and the attitudes associated with and underlying them, considered in their various modes of expression in human social life" (167).[14]

While it is easy to agree with Parsons's empirical observation of the significance of political, social, and cultural factors in the sphere of the economy, the theoretical argument that social order (in the economy) is impossible without coordinating it with ultimate ends is to be viewed more closely. The question is whether social order cannot be explained on the basis of individuated actors interested only in maximizing their utility. This is so important because the problem of order emphasized by Parsons creates the theoretical context of argument for the introduction of normative orientations in the action scheme. Parsons seems to exclude such a possibility but on the background of an empirical argument. He sees a pure exchange society as a "highly unreal abstraction" (163) because actors are always already tied into a social (normative) order. But does this argument also hold theoretically or can we think of the hypothetical case of a stable order without a normative consensus? This question is answered in the affirmative, as explained in detail in chapter 1, by the general equilibrium theory, which shows that *under conditions of the assumptions in the models* (perfect information, competition, rational actors, transitive preference order, etc.), an efficient market equilibrium is formed. This equilibrium can be described as a solution to the problem of order insofar as it brings mutual advantage to the exchange partners. It is important to note this solution of the problem of order based only on rational action orientations because it can be shown that social order in the economy is not necessarily dependent on an integration mechanism that transcends the individual interests of the actors. Nevertheless, no critique of the concept of the utilitarian dilemma can be derived from it[15] because Parsons was not concerned with social order per se but rather with the link of the postulate of the behavioral autonomy of the actors with the problem of order (Alexander 1987). In the general equilibrium theory, actors are confronted with single-exit situations and thus a situational determinism (Latsis 1972) that reduces their options to executing the optimizing alternative. Thus, it is referred back to the utilitarian dilemma outlined by Parsons, but to the side of the external determination of action and not to the problem of the nonmaterialization of order. But Parsons indirectly confirms that the problem of order is introduced into economic theory only when one moves away from the assumptions of the neoclassical model and focuses on situations with uncertainty, asymmetrical distribution of information, social power in market relations, and the like.[16]

Even if Parsons's methodological considerations of the analytical delineation of various social sciences are clearly directed against imperialistic claims of both sociology and economics, the definition of sociology as the science concerned with the normative integration of social systems can be seen as an attempt to create a hierarchy of the sciences of action. The organization of the system of action that stabilizes social order is critically dependent on its normative integration. The coordination of action demands a normative order that makes the ends of action compatible with one another. Parsons expresses this argumentation by repeatedly calling attention to the functional need of norms and values for the economy. The independence of economics from sociology applies only to the theoretical framework of the action frame of reference but not to the economy as a social sphere of action.

Yet the tendency to subjugate economics to sociology is at the same time counteracted because the action frame of reference as the metatheoretical frame of analytical disjunctions itself represents a generalization of the methodology of orthodox economics (Clarke 1991:301). The analytical system of action is developed based on the neoclassical theory of economics that is located in it, but is not regarded critically. As long as the economic model of action is understood as analytic, it does not seem problematic to Parsons in the context of the general theory of action and is thus sanctioned in terms of sociology. Here, first of all, the author's respect for the systematic consistency and the high degree of formalization of economic theory can be assumed. Parsons comments in passing that he does not consider it wise to abandon the knowledge economics has accumulated. The analytical compartmentalization of the social sciences "avoids the necessity . . . of sacrificing entirely the theoretical work of generations of economists" (Parsons 1934–35:665).

If Parsons's essential concern in his writings up to *The Structure of Social Action* is seen as defining sociology as a science with a clear subject matter and thus legitimizing it in the scientific landscape, the reference to the institutionally successful economics looks like a wise strategy politically, too. As Charles Camic (1991) showed in his study of the early Parsons, Parsons was actively involved in the debate about the institutionalization of sociology at Harvard, and, in the controversies with representatives of other disciplines, he had to learn repeatedly that sociology still had to struggle for scientific legitimacy even when the field was already established at the university (Camic 1991:XXXVff.). Parsons's attempt to legitimate sociology under the acknowledgment of an analytic understanding of the sciences of action sanctions the economic critique of an encyclopedic sociology and, at the same time, offers a solution in the action frame of reference that claims to establish sociology on an epistemologically equal plane. The alternative produced by Parsons seems almost like a deus ex machina that constitutes sociology as a science—but at the cost of acknowledging the formulation of the field of study as expressed from economics. With the perspective that sociology is complementary to orthodox economics, Parsons achieves a formal equality of the two disciplines; considered from the perspective of action theory, however, the noneconomic elements that appear in Pareto and Weber are systemically incorporated only as residual categories. At the same time, the tension between Parsons's theoretical proximity to economics and the empirical proximity to the sociological factors reconceptualized as "normative elements" also remains.

From the perspective of economic sociology, however, it must be asked, what are the consequences of Parsons's solution for the examination of social, political, and cultural aspects in economic relations? What possibilities of a sociological examination of the economic area of action exist *with the use* of Parsons's analytical compartmentalization? Starting from the action frame of reference, is it possible to analyze the connection of normative and economic elements of action in the sphere of the economy? Parsons's goal is not to construct an analytical heuristic as a metatheoretical end in itself but rather to guide understanding of social reality theoretically. But it is precisely this reference of the theory to an empirical use that is questionable. By delineating the individual disciplines analytically, Parsons blocks the development of a substantial sociological theory of the social conditions of economic processes. The processes of allocating scarce means are analyzed by economics under the postulate of maximizing profit or utility, and sociology cannot contribute anything to that. The task of sociology is to explain the materialization of ultimate ends of action. Yet, how these two elements of the action frame of reference can be brought together, remains open. The analytical separation of sociology and economics does not show how the empirical complexity and heterogeneity of economic processes emphasized by Parsons can be scientifically understood, and thus are in tension with Parsons's conviction of the significance of institutional elements for the economy. If only the combination of various analytical elements can describe economic processes, then the connection of the elements has to be shown on the theoretical level. But the relations between value integration and the rational allocation of scarce means with alternative possibilities of use cannot be studied because the definition of sociology as a science cut off from the analysis of the economic and political elements of action makes it impossible for the discipline to say anything about the mutual influence of normative political, economic, and cultural processes. There is no bridge connecting the analytically delineated economics and concrete areas of economic action.

In his critique of empiricist economic theories, Parsons correctly calls attention to the need for theory-guided research for a consideration of economic processes from a sociological perspective. It must be noted, however, that the reproach of a lack of theory cannot be presented in toto against historically and culturally oriented approaches of economics and sociology, as Parsons meant. Veblen, criticized by Parsons as the advocate of an encyclopedic understanding of science, developed theoretical concepts for studying concrete economic formations (Backhouse 1985:221; Reuter 1994:45ff.). Schmoller's (1883:979ff.) objections to the deductive analytical basis of economics by Menger did not reject all abstractions in economics but were directed specifically against the theory proposed by Menger. The concepts drafted by the institutionalists and the Historical School are not formulated on the historically unspecific level of generality of orthodox economic theory, but this is no argument that could prove per se the superiority of Parsons's analytical compartmentalization, because it involves an understanding of theory that must be regarded critically itself. Parsons seems to represent a position that claims that an empirically oriented theory has to be able to explain all facts and thus naturally can no longer be a theory but rather can only present a map on a scale of 1:1. Parsons's epistemological conclusion from that is a complete separation of theoretical concepts from empiricism so that, in principle, the former cannot be influenced by the latter. But it is not at all certain that Parsons's dichotomy—derived from the debate between neoclassical and institutional economics—exhausts the epistemological spectrum of types of theories and thus in fact we are dealing with only two alternatives.[17] Thomas Burger (1977:326) noted that Parsons's position concurs with Carl Menger's in the *Methodenstreit*. On the one hand, Parsons, like Menger, speaks out against a comprehensive social science; and on the other, he considers economic laws inaccessible to an empirical examination. Consequently, from a sociological perspective, Parsons radicalized the position taken by Weber in the *Methodenstreit* to understand economic rationality as an ideal type and thus granting it the epistemological status of a heuristic that can guide the research process. Yet Weber's position can also be understood as another alternative to the type of theory Parsons confronted, which acknowledges the need to develop theoretical approaches in the social sciences but also keeps its eye on the explanation of singular socioeconomic phenomena.[18]

The limits of the analytical approach advocated by Parsons for a sociological investigation of economic means-ends relations becomes clear also from Parsons's explanations of economic rationality. Unlike the technological concept of action, means and ends are not predisposed for the actors to some extent by external conditions and objective—that is, technologically determined standards. Instead, economic systems of action are characterized by alternative ends and a plurality of actors, who require a normative order to coordinate their individual and collective interests. While the economic model can describe an efficient allocation of resources of a utility-maximizing individual, it cannot do so for the ends of the collective, as shown by the theories of social choice (Arrow 1951). Here the separation of sociology and economics in Parsons's sense becomes precarious because the conceptualizations of rationality must themselves be seen as socially constituted, and it would be necessary to introduce noneconomic considerations into the economic theory of rational allocation of means.

A viable point for a sociological analysis of economic processes can be seen in the area of institutions cited by Parsons, with reference to Durkheim, but not specified. In the empirical field of the processes of production and allocation, sociology is assigned the task of analyzing economic institutions, thus of determining patterns of mutual expectations that normatively regulate the goal setting of the actors and impose restrictions on them in the choice of means and the determination of ends (Parsons 1991a:170ff.). Yet, in his discussion of economic institutions, Parsons emphasizes that these institutions themselves are not part of the economy, thus reinforcing the view that sociology and economics are separate from one another.[19]

The Economy as the Adaptive Subsystem of Society

The early work contains Parsons's intensive debate with economic theory and the development of the voluntaristic theory of action along with the concern for the contemporary economic controversies between the institutional and neoclassical schools in the United States. Considering the early work in terms of its contribution to formulating questions of economic sociology to link the economy and historical, social, or cultural aspects of social development, the theoretical framework developed in the action frame of reference proves to be based too much on the analytical differentiation of rational allocation of means on the one hand and normative integration on the other to be able systematically to shed light on its processes of interaction. Instead of explaining possibilities for a theoretically oriented, sociological conceptualization of the economy, Parsons's analytical separation contributes to consolidating the separation of both disciplines (Granovetter 1990:90ff.). This reflects the ambiguity of Parsons's program, which intends to resolve the controversy between two competing schools of theory of economics with a "higher synthesis" while also contributing to the legitimation of sociology by granting it an analytically defined subject matter.

The publication of *The Structure of Social Action* can be considered a conclusion of more than ten years of concern with the problem of delineating the two fields of sociology and economics in the context of epistemological debates with the status of the social sciences. But, after the conclusion of this project, where does Parsons stand, and what was the significance of a further concern with economic theory? In his autobiography, Parsons (1977:33) indicates that the theoretical synthesis explained in *The Structure of Social Action* led him to a concern with the professions. In this respect, the empirical works on the medical profession (Parsons 1954a; 1951) can be seen as a continuation of Parsons's interest in economic sociology. The link between theory and empirical work, however, must be interpreted in the loose sense of an impetus for the new thematic interest and not as an empirical use of the theoretical scaffolding. In the 1939, essay on the professions, Parsons shows that these cannot be understood in terms of maximizing economic utility, but rather that they follow a distinct type of rationality. But this argumentation is in the tradition of institutionalist considerations of economic institutions and makes do completely without the analytic plan developed in *The Structure of Social Action*. The impression that the metatheoretical considerations in the early work are abandoned is also confirmed by the two articles that appeared in the 1940s, in which Parsons once again addresses the relation of the sociological and economic theory of action. Remarkably the 1940 essay, "The Motivation of Economic Activities" (1954b), does not refer to the analytical separation between sociology and economics in the early work but argues instead in the institutionalist tradition for the inclusion of social structures in economic analysis. Parsons's turn to the theory of socialization and role theory is already indicated in that work. The second essay is a lecture delivered in 1948 at the University of Chicago on *The Rise and Fall of Economic Man* (Parsons 1949b). Here, Parsons refers to the utilitarian theory of action and criticizes it with the same arguments advanced in the essays of the 1930s on the need to include noneconomic elements in a comprehensive theoretical scheme. In this text, too, however, Parsons does not accept the proposal of the analytic separation of sociology and economics by means of ultimate goals and means-ends relations, but rather, influenced by Freud, pleads for a complex understanding of behavioral motivations in economic contexts. The expansion of the utilitarian theory of action is sought rather on institutionalist ground by enriching the system of action and not by complementing orthodox economic theory.

In sum, the conclusion seems justified that, in the 1940s, the question of the relation of sociology and economics was clearly less significant for Parsons; unlike during the period from 1925 to 1937, his work no longer developed along the lines of the questions formulated by economics. At the same time, Parsons was interested in the interaction of utilitarian motives of action and the factors described as sociological elements in the early writings, which materialized especially in the studies of the professions. The two books that appeared in 1951—*The Social System* and *Toward a General Theory of Action*—described further theoretical developments, especially the pattern variables, but were no longer based on a debate with economic theory but rather on Parsons's concern with the works of Freud, Mead, Thomas, and Erikson (Parsons 1977:38ff.).

Two reasons can be cited for the break from economics as the acknowledged point of reference for the development of his own theory. On the one hand, it must have been clear to Parsons, even if it was never explicitly posited, that the action frame of reference brings a theoretical solution to the relation of sociology and economics only on a metatheoretical plane, but cannot be reflected in the empirical process of research—especially in the question of the connection of economic and sociological elements of action. Parsons never answered the question of what a sociology concerned with ultimate values, but not with relations of means to ends, really does. This would not have had to bother Parsons anymore if he had wanted to deal only with epistemological questions. And it can be speculated that Parsons might have done that if this path had not been increasingly closed to him, or at least had not led to a dead end. This applies not so much to the theoretical development as to the institutional level. Ever since he returned from Germany in 1927, Parsons had taken an ambivalent position between two social science disciplines. At Amherst and, until 1931, at Harvard, Parsons was a member of the economics department. At the same time, he was working on problems outside the canon of the discipline. Publishing in the most distinguished economics journal, he let the reader know that he considered himself a sociologist (Parsons 1991a:153).

This tightrope act was possible for Parsons because of a strong personal support based in a few important contacts he had made in the 1920s. Along with the connection to the Harvard economist, Frank Taussig (Camic 1991: XXXI), his friendship with Frank Knight, whom Parsons met in Heidelberg, where Knight was working on the translation of Weber's economic history, was especially important.[20] The correspondence between Parsons and Knight indicates that Knight grew increasingly critical of Parsons's positions, which produced an insuperable antipathy and developed into an open debate after 1940.[21] Harald Wenzel (1990:119) even argues that Parsons's critical methodological position vis-à-vis neoclassical economics can be seen in the debate with Knight. Parsons must have increasingly recognized that his attempt to fit sociology into a frame of reference outlined by economic theory was not acknowledged by the economists. But this support was important because Parsons criticized existing traditions of American sociology as a sociologist from the perspective of economic theory, which put him in a precarious and vulnerable position. In fact, Parsons also had to debate with critics of his positions from his own department.[22] Even if it is hardly possible to say for sure what ultimately led Parsons to break with the strong emphasis on economic issues in his early work, obviously it must have been a clear decision for Parsons, as indicated in his autobiography: "I am not wholly clear about my motives, but I think they had to do with the feeling that I needed a relatively formal complete formal break with economics" (Parsons 1977:32ff.). This was also corroborated by Parsons's refusal of Schumpeter's offer to publish together a collection of essays from a discussion group organized by Schumpeter (32).

Perhaps even more surprising than the sudden break from the close relationship to economic theory is Parsons's resumption of this liaison in the early 1950s. As a guest professor at Cambridge in 1953 Parsons was invited by the department of economics of the university to deliver a series of lectures in honor of Alfred Marshall. In 1953 Parsons delivered three lectures, the *Marshall Lectures* (1986), dealing with economics in terms of the general theory of social systems. These lectures formed the basis for *Economy and Society* (1956), published three years later with Neil Smelser. These two works once again take up the problem of determining the relationship between economics and sociology, but Parsons's renewed concern with economics takes place in a completely different theoretical key. Parsons's metatheoretical framework had developed from the early voluntaristic theory of action to the general theory of social systems. He had access to the four-function scheme to examine the economy as a subsystem of society (Parsons and Shils 1951; Parsons, Bales, and Shils 1953). In the new theoretical key, the question for Parsons was which structures fill the functions necessary to maintain a social system. Some functions of society are economic and the economy appears as a social subsystem that is differentiated from other social functions.

The renewed concern with the relationship of sociology and economics appears under various aspects as a break and a continuity with the work of the 1930s. The most important innovation for systematizing the relationship of sociology and economics in sociological theory was that, for the first time, the theoretical conceptualization takes place not from a genuine concern with economics but rather as a *use of a sociological framework developed independent of economic theory*. In the *Marshall Lectures* and in *Economy and Society*, Parsons presents the hypothesis that economics can be understood as a special case of the general theory of social systems that he developed, and therefore can be reconstructed within the functionalist frame of reference that includes all the social sciences.[23]

At first glance, this break with the strategy followed in the early work of conceiving of sociology according to the scientific model of orthodox economics as an analytically delineated science also seems to contain a rejection of orthodox economics itself. The general theory of social systems is understood as a theory of society that locates economics as a functionally differentiated field, and thus also subordinates economic theory. Yet, in continuity with the early work and contrary to the expectation of a critique of economic theory from the system-functionalist perspective, Parsons holds onto the view that economic theory itself is an adequate instrument for analyzing and explaining the economic processes it studies, as he states at the end of the *Marshall Lectures*: "The farther I have gone, the more convinced I have become of the essential soundness, from a sociologist's point of view, of the main tradition of economic theory" (Parsons 1986:68). Parsons's ostensibly much more confident position vis-à-vis economic theory was directed at a new subordination of sociology in the sense that economic theory was granted a reference function for the social sciences. That is, Parsons and Smelser (1956:28) claimed the validity of their theoretical considerations with the argument that they were in accord with those of economic theory. Independent of the justice of this claim, it is implied that sociological theory can be legitimated vis-à-vis economic theory by compatibility with it.

Parsons, who delivered the *Marshall Lectures* to an audience that consisted mostly of economists, may have intended to mitigate resentment by validating economic theory in order to pave the way for an interdisciplinary discourse; but the irony of the argument naturally was also that sociology has nothing to contribute to the consideration of economics in a narrow sense but merely *locates* economic theory in an expanded theoretical framework. Parsons also saw this locating of economics as the main preoccupation of his renewed concern with the relationship of sociology and economics. The metatheoretical perspective and the functionalist argumentation of the AGIL scheme allowed him to represent economic theory as *requiring completion* from a sociological aspect, because this recognizes neither the noneconomic preconditions of the functionally differentiated economy nor its incorporation into societal functions at large. Parsons formulates his claim at the beginning of the *Marshall Lectures* in a not altogether modest metaphor, as an "attempt to sketch a 'Columbian' map of the social world, on which the main land masses can all be located relative to each other" (Parsons 1986:3). Such a map of the social sciences was to designate and fill in the sociological factors of influence, which are externalized as residual categories by economics. Thus, the commensurability of economic and sociological considerations would be shown within the framework of the general theory of social systems.

The hypothesis that economic theory can be understood as a specific case of the theory of social systems sanctions economic theory in terms of sociology. With this intention, given the fundamentally changed theoretical framework, an amazing continuity with the relationship to economic theory formulated in the early work can be seen.[24] At the same time, the cool reception the book encountered in sociology is partially explained by this program. Parsons and Smelser are not interested in a sociological reformulation of the economic concept of internal economic processes but rather in a theoretical explication of those factors of influence on these processes which are externalized by economic theory and go into the theory as ad hoc postulates. In *Economy and Society*, they did not intend any theoretical establishment of economic sociology. Instead, the goal of the analysis consisted of explaining the congruency of orthodox economic theory and functionalist systems theory, to show their mutual capacity to connect. In terms of economic sociology, the central limitation of Parsons's analysis of the economy can be seen in the acknowledgment of economic theory for analyzing market transactions—that has been described by Richard Swedberg (1987:62) as the "economy and society paradigm" of economic sociology.

Yet, at the same time, in *Economy and Society* a much stronger integration of the economic subsystem with the other subsystems depicted in the four-function scheme takes place because the system is integrated in terms of theory. Parsons's self-critical consideration of the juxtaposition of normative integration and rational means-ends relations as a differentiation of sociology and economics in the early work rejects it as a "false dilemma" and makes room for an integrative view:

> The non-economic aspects are not the resultants of the operation of one or more sets of "non-economic" variables whereas the economic aspect is the resultant of a different and independent set of variables, of an independent though abstract "theoretical system." The correct view is rather that there is one set of fundamental variables of the social system which are just as fundamental in its economic aspect as in any other. (Parsons 1986:11)

Programmatically, economics is integrated into the general theoretical framework, and the theoretical reflection of economic relations and their link to the other subsystems conceptualized within the theory of social systems must show whether economic theory can be proved within the metatheoretical system. The criterion for that is the reconstruction of economic concepts in the language of systems theory, which enables an integrative examination of the economic aspect of society and overcomes the analytic separation of sociology and economics by assigning disparate aspects of action. The essential progress for economic sociology in Parsons's renewed preoccupation with economics consists of the systematic debate with the processes of boundary interchanges between the economic subsystem and the other subsystems. Social differentiation is indeed conceived as an analytical separation of social functions, but the reciprocal dependence of these functions on one another calls attention to the view of the boundaries and interchanges of the economic subsystem. This is shown by the points of contact with other social subsystems and through the internal boundary processes of the economy, which also has to be provided with structures to deal with the four functional imperatives. The systems-theoretical framework allows Parsons to analyze the economy in its functional relations to other subsystems.

Another important change in Parsons's view of economics vis-à-vis the early work can be seen in the turn to macroeconomics as a theoretical frame of reference in economics. In his work of the 1930s, Parsons debated mainly with neoclassical microeconomics and complemented the action theory used in it. In the *Marshall Lectures* and in *Economy and Society*, Keynes's macroeconomic theory is chosen as the reference point in economics.

With regard to the programmatic *intention* of *Economy and Society*, two questions must be addressed: is the AGIL scheme a convincing outline of a social theory, and is it in fact possible to reconstruct economic theory in the theoretical framework proposed by Parsons? Whether it makes any sense to deal with the economy in terms of the general theory of social systems depends on the answer to the first question. If the theoretical framework of the AGIL scheme cannot be used as an instrument of social theory, the result is that little can be said about the bond of the economy in society from this perspective. If it is not possible to reconstruct economic theory in the four-field scheme, Parsons's claim to cite orthodox economics as a key witness for the universal claims of his theory cannot be maintained. In fact, it seems to me that both Parsons's claim of social theory and the reconstruction of economic theories in *Economy and Society* are problematic. Various sociologists have debated in detail about how convincing Parsons's theoretical outline is (Alexander 1984; Giddens 1984; Habermas 1984). In terms of economics, the problematic has never been worked out but was simply hinted at in reviews of *Economy and Society* in economic journals deploring a drastic distortion of economic concepts in Parsons's reconstruction.[25]

In the discussion in this section, both questions are touched on only marginally. The issue is neither an inspection of Parsons's social theory as such nor the interpretation of outlines of economic theory in *Economy and Society*. Instead, after a general description of the positioning of economics within Parsons and Smelser's theoretical structure, the boundary processes between the economic subsystem and the three other subsystems portrayed in the AGIL scheme is discussed. The focus is on the question of what contribution can be gleaned for the three action situations of cooperation, uncertainty, and innovation from Parsons and Smelser's preoccupation with the economy. The hypothesis resulting from this is that Parsons's debate with the boundary processes between the economy and other subsystems indicates, against his own theoretical intention, aspects of a link between both, which goes beyond the sociological determination of social conditions externalized by economic theory. The study of economic institutions, the consideration of economic rationality as a socially sanctioned approach to adaptive processes, the incorporation of the utility concept in the system of social values, the analysis of financial markets, and the consideration of motivational presumptions of economic action indicates the significance of normative structures in economic processes, which can no longer be interpreted as a mere complement to models of economic theory. The elements cited in *Economy and Society* are not elaborated satisfactorily. But this does not mean that they cannot be made productive for economic sociology. While the treatment of the economy as a social subsystem in the AGIL scheme is problematic, there are some interesting (but not well-developed) concepts for economic sociology in the book, which have attracted almost no attention to this day. This hypothesis contains a critique of the sociological reception of *Economy and Society*, which contributed to what may be a too hasty aversion to the book.

The Boundary Processes of the Economy

Parsons studies the economy as a social system of society. Social systems consist of the interaction of at least two, but usually many, actors and are distinguished both from cultural systems and personality systems. The more precise definition of social systems postulates a functionalist scheme, which states that processes in a system must fulfill four functional imperatives in order to form a stable equilibrium. These functional requirements are represented in the AGIL scheme. "A" stands for adaptive processes in systems, meaning the necessary fulfillment of the requirements approached from outside as conditions. "G" stands for the processes of goal attainment of the system that uses resources to achieve social goals. The separation of adaptive and goal-attaining functions continues the distinction of means-ends relations and determination of ends in the early work. The determination of ends is identified with the "G" aspect of the AGIL scheme, whereas the adaptive dimension of the social system is directed at the supply of resources for *whatever* system goals and thus corresponds with the means-ends relations of the voluntaristic theory of action. This separation is also considered analytic; in the system functionalist framework, however, the separation into two distinct scientific disciplines is dropped. Economics is concerned not only with the adaptive processes of society, but rather, vice versa, the processes analyzed by economics are part of the adaptive demands of society, which are studied in a general theoretical system.

In Parsons's conception, both of those functional aspects are located in a broader theoretical system, in which two more system requirements that indicate the normative framework of the functioning of the social system are represented. The processes of achieving ends and the availability of resources for these ends must be consonant with the values of society and must be coordinated with the processes in other systems in order to avoid conflicts between the parts. Parsons designated two more systematic dimensions for these requirements. The integrative aspects "I" indicate the forces of "solidarity" in a social system, which stem from the normative agreements. Finally, "L" indicates the institutionalized system of values whose task consists of system integration.

The four functional imperatives of the AGIL scheme can be used as analytic distinctions for systems on all levels. The most abstract level is "society"; right beneath it are differentiated social subsystems, whose task is to deal with each of the four system functions of society and which, in turn, also have to fulfill the four functional demands. The economy is viewed as a social subsystem that is differentiated with respect to fulfilling the adaptive demands of society.[26] In reference to the system demands of society, adaptation means the supply of resources with which material needs of society can be fulfilled and which thus contribute to achieving social ends (Parsons 1986:9). These resources of society come into being through production and contribute to social wealth or income if they are considered useful by society (!).[27]

The metatheoretical framework of the four functional subsystems and locating the economy as one of them first demonstrates the multidimensionality of functional demands and objects categorically to any (economic) reductionism in social theory. The economic subsystem is assigned a central, but limited function. Alongside it are the areas of social determination of ends and the normative integration of society. Only the fulfillment of all functional demands enables the development of a stable social order. Thus, in continuation of the critique of utilitarianism in the early work, the social scenario outlined by Parsons challenges the solutions of the problem of order that appeal to contract theory or the converging interests of selfish actors.

But with regard to economics, the theoretical systematic of the AGIL scheme also goes beyond the analytical delineation of the early work. The economy itself is viewed as a social system that must fulfill the four functional imperatives for its stable functioning. The plane of reference is not society, but rather the economic subsystem, hence the organization of the processes and structures for the provision of goods and services that are needed on the level of society to fulfill the adaptive function requirements. By making the economy itself fulfill normative demands for integration and political functions for the pursuit of ends, Parsons challenges the possibility of the norm-free functioning of the economy along with the sole "jurisdiction" of orthodox economic theory for the subject matter of economics. Yet this does not mean that Parsons would reject the significance of utilitarian economic theory itself. Instead, under the condition of functional differentiation, many processes within the economic system, but not the economy as a social system, are accessible with a theory that starts from utility maximizing. The significance of the pursuit of individual utility for economic processes depends on institutional presumptions and is not assumed as an a priori postulate of the analysis of economic phenomena. Because the four categories of the AGIL scheme represent analytic distinctions, they do not correspond with concrete social organizations. Instead, subsystems represent social structures, each specializing in one function, able to be isolated by "types of processes" (Parsons and Smelser 1956:47). Thus, in modern societies, the economy cannot be equated with enterprises, markets, or processes of production and distribution. Parsons and Smelser (1956:15ff.) distinguish functionally differentiated subsystems from collectivities (as, e.g., the enterprise), which are always multifunctional. It can be said of them only that they fulfill *primary* economic (or, e.g., political) functions. On the basis of the functional primacy of adaptation, organizations of the economy are differentiated from other social systems like the family or the school, but they are never *only* economic organizations.

Attributing system requirements to social subsystems says nothing about their empirical significance in concrete social formations; only a general framework is outlined within which empirical structures can be considered. The adaptive needs imply merely that societies must produce goods and services for their reproduction. How this happens, whether there are differentiated organizations in society for it, and what significance this function assumes in society—these are empirical questions. Parsons claims a universal theoretical framework that can be applied to the investigation of all social formations and thus enable comparative research.[28] Yet in *Economy and Society* interest is aimed at modern societies for whose adaptive processes definite structures are assumed. Thus Parsons starts from the point that, in modern societies, the economy is differentiated as a social subsystem and organizations that pursue primarily economic ends are established. Along with developing organizations in line with the adaptive functions of society, Parsons (1986:21) also assumes that, because of the significance of the adaptive capacity, the economy in modern societies attains a special importance vis-à-vis other social subsystems. However, he does not assume a specific model of relations of production.

Unlike the conception of the early work, system functionalism is not on the level of the actor but on the aggregate level of systems. This can explain why Parsons no longer chooses microeconomic theory as a reference point in economic theory but rather, in *Economy and Society*, refers to macroeconomic models, particularly to Keynes's theory. Especially momentous is the choice of the reference level of society for the notion of utility, with which Parsons and Smelser turn away from individualistic concepts of utility of neoclassical economic theory, which defines utility as an individual measure of satisfaction of need, from which demands for goods and price setting can be derived. By using society as a reference level for the term of utility, Parsons circumvents the problem known from welfare economics that individual utility functions cannot be aggregated into an optimal social utility function. Welfare economics describes the social welfare optimum by the aggregation of independent individual utility functions. The problem of welfare theory is how individual utility functions can be compared among individuals. On the basis of ordinal utility functions, no social welfare function that satisfies the conditions of consistency and transitivity can be derived.[29] Parsons and Smelser avoid this problem by applying the concept of utility as interindividual from the start. A subsystem contributes to fulfilling the functional demands of the system of which it is a part. Thus, the economy makes resources available for the fulfillment of the adaptive needs *of society*. In contrast to the model of welfare economics, utility is not materialized by the aggregation of individual utility functions but is always defined a priori by the institutionalized value system of society. The result is that the consideration of individual utility functions separate from social utility is not possible: "Since the individual is not the defining unit for the maximization of utility, it is inappropriate to refer to the measurability of utility *among* individuals" (Parsons and Smelser 1956:22). Parsons and Smelser reject a theoretical approach that aggregates individual utility functions because the individual assessment of utility is always socially determined, standards of consumption expressing themselves in life-styles. The welfare economic concept of utility cannot show clearly that "the acquisition of necessary motivations and powers for the individual pursuit of utility presumes the appropriation of a commonly shared social and cultural world in which symbolic models of realized and symbolic models for desirable life styles exist" (Sauerwein 1988:45).

The concept of utility used by Parsons and Smelser is clearly reminiscent of Durkheim's normative price theory, which saw price as always determined by "public opinion." If the ends of the economy are socially structured and value is determined by society, then there is the danger of a deterministic view of the demand curves on the basis of normative definitions. This applies especially to Parsons's systems theory because the behavior of the economic actors is understood as filling institutionalized roles. This is the opposite of the procedure of economic theory because the actors' level is seen in terms of the functional demands of society.

Viewing the economy as a functional subsystem draws attention to the equilibrium conditions of social reproduction. Thus, the starting point of the theory shifts from the "unit act" to the macrosociological study of the conditions of maintaining the system. At the same time, the social subsystems first separated analytically are integrated into a metatheory. Thus, the essential change of the view of the economy in *Economy and Society*, vis-à-vis the early work, can be seen. If the analytical separation between ultimate ends and means-ends relationships does not show how the unity of economic and sociological elements of concrete action situations can be represented, in the systems theory the analytical scheme is constructed from the unity of the system of society. The analytical separation into different functional demands, according to which subsystems are differentiated, is valid only in reference to the unity of the whole. The central question consists of how parts and wholes relate to one another. In this theoretical project, attention is drawn to the relationships between the economy and the three other social systems represented in the AGIL scheme. Thus, the analytical distinction has the status of a heuristic that sets up a theoretical scaffolding available for the analysis of intersystemic unity.

Most of *Economy and Society* deals with the analysis of these boundary processes between the economy and the three other social subsystems, as well as the internal economic boundary interchanges between the four functional imperatives of the economy. In the schematic consideration of the AGIL cross tabulations, the boundary interchanges of the economy are derived deductively on hierarchically structured levels. Parsons and Smelser study the boundary interchanges between the economic subsystem of society and the other three subsystems. The interchanges are localized on a more specific level, so that the boundary processes between a functional imperative of the economy and the corresponding functional imperative of one of the other three social subsystems are studied. In a horizontal view, the three other functional imperatives represent the "social situation" of the subsystem of the economy. The boundary interchanges are reciprocal so that a system always presents a product output and a factor input at the interface with another system. Schematically, this results in the interchanges Ag-Lg, Aa-Ga, and Ai-Ii. Furthermore, intermediary symbolic mechanisms that control the direct boundary interchanges are studied for all three boundary interchanges. From the architectonics of the theory, the horizontal order of the boundary processes is interesting because it means that a hierarchical ordering of the subsystems is renounced in *Economy and Society*. This distinguished the systematics of the systems-functionalist phase from the cybernetic control hierarchy that Parsons introduced later, in which the economy is incorporated vertically on the lowest level and is controlled by the other systems.

In the discussion of the influence of the other functional imperatives on economic processes and the significance of the economy for other functional needs of social reproduction, the incorporation of the economy into the nexus of functional demands becomes clear. Unlike neoclassical theory that shields the analysis of economic processes from cultural, normative, and historical factors and understands the economy under assumptions of the postulate of maximization as a self-regulating system, Parsons and Smelser are interested in indicating the systematic link of the economy, political community, and social value system. Thus, within the general theoretical framework, the extraeconomic contingency of economic processes is indicated on the one hand; and on the other, the factors of social influence, externalized by economic theory as peripheral conditions, are to be bound into *one* theoretical systematic with economic analysis.

The boundary processes are conceptualized in a clear analogy to macroeconomic cyclical flow theories as inputs or outputs of the subsystems. On the most general level, the output of the economy consists of the produced wealth or income that becomes available to society for its ends. The input of the economy from the other social subsystem consists of power (in the form of credit), solidarity (in the form of normatively integrated action), and respect (as acknowledgment of value conforming action) (Parsons and Smelser 1956:49ff.). Parsons and Smelser themselves call attention to the analogy of these boundary processes with macroeconomic models: for market processes guided by supply and demand, this same logic applies as for the relation of performance and sanction in social interaction generally. Yet Parsons and Smelser (9) assert that the model for conceptualizing the boundary processes is not based on a model from economic theory but rather on the view of mechanisms of interaction between social systems according to the production-sanction plan of the general theory of social systems. Thus, for Parsons, the close agreement between the general systems theory and economic theory does not represent an "economization" of sociology but merely indicates its compatibility with economic theory under the direction of systems functionalism.[30] Parsons finds here the confirmation of his thesis that economic theory is the best structured part of the general theory of social systems he developed, which legitimates this view while avoiding a confrontation with economics. This description of the theory must certainly not be seen as a refutation of the claim that Parsons's theory design is oriented to economic models, for which there are strong arguments (Sauerwein 1988; Chazel 1989). If this is so, it would not be surprising that the first "use" of the general theory of social systems falls precisely on the social subsystem of the economy. There the link between theory and the conventional conceptualization of economic processes would necessarily be strongest. At the same time, a similar process could be worked out like the one Habermas (1980) showed for the media theory later developed by Parsons—namely, that the power of persuasion of the boundary interchanges, according to the economic input-output model, recedes when intersystemic boundary processes outside the economy are analyzed.

These questions will not be pursued in the context of the debate with Parsons's economic sociology. What is important about the correspondence of the boundary interchanges viewed by Parsons with macroeconomic circular-flow models is the resulting ambivalence between substantial and analytical delineation of subsystems. From the analytical point of view, all those functions in society would be viewed as economic, which provide resources for the achievement of societal ends. Under substantial aspects, the economy consists of concrete institutions and organizations. Economic circular-flow models conceive of concrete entities—enterprise, household, and state—as recipients and senders of flows of money or goods; thus the analogy to this model substantiates Parsons's analytic distinction. Parsons does not resolve this ambiguity, but it is clear in the view of boundary interchanges that these are conceptualized based on economic theory, and the relationship between the general theory of social systems and economic theory is in fact the opposite of Parsons's claim: it is not economic theory that adjusts to the general theory pattern; rather, the boundary processes are conceived so that they do not conflict with economic theory. This must not be understood as criticism per se, but the systematic consequence is that Parsons's economic sociology always applies precisely where economics operates with psychologically based assumptions of behavior—either in case of rational action or, if Keynes's theory is enlisted as a reference, in the corresponding assumptions for the establishment of demand and supply functions that deviate from orthodox economics. The representation of guiding inputs in the economic system by processes of institutionalization allows economic functions to be viewed as dependent on social preconditions. Yet, as the following sections show, this deals only in a limited way with the social embedding of economic processes because only those elements of economic action that are externalized by economic theory are investigated. This is the central limitation of Parsons's concrete formulation of boundary interchanges, which systematically constricts the potential for the multidimensional analysis of the interpenetration of economic processes contained in the theoretical framework. Parsons is not willing to reject economic theory any further.

The Boundary Processes between the Economy and the Pattern-Maintenance System

Because they offer the first interface of the economic system with another social system of society, Parsons and Smelser study the boundary processes with the pattern-maintenance system. The social functions aimed at maintaining cultural patterns in the social system are located in this system. On the institutional level, these include the church, the school, and especially the family, which contribute to handing down existing patterns of value through socialization processes and conflict management.[31] In *Economy and Society*, the boundary interchanges considered between the two systems—following the macroeconomic circular-flow model— take place between enterprises and the family (the household). The household obtains goods and services for consumption purposes from the economy and, in return, serves as a labor force for the economic system. This conceptualization, which seems very conventional at first, obtains its specific significance through the precise location of the boundary interchange and the localization of households in the social subsystem that has the function of handing down cultural patterns.

The boundary interchanges between the two systems are localized in the respective functions of the goal attainment of the economy (Ag) and the pattern-maintenance system (Lg). This allocation shows the societal nature of the economy, whose end consists of the production of goods and services, which are available as general resources. Produced consumer goods go to the family as input and thus to an institution of the pattern-maintenance system, whose function consists of stabilizing the social system of values. Through this conceptualization, consumer goods themselves get a role in the reproduction of social structure, which consists of the possibility of the development and reproduction of life-styles (Parsons and Smelser 1956:54). By linking consumption to the pattern-maintenance system, Parsons and Smelser make it clear that consumption decisions can be understood neither on the basis of the utility maximization of atomized individuals along indifference curves nor as the result of consumer manipulation based on power relations. Thus they also object both to the microeconomic household theory and critical theories of manipulation through mass consumption.[32] Instead, Parsons and Smelser view consumer decisions as established in the generalized value system of society. Thus consumer needs are acknowledged as authentic in principle. Consumption symbolizes the culturally established life-style, lends status and prestige, and has a character in this function that is not only individual. Already in *The Social System*, Parsons had analyzed the significance of consumer goods not only as gratification within the performance-sanction scheme but in their function as expressive symbols. The expressive significance of consumer goods makes these "more significantly cultural than physical objects, because their style-patterning is more important than any other aspect of them. A good example would be style in clothing or in house furnishings" (Parsons 1951:128). Robert Holton (1986:58) correctly sees in Parsons's conceptualization the possibility for a sociological theory of consumption, which has hardly been noticed up to now.

On the basis of Parsons's construction of the boundary processes, according to the circular-flow model, the output from the economic system into the pattern-maintenance system in the form of consumer goods must be "equilibrated" by a reciprocal process through which an input flows from the pattern-maintenance system into the economy. Parsons and Smelser consider the labor force as this input. The location of the labor force in the pattern-maintenance system refers to the socialization processes, which Parsons assumes for the stable exercise of professional roles. It requires structuring and channeling attitudes, value orientations, and behavior patterns through which the individual acquires the capabilities, motivations, and orientations requisite for the functional demands of professional activity. The institutions of the pattern-maintenance system initiate and guide socializing processes that prepare the production factor labor to fulfill the functional demands of the economic system. Therefore, in Parsons and Smelser's model, this coordination of individual and organization is not an internal economic issue, but rather includes institutions with other primary functions. Because the socializing processes of learning professional roles represent the primary goal of the pattern-maintenance system with regard to the economy, the output is localized in the goal attainment field of this system (Lg). Actors are indeed prepared for the functional demands of the economy by socialization processes, but this relationship cannot lead to the complete assimilation to functional needs of the economy.

The emphasis on extraeconomic socialization processes and the incorporation of the labor force into cultural contexts of society as well as their significance for the economic process are interesting for economic sociology because it raises a problem omitted by economic theory—that is, that the sociocultural constitution of actors in the economic system has a structural significance for the operation of the economy. It is one aspect that the social preconditions for the fulfillment of professional roles and the integration of differentiated tasks of labor in enterprises have been externalized by orthodox economic theory. What is more serious is that the systematic consequences of the social construction of employee roles for the labor market have not been studied because of the dogmatic equation of wages and marginal productivity. During the past twenty-five years, there have been controversial debates within industrial sociology about the significance of normative attitudes for the labor process. Marxist-oriented empirical studies of the 1960s and 1970s have especially called attention to tendencies to disqualification and the loss of profession-specific identities as well as the increase of instrumental attitudes toward labor (Braverman 1974). The extraction of labor productivity (Bowles 1985) is guaranteed less by a control of labor relations in normatively structured socialization processes than by direct control mechanisms of management. On the other hand, studies in industrial sociology of the 1980s indicate a requalification process (Kern and Schumann 1984; Piore and Sabel 1989). Researchers in organizational sociology, stimulated mainly by international comparative studies that deal with the significance of organizational culture for the efficiency of enterprises, refer to the significance of "soft" factors for the efficient functioning of enterprises (Ouchi 1980; Peters and Waterman 1982). In connection with mechanisms of self-coordination for the control of enterprises, management literature refers to the significance of processes of identification and internalization, which can be introduced as a functional equivalent of outside controls (Staehle 1990). These discussions of organizational or industrial sociology occupy the same territory that was conceived theoretically by Parsons and Smelser in the boundary interchange between the pattern maintenance system and the economic system, and refers to the cooperation problem discussed in chapter 1.

Money, which is paid by households for consumer goods and flows from enterprises to households as wages, functions as an intermediary mechanism of boundary interchange. Parsons and Smelser see the basis for this intermediary mechanism, on the one hand, in the division of labor, which makes a direct exchange of labor and consumer goods functionally impossible; and, on the other, in the divergent interests of family and enterprise.[33] Whereas production decisions of the enterprise are oriented toward expectations of profit, consumer decisions are made on the basis of life-styles established culturally and founded on socialization processes. The differentiation of production and consumption of goods assumes the relative detachment of employment and purchase of products. Only by abstracting concrete items and storing value by means of the medium of money can production levels develop independent of the concrete demands of the employees and be adjusted to the profit motive.[34] Through the medium of money, consumers can acquire sovereignty vis-à-vis products made by themselves, which is what makes it at all possible to speak adequately about the formation of life-styles on the basis of consumption decisions. By separating consumption demands and labor demand from the concrete exchange partner, and yet binding them together on a generalized level with the generalized exchange medium of money, the different goals of economy and family can be coordinated through the market mechanism. Thus money receives a central significance for the differentiation of the two social systems of economy and family: it is unimportant for the employee what he produces as long as he can trust that the consumer goods he wants are produced by somebody else and he can acquire them with the generalized exchange medium of money. As a mirror image, it is unimportant to the producer if the labor force he pays has any interest in the product manufactured. By including the mechanism of money, the potential conflict of interest between household and enterprise is reduced to a conflict over wages. In *The Social System*, Parsons had already interpreted the use of money as the central prerequisite for shaping stable, instrumentally oriented interactions and for the functional differentiation of production. Through money, the specific obstacles of the exchange of goods can be circumvented because "the two aspects of the total interaction system in which ego is involved are adjusted to each other" (Parsons 1951:71).

INTEGRATING CAPITAL AND LABOR THROUGH THE LABOR CONTRACT AND THE PROFESSIONAL ROLE

The differentiation of the economy made possible by the introduction of money as a symbolic medium does not completely defuse the potential conflict of the two systems of household and enterprise. The reason for that is inherent in the specification of the labor market, where contracts are concluded about a "commodity" that is in principle bound up with its bearer (Parsons and Smelser 1956:141). Whereas the neoclassical labor market theory starts with the idea that the salary determined by the labor contract corresponds to the marginal product, both in the Marxist tradition and in the new principal-agent literature a central problem of capitalist market economies is seen in the specifics of labor, which is connected with the question of the efficiency of social relations relying only on interest in organizations. By examining the specifics of labor contracts in the boundary relationship between the economy and the pattern-maintenance system, Parsons and Smelser refer to an aspect of the cooperation problem of purely interest-oriented actors, discussed in chapter 1.

In Marx's theory (1967:181ff.), the specification of labor was the analytical starting point for discovering the social antinomies that were ultimately to lead to the destruction of the capitalist system. A prerequisite for the production of surplus value is the double character of labor, which appears in the sphere of circulation as a commodity, and is used in the sphere of production as living labor. The surplus value is the value discrepancy between the salary determined by a labor contract and the value created in the labor process. According to the Marxist interpretation, two scenarios can be derived from this specification. One results from the progressive process of capital concentration and technological development and emphasizes the economic contradictions of the processes of capitalist accumulation, which tend to lead to the abolition of surplus value production. The other scenario, oriented toward revolution and developed most succinctly by Georg Lukács (1971) emphasizes the reifying character of capitalistic relations of production and the potential of the proletarian classes to abolish social alienation in class struggle. The principal-agent approach has indirectly followed this problem by getting away from the fundamental assumptions of the neoclassical standard model of labor market theory that labor output would be established in the labor contract so that the realized labor output corresponds to a contractually agreed marginal product. Instead, the principal-agent approach brings into labor market economics the conviction that the employee has an interest in realizing the smallest possible labor output, which the principals can counteract only by using control measures or incentives.[35] Whereas Marx sees a structural macrosocial conflict emerging from the special nature of labor, the principal-agent approach is only interested in the enterprise as a unit of analysis.[36]

Like Marx, Parsons sees the specifics of labor as a starting point for a central structural conflict for the system stability of the market economy, but he aims at a completely different solution. Attention is directed neither at a scenario of destabilization nor to the effect of control measures—as in principal-agent approaches—but rather to the question of an institutional mechanism for *defusing* the conflict on the level of enterprises. Unlike the emphasis on control mechanisms in principal-agent approaches, Parsons's expectation is that the antagonism between employee needs and the functional demands on them in the production process is reduced by the institutionally controlled, normative integration of the actors into the general system of values, which can transcend the conflicts of interest and allows the stabilization of the social system. Conflict-reducing, normative integration is manifested in the institutions of the *labor contract* and the *professional role*. Parsons explicates the problem resulting from these two institutions in the *Marshall Lectures* against the background of role theory, by describing the boundary processes between the systems on the level of action theory as "interpenetrating boundary roles" (Parsons 1986:27).[37] Such a role is assumed at the interface between economy and pattern-maintenance system by both consumers and employees. Consumers have a role in the economy as demanders of products but are also established firmly in the family and community. Employees find themselves in a boundary role as family members and as production factors in the economy. Parsons concludes from this that, because of the boundary processes, the values of the family have a structural influence on the economy. The labor contract "must somehow integrate the values of the two systems, that of the economy in the field of efficient production; that of the family in the maintenance of an adequate standard of living" (28).

To understand how Parsons sees the labor contract and the professional role as the institutional prerequisites for dealing with the problem of integrating two social systems with at least partially antagonistic interests, Parsons's concept of institution must be examined more precisely. Parsons and Smelser define institutions as "the ways in which the value patterns of the common culture of a social system are integrated in the concrete action of its units in their interaction with each other through the definition of role expectations and the organization of motivation" (Parsons and Smelser 1956:102). Accordingly, the function of institutions in the economy consists of regulating social relations by constructing reciprocal structures of expectation that make the economic system commensurable with its environment. This happens by institutionalizing rights and duties in accordance with the general system of values as role expectations and behavioral motivations, and internalizing them in the socialization process. Regulation includes the two dimensions of conformity with institutionalized expectations and consistency of the expectations of the various systems of action.

An institutional regulation is required especially for contracts, which increase along with the division of labor and guide economic processes of factor allocation (104). Under the conditions of production by division of labor, production factors come from various sources in the economy and are subject to an economic control only on the basis of contractual relations that can bring production factors together. *Pace* Durkheim, the contractual relations that integrate production factors into the economic system have *two dimensions*: the instrumental dimension of the necessary mutual advantage of the contract for both parties; and "the socially prescribed and sanctioned rules to which such bargaining processes are subject, such as the guarantees of interest of third parties, restrictions on fraud and coercion, and the like" (105). The second dimension refers to a system of values shared by both partners to the exchange, which transcends the conflict of interest of the exchange relationship and is a basis for the stabilizing integration of the exchange relationship. This dimension indicates the real institutional significance of contractual relationships. With reference to the labor contract, this means that the contract includes not only the instrumental exchange relation of a specified quantity of labor productivity (or labor time) for a certain sum of money, but also implicitly contains reciprocal normative duties, which are built on a common system of values and are acknowledged by *both* parties to the contract. These reciprocal structures of expectation include a second performance-sanction exchange (along with labor productivity and money), which lends meaning to the material exchange on a symbolic level. This includes the prestige of working for a certain firm, and thus the social recognition resulting from the labor activity and, vice versa, the duty of feeling loyal and responsible to the firm.[38] But, in addition, the labor contract is also based on "a kind of common valuation of the functions of production in the society. From the firm's point of view it is defined in terms of the valuation of efficiency and worker reliability, from the worker's point of view it is defined on the basis of having a 'worth-while' job

(and not only in terms of wage level)" (110). The solution of the cooperation problem is thus seen by Parsons and Smelser in the normative integration of the parties to the contract, which obligates them beyond their
instrumental advantage from the exchange relation to an institutionally
regulated behavior that transcends the inherent conflict of interest.

The normative integration of action is described more precisely by Parsons and Smelser in the discussion of the role of the professions and their
institutional status. The significance of normative integration and the contract is strongly reminiscent of Durkheim, but Parsons's comments along
the AGIL scheme are much more elaborate, and his development of role
theory goes beyond Durkheim.

Contractual relations systematically refer to two other central economic institutions. On the one hand, contracts regulate *property* in things
and, on the other hand, the use of outputs, which are connected with the
institution of the *occupation*. Accordingly, Parsons and Smelser distinguish between three economic institutions: the contract that regulates the
exchange process; property, which fixes the right to nonsocial objects;
and occupation, which determines the use of labor productivity. By developing the institution of the occupational role from the general concept of
contract, Parsons and Smelser produce a hierarchization of institutions in
which the contract appears as the central economic institution, but which
also leaves the distinction between labor contract and occupational role
vague. Terminologically, the concept of the occupational role refers more
strongly to the external economic socialization processes that precede the
labor contract. However, the functional problem for both institutions
consists of the necessary integration of the three participating systems of
action—enterprise, family, and personality—whose partially antagonistic
interests cannot be abolished through the generalized medium of money.
This is only possible with material relations within the economic system.

As *occupational roles*, Parsons and Smelser designate "the role of an
individual within an organization in so far as it commits him to productive functions on behalf of the organization through personal performance and in so far as the commitment is established and/or maintained
by an explicit or implied contract with the organization" (Parsons and
Smelser 1956:114). The concept is used mainly in the discussion of the
problem of the specification of economic functions. Occupational roles,
as Parsons (1986:50) explains with reference to Weber, must be adequately specified and differentiated from broader role expectations to be
able to contribute efficiently to the adaptive performance of the economic
system. The development of occupational roles is partly an internal organizational process and partly a general socializing process that is traced
in the various stages. The quasi-biographical pursuit of the specification
of general skills to the performance of concrete tasks on the job explains

the extraeconomic origin of the performance of occupational roles. Preparation for the occupational role begins in the socialization process with learning general productive ability and motivation in the oral phase of childhood development. Later, formal training leads to qualifications that enable participation in the labor market. The interface between the general socialization process and organizational work specification is achieved in the firm with employment regulated by the labor contract. In the organization, the work specification is made by occupying a special position with fixed tasks. The process of role learning shows clearly that the occupational role always includes an integration of general values with specific abilities tailor-made for the economic system. "Labor services . . . are not generated within the economy at all but in the household and the educational system" (Parsons and Smelser 1956:135). While role learning is first initiated outside the economy, the internal stages of functional specification in the organization are aimed solely at the economic dimension of the efficient allocation of production factors. The specification of the labor force also includes a process of differentiation through which "freedom from ties which would inhibit the 'efficient' devotion to a specific functional goal" (Parsons 1986:50) is achieved. Hierarchical relations and obligations vis-à-vis other members of the organization remain limited to the occupational sphere and separated from family duties. Successful role learning in the socialization process guarantees the defusing of the conflict between capital and labor by an internalized and hence stable orientation of action to the interests of economic productivity.[39]

But defusing the conflict by institutionalization does not imply only an adaptation of the employee to the functional demands of efficient use of production factors in the production process. Successful institutionalization also implies the development of *reciprocal* obligations, including those of the firm vis-à-vis the employee. Only under this condition can the institutions of the labor contract and the occupational role integrate the three action systems of organization, household, and personality. The household must allow the performance of the occupational role, and, vice versa, the structure of employment in the organization must permit the performance of family functions, through the prospect of a stable family income.[40] At the same time, the organization has the right to impose sanctions, especially through dismissal. On the symbolic level, integrative inputs are expected from the employee "to develop a sense of organizational responsibility" (Parsons and Smelser 1956:116), and, vice versa, the firm confers prestige connected with the occupation and status in the organization. Only through the performance of the respective functions of effective production, or "to be a 'good provider'" (117), do the roles merge into a stable system.

If the wage structure and the sanction mechanisms are dependent on the institutionalized system of values, then the approach of neoclassical economics, which views salary as monetary compensation for the marginal product, is wrong. Then, salary distinctions had to be explained instead by the institutionalized structures of expectations in society. Parsons and Smelser seem to have such an interpretation in mind when they try to explain the income level of various labor market groups from the different expectations of an appropriate standard of living generated in the pattern maintenance system. They therefore distinguish between the market for blue-collar and white-collar workers with minor organizational responsibility, for managers, and for professionals. The different institutional structure for each labor market group explains the variously defined conditions for the organizational membership and salary of each group. For the different labor market groups, there are always *distinctive* deviations from the assumptions of the economic model, on the basis of their specific incorporation into normative structures. The first segment— blue-collar and white-collar workers with fewer qualifications—was to some extent a model for the already discussed qualities of the labor market. The role of management is distinguished essentially by the greater organizational responsibility, which reverberates on the household. The wife must take a greater responsibility in the family in order to compensate for the manager's tighter incorporation in the organization.[41] Parsons interprets the manager's salary as based on his culturally defined higher standard of living, which also leaves the aspect of security—which is uppermost for the worker—relatively insignificant. Clubs influence the public and provide the group of managers with a functional equivalent of the trade union (Parsons and Smelser 1956:150ff.). The group of professionals deviates even further from the ideal of the perfect market because of its institutional regulations. That is, the values of the profession cannot be subordinated to the efficiency demands of the enterprise. Instead, the enterprise must respect the rules of the profession, which are set outside the economy and represent another integrative problem for the labor market. The pursuit of economic interests is restricted by professional standards (Parsons 1954a; 1951).

The emphasized normative factors of influence of the pattern-maintenance system prevent the functioning of the labor market according to the neoclassical model. Even an approach to this model can be expected only from markets set within the economic system. The labor supply function cannot be described as a function of the wage rate as in neoclassical theory because decisions about the labor supply start with the family, thus a system of action outside the economy. Moreover, the labor contract is influenced not only by the interests of the parties to the contract but especially by their institutional embodiment in the general value system of the society.

This can lead to the conclusion that Parsons and Smelser saw their theoretical model in this place in opposition to economic theory. But this is only conditionally the case. Parsons vehemently contradicts neoclassical microeconomics, but he does consider the theory of the institutional determination of the wage rate as thoroughly compatible with Keynes's labor market theory. The Keynesian theory had developed as a critique of the neoclassical equilibrium theory and states that the labor supply function does not change in a straight line with the price for labor. Parsons and Smelser can continue this postulate of Keynsian economic theory. Keynes had started with the idea that, from a certain mathematically undetermined wage rate, the quantity of supplied labor would sink abruptly to zero, instead of continuing to fall in a straight line, as assumed by the neoclassicists. The background of this approach entailed behavioral assumptions derived from psychology. Parsons and Smelser try to connect with this problem, known as the "stickiness" of wages, by claiming to explain it sociologically. They see their task as replacing Keynes's psychological assumptions with a sociologically determined labor supply function, in which institutional rigidities function as independent variables.[42] The starting point consists of the assumption that the institutionalization of occupational roles limits the adaptability of the wage scale of the labor force beyond the limit of the material subsistence levels cited in economics. Pay represents not only a means for the material survival of the labor force and the workers' families but also symbolizes status both inside and outside the world of labor (Parsons 1986:52).

If decisions about the labor supply are not set within the economic sphere, it can be understood why a market-clearing equilibrium is not achieved, contrary to expectations of neoclassical economics. The labor supply is taken from the market if the supply sets in only at a wage rate that would represent a violation of status. But, interestingly, Parsons and Smelser do not consider the imaginable case that a wage considered unfair must be accepted on the basis of the unequal distribution of power between capital and labor. In this case, a contract would be achieved, but this would not enable the employee to reach the goal of maintaining a culturally defined and institutionalized standard of life. Thus a discrepancy would be produced between goal attainment and goal expectation. The result, as Parsons and Smelser remark rather laconically in another context, would be that the "usual symptoms of disturbance and frustration may be expected to appear" (Parsons and Smelser 1956:63).[43]

This leads us to the critique of Parsons's idea of the normative integration of labor market relations. The explanations show clearly that Parsons believes the institutions of the labor contract and the occupational role are capable of the normative integration of the conflicting parties of the labor market and thus thinks the conflict of antagonistic parties in cooperation relations can be solved. In Parsons, too, the reference to normative integration naturally confronts the problem dealt with in the chapter on Durkheim, of having to explain why actors orient themselves in their actions on the general system of values if it is advantageous for them not to do so. By staking so much on processes of internalization, Parsons assumes that the behavior is socially determined to a large extent. (But what happens when some do defect and thus increase the costs of cooperation for the cooperating actors?) One theoretical problem that emerges from this is that the freedom of action of the actors is strongly restricted. This is why Dennis Wrong (1961) reproached Parsons for using an oversocialized concept of action. Jeffrey Alexander's (1984:234) critique aims from another direction—that the emphasis on the normative dimension of labor relations ignores that normative orientations do not determine action in the labor market but rather "economic class-position and material resources."

Even accepting Parsons's opinion that the neoclassical labor market theory does not sufficiently explain the actual wage structure, it does not follow that this can be explained by reference to a general value system firmly established in an institutional structure. The systematic exclusion of power relations must be turned critically against Parsons. This can be illustrated especially clearly with Parsons and Smelser's view of the function of labor unions. According to both authors, this consists, on the one hand, in reinforcing the basis of negotiations of employees vis-à-vis the enterprise. But the real function is seen on an integrative level, which is achieved through union "rituals, political campaigns, and therapy" (Parsons and Smelser 1956:149). The union integrates the employee into a larger collectivity, in which fears are removed, and through its ritual activities, the self-respect of the members as well as their confidence in the successful prospects of the occupational role rises (148ff.). Only when the symbolic mechanisms of social controls are no longer effective does the latent conflict of interest erupt into the labor struggle.

It can be argued convincingly that union organization cannot be understood fully as a rational interest group because rational individual action orientations represent an insufficient basis for collective action (Olson 1965), but it does not follow that the primary function of union organization consists of the normative integration of the members. Claus Offe and Helmut Wiesental (1980:183) point out that, because of the rationalist dilemma of collective action, unions rely on forming a collective identity of the members in order to be able to represent the instrumental interests collectively. "Worker's organizations in capitalist systems always find themselves forced to rely upon non-utilitarian forms of collective action, which are based on the redefinition of collective identities, even if the organization does not have any intention of serving anything but the member's individual utilitarian interests."

Thus, the conclusion from observing *union rituals* to a *ritual function of unions* is hardly inevitable. Instead, the overemphasis on integrative institutions in the economy criticized by Alexander can be seen in Parsons and Smelser's characterization of unions. The specific interpretation of union activity can be seen as a reaction analogous to Durkheim's to the social expansion of instrumentally oriented areas of action. It is doubtful whether Parsons and Smelser can in fact show that what Marx, the principal-agent approach, *and* Parsons himself considered the central structural conflict between capital and labor can be solved by normative adjustments of values alone. Parsons underestimates the significance of interests articulated instrumentally in power clashes as structuring variables of the economic process of reproduction. However, from the perspective of the question about the preconditions of social order in a functionally differentiated social system, Parsons and Smelser show that the expansion of economic rationality collides with functional limits when this leads to compromising the functionality of social subsystems on whose functioning the economic system depends as input suppliers. The reference to institutional structures introduces *one* essential element for the solution of the cooperation problem.

THE CULTURAL INTEGRATION OF THE CONSUMER GOODS MARKET

Parsons and Smelser also study structural limitations of the market mechanism for the consumer goods market. The view is based on the difference between goods and services, which are analyzed separately. Because services cannot be detached from the provider as the bearer of the labor force, they are analyzed as part of the labor market (Parsons and Smelser 1956:157). This distinction is interesting for economic sociology because it indicates that an economy oriented more strongly to services is subject to other sociocultural limitations than one that is based mainly on the production of goods. Whereas the specific features for material goods are limited to the production process, in the case of services these special features also apply to the market allocation that coincides with the provision.

Parsons's procedure in examining the consumer goods market is analogous to the one he used in his study of the labor market. Interest is focused on institutional structures that are anchored in the general system of values and enlisted to explain the integration of divergent interest of the parties in the market. In the institutional regulations, the normatively sanctioned public interest is expressed to enable a higher adaptive capability of society. The problem in principle is formulated in the statement:

"For there to be stability in the retail consumers' market there must be an integration between the values and norms on the one hand of the economy, on the other of the family" (Parsons 1986:28). Parsons examines two institutions that enable this integration: setting prices by the manufacturer or retailers, which excludes the possibility of finding a price through bargaining between sellers and prospective buyers; and signals of quality sent by the manufacturer in the form of brand name images and by providing guarantees.

Due to fixed prices, only two decisions remain with the buyer: to acquire the goods or not and to determine the quantity. The seller is then prevented from reacting to different social situations with changing prices. But how is price setting functional for increasing the adaptive capability of the economy, which Parsons sees as critically dependent on constantly increasing consumer demand? Can the turnover not be increased by situational price changing? Parsons sees the system of fixed price setting as an expression of the differentiation of the economy from other social systems and as a tendency to universalist structures. The situational setting of prices, dependent on the social situation (especially the person of the buyer), expresses a "particularistic nexus of relationships" (59), which also includes obligations beyond the economic transaction. If the buyers have a social obligation to acquire goods from a specific source of sales and the seller's price is set dependent on the social relationship to the person of the buyer (relative or stranger, poor or wealthy, etc.), the competition between goods suppliers is effectively ended. By fixed price setting, the economic transaction is liberated from particularistic limitations, and the competitive behavior of the consumers is guided to alternative sources of sales. In comparison to regulating prices through bargaining, the institution of price setting turns out to be more efficient, if prices are controlled through market competition. However, this agreement with economic theory does not mean that the institution of price setting can be *explained* by economic interests. Instead, the process of differentiation of the economy and interest in increasing economic capability in society itself must be culturally legitimated in the general value system.

The second aspect, securing constant consumer demand and thus a higher adaptive capacity of the economy, consists of signals of quality in the form of image building and guarantees from the manufacturer. The function of these signals consists of reducing the risk in purchasing decisions for the buyer stemming from the asymmetrical distribution of information. The quality of technically complex, long-term consumer goods, especially, cannot really be judged by consumers. In Parsons's conception, the confidence the consumer "invests" in the products with the decision to buy is offset by guarantees and the long-term image building of the enterprise, which represents the product as reliable and at the same time prevents the enterprise's opportunistic orientation to an interest in short-term profit and thus enables cooperation in exchange relations. Parsons and Smelser (1956:160) did not judge the signals from the manufacturer as guided by pure economic interests, but rather as an expression of a consensus of value connected with it, in which "industry not only accepts the public interest in high consumption levels as a 'good thing,' but takes over a certain degree of direct responsibility for the content of the style of life."

Parsons's emphasis of the normative nature of institutionalized rules for the consumer goods market can be analyzed critically, analogous to the discussion of institutional rules of the labor market. Starting from the notion that price setting and signals of quality lead in fact to an increase in demand does not allow their normative character to be concluded. The question is whether their establishment in fact *requires* a common system of values of buyer and producer, or whether the economic interest of one party is sufficient. In chapter 1, the cooperation problem was used to discuss the emphasis of the reputation effect in game theory, which made it clear that, under certain informational conditions, cooperation can be explained by the interest of *one* party in long-term exchange relations.

One clue to clarifying the question of the need for normative integration is found in a comparison of what Parsons calls institutionalization of the consumer goods market with market structures in which there is neither price setting nor signals of quality through guarantees. From an anthropological perspective, Clifford Geertz (1992:227) explained both institutions of intensive seller-client relationships and negotiation in bazaars as a rational reaction to structural information problems. Buyers in bazaars have information that is "poor, scarce, maldistributed, inefficiently communicated, and intensely valued." By establishing a solid relationship with a seller, the buyer intends to avoid the risk that emerges from the information situation; in the process of negotiating a price, the buyer tries to acquire more information about the article, not only to influence the price. If the institution of bargaining and the firm relations between seller and buyer are rational reactions to definite structural qualities of the market, it can be expected that changes of these structural conditions also entail institutional change. Such a structural change would be the improved information situation that is to be expected under the conditions of standardized mass production because the quality of the product is homogenized. But if Geertz's interpretation is correct, and both bargaining and particularist relations between traders and buyers in bazaars are an expression of the specific information situation, then the universalization of economic relations and price settings can be explained as a reaction to the structurally modified information situation without having to resort to a shared system of values.

Parsons and Smelser, however, correctly introduce the problem of the increasing complexity of technical products, which also involves an intensification of the information problem. Why does it not lead to a renewed particularization of economic relations? Because it is obviously possible for the producer to send signals, through image building and guarantees, that lead to risk reduction for the buyer. But if it is possible for enterprises to improve the information situation unilaterally, the economic interest of the enterprise would be sufficient for such measures and the corresponding institutional changes. This conclusion is valid under an assumption indicated by Michael Spence (1973). Competitive advantages can be achieved through signals of quality when the costs of sending the signal are lower for producers of high-quality goods than for the producers of inferior products. This is valid because otherwise, the signals would contain no additional information for the buyer. Under that assumption, the universalization of economic relations and the development of both institutions cited by Parsons could be explained without reference to a common system of values but simply by structural changes and the interest of enterprises. While Parsons's argument of a common interest in the economic capacity can be followed (but why as an expression of a system of values and not concurrent economic interests?), the assumption of an entrepreneurial responsibility for the life-style of consumers must be dismissed as rather naive. Instead, the differentiation of the economy must also be understood so that such a responsibility cannot guide action.

Parsons and Smelser want to find a connection to economic theory for the discussion of the consumer goods market, too. The starting point here is once again Keynes's economic theory. For the consumer goods market, a sociological supply function is to be outlined that assumes the social restrictions of this market in a formalized form. Thus we come back to the connection cited at the beginning of this section of consumption decisions and the ideas of family life firmly established in the pattern-maintenance system. Parsons and Smelser do not view consumption expenditures primarily in their function of satisfying biological needs for reproduction but rather as reflecting role expectations of a culturally defined standard of living in society. Through consumption expenditure, the social system of the household fulfills the institutionalized demands of the standard of living and the constitution of a life-style. The level of expenditure is determined by the culturally defined basket of goods, which represents the "cultural survival" (Parsons and Smelser 1956:221) of the household. Expenditures for entertainment, leisure, and vacations are also granted a function because internal family conflict management and status symbols have an integrative function by positioning the household in relation to other households and thus symbolizing belonging.

To formalize the consumption function, Parsons and Smelser refer to Keynes's consumption function, according to which the portion of consumption expenditure drops as income rises but increases in absolute terms: "The fundamental psychological law, upon which we are entitled to depend with great confidence both *a priori* from our knowledge of human nature and from the detailed facts of experience, is that men are disposed, as a rule and on the average, to increase their consumption as their income increases, but not by as much as the increase of their income" (Keynes 1964:96).

Keynes had based this course of the consumption function on psychological assumptions of behavior, which was rejected by Parsons and Smelser as a reductionist procedure that avoids the social complexity by an ad hoc postulate. The relative stability of the consumption function vis-à-vis short-term fluctuations in income assumed by Keynes is explained instead by the relative stability of role expectations. When family income falls, the extensive maintenance of consumption expenditure can be expected by eliminating savings reserves and raising credit. When income increases, on the other hand, increases in expenditure are to be expected because the household complies with "pressures to symbolize a rising class position" (Parsons and Smelser 1956:226). Social factors determine both the increase as well as the position of the consumption function. From its course, the situation of the household and the changed situation of its income can be gauged in light of cultural standards.

According to Parsons and Smelser, the model of a consumption function for various social groups in society structured by institutionalized expectations should be able to be connected to economic models as "theoretically determined" (226). Saurwein indicates correctly that the claim of the "derivation" of a sociological consumption function cannot be maintained. The consumption function "is distinguished neither by an especially compelling interpretation of the effects of sociological variables nor are these brought into an explicit arrangement" (Saurwein 1988:49). The model does not clarify the relation between consumption standards, status differentiation, and role expectation or how these are concentrated within economic parameters. Parsons and Smelser do refer correctly to the indeterminacy of Keynes's consumption function, but they cannot show that they themselves have a theoretical instrument that allows them to make such a determination. Taking account of this critique, what remains of Parsons and Smelser's explanations is ascertaining the significance of cultural standards for consumption decisions, which, in light of the primarily individualistic determination of consumption in economic theories is at least an important insight, even though the claim of formalization and thus the connection to macroeconomic theory must be lopped off.

The discussion of the institutional regulations of the labor and consumer goods markets shows how Parsons and Smelser want to answer the question of the possibility of overcoming principal-agent problems. Parsons sees that market relations alone cannot develop a stable order. But unlike Marx and the principal-agent approaches, he does not see the antagonistic interests of the actors integrated by control, power, or incentives. Instead, the economic interests of the partners to the contract are bound up with a value order defining individual interests, which enables the stability of the capitalist market structure by exercising a structuring influence on behavior.

The Boundary Process between the Economy and the Goal-Attainment System

In the articles of the 1930s and in *The Structure of Social Action*, Parsons had distinguished the disciplines of sociology and economics by means of the respective dimensions of the action frame of reference dealt with by each of them. Economics deals with the rational allocation of means to achieve desired goals, sociology with ultimate ends. This distinction recurs in the AGIL scheme in the differentiation between the adaptive system and the goal-attainment system. But because the distinction in the systems' functionalist theory no longer aims at separating two scientific disciplines, it is possible to ask about the mechanisms that transmit the economic goals of the society to the economic system. This happens in *Economy and Society* with the examination of the boundary processes between the economy and the goal-attainment system, which are analyzed as a second link of the economy with a subsystem of society. Parsons and Smelser locate the interface of the two subsystems in the respective adaptive functions (Aa and Ga). As the economy is the adaptive subsystem of society, the model designates a functional need for the individual subsystems to adapt to externally given functional conditions. The adaptive problem for the economy is seen as the necessary disposal of capital that is used to obtain resources for the production process. From the perspective of the theory of social systems, goal determination of the economy does not mean the qualitative exertion of influence over internal economic resource allocation, which would set externally what is produced and which production factors are used. Instead, goal determination means the determination of the relative significance of economic capacity in a society by determining the portion of socially disposable resources that are supplied to the economy. The decision is between economic growth goals and alternative possibilities of using social resources. Resources can also be

spent or consumed for financing noneconomic objects like schools or leisure institutions (Parsons and Smelser 1956:57). Thus, once again, *Economy and Society* clearly asks how the economy functions in view of the
reproduction of *society*. The analysis views the economy in its function
"*for society*" (125; emphasis in original) and is not aimed *at* society from
the economic system.

The goal-attainment system, which is assigned the function of determining social goals, is also delineated *analytically* by Parsons and
Smelser. The substantial significance of the term is not clearly established,
which allows for ambivalent interpretations of the boundary process with
the economy. The unclear institutional determination of this functional
realm represents a central problem in the conception. To explain the
boundary process, however, an approximate paraphrase will do for the
time being. Parsons and Smelser talk of the polity as the institutional complex that is included in the goal-attainment system, but the subsystem is
not to be identified explicitly with either the government or the state
(57ff.). In general, the system can be delineated through power as the
medium of communication, which regulates the boundary process. In reference to the boundary process with the economic system, this means that
the goal-attainment system has means available for the "imposition of
social controls" (56), which gives it access to resources for the production
process.

If the decision to use general resources for specific social goals, of which
economic goals are only one part, is located in the goal-attainment system,
then the intersystemic boundary processes, which regulate the adaptive
capacity of the economic system (Aa), must be considered. The mechanism provided for that is *credit*, as the factor input entering the economy
from the goal-attainment system. The term credit is used in a problematic
double meaning, which intends to connect with macroeconomic theory
but also identifies credit with power, thus granting the term a metaphoric
use (56). The disposal of credit is a prerequisite for obtaining production
factors (labor, machines, raw materials, etc.); therefore the capacity of the
economic system can be guided by credit allocation. By providing capital,
economic organizations acquire general purchasing power and thus
power in the sense of the possible disposal of means of production in the
investment process, which is analyzed as an internal economic matter of
the efficient allocation of means. The supply of the economy with capital
thus depends on the social goals located in the goal-attainment system.
Only by disposing of capital can production factors be arranged for productive ends. Linking economic resources (purchasing power) and political resources (power) in the metaphor of credit enables the processes of
interpenetration, which make the two subsystems commensurable. This
systematic is problematic because guiding economic capacity is located in

the goal-attainment system of *society* and hence is not analyzed as guided by internal economic interests.

Analogous to the boundary process at the interface between the economy and the pattern-maintenance system of society is the boundary process between the economy and the goal-attainment system also controlled by two symbolic mechanisms. First, Parsons and Smelser conceptualize as such mechanisms of political and legal sanctions that support productivity increases. These include regulations in tax law, subsidies, economic policy in general, but also government guarantees of protection from competition (73). These regulations originate in the legislative and administrative area of government. The second intermediary mechanism consists of granting intervention rights for creditors. The credit metaphor contains the dimension of a kind of social "advance" on an expected service in return,[44] which consists of the desired rise of productivity by introducing capital. Increased productivity raises the capacity of the economy and thus the means available for social goals. The expectation of goal attainment is symbolized by the interest rate. Disturbance of the economic equilibrium must be reckoned with if the expectations are not met (63ff.). Parsons and Smelser elucidate this correlation in the explanation of the second intermediary mechanism determining economic control over capital. The rights of intervention consist of the claim for the payment of interest and the right to demand the return of the capital that was lent. However, this emphasizes not the monetary dimension of interest payments as a guiding instrument for capital allocation but rather the symbolic significance of interest. Interest indicates the ability of the borrower to dispose of capital; however, interest also symbolizes the power of the creditor to influence the business of the borrower and thus establishes prestige for the creditor, analogous to the symbolic significance of a high income (75). Parsons and Smelser also see the symbolic significance of interest in altered interest rates of the central bank, which function as a signal for the investment decisions of enterprises. "Raising the interest rate is a signal that productivity must increase at a sufficiently higher rate in order to justify the current level of credit; lowering the interest encourages enterprise by symbolically communicating that the rate of productivity increase need not be so high" (75ff.).

The power based on "reputation" or "credit standing," which debtor and creditor mutually admit by granting credit, indicates the element common to the two intermediary mechanisms. "Credit standing" controls the allocation of credit and also represents the interest of the political community, because the credit basis is expanded only when the expected rise of productivity does in fact occur.

By emphasizing the symbolic significance of interest, Parsons and Smelser again explain their position that movements of capital are not an internal economic issue. Instead, through interest symbols, the political community signals social goals to the economic system. Parsons had expressed the thesis of an extraeconomic influence on the capital market at the interface between the economy and the political community in the *Marshall Lectures* much more clearly than in *Economy and Society*. The question at this interface was "how much to weight the social interest in production as against other interests" (Parsons 1986:29).

Parsons and Smelser try to prove the social nature of investment capital in principle by reconstructing a specification process of capital, conceived analogously to the specification of the labor force. Capital must also be "produced," although not in an economic process but rather by acquiring technological know-how "to control natural processes in the interests of productivity" (Parsons and Smelser 1956:131). General purchasing power emerges from the bond of this technological knowledge with the power factor of the political decision on its use. The bond of economically instrumentalized knowledge with the political community as an assumption of the fulfillment of the adaptive function of the economy guarantees the general acceptance of the use of capital in society because in the goal-attainment system it is not particularistic economic interests that are articulated but *social* ends.[45]

By emphasizing the political control of the relative significance of economic functions in society, Parsons and Smelser object to theoretical outlines that see social development as determined by the requirements of economic functions. They oppose this with a concept that starts from the control of economic functions by the polity. Clearly, Parsons can refer to various sociological theories for the rejection of economistic social theories. Before Parsons, Durkheim and Weber, in particular, criticized the monism of such theories and tried to show that social development cannot be understood solely as enforcing economic interests. Now, in *Economy and Society*, Parsons and Smelser do not cite other theories of society for the thesis they advance, but, by conceptualizing the boundary interchange between economics and the goal-attainment system, they develop independently a theoretical scaffolding to explain the systematic incorporation of economic functions into societal ends. But how convincing is the theoretical conception of the regulation of economic functions in society by controlling the processes of capital allocation?

If we accept the premise that capital represents the central independent variable for the regulation of economic capacity, then two critical questions result from the conception. First, what precisely does Parsons mean by the goal-attainment system? Second, is it correct that capital allocation in the economic system starts from the goal-attainment system and can be controlled by it? The first question concerns the sources of influence on economic processes. How much the economy can in fact be regulated from outside, or whether it does not operate self-referentially much more strongly and can thus be in a conflicting relation to the goal-attainment system depends on the answer to the second question.

It has already been noted that Parsons and Smelser did not define the term goal-attainment system unambiguously. The system is delineated analytically, but Parsons makes the definition concrete by assigning the polity, the government, and the state to the goal-attainment system. But these institutions do not indicate the whole and therefore cannot be identified with the system as such. This ambiguity is deliberately maintained to defend the thesis of the social regulation of capital allocation in view of a clear weakness. That is, if we consider which *organizations* allocate credit, it becomes clear that the power of deciding the use of capital resources is only partially in the hands of the government and, at least in capitalist societies, an essential part is also organized privately. Organizations like banks, insurance companies, and other institutional investors are involved in the process of the allocation of capital. This led to the criticism of Alexander (1984:198) and Holton (1986:70ff.) that Parsons overestimated the significance of the polity for controlling the economy because the internal financing of enterprises and the private external funding represent significant intraeconomic forms of capital supply, which effectively "circumvent" the goal-attainment system. Yet Parsons could refute this apparently plausible critique with a reference to the analytical nature of the delineation of the goal-attainment system, which cannot be identified with any concrete organizations.

Parsons and Smelser negate the difference between government and private economic organizations of credit allocation by referring repeatedly to their establishment in the goal-attainment system in *this function*. And emphasizing the analytical delineation of systems always lets economic organizations exist as part of the goal-attainment system of society. Moreover, Parsons and Smelser keep referring to the fact that organizations are collectivities, which can indeed have an economic priority, but are never purely economic. But this scholastic argumentation can be rejected by showing that the polity has little influence on internal processes of capital allocation, but that these are oriented to economic considerations (Holton 1986). A reference point for the allocation of credit to private organizations involves economic criteria of profit expectation including the risk estimate, and not societal goals. This casts doubt on the usefulness of the credit analogy for the objectives of the general theory of social systems. Its applicability is best given for government-guided economic plans. Obviously, the economic system can operate self-referentially much more strongly than is conceded by Parsons's concept of interpenetration processes. Capital allocation must not be understood as a boundary process between economics and a noneconomic subsystem of society but rather as an internal economic problem.

Parsons and Smelser forestall these objections by emphasizing the government influence on the private economic organization of the capital market, which keeps them connected with the goal-attainment system. The relative concentration of the banking industry and its control by the central bank, as well as banking supervision, represent structural deviations from the model of perfect capital markets that protect the social interest. Institutional regulations limit the extremely volatile reactions of capital markets and guarantee the interests of the investors and the public by preventing economic crises caused by the capital markets (Parsons and Smelser 1956:239). Deviations from the model of perfect markets are an expression of the public interest represented by the banks, which conflicts with a purely economic logic. The action of private organizations in the allocation of capital is institutionally embedded and thus remains linked to the goal-attainment system.

Therefore, Parsons and Smelser's argumentation is constructed so that it cannot be denied simply by citing the internal financing of enterprises or the power of commercial banks. On the one hand, Parsons would refer to the fact that government interest rate policy also resorts to these possibilities of financing by influencing opportunity costs through changing interest rates by the central bank. On the other hand, the regulation of banking as well as the institution of investment contracts is interpreted as an expression of the entrance of noneconomic goals into private processes of capital allocation.[46] Yet it can legitimately be objected to Parsons's use of the symbol of interest rates that the material, internal economic dimension of structuring economic conflicts about scarce capital through the interest rate is not taken into account (Alexander 1984:235).

The partly substantial and partly analytic definition of the goal-attainment system was mentioned earlier. The problematics of interpreting the boundary process of Parsons's theoretical model in analogy with economic concepts is expressed in this ambivalence. Parsons had prepared for the *Marshall Lectures* by reading Keynes (Smelser 1981), and *Economy and Society* also referred to Keynes's economic theory. Keynes's macroeconomics is centered on the conviction that economic growth and economic cycles can be regulated by an anticyclical governmental policy of expenditures and the interest rate policy of the central bank. The monetary policy of the central bank can be used as an instrument of economic policy, with which general social goals, like economic growth, full employment, and the rate of inflation, are influenced on the macroeconomic level. Parsons and Smelser see government influence on macroeconomic processes in Keynes's concept as confirmation of the thesis formulated at the beginning of *Economy and Society* that economic concepts can be inserted into the theory they developed. The ambivalence between a substantial and an analytical version of the goal-attainment system refers to a discrepancy in this comparison. For Keynes, it is unambiguously the state that influences economic processes through monetary policy, whereas Parsons's four-function scheme is conceived as an analytical scaffolding that implies it cannot be identified with concrete institutions. By referring to Keynes, such a substantiation of the goal-attainment system takes place subliminally. The ambivalence maintained by Parsons and Smelser is to safeguard their own theoretical framework, on the one hand, but, on the other, to make the possibility of incorporating Keynes's theory plausible.

The assumption that Parsons and Smelser substantiate the really analytically structured distinctions by emphasizing governmental influence on economic processes is also confirmed in the view of the reciprocal boundary process that "balances" capital input. The output of the economic system is also directed at the adaptive functions of the goal-attainment system of society. The exercise of power that can set goals with a chance of realization is based on resources for sanctioning behavior. This includes government force, which can prevent the disturbance of goal attainment to some extent, but also requires means for positive sanctions that can induce cooperation (Parsons and Smelser 1956:59). These means are available to the adaptive subsystems of society. So there is a reciprocal interest of economy and polity in the success of the other system. Whereas the economy relies on power in the form of capital for disposing resources, the polity is interested in the productivity of the economy for the maintenance of its own power base. The goods produced and the potential for the production of goods expressed in productivity are at the disposal of the goal-attainment system for the pursuit of system goals (73). However, it is not clear in the implementation whether the political interest refers especially to tax revenues (Alexander 1984:87). Parsons and Smelser's primary reference point (in the 1950s!) seems to be the latent availability of material resources for dealing with political crises. Thus, using the example of war production, they talk of the quantitative dimension of production capacity and available resources of goods as well as the ability to generalize from investments, which *can* switch production to achieve political goals (Parsons and Smelser 1956:59). It can be assumed that this reflects the contemporary experience of the authors: the significance of the government in the American war economy of World War II, the political significance of key strategic industries at the height of the Cold War, and the modernization of the Soviet Union under a government-controlled, planned economic system.

Although these remarks refer to the strong emphasis of the role of government for economic processes, it would nevertheless be wrong to use the conceptualization of the boundary interchange to reproach Parsons and Smelser for identifying the goal-attainment system with the government. The interpretation elaborated in the discussion of the process of institutionalization in the investment contract of the link of capital use and social values as interests in the rise of the adaptive capacity of society shows a much broader understanding of the goal-attainment system. The economic system performs adaptive functions not for the government but rather for the pursuit of desirable social goals. That is why institutionalized social claims on the economic system for optimal use of available resources can be restricted to the potential conflict over balancing the use of investment purposes and consumption. Only performance handicaps for rises in productivity are directed at the economic system, symbolized by the level of the interest rate, which does not express particularistic government interests.

But if the sociological interest relates to viewing the combination of social and economic interests, as well as their mutual influence and conflict, then Parsons and Smelser's concept is too abstract. The point of elucidating economic distribution decisions in the tension between economic, social, and government interests is wasted with the socially oriented perspective that asks about the provision of resources for desired goals in the concept of the boundary process. Is it true that the question of capital allocation refers sociopolitically only to efficient dealing with resources? Or does the concept conceal the controversial question of the power to dispose of capital? Are the economic conflicts in modern industrial societies integrated by the normative agreement of a general orientation to economic growth? Is there no public interest in the qualitative side of production, in what is produced? And does the polity not deal essentially with how social wealth is distributed? A critical consideration of Parsons's analysis must start with these questions.

The counterclaim is that the question of the use of capital and the decision-making power over the disposal of economic resources results in social conflicts that would be sociologically interesting to study. Parsons gives away the theoretical means to study them since his concept of power as a generalized medium of communication is itself not conflict-oriented. If power is considered as "generalized media of mobilizing resources for effective collective action, and for the fulfillment of commitments made by collectivities" (Parsons 1963:240), conflicts over setting goals or the use of capital resources between various interest groups of society are overlooked. Nor does Parsons see that economic growth itself can become an object of political controversy in highly industrialized countries, which results in conflicts. Conflicts about the concrete allocation of capital that hide behind the general consensus are also overlooked. This last point is admitted by Parsons and Smelser (1956:129) in a footnote, but the problem does not find its way into the theory in a systematic form. The term of public interest used by Parsons is constructed in a way that leaves the potential of the thesis of a connection of economic rationality and social goals unused for economic sociology, essentially by emphasizing the security of investments or the increase of the adaptive capacity of the economic system. The contingency postulated for these goals is hypothetical. Thus, economically rational investment decisions, which seem suited to increase productivity, are understood as an expression of the public interest. In Parsons's concept, the social significance of the boundary interchange is systematically muted, by assuming a harmony of interest between economic system, government, and societal ends. Thus, the theory that directs its attention to the common values of investors and enterprises remains far behind what could have been achieved by an examination of the interaction of various social systems.[47]

The overlapping of the economic system with social structures appears mostly on the level of internal economic market processes. Although on the level of society the economy looks like a mechanism of efficient production, which is incorporated into the general system of values only through the abstract interest in fulfillment of adaptive functions, the discussion of the institutionalization of financial markets and the structural imperfection of the "market" for productivity refers especially to the systematic influence of social structures in concrete allocation decisions of economic actors. Parsons and Smelser conceptualize financial markets as internal economic markets. The investor is not bound by the interest of the public community but can operate independent of social bonds, oriented solely to maximizing criteria. Paradoxically, the necessity for institutional regulation of decision making results precisely from this lack of social structuration of financial markets. Here, Parsons takes up the problem discussed in chapter 1 of action under conditions of uncertainty. In financial markets, there is a maximum of alternative possibilities of decision making, and a minimum of normative predispostitions, which results in situations involving risk and uncertainty (Parsons and Smelser 1956:234). But how is the capacity for action enabled under these conditions?

Once again, Parsons and Smelser refer to Keynes (1964), who had referred to uncertainty to explain the orientation to conventions and the significance of mimesis in financial markets. Here, Parsons and Smelser link up directly with Keynes but then go beyond him by relying on anthropological findings on action in situations with uncertainty. The origin of magic and superstition is located in situations with uncertainty. Comparable mechanisms can be observed in financial markets: investors are oriented not to facts but to the *opinion* of those whose expert information is trusted, or they make decisions by rule of thumb. Stock market panics and sudden crashes in financial markets are interpreted as "irrational mass phenomena and deviance of several types" (Parsons and Smelser 1956:237), caused by a failure of social control mechanisms. Keynes had granted the stabilizing function to leading figures of the financial markets, to produce trust in the stability of the market by public testimonies. Naturally, starting here, a great deal more can be said about the connection of uncertainty and institutionalization in market contexts; and the explanations in *Economy and Society* are very laconic. By introducing social mechanisms that stabilize expectations, it is shown in principle that non-economic elements have a constitutive influence in the internal economic market and sociological theory can contribute to the systematic understanding of the functioning of financial markets by locating these social mechanisms. Here another starting point for economic sociology that was not adequately appreciated in the reception of *Economy and Society* can be seen.

As for the market for productivity, Parsons and Smelser (1956:169ff.) refer to government support of important strategic industries and the subsidizing of new industries, which intervenes in market mechanisms. These interventions are politically motivated and *per definitionem* do not follow an internal economic rationality. For Parsons and Smelser, examples of deviations of markets from models of perfect competition do not have the normative implication of economic theory that these had to be reorganized into perfect markets in the interest of more efficient allocation of resources. Instead, the imperfection of markets shows the incorporation of the economy into society and thus proves the connection of economic rationality and social structures.

The Boundary Interchange between the Economy and the Integrative Subsystem

Along with the two interfaces of the economy already discussed, as a third boundary relationship Parsons and Smelser study the processes between the integrative subsystem of the society (Ii) and the economy (Ai). The dynamic processes of adjustment of the economy are localized on this interface. As a subsystem of *society*, the integrative system has the function of connecting the motivational structures of the actors with the general system of values. Thus, the normative integration, which Parsons assumes for the internal stability of society, is achieved. Solidarity functions as the generalized medium of the integrative system, aligning action with the integrative system requirements (Parsons 1951).

As society has to fulfill integrative functions, so do the subsystems of society themselves. Integration in the economy refers to the combination of available resources for the production process and to changes of factor combination—thus, product innovations (Parsons and Smelser 1956:26).

On the one hand, Parsons and Smelser refer in their analysis to Alfred Marshall (1961 [1890]), who included organization in the economic analysis as the fourth production factor along with land, capital, and labor. Through organization the existing production factors are combined, and these combinations are institutionalized. Thus the significance of the enterprise for economic processes is referred to in economic theory. On the other hand, they refer to the function of the entrepreneur in Schumpeter. Schumpeter (1950) saw the "creative destruction" by the entrepreneurship of the "heroic" individual, particularly in the early stages of capitalist economic development as being of central significance for overcoming resistance against dynamic processes of economic change surrounding traditional societies. In Parsons and Smelser's theory, new factor combinations are interpreted as sources of solidarity because they go against economic disequilibria with their socially disintegrative effects, which result from the over- or underemployment of individual factors. Innovations thus contribute to the normative integration of society (Parsons and Smelser 1956:65ff.). This interpretation, however, is questionable insofar as the dynamic processes are also responsible for the economic disequilibria that would not result in a static economy.

More interesting for economic sociology is the conceptualization of the output from the economy at the boundary to the integrative subsystem as a contribution of the economy to the integrative functions of society. Product innovations, the result of new factor combinations, lead to a qualitative change of demand and thus contribute to the formation of life-styles, thus attaining symbolic significance outside the economy (66). This function is integrative insofar as life-styles represent common symbolic reference points that contribute to muting conflicts of economic distribution.

As intermediary mechanisms of this exchange, Parsons and Smelser (1956:78) describe profit as monetary compensation for entrepreneurial performance as well as the demand for the new products through which these products are sanctioned by consumers. Finally, the introduction of new products assumes that consumer patterns are freed from tradition. Parsons and Smelser do not explain to what extent they make the innovative function of the modernization process of capitalism itself responsible for the differentiation of life-styles. Yet the conception does seem to make the "colonializing" effect (Habermas) of the permanent change of consumer goods less dramatic by interpreting the market success as voluntary sanctioning by households. Thus, Parsons's already discussed position can be seen to view consumer decision making as authentic in principle.

The significance of the integrative functioning of social systems in linking the motivational structures of the actors with the general values has been seen earlier. This linking is clearest in Parsons and Smelser's discussion of the expectation of profit as the second intermediary mechanism, which is studied as an essential motive for entrepreneurial activity. The functional requirement for processes of innovation must encounter structures in the personality system of the actors that support the fulfillment of the function. Only thus can tensions between the functional imperatives of the social system and the personality system be prevented. The orientation of actors to the possibilities of profit seems to guarantee such integration, but that would imply understanding processes of innovation from a utilitarian perspective. Here, once again, Parsons's procedure suggests accepting economic explanations of economic processes in their result, but also supplementing economic analysis with sociological assumptions. Thus, the profit motive is indeed decisive for the motivation to innovate, but "the prospect of profit does *not* account for the *genesis* of the motivation to innovate" (266; emphasis in original). Instead, Parsons and Smelser suggest a theory of innovative action that studies the motivation for innovations in an interpersonal conflict between the pattern maintenance system and the integrative system, and thus reject the utilitarian explanation. The inherent idea in this is important for the context of this work because innovative action was identified in chapter 1 as one of the three areas of action in which the action model of economic theory breaks down.

The normative explanation of innovative activity, which is proposed as an alternative to the utilitarian theory of action, sees the starting point of innovations in dissatisfaction with the institutionalized form of labor organization. The inefficient use of production factors allows a conflict to emerge between the integrative system of the economy (where the institutionalized forms of labor organization are located) and the personality system of the actors, which is "calibrated" for an efficient use of resources. The innovative process is then interpreted as an expression of the dynamic treatment of this conflict, which is solved by changing the integrative system, and thus introducing new forms of the factor combination in the production process. The dissatisfaction at the outset is steered into channels that harmonize it with the institutionalized value system. For Parsons and Smelser, therefore, the orientation of action toward chances of profit cannot be understood as individual utility maximization; rather it results from normative action dispositions that are firmly established in the personality system.

For this argumentation, Parsons and Smelser refer to Weber's thesis of Protestantism, but without accepting Weber's longitudinal analysis of it in the form of the bureaucratizion thesis. Weber, as is well known, had studied the development of Western capitalism in its relationship to the religious doctrines of Calvinism and thus combined entrepreneurial modes of action with the value system of society. Yet, longitudinally, Weber noted that the capitalist economic process can become increasingly remote from its religious mooring and, as modernization progresses, it no longer depends on that base. This scenario is adopted by Schumpeter, but not by Parsons and Smelser, which can be seen in the discussion of the process of innovation in *Economy and Society* and the reference to Schumpeter. Congruent with Schumpeter's distinction, the process of innovation is subdivided into three phases: visionary ideas, proposals for technological changes, and use of the changes in the process of production (Parsons and Smelser 1956:265ff.). But unlike Schumpeter, who predicted, with a reference to Weber's thesis of rationalization, a process of routinization of entrepreneurial functions, during which the entrepreneur emphatically loses significance, Parsons and Smelser see the entrepreneurial function as a continuous need of modern society. Whereas Weber diagnosed a development of economic and bureaucratic functions in modern capitalist societies that detached them from their religious and cultural conditions of emergence, Parsons sees the incorporation into nonpecuniary tendencies of the personality system as a constant that cannot be dispensed with. Thus, for Parsons and Smelser, innovations remain linked to the entrepreneur and cannot be replaced by systemic self-regulation.

Considering research on innovation since 1945, the dominance of Schumpeter's evaluation, strongly shaped by Weber's theory of bureaucracy, can be seen in the social sciences for quite some time. The perspective asserts replacing entrepreneurial functions with bureaucratic structures (inter alia, Staehle 1990). But, during the past twenty years, this tendency has run counter to a trend in a renewed attention in the social sciences to the function of the entrepreneur (Kirzner 1985), a result of not only the clear presence of successful entrepreneurs, particularly in the newly emerging industries of microelectronics and biotechnology, as well as in the media, but also the decentralized reorganization of enterprises (e.g., profit center and decentralized networking structures), which project a reinforcement of entrepreneurial functions. This seems to confirm Parsons's evaluation of the continual presence of entrepreneurial functions and to contradict Schumpeter's thesis of the loss of significance of entrepreneurs. One explanation of this is no doubt in the increasing dynamic of economic processes, which make decentralized, adaptable and flexible structures functionally superior to the rigid structures of Weber's model of bureaucracy.

Yet Parsons's model to explain the motivation for innovative activity, which seeks to locate this in the norm of efficient use of social resources, is to be examined separately. This conceptualization of a mutual relationship between social values and individual action dispositions is different from Weber's much more concrete thesis of the link of the Calvinist doctrine of predestination and motives of economic action. But to what extent can the value of efficient use of resources substitute as a functional equivalent for the existential question of "calling" in a society that is shaped profoundly by religion? It is to be assumed that these notions of value influence individual action to a very different degree.

Referring to the general value system to explain the motivation for innovative activities once again shows the significance Parsons ascribes to the normative integration of society; but it is not convincingly explained how values can affect behavior. Parsons infers the action of the actors directly from the system of values, and thus the conflicts resulting from the social processes of action remain rather dim. The process of innovation can show this by example. The orientation toward the efficient use of resources can result in internal economic conflicts when the projected innovation changes the structure of work organization and eliminates jobs. The profits of social efficiency do not mean an equal profit for every participant. The internal conflicts, which can be manifested as resistance to the process of innovations, result from situations of loss. Parsons's perspective is directed at the level of society, and overlooks these conflicts. To some extent, he confronts the mirror-image problem of welfare economics: no optimum for every individual actor results from the optimal welfare gain of society. But the resulting conflicts between the actors had to be considered in the theory without assuming that the system of values had already transcended them.

The Institutional Establishment of Economic Rationality

The boundary processes discussed throughout *Economy and Society* constantly emphasize the stabilization of economic processes through normative integration. This also continues in the discussion of economic rationality. Parsons disputes neither the significance of economic functions for modern societies nor the empirically verifiable orientation of actors to expectations of profit. Only an explanation of economically rational action from motives of *individual* maximization of utility is rejected. The outstanding significance ascribed to the institutionalized value system for the orientation to economic motives is underlined in the architectonics of *Economy and Society* by granting a special place to the pattern maintenance system of the economy. In the analysis of the three boundary processes in *Economy and Society*, three of the four subsystems are discussed, but not the pattern maintenance system of the economy (Al). This results from the formal construction of the theory, which logically admits only three boundary processes with the other subsystems of society. But what is deduced from Parsons and Smelser's argumentation is that this special position does not simply result formally but is substantively deliberate: the pattern maintenance system of the economy is concerned with a "cultural boundary" (Parsons and Smelser 1956:69), which is not isolated institutionally from the other subsystems but is integrated with the general system of values of society.

The value system of the economic subsystem is described with the concept of economic rationality. On the one hand, economic rationality includes an affirmative attitude to economic goals, which consists of respect for productivity and the "appropriate controls over behavior in the interest of such goals" (176). On the other hand, economic rationality means the degree of realization of the economic principle—thus the maximization of the quantity of output in relation to the investment. The significance of the pattern maintenance system for the rationalization of economic processes consists of the institutionalization of the *relative significance* of economic goals in the social structure. Here, Parsons and Smelser see serious empirical differences between various social orders and assume a strong orientation to economic goals, especially in modern Western societies.

Economic rationality is not introduced into the analysis of economic processes as an a priori postulate but must be firmly established in social values and in the motivational structure of the actors. Thus, the validity of economic analyses that start from the postulate of utility-maximizing is always dependent on the actual establishment of specific social preconditions. Whereas, in *Economy and Society*, Parsons and Smelser essentially assume the significance of economic contexts of action in society and direct the discussion to discovering the social mechanisms that reproduce and guarantee an economic action orientation, in the essay "The Motivation of Economic Activities" (1954b [1940]) and in *The Social System* (1951) the contingent nature of economic action orientation is emphasized much more. In *The Social System*, Parsons qualifies the significance of (orthodox) economic theory as dependent "on the scope of exchange relationships where the settlement of terms can operate independently of the institutional variables of the social system and political power" (Parsons 1951:125). By classifying social formations along a continuum of the significance of economic rationality, Parsons breaks away from economic theories that consider a rational-action orientation as universally valid and also opens the problem of economic rationality to a comparative empirical analysis.[48]

Saurwein (1988:32) notes that the emphasis of the institutional assumptions of economic rationality represents a departure from Parsons's position in the early writings of the analytical separation of sociology and economics and refers to institutional concepts of economics that were rejected in the works of the 1930s. This impression could have resulted from the fact that, in the two works of 1940 and 1951, Parsons was especially interested in the empirical realization of the principle of economic rationality. In *The Social System*, Parsons argues that the significance of economic theory for a society in which no differentiated sphere of economic exchange exists was in studying the economic *consequences* of the allocation of resources.[49] From this expression, it can be seen that Parsons is still pursuing an analytical theory systematic but is now much more interested in the social genesis and cultural establishment of economic action. Thus, he tries to incorporate economic theory into his own theoretical framework, which allows the study of the cultural assumptions of economic rationality. In *Economy and Society*, Parsons and Smelser start from a functionally differentiated economy, whose analysis is available to orthodox economic theory, and study the institutional assumptions and limitations of orthodox economics in the boundary interchanges. For modern market societies, economic theory is an unproblematic instrument of analysis because with the gain of significance of adaptive functions, economic action orientations obtain a greater prominence in comparison with premodern societies (Parsons 1951:548). Here, there is a convergence with Weber (1988), who linked the dominance of purposive rationality to historical assumptions, particularly the implementation of the monetary system. Weber saw that the relevance of neoclassical economic theory limited to the market-dominated economics where the purposive, rational-action orientations of economic actors had been established.

Yet, because of the analytical concept of the subsystem of the economy, Parsons's theoretical concept in *Economy and Society* cannot be understood as institutional. The social sphere in which the economic action orientation is legitimated varies according to the social structures. But the compartmentalization into subsystems allows the emergence of an outside-inside perspective, which negates the significance of economic theory for the analysis of internal economic processes *only* for the borderline case of a perfect absence of economic differentiation, and, vice versa, assumes the redundancy of a sociological view of social factors on internal economic processes only for the inconceivable borderline case of a pure economic structuring of society. Even if economic theory is clearly restricted, it is also relevant for the analysis of premodern economic formations, as soon as spheres of economically rational-action orientation are already legitimated in them. But, even in modern, functionally differentiated societies, there is never an exclusivity that would make sociological views superfluous and justify talk of an economic structuring of society. Instead, the significance of the social sphere of action of the economy depends on processes of institutionalization, which are understood as cultural embedding of the economy, and on which the processes of functional differentiation themselves depend.

The principle of economic rationality must not be established only in the pattern maintenance system but also in the personality system of the actors. Only thus can the motivational structure emerge, which harmonizes social roles with the needs and interests of the actors. The motivation for economic action originates not only in the internalization of value patterns in socialization processes but also in sanction mechanisms that work to stabilize behavior. Thus, in a continuation of the position taken in the early writings, Parsons objects to the psychologism of economics, which considered individual striving for advantage as firmly established in "human nature." In *The Social System*, Parsons discusses the assumptions of economic-action orientation under the title of "Profit Motive." Against ontological explanations of the universal significance of action oriented toward advantage, he argues that the profit motive was "a situationally generalized goal which is learned in the course of what has been called the secondary socialization process. It is not general to human beings, but very specifically culture-bound to certain types of roles in specific social systems" (Parsons 1951:243).

Through the mechanisms of socialization, the compatibility of the personality system with the institutionalized value pattern of the social system is achieved and the interpenetration of both systems is allowed (Parsons and Smelser 1956:176ff.); the action motivation located on the level of the personality system integrates the functions defined as roles on the level of the social system with the expectation structures of the actors. In the 1940 essay, "The Motivation of Economic Activities," Parsons names "satisfaction" as the most general aspect of the motivation of economic activities. He thus distinguishes between self-esteem, recognition, prospects for monetary income, desire, and need for affection as five components of this satisfaction (Parsons 1954b). At the time this essay was written, Parsons did not yet have the AGIL scheme available, but the five components show that he analyzes the motivations of economic activity as a function of both material interests as well as social aspects of recognition and social integration. Later, in *Economy and Society*, Parsons and Smelser start with the premise that the internalization of economic values motivates the actors to fulfill role expectations, and such values are at least partially independent from short-term rewards, which is why the normative elements of action orientation cannot be reduced to the instrumental attitude. Motivation consists of the internalized obligation of role fulfillment, which includes a responsibility toward the organization. In the 1940 essay, Parsons spoke even more clearly of an altruistic element of obligation: "It is the result of the 'identification' with a general model with which it is 'right' to agree" (Parsons 1954b:144). But this does not also mean that integrating action into the functional demands of the enterprise could be done without positive sanctions. In this connection, what is most significant is the income with which obligations can be satisfied in the family and which also functions as a symbol of recognition (Parsons and Smelser 1956:179). Money is the means to acquire goods and services that can represent life-style and social identity externally. Here Parsons refers explicitly to Thorstein Veblen's (1979 [1899]) famous description of conspicuous consumption. But he also sees that possessing money can itself take over the function of symbolizing prestige (Parsons 1951:244).

Clearly, the purposive rational-action orientation must itself be legitimated in institutional structures and can guide behavior only under this assumption. "It is the normative models which define what forms of behavior or what social relations in a given society are considered appropriate, legitimate, or expected" (Parsons 1954b:140). This can also be seen in parts of *The Social System* where, more precisely than in *Economy and Society*, Parsons denotes the institutionalized roles for which an orientation to profit is socially legitimate. These especially include the role of businessman, but those organizational roles that are concerned with market exchange also belong to this category. Examples are the financial administration of a hospital or the sales staff in an enterprise. Excluded are the professions and most organizational roles in enterprises as long as they are not concerned with market transactions *for* the enterprise. The roles in which an action attitude oriented toward profit is legitimate are thus relatively narrowly circumscribed. Parsons (1986:47) leaves no doubt that this motive is not legitimate in most social roles, citing the family as an example.

An interesting special position is occupied by what Parsons called the possibility of profit aspiration as a purely personal orientation. This does not have a basis in any institutional role, but rather reflects opportunities as they "necessarily arise in a money economy" (Parsons 1951:245). This suggests that money itself can be ascribed a behavior-molding force that allows its social significance to go beyond the simplification of exchange relations and the symbolic use emphasized by Parsons. The applicability of the economic model to all social relations assumed by representatives of an "economic imperialism" is rejected by Parsons and Smelser (1956:141), but as a borderline case. A prerequisite for that would be the destruction of the household (family).

Yet what is decisive for Parsons's theoretical system is not the *concrete* shaping of the institutionalization of roles in economic systems but rather the necessity of institutionalization itself, which completely changes the status—not necessarily the empirical relevance—of the economic theory of action. Rational action is not a premise of the theory but is to be analyzed itself in its social preconditions. That is, an orientation to selfish interest and the action coordination in society deduced from utilitarian economic theories cannot simply be assumed, but is itself a result of socializing processes and cultural structures (Parsons 1951:246). At the same time, generating economic motivation is very significant for societies with high claims to the adaptive system because the integration of the production factor of labor depends on it. That this is a risky venture in principle with a potential for social friction becomes clear from the demands that result from the necessary integration of the most disparate role expectations and the interpenetration of personality systems with the social system. Thus, Parsons's theoretical system is open in principle to the potentially conflictual nature of the functionally differentiated organization of economic activities in modern societies. However, what is hardly surprising is that, against the background of the theory directed by and large at a successful social integration, in the descriptions of the boundary process, he starts from a functioning integration. Economic action in modern societies, on the basis of institutional and motivational structures, is directed at allowing the efficient fulfillment of its function.

The discussion of the pattern-maintenance system of the economy once again expresses Parsons's conviction that the economy cannot be viewed as an autonomous area of society. The market can indeed function as a pure money nexus but only under cultural assumptions that are not considered by economic theory. Here the reference to Weber is expressed, who also considered instrumental rationality as based on a cultural presumption that is the instrumental attitude itself. But Durkheim's analysis of the significance of the normative order for contractual relations also plays a part. Yet the normative embedding of economic action is conceived in principle in light of a *supplement* to existing economic theories. Parsons endeavors to show how, through socialization processes and sanctions, actors are prepared for an action that corresponds to the premises of economic theory.

Cooperation and Interpenetration

Parsons's functionalist examination of the economy in the 1950s represents one of the few attempts of systematic analysis of the economy from the perspective of a sociological frame of reference. Right at the beginning of this chapter, it was indicated that in *Economy and Society*, Parsons and Smelser are not interested in formulating a sociological theory of economic processes and structures. Rather, they want to show that concepts of economic theory can be reconstructed in the theoretical pattern of the general theory of social systems and that systematic junctions between economic theory and the general theory model can be found. This program was criticized from the perspective of economic sociology. Mark Gould (1991) accused Parsons of "failure of will" and argued from the perspective of the voluntaristic theory of action that *Economy and Society* did not exhaust the potential contained in Parsons's theory for a sociological concern with the economy. Gould sees the main reason for that in Parsons's exaggerated respect for economics. But the criticism which was also advanced by Swedberg (1987) argues too strongly from the theoretical systematic used in *Economy and Society* and is involved only insufficiently with the content of the explorations of boundary interchanges of the economic subsystem with other subsystems of society.

From the detailed discussion of boundary interchanges in this chapter, it becomes clear, on the one hand, that Parsons and Smelser try to show the possibility of integrating economic theory into the general frame of reference of systems theory, but they also refer far beyond economic theory to the systematic interpenetration of political and normative elements with economic structures and processes. This influence cannot be understood simply as a supplement to economic theory, but rather affects that model itself. The result is ambivalent to some extent: Parsons cannot show convincingly that concepts of economic theory in the framework he outlines can be reconstructed without grossly distorting them; the analogies produced are metaphors rather than substantive equivalents. On the other hand, the progress in Parsons's concept is having developed a theoretical framework in which the social embeddedness of economic functions is systematically explained. This does not mean that the concept of incorporating social factors in economic processes developed in *Economy and Society* with the use of the AGIL cross tabulation would always lead to acceptable conceptualizations. On the contrary, Parsons and Smelser's discussion of interchanges carried out between the subsystems has led to critical results in many places. In general, the boundary interchanges discussed seem very selective. The differences between internal economic exchanges and boundary interchanges with other social subsystems cannot, in fact, be maintained unconditionally. But, with the AGIL scheme, Parsons possesses an instrument that allows the theoretical study of the incorporation of the economy in specific functional demands of social reproduction. If this theoretical framework is detached from the idea of a necessary connection to economic theory models, it can be used as a flexible instrument of studies in economic sociology. This is also valid because the specific limitations, which had resulted in the early works from the distinction between means-ends relations and goal determination as a delineation of economics and sociology, are overcome by concentrating on boundary interchanges. Hence, criticism must be directed less against the AGIL scheme than at some of the concepts derived from the investigation of concrete boundary interchanges.

But what is the significance of Parsons's concept for understanding the question of how actors cross the limits of individual utility maximizing and can thus achieve cooperation? Incorporating the economy into a theoretical scheme with the three other subsystems and the boundary interchanges between them shows systematically that Parsons starts from transcending purely economic interests through the interpenetration of various social systems and the personality system. Cooperation is made possible with a system of mutual rights and obligations, which regulates the boundary processes of inputs and outputs between the systems, making the interaction partners bearers of a common normative orientation. If the differentiation of the economy from other social areas of action can never be perfect, which Parsons expresses in the concept of interpenetration, there is a chance of solving the problem of cooperation, which gives economic theory so much trouble. What is significant here is that these boundary interchanges are always aimed at reciprocity, so that an image of society emerges that categorically rejects an assimilation of other functional areas into the economy. But this also explains that an assumption for the solution of cooperation problems based on the achievement-sanction pattern rejects the notion of purely individual action orientation. Institutionalizing boundary interchanges generates a perspective directed at the functional requirements of society in which considering the functional requirements of other subsystems is a prerequisite for obtaining the resources necessary for the reproduction of the economy.

Although it can be asked against the notion of institution of both Parsons and Durkheim whether institutions cannot effectively be undermined by free riders, the significant progress seems to me to reside in two aspects. First, Parsons no longer asks about the presumptions of a *just* social order. Instead, Parsons focuses on the functional requirements of the adaptive system. Because the economy is located in a social whole, it can function only if it takes account of the functional requirements of other social systems and personality systems, which is insured by norms that are moored in a common, obligatory system of values. Second, Parsons develops a much more differentiated theoretical framework, in which the institutionalization of economic actions and the social incorporation of economic functions are precisely represented.

Normative integration on the basis of a common system of values is a central explanation contributed by sociology to solve the cooperation problem. But, finally, two objections to Parsons should be formulated. On the one hand, the emphasis of normative integration of economic functions is one-sided in Parsons. That is, the stabilizing effect of self-interest and social power is omitted. Parsons's theory is constructed from the normative ideal of a conflict-free social integration. Conflicts are deviations from an equilibrium for which there must be mechanisms that lead back to the state of equilibrium. At the same time, the market-based economy is a social sphere implemented structurally with antagonistic interests that can potentially cause massive social conflicts. Parsons does not believe in the possibility of integrating opposing interests—either by a Leviathan or by the common, enlightened self-interest of the actors—and, referring to Durkheim, he emphasizes the functional necessity of normative integration. This leitmotif leads Parsons to some problematic interpretations of economic relations, which sees them as ultimately normatively controlled. This is clear in the discussion of union functions, the determination of economic goals in the polity, and the assumption of socially integrative contributions of economic organizations through the production of consumer goods. Although all these aspects are interesting for economic sociology, in Parsons's explanation they achieve a dominance in which the self-organization of economic processes and especially the significance of social power in economic structures are systematically overlooked. But it would be interesting for economic sociology to study precisely the tension between interests, power, and normatively legitimated action.

On the other hand, the concept of value integration that relies strongly on internalization processes leads to a passive concept of the actor, which starts with a control of action by a normative model. The normative integration of the person is given through processes of internalization in childhood socialization, which are conveyed to the person by cultural patterns. In the socialization process, persons are provided with values that enable them to fulfill social roles. The assumption of processes of internalization, based strongly on the debate with Freud, allows Parsons to describe economic processes as normatively integrated. Referring to the critique of Parsons by Dennis Wrong (1961) and Harold Garfinkel (1967), Mark Granovetter (1985) has indicated that the strong normative control of actors brings the concept of actor astonishingly close to the individualistic actor concept of economic theory. The "oversocialized" actors appear as "cultural dopes," who are released from producing reciprocal capacity for interactions as an ongoing task. But it is unlikely that cooperation in modern economic contexts can be built only on an unquestioned repertoire of cooperation norms. Instead, because of the material advantages resulting from noncooperation, the erosion of these norms would be expected. Because Parsons considers social order impossible without the integrative achievement of a value system in society, he does not sufficiently consider how cooperation is stabilized through interactive engagement in the situation itself.

FOUR

NIKLAS LUHMANN: THE ECONOMY AS
AN AUTOPOIETIC SYSTEM

Thinking economically means the ability to
translate into the language of price.
—*Niklas Luhmann*

IN the debate over the works of Émile Durkheim and Talcott Parsons
in the field of economic sociology, it was clear that, in the context
to explain the development of stable social structures of order, both
authors deal with questions of cooperation, which can be connected with
the problems of economic theory discussed in chapter 1. For Durkheim,
the paramount issues involved not questions of the efficiency of economic
structures but rather considerations about overcoming the contemporary
socioeconomic crises and the demand for a just social order. For Parsons,
too, the starting question on a metatheoretical level was inherent in the
problem of explaining social order, but the works in economic sociology
of the 1950s try to show that the social embedding of economic structures
is also a necessary prerequisite for the efficient fulfillment of adaptive
functions. Both authors refer to the significance of socially obligatory
norms or a system of values, and the significance of social structures—
even though it was not well developed—is emphasized by Durkheim. The
theoretical tradition represented by Durkheim and Parsons shows the significance of the institutional stabilization of interaction and social structures for overcoming the action dilemma so clearly underlined in game
theory. Moreover, the concept of interpenetration in Parsons provides a
theoretical understanding of why action in economic contexts can never
be completely detached from the rationality of other social areas and why
economic institutions are influenced by the functional needs of other subsystems. The conception that concentrated on examining boundary interchanges helps to understand why the economy is not to be conceptualized
as an autonomous and separate sphere of action, as in orthodox economic
theory, but is always to be examined in the context of reproducing the
social order as the embedding of economic action represented in the concept of interpenetration allows a positive answer to the question of the
possibility of introducing values and socially shared norms into situations
of economic action, which can also be a prerequisite for cooperation.

But what about the problem of action under conditions of fundamental uncertainty? The problem for economic theory that results from uncertainty, as was argued in chapter 1, was that it is not possible for actors to deduce the optimal choice because the assumptions for the maximizing postulate are not given. The question resulting from this was how actors who are interested in maximizing their individual utility or profit make decisions under this condition. What do we do when we cannot know which decision maximizes our utility?

In classical sociological theory, a concern with this problem is only suggested. In Durkheim, a debate with the economic theory of action takes place only in reference to the question of explaining social order on the basis of utility maximizing. But the assumptions of economic theory are not questioned critically with regard to the information available to the actors. Only in one place, in chapter 7, book I of *The Division of Labor in Society*, does Durkheim (1984:160) mention the impossibility of anticipating all possible contingencies when the contract is made, and this leads him to derive the need for protection of property rights through law.

The debate with the informational assumptions of economic theory achieves greater significance in the works of Max Weber. The problem of uncertainty deriving from causal relations represents an important starting point for Weber's argument for rejecting a deterministic type of theory in the social sciences modeled on physics. In the essay, "Objectivity in Social Science and Social Policy" (1949 [1904]), Weber seeks a notion of law for the social sciences that fits the epistemological character of their subjects. For Weber it is clear that social facts, unlike causal relations in nature, do not have a deterministic character, which is why attempts of economists to emulate the natural sciences must be doomed from the start:

> Accordingly, the fantastic claim has occasionally been made for the economic theories—e.g., the abstract theories of price, interest, rent, etc.,—that they can, by ostensibly following the analogy of physical science propositions, be validly applied to the derivation of quantitatively stated conclusions from given real premises, since given the ends, economic behavior with respect to means is unambiguously "determined." This claim fails to observe that in order to be able to reach this result even in the simplest case, the totality of the existing historical reality including every one of its causal relationships must be assumed as "given" and presupposed to be known. (1949 [1904])

Weber's skepticism about the notion of causality and the informational assumptions used in economic theory is manifested clearly when Weber talks of a "chance" or of the "probability" of the occurrence of a certain result.[1]

In his works on economic sociology, which sees one crucial basis of modern market economies in rational calculations, Weber uses the topic of financial speculation to discuss uncertainty. In speculative transactions, objective chances and subjective expectations fall apart unpredictably, resulting in the acceptance of an "unpredictable risk" by the speculator; unlike Frank Knight's clearer separation between risk and uncertainty, Weber sees the transition from rational to speculative calculation as fluid: "The distinction thus has reference only to a difference in the *degree* of rationality" (Weber 1978:159). In the essay, "Die Börse" (1894), Weber objects especially to the view widespread in his time that speculative transactions were unethical and incompatible with the calculative bases of the modern market economy. Weber refers to the significance of dealing in futures as part of rational business planning. The renunciation of the insurance mechanism contained in dealing in futures would establish uncertainty *in business*, and thus make the entrepreneur into a gambler, the role that makes the speculator discredited.

The problem of uncertainty figures much more prominently in the work of Talcott Parsons. In the early book, *The Structure of Social Action*, in his critique of the utilitarian theory of action, Parsons (1949a:45ff.) discusses the problem of the "possibility of error." For Parsons, one of the central implications of the "unit act" is that ends and means cannot completely determine action: "The fact of a range of choice open to the actor with reference both to ends and means, in combination with the concept of a normative orientation of action, implies the possibility of 'error,' of the failure to attain ends or to make the 'right' choice of means."

The question posed by Parsons in a critical debate with the tradition of positivistic theory is how deviations from the rationality postulate of utilitarian theory can be explained within the frame of positivistic theory. To this end, Parsons divides the notion of error into two categories: either the situation is so complex that no assignment of rational means to ends is possible. This would be the case under conditions of uncertainty. Or the actors do not perceive their objective conditions of action correctly and therefore choose objectively wrong means. Quite in accordance with the notion of "irrational behavior with regret" (Frank 1990), introduced in chapter 1, actors would choose other means if an observer of the situation points out their error to them. The explanation for deviations from the objectively optimal selection of means within the positivistic theory is possible for Parsons only by giving up the voluntaristic perspective in action theory:

> If the explanation of irrationality on a positivistic basis must lie in factors not in fact known, but intrinsically capable of being known scientifically to the actor, then these factors must be found, on analytical generalization, to lie in categories capable of nonsubjective formulation, that is in the *conditions* of action. Thus, remarkable as it may seem, departure from the utilitarian posi-

tion, so long as it remains within the positivistic framework leads in both the major problems, that of the status of ends and that of the norm of rationality, to the same analytical result: explanation of action in terms of the ultimate nonsubjective conditions, conveniently designated as heredity and environment. (Parsons 1949a:67)

In the remarks on the utilitarian dilemma, Parsons shows how utilitarian theory breaks away from a voluntaristic concept of action. This is the only way the empirically ascertainable deviation of action from the normative ideal of optimization can be explained. If Parsons's explanations are examined more closely, it can be seen that the objectifying solution he presents can be claimed only for action situations in which an optimal way of acting is available, at least for an observer. Parsons does recognize the problem of uncertainty in the classification of the notion of error, but it does not gain entry into the broader systematic of the argumentation. Uncertainty in the definition used here—which must have been familiar to Parsons from his friendship with Frank Knight—means precisely that from no position ex ante can it be said by which means an end can be achieved; the notion of "error" can therefore be introduced only as an ex post evaluation. Parsons (1949a:65) excludes uncertainty for the solution he produces, by explaining it briefly in a footnote as unimportant: "This case is not theoretically important in the present context." But unimportant is out of the question because criticism of the positivistic theory of action can be stimulated with reference to the problem of uncertainty not only because the withdrawal from the voluntaristic dimension of action is deplored but rather the *possibility* of the objectivizing solution is itself in doubt. Parsons's argumentation in the early works is too limited in the debate with the problem of uncertainty, because he still starts from the objective existence of an optimizing alternative.

In the 1950s, however, Parsons once again posed the problem of uncertainty. In the "General Statement," written with colleagues, that introduces the collection, *Toward a General Theory of Action* (Parsons and Shils 1951), Parsons formulates the problem of double contingency as a fundamental starting problem for social systems. The problem of double contingency means that no action takes place if Alter makes his action dependent on the action of Ego, which is, on the other hand, to be contingent on the actions of Alter. So, the question is, How can actors reciprocally connect their actions under the condition of radical uncertainty about the action intentions of the interaction partner?

There is a double contingency inherent in interaction. On the one hand, ego's gratifications are contingent on his selection among available alternatives. But in turn, alter's reaction will be contingent on his selection and will result from a complementary selection on alter's part. Because of this double contingency, communication, which is the precondition of cultural patterns, could not exist without both generalization from the particularity of the specific situations (which are never identical for ego and alter) and *stability* of meaning which can only be assured by "conventions" observed by both parties. (Parsons and Shils 1951:16)

By characterizing the problem of double contingency and asserting that the uncertainty for the actors contained in this situation must be overcome for the establishment of social order, Parsons and Shils formulate for the first time for sociology the full scope of the problem of the contingency of action situations. But what is to be argued here is that Parsons and Shils do not adequately deal with the problem they pose. Their answer to the solution of the problem of double contingency falls short. According to Parsons, the social value system or rather the role models instilled and internalized in the socialization process introduce the reciprocal action expectations into the action situation; these expectations allow social actions to be materialized and to solve the problem of double contingency. But on a theoretical level, as shown by critiques of Parsons from the 1960s, such a program runs the danger of falling into a normative determinism that makes the autonomy of action of the actors disappear (Garfinkel 1967; Wrong 1961). The solution of the problem of double contingency based essentially on norms is especially problematic for economic contexts: if, under the condition of uncertainty, no unequivocal action alternative can be discerned from the maximizing postulate because in strategic action situations Ego cannot foresee the reaction of Alter, then it is a contracting assumption that Alter will orient itself to deducing an action alternative simply from norms. The objection to this is that, through the market, strategic action that deviates from established norms is rewarded. The dynamic of economic development in capitalist societies demands *going beyond* established conventions (Child 1972; Oliver 1991). It can also be argued with Harold Garfinkel that behavior cannot be derived from norms unconditionally because it always requires the reflexivity of the actor to apply a norm in the concrete action situation. A theory that builds on determining action only by norms and values is formulated too narrowly. Instead, a sociological theory that poses the problem of uncertainty must take account of the possibility of the radical contingency of action by conceptualizing various social arrangements to reduce contingency and by emphasizing the active nature of human action.

Starting points for the debate with the problem of uncertainty can be found in the works of the authors of the classical phase of sociological theory, and especially in Talcott Parsons. Yet altogether it can be concluded that neither in classical sociology nor in Parsons is there a satisfactory solution to the problem of double contingency.

No sociologist has presented an outline of social theory—which has meanwhile also been applied in many ways to economic issues—constructed so strongly and systematically from the problem of uncertainty as that of Niklas Luhmann. The problem of double contingency and the resulting need to reduce complexity are the systematic starting problems Luhmann poses and, from them, he develops the theory of self-referential systems. This systematic starting point makes Luhmann's theory a suitable reference within sociological theory to find an answer to the question of how actors achieve the ability to act under conditions of uncertainty.[2]

As for the status of economic issues in the development of Luhmann's works, the debate with economic theory is not the central starting point, unlike Durkheim's and Parsons's early work. Instead, Luhmann's economic sociology is a much stronger application of theoretical tools originally developed by observing the functioning of bureaucratic structures. This confirms the tendency of sociological theory no longer to obtain its systematic stimuli from economics and the economy, but rather to regard the economy merely as an *area of application* of theoretical tools. Of all current social theorists, however, Luhmann is among those who have investigated economic issues most comprehensively. Back in the early 1970s, Luhmann outlined the implications of his theory, which starts from the problem of the reduction of complexity, for a sociological conceptualization of the economy (Luhmann 1970); on that foundation, several essays appeared on that subject later, in the 1970s and 1980s. The most comprehensive debate with economic subjects is in *Die Wirtschaft der Gesellschaft* (1988a), where many of the earlier essays are collected. Shortly after, an essay appeared that dealt especially with the problem of risk and uncertainty in the economy (Luhmann 1991). Moreover, there are several works by Luhmann's students dealing with special areas of the economy—banking and enterprises among others—starting from the concept of autopoiesis,[3] as well as more applied works that refer Luhmann's concepts to specific problems of organization and management.[4] The widespread reception of Luhmann's concepts in economic sociology—at least in the German-speaking context—is in clear contrast to the extensive disregard of Parsons and Smelser's book of the 1950s.

In this chapter, I examine the theoretical conception of the economy in the framework of the theory of autopoietic systems.[5] In the first part, I talk about the evolution of the functional differentiation of the economic system from the problem of double contingency. In connection with this, the mechanisms of preserving and reproducing systems is explored based on the concept of autopoiesis. The second part of the chapter examines programs and structures in economic organizations. This is intended to clarify how payment decisions are determined and how external referentiality enters the economic system. Providing reasons for payment decisions refers to the environment of the economic system and the elementary overlapping of systemic events (payments) with the environment of the system. In representing the mutual connections of self-referentiality and external-referentiality, a line of criticism of Luhmann's system-theoretical conceptualization is countered, which states that the economic system would lose its connection to normative and moral issues (Münch 1990; 1994). Against this criticism, I emphasize, as a strength of Luhmann's economic sociology, that the problem of uncertainty is posed explicitly. But, at the same time, the critique of Luhmann's theory is aimed in another direction: the weak point of the theory is not the exclusion of supposedly normative motives of economic actors but rather the loss of the dimension of action. From Luhmann's conception of economic sociology, we can learn something about the *systemic* reactions with regard to complexity, but there is no theory in it to help us understand what *actors* do in situations of uncertainty in active debate with the situation. A consequence of the subject-free notion of action used by Luhmann is that the theory does not allow an understanding of innovative processes in the economy, and that knowledge gained about the question of solving the cooperation problem is lost once again.

The Self-Referentiality of the Economy

Double Contingency

Because Luhmann's social theory is constructed from the problem of contingency of social interaction, it is reasonable to approach the theory from this starting point. In the context of the systematic of this work, this must also be the chosen vantage point because it concerns the question of to what extent Luhmann's theory can explain how actors in situations of uncertainty can act, and thus how actors refer to one another with their actions and coordinate individual economic decisions with one another under conditions of radical contingency.

This problem of double contingency connects directly to the economic problematic of action under uncertainty discussed in chapter 1. A strategic situation in which, through his own selection, an actor opens to other actors several possibilities of action that have different utilities for him, without being able to foresee unequivocally which alternative the other actors will choose, makes the outcome of a decision unpredictable, resulting in the discussed possibilities of market failure. The notion of double contingency is connected with the principal-agent problems emphasized in chapter 1, as well as the problems of moral hazard and adverse selection that are the focus of the economic discussions concerning the Arrow-Debreu model of the general equilibrium theory. Situations deliberated under this rubric are distinguished by incomplete and asymmetrically distributed information. Here, too, however, the economic model holds onto the action theory of *homo oeconomicus* but, under the conditions specified in chapter 1, either can give no unequivocal recommendations for action or have to concede the possibility of non-Pareto-efficient equilibria.

The central difference between the modeling techniques of the new microeconomics in dealing with both uncertainty and asymmetrical information and Niklas Luhmann's theory develops along the assumptions of maximization. While economic theory holds onto the possibility of optimizing decisions, the core of an application of Luhmann's theory to economic contexts can be seen precisely in the rejection of this postulate. The difference of Luhmann's theory from economic theory can be understood in this statement: complexity is a reason for the *impossibility* of maximizing decisions. Even though Luhmann has rearranged his theory along different basic concepts since the early work of the 1960s, the rejection of the possibility of the description of action on the basis of the means-ends scheme can be followed as a leitmotif.

In *Zweckbegriff und Systemrationalität* (1968a), Luhmann asks about the *function* of the description of actions according to the means-ends scheme and the model of causality, which differentiates between cause and effect and must be distinguished from the means-ends scheme. That is, the rationality of action results cannot be ascertained simply on the basis of causal laws against the background of fixed ends. Instead, in modernity, a "subjectivation of ends" (Luhmann 1968a:9) emerges, which tends to dissolve the intersubjectivity of the representation of social reality and which allows an awareness of the possible contingency of ends to emerge. For the notion of causality it is valid that laws of cause and effect can exist only in exceptional cases because effects can usually not be traced unequivocally to causes and causes can evoke extremely uncontrollable effects. Against the background of this interpretation, Luhmann sees the function of the means-ends scheme and the causal interpretation of effects in their achievement of establishing a cognitive order. "The meaning of schematizing possible experience through the category of causality consists simply of systematizing them in the potentialities of experience and behavior that appear in natural experience and interpreting them so that they are available for comparative ends, hence can be rationalized" (17).

The notion of causality is interpreted as heuristics, which stimulates the search for alternatives. The causal explanation of action "can unlock the tenacious conservatism of natural experience for innovations by initiating possibilities of variations that can be controlled in specific respects" (16). The causal interpretation of action also enables the reduction of complexity by attributing causes to effects and the controlled introduction of complexity, in which both effects and causes can be treated as variables. "The multitude of causes and effects that are combined in every actual causal event enables first abstracting identification of a cause or an effect in the sense that cause A does not lose its identity when it generates the effects a, b, c, e, f, g in an altered general constellation instead of the effects a, b, c, d, e, f" (15).

The discovery of alternatives with the help of the causality principle can be explained with reference to a production function in which the production outcomes can be observed as a result of altered quantities of input. Luhmann also analyzes the means-ends scheme in its function of complexity reduction. In view of the infinity of possible decisions, it needs the setting of ends to preserve the ability to decide. Ends or values take over a function as external selection criteria, which are set as constants, but can still be changed in principle. On the background of this interpretation of the means-ends scheme and the causality principle, statements about orthodox economics can now be made. Its notion of maximizing appears as a heuristic principle on the basis of which no empirical statements about the motives of action are made, but, quite the contrary, the motives of setting ends can be expelled from the semantics of science. But this fundamentally changes the status of the postulate of maximizing: the assumed causal relations do not have the status of natural laws but are cognitive structures that serve only to reduce the contingency of the situation.

Nevertheless, values can naturally not be excluded from economic theory because the actors' preferences are shaped on the basis of notions of value. Values have an ordering function for allocation decisions. The limit of the achievement of order by values, however, is inherent in the possibility that they can be contradictory in the requirements for action. Economic theory reflects this problem by assuming a utility function that fills the condition of transitivity in which it thus gives an unequivocal rank order of values. If A is preferred over B and B over C, then A must also be preferred over C. The rank order of a hierarchy of values is to make unequivocal decisions possible, but Luhmann refers to a concomitant problem: in the complex situation of concrete human action, a transitive utility function would not be rational "because it is too rigid and does not correspond to the conditions of meaningful value orientation" (24). However, the condition of transitivity is central for the maximizing postulate of economic theory. If the condition is given up, because of the mutual dependence of values, no consistent preference order can be established, which is itself a prerequisite for optimizing decisions. The limits of the laws of causality postulated by economic theory can thus be gathered from the necessary additional theoretical devices that are needed to make them plausible. Either given alternatives must be defined away by using the ceteris paribus clause or the strict causal nexus must be glossed over with a reference to probability.

Luhmann's critical examination of the means-ends scheme is not intended to create an altered description of action within the framework of action theory, but rather serves as a foundation for a systems theory of society. That is, setting ends is not only a pattern for reducing the complexity of the action situation but is understood as a process of drawing boundaries that allows the emergence of the rigid complexes of processing meaning that are called systems. "Ends fix certain estimated effects in terms of systems in order to be able to explain other value aspects of the results of actions as irrelevant. The side-effects are thus ushered out of the area of the relevant causal structure of recognized motives and justifications" (31).

The systematic significance of the contingency problem continues in Luhmann's (1995a) later theoretical works, focusing on the notion of autopoiesis. Here, referring to Parsons and Shils (1951), Luhmann analyzes the problem of the emergence of social order from the improbability of the rise of social systems under conditions of double contingency. Unlike Parsons, Luhmann (1995a:103) tries to solve the initial problem of social order, understood in the problem of double contingency, not by incorporating a normative frame of reference, which allows structures of mutual expectations to be introduced into the action situation. Instead, Luhmann assumes the solution of the action blockade with an "order-from-noise principle," which links the improbability of reciprocal action connections with their simultaneous arbitrariness:

> If everyone acts contingently, and thus everyone could also act differently and knows this about oneself and others and takes it into account, it is, for the moment, improbable that one's own action will generally find points of connection (and with them a conferral of meaning) in the actions of others; self-commitment would presuppose that others commit themselves and vice-versa. Along with the *improbability* of social order, this concept explains its *normality*; under the condition of double contingency, every self-commitment, however accidentally arisen or however calculated, will acquire informational and connective value for the action of others. (Luhmann 1995a:116)

Therefore, communication and the rise of a social system are based on an initially accidental determination that is explained neither by recourse to normative patterns of value or collective practices, nor as an expression of aspiration to utilitarian maximization.

The accidental determination of an action alternative preshapes the selection horizon of Alter, whose meaningful reactions are reduced by Ego's action. Reducing complexity by selections that themselves, in turn, represent connections for the progress of communication is the central prerequisite for the rise of social systems and also paves the way to explain the functional differentiation of society into subsystems. Complexity here means that the situation consists of so many elements that these can only relate selectively to one another. It requires a procedure that establishes the model of the selection of relations and thus also excludes other possibilities from the combination (Luhmann 1995a:195). Such structurings are called systems. They allow *differences* that enable the mutual connection of action in an overcomplex environment to be created. Like every other system, the economic system also operates according to its own rules of selection, which allows it to perceive and digest events in a specific way, and thus to distinguish itself from all other models of selection that become the environment of the system.[6]

On the one hand, it can be ascertained that the problem of double contingency can be connected to problems dealt with in economic theory. At the same time, the concept as Niklas Luhmann uses it has a radical openness, because Luhmann readily gives up the maximizing postulate of economic theory and the notion of normative orientations introduced by Parsons. The result is that the selection horizon of the actors is no longer determined by a single action alternative. Luhmann's theory thus eliminates all the problems of economic theory addressed in chapter 1, even regarding the deduction of optimal action alternatives through elaborate probabilistic calculations. The interpretation of uncertainty is no longer stipulated to interpret this merely as a complication of a process of decision making that is valid in principle, but rather the theory takes its own justification from the analysis of the impossibility of optimizing decisions. In chapter 1, it was demonstrated that under sufficiently complex conditions, deducing optimal models is not only a matter of mathematical problems; rather, it becomes increasingly unlikely that actors recognize the optimizing alternative in decision-making situations. In Luhmann, giving up the rational-actor model, however, goes along with abandoning action theory itself and conceptualizing sociological theory as systems theory.

Using Luhmann's conception of economic sociology, the issue discussed in this chapter is how increased efficiency of economic functions is enabled by forming a system that leads to a separation of economic communication from other social semantics. Based on that, Luhmann's perspective of the functioning of a self-referentially controlled economic system is discussed using the concepts money, code, and autopoeisis. These comments show clearly that Luhmann makes uncertainty into a paradigmatic starting point and thus creates a perspective that allows examining in principle all conceivable mechanisms of reduction of complexity in economic contexts of action. Sociological criticisms of Luhmann's economic sociology have especially rejected the separation of economic communication from moral and political semantics as a misinterpretation (Münch 1990; 1994). Here, on the other hand, it is to be shown that this critique has only limited relevance because the overcomplexity of the market leads to the institutionalization of *programs* that bring back the "excluded third" for the allocation of code values in payment decisions. Vis-à-vis external referential elements in the economic system, Luhmann's position is normatively ambivalent at best, but the theory itself demands integrating programs that can also move moral or political concerns into the economic system.

The Functional Differentiation of the Economy

Luhmann (1988a:14) understands the economy as a functionally differentiated subsystem that arose from the process of the internal differentiation of society and deals with the specific communication problem of regulating access to scarce goods. The problem of scarcity means the *social* perception of the limited accessibility of goods and services, which demands social regulation of access. The economy is assigned the task of meeting the future need for material goods. This is a constitutive problem whose social significance produces enough communication to differentiate a functional subsystem (Baecker 1987; Luhmann 1981:394). This description of the function of the economy relates to the neoclassical definitions of the subject matter of economics but intensifies its axiom of scarcity: if the task of the economy is to ensure the satisfaction of future needs in the present, then the present scarcity is increased because stocks for later have to be created today and, therefore, are not available for current consumption.[7] The prevailing institutional arrangements in the economic system are consequently explained as instruments to carry out the function entrusted to the economic system.

The basic problem of the economy can in principle be treated variously. Organized in segments, archaic societies perform their economic functions in a network of multifunctional social institutions that are not separated according to specific areas of specializations. In this type of society, the strategies of securing subsistence consist of "stockpiling supplies and maintaining social relations of mutual support" (Luhmann 1970:208). These two strategies avoid the risk of a purely individual allocation of goods but also represent the specific limitation of fulfilling economic functions in archaic societies: the obligation to help out that is institutionalized in social relations of reciprocity, which distributes scarce goods according to moral criteria, prevents the formation of purely economic capital. Controlling the fulfillment of economic functions by social expectations of reciprocity does not allow the differentiation of a system of economic functions because cultural, legal, and kinship expectations are mixed with economic motives. Archaic societies do not succeed in separating communication about access to goods from other social semantics; instead, they link these with social expectations of reciprocity, family considerations, or moral prohibitions. It is easy to imagine, for instance, that an economy is more efficient if the interest on borrowed money is not subject to any moral prohibition; thus morality as a scale of reference is excluded from the horizon of meaning of the economic system.[8]

This nexus of increased efficiency and exclusion of certain communications results from the central assertion of the new systems theory that a system increases its efficiency by merely selective perception of its environment. This assumption contains the functional (not genetic!) cause for differentiating society into functional subsystems, whose distinguishing feature is that the range of meaningful possibilities of communication is reduced in them.[9] By differentiating the economic system, a boundary is drawn that establishes a difference between system and environment, which reduces the complexity of the environment in the system. Systems then perceive the environment "in a categorically preformed way" (Luhmann 1989:12), and through their selection mechanisms, they determine which aspects of the environment are relevant for their operations. By observing it, the system "invents" (von Foerster 1985) its environment, which is not given a priori.

In the early works in economic sociology, Luhmann, clearly referring to Weber, links the process of differentiating the economy to the three developments of the emergence of markets, the separation of household and the firm, and the emergence of the monetary system. Markets enable a differentiation of roles, which institutionalize a "novel form of surplus utilization and commodity supply" (Luhmann 1970:209) along with the established criteria of social reciprocity. The market possibilities of comparison lead to impersonal relations oriented to equivalent values that can allow abstracting from other social roles of the exchange partners. The rise of firms that are freed from the household and their market-regulated boundary interchanges establish organizational structures that operate according to their own logic and create a consciousness of the systemic functioning of the economy.

In his later works, Luhmann moves money to the foreground as the central institution of the emergence of the functionally differentiated economic system.[10] The symbolically generalized communication medium of money operates as a special language and enables the differentiation of the economic system by limiting meaningful communication.[11] Because of the emphasis on the self-referential closure of systems, communication media in Luhmann's systems theory necessarily have a different significance than they do in the work of Parsons, who conceptualized media as instruments for conveying the boundary processes between systems. For Luhmann, on the other hand, the function consists of conditioning the selection of communication (Luhmann 1995a:162). Money enables the situationally independent reconciliation of the difference of Alter and Ego, which initially makes communication unlikely, by creating a context of commensurability:

How can it be . . . imagined that the always more special, always less probable, always more "private" selection of the actor also has motivational value
for another? How can individuals be willing to cooperate in situations with
double contingency and to integrate them for themselves . . . when it becomes
increasingly clear that the selection follows interests that are private, cannot
be influenced, and finally are often unknown? (Luhmann 1988a:238)

Money is independent of situations insofar as it reduces all goods or
services that are considered for economic uses to a quantitative expression. Money enables exchange processes to refer solely to the economic
dimension and to be free of cultural embedding. Moral, legal, scientific,
and other such aspects are excluded. The system is thus independent of
reciprocity and escapes a moral codification. Through the medium of
money, the economy forms its own values, ends, and norms, to which the
decision making is oriented in this area.[12]

But the probability that communication will be mutually linked in the
economic system is increased not only by the independence of normative
structures, but also because money—if we assume trust in the stability of
the value of money—can contribute to the solution of the two basic problems of exchange processes: to finding an exchange partner and to determining the quality of the exchanged commodities. The first problem
refers to the fact that money as a general exchange medium is free of the
restrictions of barter, in which one of the exchange partners may have no
interest in the articles offered by the other. This produces either exchange
blockades or leads to transaction cost intensive multilateral exchanges.
Money also facilitates solving the problem of the type of the exchange
commodity. It must be determined how much money is paid, but it is
established that the service in return will be money (Baecker 1988:99ff.).
On the macroeconomic level, money enables price formation which
makes observing the action of other actors easy. Prices and markets can
emerge because of money.

The most important structural feature of money consists of the money-
induced possibility of reducing complexity while simultaneously maintaining the contingency of transactions in principle. The use of money is
determined only at the moment of the transaction. Afterward, the money
is immediately available again for the purchase of any good. Giving up
the ability to pay always also means increasing another actor's ability
to pay, and this is how the economic system's ability to reproduce is
maintained.

By introducing money, payments can develop as a code in the economic
system that leads to the separation of the economic system from other
social semantics. *Codes* can be understood as the controlling behavioral
pattern of a system, the distinction, so to speak, that it uses to classify the

world (Willke 1987a:109).[13] In codes, social systems define their specific modes of operation and control "which meaning-units enable internally the self-reproduction of the system and thus are repeatedly to be reproduced" (Luhmann 1995a:34). The economic system is first codified by the code of property, which distinguishes the totality of communication by means of the guiding difference of owning or not owning. It is coded "secondarily," with the development of the money medium by the code of paying or not paying. This means that every transfer of goods and services involves a countertransfer of money, which enables the full functional differentiation of the economic system: the system is no longer oriented to social bonds but only to the price information generated by its own code in the language of the medium of money itself. The communications that occur in the environment of the system and in the system itself are perceived by means of this binary schematization and brought into a form that enables decision making by thus reducing complexity.

In the context of the argumentation of Luhmann's theory, the formation of markets must be another prerequisite for the differentiation of the economic system, because payments are regulated by prices that are shaped in markets. Markets are thus understood as an internal environment of the economic system (Luhmann 1988a:94), which enable the self-observation of the system. In this sense, Baecker (1988:205) talks of markets as "representations of the economy as a whole in the horizon of the participating subsystems." Participants in the economic system, like enterprises and households, can observe the payment operations of the other participants in the market by means of prices. Seen from the level of the observer of these observations, these observations are self-observations of the economic system. Prices thus have the function of generating information for communication processes that can be used to make decisions about payments (Luhmann 1988a:18). By appearing as a market for the individual participating systems, the economic system succeeds in obtaining an orientation for the communication with other internal economic subsystems. Through the market, it can be observed how other participants react to prices, which creates clues for one's own payment decisions. What is important here is that prices generate only internal economic information but not information about the relationship of the economy to its environment (35).

With the communication medium and the code, functional subsystems have their own standard of selection, which reduces for them the complexity of possible meaningful communication beyond what is determined by language.[14] Subsystems construct society in a specific way for themselves—using their binary code—and thereby produce their own claim to the reality of the subsystems. The semantic structures (codes) force systems to bring their communicative operations into a self-referential, recurrent orbit and thus produce an operational closure (Kasper 1991:16). The components of the system are linked in a circular way to one another in a circle that reproduces itself. This consistency is understood with the term autopoiesis, which refers to the fact that systems are not produced and maintained from outside but are understood rather as units that produce and reproduce themselves recurrently from inside (Luhmann 1995a:35). The economic system survives by payments and by maintaining the ability to pay. Thus, there is no difference for the economic system as to why payments are made; it does not influence the system itself. What matters for the demand for a good is only whether the demander can pay and if the exchange partners can agree on a price. It does not matter if Alter is a beggar or a millionaire, a believer or an atheist, beautiful or repulsive. This elasticity is opposed to the rigidity of the conditions of the framework, because every communication that cannot be represented in the code represents no information for the system, but in any case produces an incomprehensible noise. The highly selective specialization of subsystems is enabled by "operational blindness" (Berger 1990:233), because the systems can observe and describe their environment only by means of the guiding difference presented in their own specific code.

In this understanding of system, social systems react primarily to their own self-produced conditions and cannot be influenced directly from outside. The examination of the economic system is not directed to its boundary relation with relevant environments, as in Parsons, or to its environmental determination, as in the population ecology approach (Hannan and Freeman 1977), but rather to operational closure. Attention is drawn to the internal horizon of the economic system. What is emphasized is the internal determination of the structure of the system, which has to organize its own continuity.

The Re-Entry of the Excluded Third Party

The concept of autopoiesis does not imply that systems exist as quasi monads next to one another without being in contact with one another but simply that a direct intervention in the system by another one is categorically excluded. Autopoietic systems are not independent of their environment. Instead, it is argued that operational closure is required as a prerequisite to create the conditions under which perceiving the environment—that is, external referentiality—is possible. "Self-referential systems acquire information with the help of the difference between referring to self and to something other (in short, with the help of accompanying self-reference), and . . . this information makes possible their self-produc-tion" (Luhmann 1995a:448).

This section deals with elaborating how far Luhmann's theory, which emphasizes the operational closure of systems for one thing, can concep-tually integrate the opening of the economic subsystem to elements of the environment. The starting thesis of this book is that it is precisely the social embedding of economic action that enables economic efficiency. Thus a theory that disputes this possibility would contribute little to es-tablishing economic sociology based on this premise. First, I examine the relationship of the economic system and the environment, which clarifies Luhmann's skepticism about external-referential influences on economic communication. In a debate with the critique of Luhmann's understand-ing of economics presented by Richard Münch (1990; 1994), I then try to show that Luhmann's theory definitely does offer a possibility of inter-pretation that takes account of the social embedding of payment deci-sions. For this, it requires the inclusion of "programs," which is the sub-ject of the following discussion. In the last part of the section, I relate the theoretical considerations to enterprises as central subsystems of the economy.

Economic Systems and Environment

The relationship of the economic system and the environment is ambiva-lent with respect to the entrance of external-referential elements into the operations of the economic system. Systems cannot be defined by their environment, but the environment is assumed as a condition. On this background, Luhmann says that the economic system is both closed and open at the same time. Nor is it a contradiction if Luhmann calls the relationship of system and environment "the central paradigm" (Luh-mann 1995a:176) of the new systems theory. The differentiation of sys-tems assumes that, in their operation, these can refer to their own ele-ments, for which they must produce and use a description of themselves. They succeed in this only insofar as they can use the difference of system and environment "within themselves [the systems] for orientation and as a principle for creating information" (Luhmann 1995a:9). The operation of this identity-constitutive knowledge is observation, which, as defined by the theory of autopoietic systems, means the determination of a differ-ence (Willke 1987a:94). Systems observe in their difference schemes both themselves and their environment (external observation).[15] Wimmer (1989:140) explains the relationship of simultaneous dependence and in-dependence of systems on the environment in terms of mode and event: systems are independent of their environment with regard to the "specific mode of self-guidance" and dependent with regard to the "current events in the environment, from which they can obtain information and meanings which are imperative to maintain and develop their own identity."

This view of the system-environment relationship, which first appears as an opening of the conception of systems theory, is also decidedly modified. Because the observations and the subsequent descriptions[16] must correspond to the logic of the observing (!) system and its cognitive structure and not to that of the observed system,[17] the perceived communication is reduced to the guiding difference appropriate to the system. In observation, the observing system constructs the observed object from the perspective of its own semantics. Information therefore is the self-product of the system and not a fact of the environment, which exists independent of observations.

The ability of the economic system to resonate is thus extremely restricted.[18] Through payments, the economy keeps reproducing only the ability to pay and thus refers to connecting payments.[19] Only on condition that any external influence complies with the "language of prices" can the economic system derive information from it that can be introduced into the payment operation. Thus, a compatibility with the internal economic operations that does not rely on any code of the environmental system but rather shows an *economic motive* for consideration must be achieved. "The economy cannot react to disturbances that are not expressed in this language" (Luhmann 1989:62); they merely produce noise that may have dysfunctional consequences. Thus, in connection with ecological communication, Luhmann (20–21) states that an appeal to more environmental awareness in the economic subsystem can lead to an "effect explosion" that influences society in uncontrollable ways. A dysfunctional process of mutual build-up can occur in the reactions of the subsystems: systems react to disturbances of their autopoiesis with noise by building structures that enable their further autopoiesis. This process includes a thoroughly ironic dialectic: That is, systems also influence their environment and can change it so that they can no longer exist in this environment (14). The logic of this systemic self-endangerment resides in the systemic functioning itself: the next step is more important "than concern for the future, which indeed is not attainable if autopoiesis is not continued" (14). Luhmann thus thoroughly acknowledges the socially problematic nature of this model of selection: "In the price information supplied to the economy, information about the effects of the economic operations in the social environment [are] systematically overlooked" (Luhmann 1988a:blurb). Yet this does not change anything about the analysis itself. External noise can lead to "effect explosions" which cannot be controlled and thus whose consequences are unpredictable.[20]

This discrepancy is intensified by the specific time horizon created in the economic system, which corresponds to its operational logic and is not coordinated with the social or natural environment (Luhmann 1989:57). Despite the increasing scarcity of fossil fuels, the price of crude oil can go down. The time horizon of the economic system is directed at the present, whereas environmental groups may be concerned for the life of future generations. The summary is laconic: "Society [is] not informed by its economy about environmental problems triggered there" (Luhmann 1988a:35).

The perspective of the self-referential functioning of the economy has triggered the most protest in the discussion of Luhmann's concept of economic sociology. Richard Münch (1990; 1994) has especially objected to the idea of separating the economic system from the moral discourse of society. Thus, against the background of Parsons's theory, Münch (1990:305) characterizes the thesis of the autopoietic functioning of the economic system as "simply not true," referring to the incorporation of economic functions into societal references: "In empirical reality, the self-reproduction of the economy [is] not an automatically continuous process of payments, but rather a boundary interchange between economic, political, legal, religious, scientific, and other thoughts and acts, which must constantly be redefined and is socially contested."

Münch confronts the idea of the self-referentially consistent functioning of the economy with Parsons's term of interpenetration, which is to indicate the overlapping of economy and morality. For Münch, the differentiation of the economic system itself becomes a result of the use of moral yardsticks in economic contexts, which is explained by the institutionalization of property laws and occupational roles. Referring to Weber's thesis of Protestantism, Münch points to the ethical foundation of work in the Reformation and in Calvinism. *Pace* Weber, Münch sees that the ethically obligatory character of the calling has been assumed in the developmental process of modernity, but today work is also "shaped by a professional ethic whose demands are determined by the prestige of a profession and whose performance fulfillment decides on the respect for the worker in the profession" (Münch 1994:389). In this sense, social respect and economic achievement always dovetail. Münch also sees the moral embedding guaranteed in the marginal case of an action oriented purely to economic motives. "Doing good means producing services that create economic value" (394). On the other hand, a moral regulation of the economy takes place through the law, "which brings moral considerations into the enforcement of economic calculations" (398).

Münch's desire to refer to cultural and institutional assumptions for shaping economic rationality and the influence of legal regulations on economic payment decisions is not to be criticized. This assumption is part of the core of thinking in economic sociology and can also be clearly verified empirically. Therefore, we can also agree with Münch especially because he acknowledges the systemic constraints to which economic decisions are subject. "A manager of industry can certainly not change the laws of the economy, he must master the language of prices" (389). But the question is whether these considerations contradict the concept of Luhmann's theory, as Münch asserts. That is to decide whether a critique of the idea of a self-referential reproduction of the economic system should start with *these* critical objections. At first glance, Münch's critique seems plausible because Luhmann sees the progress in increased efficiency of the differentiation of the economic subsystem among other things in its separation from moral discourse.

But if Luhmann's concept is examined more closely, it can be seen that the self-referentiality is located on the level of the code and does not yet include important determinations of the operation of the economic system. The question of *what* payments are made *for* is not yet considered. For the autopoiesis of the economic system, it does not matter in principle which payments are made, as long as the existence of the system is not jeopardized by those payment decisions. This happens when the ability to pay can no longer be maintained. But to what extent can the observation of prices as well as payments actually contribute to guiding payment decisions?

If we stay first with enterprises, whose payment decisions are oriented toward the goal of profit maximization, then only under the conditions assumed by neoclassical economic theory can prices contain the necessary information for establishing the production function of the demanded quantity of impact factors and the planned quantity of output. Under conditions of uncertainty, prices cannot contain total information because—aside from uncertainty in the production process—the market size or the market price cannot be anticipated.[21] Prices cannot then be a structural source to determine decisions for firms interested in maximizing decisions. Assuming the absence of uncertainty, households can also make optimizing decisions only on the basis of price information and a preference order. But if, in economic sociology, we are also interested in the question of action in situations with uncertainty, then it is not enough to refer to payments and the information contained in prices in order to understand why payments are made. The code "payments" is informative because, on the one hand, a systematic limit is indicated in it that defines under which conditions actors can participate in the economy,[22] and because, on the other hand, prices can clearly reduce the complexity of the information from the environment; at the same time, keep in mind that, through the code "payments," a reduction in complexity is obtained only insofar as a language for the resonance capacity of the system is claimed. Just as a natural language does not prescribe concrete expression, so the communication medium and the code contain no motive for concrete payment decisions. Instead, the complexity of the language horizon continues undiminished. The next question, therefore, is through what mechanisms are actors (systems) moved to a position to make decisions for concrete payments if, in situations with uncertainty, prices do not necessarily induce any selections. This does indicate that the purely formal level of payments must be supplemented by a substantial level. The following section shows how what appears initially as a rigid definition of the economic system in Luhmann's remarks can be amplified by elements of external referentiality that also allow it to integrate into Luhmann's theoretical concept the political and moral influences on payment decisions demanded by Münch.[23]

Programs

The remarks about the relationship of economic system and environment at first confirm Richard Münch's critique that, in Luhmann's concept, the economic system is (incorrectly) divorced from moral and political discourse, by shielding it from information that does not comply with the language of price. But it has already been shown that Luhmann also sees the assumption for the institutionalization of the differentiated economic system in legal regulations. What is more important, however, is that the reduction of information to "the language of prices" must not necessarily be interpreted as excluding moral and political influence on economic payment decisions but rather merely as *formulating conditions for their articulation*. The transformation of moral criteria into price information is required to allow them into the self-referential operation of the economic system.

But this description of the functioning of the economy as such gives hardly any ground for criticism. On the one hand, it contains experience that is easy to confirm empirically: allocation decisions in the economic system can be influenced by the change in price. The politics and jurisdiction involved in controlling economic activities operate with the influence of factor prices through monetary incentives (subsidies) and negative sanctions that influence prices and thus steer economic decisions into a politically desirable direction. Environmental groups, for instance, can expect success when they have the possibilities of inflicting monetary sanctions on the companies whose policies they oppose. On the other hand, the idea that the economic system is sensitive exclusively to money must also not necessarily be rejected normatively for two reasons: the resonance of the economic system adjusted to price professes a mechanism whose knowledge allows actors to have a focused influence on allocation decisions of the economic system. This might enable more targeted interventions than more diffuse mechanisms to influence economic decisions.

But it must also be reflected that the functional differentiation of the economy and its "operational blindness" (Berger 1990) lead to an increase in the adaptive capacity and thus allow producing more resources that find a use in other social subsystems. If the lack of differentiation of the economy is linked to a lower production of wealth, this must itself be reflected in normative terms.

This argumentation starts from the notion that prices and their observation can sufficiently steer economic decisions. It has already been argued that this assumes the adoption of the assumptions in neoclassical theory. Yet in situations with uncertainty these assumptions are refuted. But how can the pursued thesis that Luhmann's theoretical concept is especially relevant for a sociological understanding of action under conditions of uncertainty be defended?

The crucial step here consists of including programs. Communications media and codes are not sufficient assumptions to control the allocation of resources. In the remarks so far, it has always been as if allocation decisions would result from price information. Yet the analysis of this assumption shows that the economic system is dependent on additional assumptions for the explanation of allocation if the maximizing assumption is given up. A comparison with neoclassical economic theory explains this: this theory also begins with property rights and the problem of scarcity, and also assumes action oriented to factor prices, but with the additional assumption of utility-maximizing actors who have an unequivocal preference order available. This last element introduces a *motive* for specific allocation decisions into the theory. The actors always reduce the decision contingency of the situation by choosing optimizing alternatives on the basis of their preferences. But an equivalent to that is lacking in Luhmann's concept of systems theory because the theory begins with the notion that it is precisely the overcomplexity of market information that prevents maximizing choices. Prices and payments observed in the market convey only data that appear in the horizon of meaning, which is processed in the economic system and which keeps stimulating payments. The perspective not yet addressed is that information appearing as prices must first be interpreted for payment decisions. This goes beyond the level of the code because the code is indifferent to its molding (paying or not paying), and thus is not a "criterion of selection" (Luhmann 1989:40). The economic system has no endogenous preference for payments or nonpayments in view of price information. Because Luhmann's theory starts from the overcomplexity of action situations, it cannot fall back on the postulate of maximizing to explain payment decisions in the economy.

As a systematic substitute for the maximizing postulate of neoclassical theory, the problem of permanence (*Bestandserhaltung*) is introduced into systems theory. This "final problem" taken from biology directs attention to the possibility of systems to survive in a complex environment by specific performance achievements. The "themes of the difference between system and environment, complexity, self-reference, and the temporal combination of irreversibility and reversibility (process and structure) can be interpreted from a methodological viewpoint as an articulation of the problem of permanence"; maintaining permanence means maintaining the consistency of the system by reproducing elements from elements "that pass away in their very emergence" (Luhmann 1995a:54).[24] This can easily be applied to the economic system: the existence of the economic system depends on payments; autopoiesis would then be destroyed if the capacity to pay were interrupted. This logic must be respected in the allocation decisions of the economic system and also obeyed as a limitation of possible interventions. Conditions for the consideration of demands of other social subsystems, the natural environment, or mental systems in allocation decisions can be derived from this systemic criterion. Payments must be calculated so that the ability to pay can be regenerated by them. Ecological concerns from outside the system, for instance, can be apprehended only under two conditions: first, if they open new markets, and thus create possibilities of income (this is the case, e.g., with enterprises that produce technologies for environmental protection); second, if they can pass on the costs as prices (Luhmann 1989:56). A more macroeconomic argument can be found in the description of the function of the economic system: if it is the function of the economic system to provide for future needs, then allocation decisions must be oriented to accomplish this task.

Yet these general determinations cannot give any concrete instructions for allocation decisions because they profess only abstract directions; however, they cannot be translated easily into concrete instructions for payments under conditions of radical uncertainty. Luhmann's notion of systemic rationality is not determined in any way. The existing difference between systemic survival demands and concrete allocation decisions can be read clearly in Luhmann's (1988a:12ff.) discussion of action under risk: the recommendation here is to make only those allocation decisions that do not jeopardize the autopoiesis of the system even in the event of the worst-case scenario. Thus, it turns out that a few allocation decisions are excluded by the criterion of the system survival, yet it does not allow any determinate instructions for action to be deduced. An openness in principle exists with regard to concrete allocation of money. But how can this contingency in the economic system be reduced?

From the pressure of this problem, Luhmann introduces another analytical level, along with the level of the communication medium and the code, whose function is to explain the allocation of the code values. This level requires not only the price but also the interpretation of the information contained in it. Introducing this level significantly supplements the pure price orientation of economic decisions, and initially excluded variables can be reintroduced into the economic system. This refers to *programs* that are established on another level of the operation of systems and have the function of overcoming the *meaning emptiness* of codes. Programs can "be understood as the forms in which any code can be worked off in arbitrary differentiation" (Willke 1987a:109). Programs that operate in the framework of a specific code and determine its functioning more precisely with regard to the criteria, premises, and preferences of the system thus indicate possibilities and limitations (Luhmann 1989:48ff.). If the systematic position of programs is considered, this concerns second-order self-observations, which "do not depend on linking, extracting, and processing their information to the code's binary schema" (Baecker 1988:182). Programs in the economic system indicate reasons for payments and consist of needs, expectations, and structures. Needs circumscribe the contingency of possible allocation decisions. Expectations "prepare possibilities of future events" (Baecker 1988:121), thus reducing the contingency for what payments are made without being deterministic: expectations can be disappointed. Structures are determined in systems theory with regard to the notion of expectation.

The level of programs introduces a crucial additional dimension into Luhmann's concept of economic sociology, which refers to the contingent nature of decisions in principle in view of existing market price information. Even under the conditions of a functionally differentiated economic system, this still remains dependent on elements that are excluded from the system initially by the media of money and the code. Programs enable the reentrance of the *excluded third party*—"but only to co-steer the allocation of the code-values on which it primarily depends" (Luhmann 1989:41). If the code of a system is seen as the grid in which information is generated, the task of programs consists of filling the code with content that is effective as selection criteria. Through programs, it is decided *what* payments are made *for*. As long as these payments are suitable to reproduce the payment capacity of the system, it is immaterial in principle for its autopoiesis what they are made for.[25] By attaching the self-referential code closely to programs, payments are linked to reasons "which ultimately refer to the environment of the system" (Luhmann 1988a:59) and express the openness of the system. Systems are closed in reference to their code. A change of the code would destroy the basic circularity and thus the identity of the system; autopoiesis would be prevented. The system is open with reference to its programs, which can be changed, but must always be proved with regard to the code.

At the same time, Luhmann assumes a normatively ambivalent posture with regard to steering payments through programs. While he emphasizes the reciprocal reference of self- and external referentiality that is inherently necessary in the theory, he tries to downplay its structural significance for the self-referential functioning of economic processes. This can be explained with two examples. First, in the discussion of needs as structuring elements of the economic system, Luhmann (1988a:62) distinguishes between elementary, luxury, and production needs, in which these forms can also indicate an evolutionary sequence: production needs (secondary needs of the economic system) gain significance in modern economic systems because the economy is increasingly dependent on itself. In this assessment, the distance Luhmann takes toward external referentiality introduced into the economic system by programs becomes clear. To a certain extent, emphasizing the significance of production needs again revokes the external referentiality introduced by programs by incorporating needs into the economic system itself. Second, Luhmann's ambivalence about elements of external referentiality is even clearer in the discussion of profit. Profit is understood as realization of the intention to improve one's own payment position for future payments by payments (Luhmann 1989:51ff.). By adapting the economic system to profit, it controls itself and is independent of private motives and esteem, which overcomes the specific *deficiency of motive* of the code "payment" that has no goal itself.

Now, the question is at what level does the profit motive enter the economic system. On the one hand, Luhmann (1988a:56) talks of profit in terms of self-control and the delineation of the economic system from private motives, which assumes a function mechanism inherent in the system to be inferred; on the other hand, the profit motive is introduced as a *reason* for payments and is thus on the level of programs in the economic system. If profit is a program, then it is established firmly in the environment of the system, requires an extraeconomic legitimation, and is an element of the external referentiality of the system. Thus, the self-motivating function of money is questioned: striving for more money is not determined as inherent to the system, but is rather an external contingency. An economic system could also be functionally differentiated without being oriented to profit. Unlike neoclassical economics, which establishes profit or utility maximization of the actors as an axiom, Luhmann's theory is open with regard to the action motives of actors, which must be proved merely with respect to the autopoiesis of the system. It still requires the mutual reference of self- and external referentiality, because this is the only way motives and expectations can be introduced.

The construction of the system as closed and open at the same time refers to the radical contingency of economic payment decisions that rest on the basis of perception of price information controlled by programs. Only because the economic system refers to needs and expectations that find entry as programs can the lack of motive of the medium of money be overcome. The medium of money itself can induce no payment decisions. Price information says nothing about the results of the selective observation of the market or about the concrete payment decisions to be made on the basis of price observation. If it is irrelevant to the system why payments are made (as long as the capacity to pay is maintained), the interest of economic sociology shifts to the structures, expectations, and needs that decide about the allocation of code values. Therefore, the theory has the potential for an openness limited initially only by the criterion of survival, in which the essential advantage vis-à-vis economic theory is for understanding action under conditions of uncertainty. With his statements about the overcomplexity of the market, Luhmann emphatically objects to rational-actor models of utility maximizing. Evidently, the concept of the theory is not only able to integrate uncertainty theoretically but also recognizes uncertainty as a prerequisite for the functioning of the economic system.[26] The "situative determinism" (Latsis 1972) of neoclassical theory is eliminated for the explanation of allocation decisions. Decisions always remain risky because expected consequences need not appear. The mathematical calculations of economic models of action under conditions of uncertainty cannot achieve in principle what they claim to carry out: to produce decisions that guarantee optimal results. Rejecting the normative action models of economic theory as a starting point for a theoretical conceptualization of economic processes—in reference to the imperceptible complexity of causal relations—is the central gain of knowledge of Luhmann's new systems theory for economic sociology.

Contrary to Richard Münch's critique, reducing the economic system to payments does not prevent incorporating political and moral regulations into the differentiated economic system. These appear on the level of programs on the basis of which market price information is judged. These include needs and expectations, with regard to both the action of a third party, and causal relations, as well as the structures of the economic system. To a certain extent, the idea of the autopoietic reproduction of the economic system is an illusion produced by the construction of the theory, which is also undermined. The radical circumscription of the scope of communication of the economic system refers precisely to the elements that are banished in the environment of the system, but it cannot get away from them. Terminologically, the theory can sidestep the significance of the *material basis* of scarcity and the *motives* for payments by emphasizing the code, but the theory construct of self-referentiality still remains dependent on external referentiality. Luhmann (1988a:59ff.) makes this explicit theoretically, but its potential is not exhausted. Instead, he emphasizes the aspects of self-referential closure, orientation to prices through market observations, and the evolutionary advantages of excluding social bonds from the economic system. But instruments contained in the theory of self-referential closure can be shown that leave open the extensive possibilities of incorporating elements from the environment.

To explain the possibilities of using Luhmann's theory for economic sociology, I now turn to the example of business firms to show how programs systematically enter into economic decisions of payment or non-payment.

Economic Organizations and Payment Decisions

In Luhmann's language, organizations are systems that consist of decisions.[27] Decisions are understood as a special form of communication in formally organized social systems, which are characterized as a reaction to prevailing expectations. Thus Luhmann (1988a:278) brings decisions into a systems-theoretical difference scheme: "An action, then, [is] always to be seen as a decision when it reacts to an expectation directed at it." Actions assume ambiguous situations in which a decision must be made that allows one either to fill or to contradict expectations. Expectations brought into the organization from outside can be understood and obeyed only when they are compatible with the expectation structures of the organization. They must find access "to the internal network of decision production" (Kasper 1991:19). But at the same time, decisions are also those operations in which selective motives from the system and its environment merge (Luhmann 1988a:277). Both before and after the decision, contingency (the situation of choosing) and the difference of system and environment exist.

In this understanding of organizations, expectations are structures that are brought into actions as assumptions of behavior that provoke decisions (Kasper 1991:21). They allege a scope of possibilities that make up the structure of the organization, either as formal rules or as well-established habit. Generalized expectations are manifested in enterprises as cognitions or norms that are distinguished from one another by different predispositions for the case of disappointment. While norms can be held onto even in case of disappointment, unrealized cognitive expectations are more easily revised (Luhmann 1969). Through confirmation and disappointment of expectations, decision structures are developed in organizations, which gradually transform accidental events into solid orders, but thus are also always subject to changes.

Thus, expectations represent a form of rigidification of payment decisions in enterprises. The category of expectations abstractly names the central mechanism for reducing complexity in enterprises. The question of how enterprises make payment decisions in situations where the maximizing criterion of economic theory cannot be applied because of the uncertainty about optimal decisions is answered with the assumption of the orientation to relatively rigid structures, which circumscribe flexibility. Although this is initially a purely formal determination, which represents merely the mechanism of complexity reduction, without determining the content of predispositions, such specifications can be derived from the function of enterprises as actors in the economic system: the social function of the economic system consists of providing for future demands. Enterprises can contribute to this function by reconciling the "asymmetrical relation of production and consumption" (Luhmann 1981:398) and through capital formation. By planning, economic organizations adapt to the fact that "customers arrive at previously unknown times with previously unknown wishes and yet can be made to find what they thought they wanted" (399). In addition, enterprises can realize profits through cost-favorable organization and thus form capital. Capital allows the satisfaction of abstract (economic) needs in the future. So, Luhmann sees the functional significance of economic organizations as a contribution to the social function of creating freedom of disposition. But the orientation of the enterprise to these functions is also induced by the environment of the enterprise, which demands generalized resources in the form of taxes, wages, and profits, which is legally enforced if necessary.[28] Therefore, expectations in enterprises are determined by social functions communicated from the environment of the economic system but also remain oriented to the autopoiesis of the organization and maintain the ability to pay, without which the performance of social functions would not be possible.[29]

If enterprises are dependent on earning surpluses, then the useful decisions are limited to those that seem suited to filling this goal, which results in specific ideas of rationality in enterprises (402). This, however, does not propose a conception of enterprises as rational actors, whose decisions are determined by production functions. On the contrary, the neoclassical theory of the firm is again rejected as incorrect, because "the social environment presenting itself as a market is too complex" (ibid.) for rational decisions of the economic organizations. It is necessary for enterprises to make decisions in the present about future supply, without knowing future states of the market. Thus, theoretical interest focuses on the problem of uncertainty. Luhmann's attention is directed to observation of enterprises with which they process contingency. This cannot be based only on prices. Organizations must "produce their own structure-specific reduction capacities, which are not determined by the social environment (e.g., through prices). The gap between the possibilities of system formation and system complexities on a societal and organizational level is, on the one hand, a problem because society is an environment for organizations; on the other hand, it is an opportunity because this is how organizations can produce their own capacities for the reduction of complexity based on system-specific environments and system-specific structures" (ibid. 402). Therefore, enterprises are not considered determined in their decision by the market; rather companies build up specific structure—that is, there is organizational latitude[30]—which is limited only by the autopoiesis of the system. Although the complexity of the action situation never allows it to seem certain that the right decision has been made (Luhmann 1988a:227), the ability to act can be maintained by programs that make decisions expected but without diminishing the risk.[31] The optimal pre-condition for dealing with uncertainty is possessed by those participants in the economic system, who have power and staying power, thus, "robustness . . . the ability to survive the mistakes of others and oneself" (1988a:122).

> The procedural effort in individual decisions does not aim at the goal of making the right decision, that would be in vain, but to the attempt to make a decision that can be declared correct in retrospect, because one has considered what could be considered according to the state of things and the condition of knowledge. Thus, one must take care that the expected consequences of the "right" decision are attributed to a good decision and not an accident, and the surprising consequences of the "wrong" decision can only be attributed partially to it and mostly to other influences. (Baecker 1988:133)

But economic organizations also limit the complexity of the economic system. The initially unlimited investment possibilities of money are circumscribed drastically by the capital investments of enterprises. Scarcities are patched up by organizations and transformed into small-format decision problems that can be controlled better (Luhmann 1981:407). By building internal complexity, organizations contribute to *structuring* the economic system and reducing market complexity. This structuring is not induced by the market but is a specific capacity of the organization, which must prove itself simply with regard to the autopoiesis of the system.

The complexity-reducing capacity of organizations is discussed by Luhmann (1988b) in the concepts of medium and form. Medium means money; form means the organizations of the economic system. Through investments, enterprises determine what money is to be paid for—which binds their money while working against a background of maintaining their own ability to pay—(Luhmann 1988a:309). Thus, "more rigid complexes" emerge in the economic system, whose decisions about payments are determined extensively by the specificity of the investment. "The 'how' of the use of money is always decided down to a relatively small remnant which is necessarily left free for the transaction of payments" (312). But the combination latitude of money is specified again not only by investment decisions, but also by the organization itself. Part of the means of payment is used to buy labor, which, to some extent, transfers money into another medium, that is, into power. Money can win members for the organization and motivate them through the advantages of membership to orient their behavior to the goal of the organization (302). In the form of hierarchy, money is transformed into power, which overcomes the specific *motive risk* of the money medium within the firm. Consequently, an organization (hierarchy) relieves the economic system from "combining all contributions of individuals exclusively through markets and market related marginal utility" (Luhmann 1981:408).

Through payment decisions, organizations control their own capacity to reduce complexity and change their sensibility to the environment by increasing the variety or redundancy through which the correspondence between events in the environment and events in the system change.[32] As a means of condensing internal decision contexts—thus increasing redundancy—organizations have three possibilities available to concentrate the premises of decisions and thus structurally circumscribing decisions:[33] establishing paths of communication; formulating programs, by which the correctness of decisions is judged by the organizations; and persons. This formal structuring of organizations is depicted in the notion of *position*, which combines all three of the structural circumscriptions of decisions mentioned. Yet this definitely does not say anything about the *consequences* of such oscillations for the autopoiesis of the system.

The structures of the organization must enable its reproduction. A prerequisite of the autopoiesis of the enterprise is that it produces the capital (money) it needs. The programs of the enterprise are flexible only to the extent that this goal must be achieved and must also find the measure of environmental openness through which it can achieve this goal. Observations therefore cannot be limited to market observation and self observation, but must, if need be, include functionally necessary observations of other subsystems, including psychological systems, and the natural environment to construct internal "ideas about the possibilities of the continuation of its self-reproduction" (Luhmann 1988a:123). How far enterprises succeed in this depends on their own structures, which are the starting point of changes and which cause rigidity in the form of positions but also informally through the history of the enterprise and through cultural models (Kasper 1991:27) that cause their limitation only in terms of ability to communicate.[34]

In the remarks on the rigidification of organization structures, the environmental openness of enterprises becomes clear. Here, the focus is on the dimension of external referentiality. Through expectations and structures, enterprises can process the overcomplexity of market and environmental information so that sequences of interaction can develop. But this increase of redundancy is a special capacity of the enterprise and is not determined externally. The code payment or nonpayment cannot induce whether a payment should be made or not, but can simply state what happens when one or another decision is made. *Selection criteria* are fed into the enterprise only through *programs*, which create the reasons that motivate payments.

The legitimatory preconditions for differentiating the economic system and its ability to function, emphasized by Richard Münch, can also be integrated into this principally open structure of the economic system. Programs that introduce rigidities on whose bases payment decisions are made allow sensitivity toward the semantics found in the environment of the system. This corresponds with Münch's (1990:386) argument: "The delineation of economic action requires cultural legitimation, legal protection, solidary support, and political execution." With the notion of autopoiesis, however, Luhmann's theory also refers to the conditions of reproduction of the economic system, which always remains dependent on regenerating the ability to pay. But, the systemic criterion—and this is the essential advance vis-à-vis the neoclassical assumption of maximization—does not have a deterministic nature, but simply claims a limitation. This conceptualization allows the reduction of contingency to be understood as a task that must be continually fulfilled by economic organizations, which is possible only through openness vis-à-vis the system environment; but at the same time, the systemic assumptions of reproduction may not be ignored.

If this model of enterprises is assumed, which is both closed (with respect to the code) and open (with respect to the structures), this opens the possibility of examining the reduction of complexity in the enterprise as a contingent relation of enterprise and environment. The network of expectations manifested in an enterprise results from the history of development of the enterprise and is manifested in the structures of the organization, its culture, and the style and personality of the leadership, among others, which all contribute to reducing the complexity of the environment in ways specific to the enterprise. But only those programs can be maintained that select code values that allow the ability to pay to be reproduced. Programs that do not fulfill this condition and thus lead to disappointments (losses) must be abandoned.[35]

In shaping specific structures and expectations, the enterprise determines its perception of the environment. But which aspects are perceived and which are not and how the information generated by observations influences decisions is presently determined only through existing rigidifications. This makes it understandable why Luhmann (1988a:314) trusts "strong leadership personalities who think they know what they want" to reshape organizations. A prerequisite for that is the given flexibility of the enterprise on the program level with regard to the expectations prevailing in it, which can be altered by the change of management. The selection mechanisms on the program level that establish the organizational expectations and thus steer decisions in prearranged directions are diverse. Thus the plurality of programs in enterprises allows only a limited rigidity to emerge, so that decisions are restricted but not determined. The variance held onto here can be considered as a latitude of activity which brings a voluntaristic element into enterprises beyond the changeability of programs in principle: decisions can be made with reference to various expectations.[36] The latitude of action arising from the variance can thus, paradoxically, fill the gaps that emerge only through variance—the incomplete program determination of decisions. In this sense, Schreyögg (1991:283) speaks of the "stopgap function of *leadership*," which absorbs the complexity of the environment in the last resort and transforms it into payment decisions.

The comments show that the problem of reducing complexity does contain the postulate of selective observation of the environment but does not mean the monadic delimitation of the economy from other social semantics.[37] Shaping programs can be understood only under the inclusion of the structure of the environment because enterprises must make decisions about future supply without being able to read the necessary information from prices alone. At the same time, understanding enterprises as autopoietic systems explains the limit of the capacity for resonance: enterprises must perceive their environment selectively and on the premise of the reproduction of their own ability to pay. The resonance of the environment in the system assumes that structures are formed on the program level of enterprises, which correspondingly form perception. Therefore, the self-description of the intervening systems must be reconstructed (Willke 1987b:351) and the environment can only be understood based on the use of this guiding difference. Johannes Berger (1990:233) sees this project already initiated because "the long-term observation of economic decisions by society leads to a stronger opening of the economy to the interests of its environment."[38] The selective perception of the environment is also a constitutive assumption for the continuation of the autopoiesis of the enterprise. This produces a perspective that does avoid a deterministic understanding of economic decisions but nevertheless recognizes systemic limitations for freedom of decision and thus categorically rejects *subsuming* economic action under other social semantics, which also suggests a theoretical statement for the socially conflictual nature of the behavior of enterprises.

Establishing the possibility of intervention in the system resulting from programming says nothing about the results for its autopoiesis. In this context, Luhmann is thoroughly skeptical. He sees the danger not so much in the fact that too little resonance for the environment is summoned up in enterprises—even though he does leave this possibility open (Luhmann 1988b:175)—but rather in an excess of resonance: "There can be *too much resonance* and the system can burst apart from internal demands without being destroyed from outside" (Luhmann 1989:116). Luhmann cites politically motivated, unprofitable investments that enterprises are forced to make by their environment, which can destroy the autopoiesis of the economic system (1989:59ff.); in the background of these warning statements is the assertion that resonance of the environment in the economic system can itself "trigger one of those 'effect-explosions'" (62). Willke also called attention to the fact that interventions in a system "depend on achieving calculable effects in a basically uncontrollable field" (Willke 1987b:351).[39]

While the impression of the normative nature of the warnings of the dysfunctional results of too much environmental influence cannot be resisted in Luhmann, the approaches that demand a restless flexibility of expectation—and thus complete variance in enterprises or in the economic system—neglect the problem of the necessary reduction of complexity in an overcomplex environment as the initial problem of the theory.[40] But, ultimately, only empirically can it be clarified how much resonance the economic system must or can summon up under dynamic environmental conditions in order to continue its autopoiesis.

If the warnings of possible incalculable effect-explosions are justified and one wants to avoid negative results of interventions, two possibilities remain. One consists of enterprises orienting their payment decisions only to the environment, if there is an economic motive for it. This would be given if the ability to pay increases (profit), or is at least not decreased. The second option is more far-reaching: enterprises themselves introduce the difference of system and environment into the system and thus orient themselves not to their own identity but to the difference to their environment. Thus, enterprises could "charge the reactions to its environmental effects to 'themselves'" (Luhmann 1989:131). On the other hand, the environment itself had to reflect in its claims the results of its resonance for enterprises. This "understanding," as Willke emphasizes, still does not make "the effects of intervention controllable, but it does make them calculable" (Willke 1987b:351). Johannes Berger (1990:241) calls this a sensitizing strategy: "Sensitivity can be achieved by the relevant actors developing in their own interest behavioral norms of a moderate pursuit of their goals, which lead to a stronger consideration of the action problems of the 'fellow players.'"

System and Action

The discussion of programs as contingency-reducing structures of the economic system should have shown the specific achievement of systems theory for economic sociology. Situational complexity becomes the central starting problem for considering decisions in economic contexts where the possibility of maximizing action is firmly rejected. By no longer conceiving decisions as optimizing, systems theory avoids problems of deducing the "right" choice that results from complex action situations characterized by uncertainty. That rigidification and selective perception of the environment are central mechanisms for handling uncertainty eludes economic theory, which expects the actors to make ever more complicated mathematical calculations to deduce maximizing alternatives. Unlike Parsons, Luhmann's solution to the problem of double contingency is not seen in the existence of an institutionalized and internalized system of values but is rather much more broadly constructed. Limiting the range of semantics through codes and building structures creates rigidification that reduces complexity. The breadth of possible programs shows that the separation of the economic system from other social semantics applies only with regard to the code. The economic system remains linked with its environment through programs that decide about the allocation of code values. The entrance of political, moral, religious, and scientific elements into payment decisions can be studied within the theoretical framework outlined by Luhmann. However, it always requires a *translation* of the intervening semantics. By emphasizing the development of more rigid decision complexes, the theory shows an important way to explain allocation decisions in situations with uncertainty.

But can we also use Luhmann's theoretical conception to understand the two other problems of cooperation and innovation, discussed in chapter 1? Assessing the achievements of systems theory for understanding the two action situations confronts the difficulty that Luhmann does not explicitly discuss either of them.[41] A critical, metatheoretical concern with the postulate of self-referentiality is required to be able to measure Luhmann's contribution to these two problems. The thesis is that giving up the intersubjective horizon of reference of an always socially constituted subject and renouncing a notion of action prevent a sufficient understanding of cooperation and innovative processes.

Cooperation and Intersubjectivity

In the theory of autopoietic systems, each system constitutes its own horizon of meaning, which allows it to differentiate itself from its environment and to perceive other systems only as material for self-referential observations. If we understand actors in the economic system (enterprises, households) as systems, each of these constitutes for itself a distinct partial perspective in the observation of the actions of other systems and the market. The consistency of the economy is represented differently from the perspective of each of the participating systems. The self-referentially operating subsystems must give up a common perspective from which "the economy" or "the society" can come into view. It is precisely in this in-commensurability of functionally differentiated social systems that Luh-mann sees the development of the specifically modern structure of society realized, which is thus distinguished from premodern societies in that it no longer gives a privileged point from which a control of social development would be possible. Modern societies form no logical identity in the sense that the consequences of actions for the subsystems in the environment are reflected and thus can be controlled by a societal rationality. The mode of reproducing the system is oriented to the criterion of enabling the con-tinuation of its own autopoiesis. Systems can only observe one another, and in an endless increase of this operation, they observe the observation of observations. By means of observations, expectations can be shaped on the basis of which decisions are made, which are observed in turn in the horizon of meaning of the other systems and give a reason for con-firming or revising one's own expectations. The interesting question here is not whether to affirm or criticize Luhmann's description of the func-tional logic of self-referential systems.[42] The question is whether in the economic system relations of cooperation can be imagined between the subsystems that can affect one another contingently only from outside, without having an intersubjectively shared horizon of meaning, which functions as a mechanism to ensure the commensurability of their mutual observations.[43]

The cooperation problem in economic theory is that, through a one-sided advance to another actor, an actor opens several options, only part of them in his own interest, without Ego being able to control the decision of Alter. The actor will produce the advance only if he expects that Alter chooses an action that is in his interest. Thus, it requires an observation of the way Alter acts. But the decision for cooperation always involves the risk of the disappointment of the expectation. The observation of Alter is necessary to lessen the risk of disappointment as much as possible, but is also linked with costs. Alter's action must be observed in compara-ble interaction situations with other actors, such as the ability to observe the interaction through a third party (reputation effect). Thus, all the problems are posed again that were already examined in chapter 1. The possibility of mutual observation under conditions of the uncontrollabil-ity of the decisions of Alter increases the probability of cooperation through reduction of the risk involved in it. But it does remain dependent on stable structures or it generates high transaction costs.

The situation changes with the assumption of a common horizon of meaning of the actors, which allows reducing the need for observation. Such a common horizon of meaning can exist in a value system shared by Alter and Ego, which does not leave the definitions of situation in the arbitrariness of the "contingency of the world" and their exhaustion through mutually observing social systems, but represents a common third party, to which social behavior can be oriented. The reduction of contingency, then, is not a separately posed task of every subsystem but rather takes place in the context of a world already experienced as socially structured. Values (Durkheim, Parsons), intersubjectivity (Mead), or discursively obtained consensus (Habermas) then assumes the function of insuring a social background, which can stabilize expectations and allow the reciprocal ability to calculate the actions of other actors. The commonly shared horizon of meaning allows the shaping of expectations of Alter's reaction to cooperative advances, without requiring the observation of the *concrete* Alter. Hence, it is an abbreviated assumption of Luhmann when he says that the problem of mutual respect in exchange is a "triggering factor" (Luhmann 1995a:240) for coordinating the individual contributions. Rather, it is the embedding of exchange acts of the social system in a common horizon of meaning that can achieve an essential contribution for the autopoiesis of the economic system by increasing the probability of cooperation.[44] Belonging, according to this assumption, is a central category for understanding cooperation relations.[45]

Luhmann's social theory is designed precisely from the rejection of the idea of the possibility of an intersubjective (intersystemic) shared context of meaning,[46] but the question about the possibility of such a "common third party" does not have to be decided here. What is sufficient is the finding that the cooperation problem cannot be solved any further within the concept of autopoiesis than is already done in economic theory. In the critique of the economic approaches, it was shown that, under specified conditions, they can explain the solution of the cooperation problem, but the crucial step is a reference system that is binding between the actors, which can be called norms of cooperation, trust, or social capital. The mutual observation of social systems that offer environments for one another cannot be a functional equivalent for this. To this extent, for understanding cooperative relations in the economy, the concept of the self-referential mode of operation of social systems remains behind the theories of Durkheim and Parsons, which presented concepts for an intersubjective horizon of reference in the moral order, in the general system of values, and in the concept of interpenetration of social systems, which could contribute to explaining the stabilization of contexts of cooperation.

However, in the late 1960s, long before the restructuring of his theory on the basis of the concept of autopoiesis, Luhmann dealt with the problem of trust and thus studied the cooperation problem.[47] The considerations elaborated in the book *Trust and Power* (1979), are more easily connected to the problems developed here of explaining cooperation in economic theories. In the study of trust, Luhmann also carries out a radical reversal of the question. The question asked is not how actors can overcome the risk involved with cooperation, but rather what is the *function* of trust for the reproduction of social order. Trust opens possibilities of action that remain closed without it since, because Alter's reaction cannot be foreseen, Ego would not get involved in one-sided advances. Trust enables muting the risk involved with the action, yet without reducing the risk itself. The cognitive act enables advances by making the actors blind to the risk of exploitation; the danger of Alter's withdrawal is not considered, which reduces the complexity of the action situation (Luhmann 1968b:23). Interest is not directed, as in economic theory, to the calculation. The question of why actors decide on the cooperative relation is not answered with reference to long-term utility expectations or stochastic considerations, but with reference to *indifference* and its function. Stabilizing trust takes place with regard to the consequences of nontrust, which are either so great that the very idea is not allowed or are so minor because of differentiation that the disappointment of trust by Alter can cause only minor damage (25). But, with regard to the rationality of decision processes in the sense of an optimal allocation of resources, trust ultimately cannot be substantiated, even if reasons are given by the actors as social justification.

What is important is that, in considering cooperation, in his early work Luhmann emphasizes the significance of intersubjective social contexts that promote relations of trust. These include the relative duration of the relation and the mutual dependence of the actors. The social structure in which the relations of trust are embedded—as Durkheim had already indicated—can compensate at least partially for the lack of information at the starting point of the cooperation problem. The experience that one-sided advances that *can* be exploited do *not* get exploited leads to stabilizing contexts of trust. But Luhmann also refers in the book to socially shared values: only if there are possibilities of sanctions, part of which are social disapproval, can the expectation of the persons involved, who "have to meet again at a later point," become a fertile ground for relations of trust. Moreover, Luhmann refers to the significance of early childhood socialization processes for the development of the ability to trust (26ff.).

Innovation and Intentionality

In the critical examination of a market-determined understanding of technological progress in orthodox economics in chapter 1, the significance of uncertainty for innovative processes was indicated. It was emphasized that the dynamic of technological progress follows "technological trajectories" (Dosi), which can be explained in part by the need to reduce highly complex action situations. But at the same time, innovative processes are not to be understood as a passive adaptation to prevailing structures, but rather require the creativity of actors who are involved in the process of research and development. In his theory of enterprise, Schumpeter points out that we cannot understand the behavior of entrepreneurs from a purely instrumental action orientation because it includes elements of value rational and charismatic action. These elements of understanding innovations in economic contexts call attention to two requirements of a theory of technological change: the theory must include dimensions of structure *and* action, yet a purely instrumental notion of action is insufficient.

If we examine the theory of autopoietic systems against the background of these requirements, it can easily be shown that it introduces structural rigidity as an explanatory variable for systemic events and can also explain with its notion of structure why technological change moves along trajectories. In processes of social change, structures emerge that preshape the selections themselves and are bases for all further structural changes, so that an internal context emerges, which "can be described as the attainment of structures with greater improbability" (Luhmann 1995a:355). But what about the notion of action introduced by Luhmann?[48] Luhmann conceives of actions as "prefabricated and symbolically marked systems . . . assumed by the actors as unproblematic previous knowledge" (Esser 1993:507). This understanding of action connects to the phenomenological tradition of Alfred Schütz, who described the act (*Handlung*) as a "closed unit," a "finished product," "a well-defined experience,"[49] but who also introduced a notion of "action" (*handeln*) into his theory which describes the sequence of the actual behavior. Action as defined by Schütz, at least in the broader sense, agrees conceptually with the notion of action used in sociology since Max Weber, in which action refers to "subjective meaning." What is decisive now is that Luhmann's theory does have access to a notion of "act" but not to one of "action." Accordingly, the act is ascribed to the system and not the person, which is left out of the autopoietic reproduction of the system: "Observers can predict action better by knowing a situation than by knowing people, and, correspondingly, their observation of actions often, if not always, is not concerned with the mental state of the actor, but with carrying out the autopoietic reproduction of the social system" (Luhmann 1995a:166). The notion of act introduced by Luhmann is not linked to the intentionality of actors because it includes not more than an event that other events can connect with. This also means that the question about the types of action is not even raised.

Innovative processes in social systems are studied by Luhmann under the rubric of social change.[50] This is not understood from the perspective of action theory as a result of an intervention in a social system that changes its structures but rather as a self-referential process in which the change of structures can be read in the change of communicative events (Luhmann 1995a:344ff.). Change means the change of expectations in a system, which leads to changed communications. Thus, it can involve an adaptation to a changed environment, accidental events, but also an anticipated structural change. On the level of abstract theory, Luhmann must not be contradicted in the description of social change. Innovations are structural changes on the basis of which systems react with changed connecting communications to environmental events. Innovations can be marked as differences only because they are first known as such when they are selected and, if possible, already represent routines (de Vries 1997). But such an understanding of innovative processes also remains peculiarly empty because the processes located in the acting subjects, which give rise to changed expectations, are not discussed at all. This indicates the weakness of the notion of act introduced by Luhmann, which does not make the contribution of the actors visible for understanding innovative processes. What interests us about innovations is not only the assessment made from the observer's perspective that processes have changed but especially the considerations used by the actors, their motives and their assumptions, which are all together a basis for their creativity in innovative processes.

Luhmann's action model is not developed on the background of understanding creative processes but focuses instead on routines. Dealing with files by a government bureaucrat can be understood at least in large part as an adaptation to prefabricated action sequences for which we do not need to know anything about the person of the official. In this case, too, the act does proceed from the concrete individual person, but it is much more informative to ascribe it to the system and not to the person, which can justify a notion of act that conceptualizes the actor solely as an executor of systemic reproduction. Such strong parallels might exist between dealing with files and the event of an apple falling from a tree that these can be combined into one category. But this definitely does not apply to innovative processes that intentionally break through patterned sequences of action. These can be grasped from the result in the theory of autopoiesis, but the theory remains silent about the question of how new structures come about. The reference is mainly to adaptation, errors, and misunderstanding. What had to be explained was how intentional social change or planned innovations materialize. This would require a much stronger inclusion of processes of consciousness and an understanding of the creativity of actors, which could have been gained by looking into the black box of changed communicative connections.

The discussion of Luhmann's theory with regard to the problems of cooperation and innovation shows that giving up a notion of intersubjectivity and marginalizing the role of actors in systems theory represents serious limitations for the question under discussion here. If the systemic self-logic is all that matters, the process of creative engagement of subjects capable of acting is removed. While the contingency-reducing role of structures indicates a central element for solving problems of acting under conditions of uncertainty, the theory falls short of including the constitutive contribution of actors. This applies because the operation modes of social systems cannot be carried out independent of the actors, although they act against the background of an already structured horizon of experience.

The demands for a theoretically based economic sociology that is to deal with the problems of cooperation, action under uncertainty, and innovation can be formulated more clearly from the discussion of Luhmann's theory. In the discussion of chapter 1, it was claimed that such a theory has to give up the maximizing postulate of economic theory. At the same time, as was shown in the discussion of Luhmann's concept of economics, the theory does not need to lose the action theoretical reference point by observing only the reproduction of systemic structures. It requires an action theory that goes beyond the understanding of rationality of economic theory. But the theory must also possess a notion of intersubjectivity to explain how actors can shape binding behavioral expectations. At the same time, structures, as central elements of the intersubjective shaping of expectations and the reduction of complexity, must be considered prominently in such a theory.

FIVE

ANTHONY GIDDENS: ACTOR AND STRUCTURE

IN ECONOMIC ACTION

Formulating a theory of action in the social sciences demands
theorizing the human agent.
—Anthony Giddens

STUDYING the theories of Durkheim, Parsons, and Luhmann showed that we can infer elements from their sociological concepts of economics which at least partially go beyond the limits of economic theory presented in chapter 1. Yet none of the three theoretical outlines turns out to be sufficiently inclusive to be able to interpret it as a comprehensive solution to the problems cited. The insufficient emphasis of the active and creative role of actors appeared in each of them in a different form as a serious limitation. For the solution of the cooperation problem, Durkheim and Parsons refer to the shared notions of morality or the general system of values. It can be maintained with Durkheim and Parsons that the solution of the pervasive free-rider problem and the prisoners' dilemma requires social norms, but the question of how these norms can guide action in economic contexts of modern societies if they are not effectively assumed by custom or a process of internalization is still open. A theory that wants to answer this question must consider the reflective involvement of actors in the action situation—at least according to the assertion that is yet to be proved.

The discussion of Luhmann's theory showed the significance of structural rigidities for the ability to act in situations with uncertainty. Here, clear connections can be found to the new economic sociology but also to institutional approaches of economic theory. Eric Leifer and Harrison White explain the existence of social network structures in economic contexts with direct recourse to the problem of uncertainty:

> Structures exist and reproduce themselves in part because information needed to pursue maximization and efficiency is not available. In other words, an individual frequently does not know in advance which option will produce, for example, the highest profits or the lowest costs. In these circumstances, the only tangible guidance available to the actor is that which can be inferred from the patterns and outcomes which emerge from relations among actors. (Leifer and White 1986:86)

Institutional organization theory, one of the most important developments in organizational sociology since the 1980s, refers also to institutional rigidification as an explanatory variable for organizational behavior and thereby contradicts the notion of market-determined striving for efficiency. One example is the work of Paul DiMaggio and Walter Powell, "The Iron Cage Revisited: Institutional Isomorphism and Collective Rationality in Organizational Fields" (1983), which is considered one of the classics of institutional organizational theory. DiMaggio and Powell attempt to explain why organizations in their development follow homogenizing tendencies that make them more alike. The rationalization processes of organizations, according to the thesis, are not (only) market-determined but rather are subject to several cultural expectations, legal requirements, the imitation of allegedly successful models, and a normative pressure exercised by professionalization. That these institutional elements can also influence the development of such organizations that are exposed to the pressure of market competition (and therefore must satisfy efficiency requirements) is explained, inter alia, by uncertainty. Uncertainty does not allow actors to deduce optimal structures. Under such situational conditions, imitation of successful organization models can gain acceptance as strategy.

By emphasizing the connection between uncertainty and institutional rigidification, these sociological approaches also agree with the new institutional economics. Oliver Williamson (1975; 1985) explains the emergence of organizations (hierarchies) from market failure caused by transaction costs in contract relations. Hierarchy enables a controlling influence on the action of Alter and is thus, under specified conditions, more transaction-cost-efficient than the market organization of economic activities. Unlike institutional organization theory, however, in the transaction-cost approach, the structure of the organization is understood as an efficient adjustment. The economic historian Douglass North (1990) also sees the function of institutions in economic contexts in their ability to establish stable exchange structures by reducing uncertainty. However, North does not conclude that this efficiency advantage of institutional regulations means that the institutions themselves have to be efficient. Because of political interests and path dependency, institutional design is not only oriented to economic criteria of efficiency. The examples cited here show that extremely varied theoretical approaches examine the relation of uncertainty and institutional rigidification as a decisive variable in explaining the organization of economic activities. These theories, which can be classified with Robert Merton's term "middle-range theories," can attain confirmation on an essentially higher level of abstraction with the help of Luhmann's systems theory.

A criticism cited against Luhmann has been the marginality of actors in this theoretical concept, which brings the theory up against limitations in its understanding of cooperation and innovation. This stands in an interesting agreement with critics of the institutional approach of organization theory and the concept of embeddedness of new economic sociology, who complain about a deficient notion of action in these approaches. Critics of institutional organization theory comment that this theory places too much emphasis on tendencies of homogenization and thus loses sight of the possibility of "strategic choice" (Child 1972) by interest-oriented actors (DiMaggio 1988; Powell 1991; Scott 1991, 1994). If organizational change is understood as a mimetic process, strategic aspects of the achievement of efficiency advantages moves to the background. Institutional forces themselves then become explanatory variables of the dynamic of organizational structures. Richard Whittington (1992) opposed the concept of "embeddedness" introduced by Granovetter (1985), claiming that it was applied too passively and thus left too little room for strategic decisions of managers. The network approach pursued by Granovetter centers on social structures but neglects the structuring significance of action.[1] This agreement with the critique of the concept of autopoietic reproduction in Luhmann's theory is accidental because Luhmann, the institutional organization theory, and the new economic sociology hardly refer to each other; but it does indicate clear parallels in the problematic of these theoretical approaches that start from structural rigidities and tend to reduce the perspective of the actor. Strategic choice after all means that either a choice is made between various existing options or that actors reflect on their decisions on alternatives beyond already realized institutional models.

With the second element, the aspect of innovative activities comes into view. The transition from the theory of organization to the problematic of innovation can easily be produced because one of the two central aspects of innovative activities consists of creating new methods of production—for example, changing the structure of the organization. The distinguishing feature of the institutionalization of new organizational forms is that existing structures are not reproduced but that these are exceeded by new combinations. This going-beyond-the-existing is naturally the defining characteristic for process innovations in general, as well as for the second systematic area of innovative activity, the provision of new products. Innovative activities remain linked with the problematic of uncertainty because the results of the innovative activity remain unknown ex ante. But, at the same time, innovations go beyond the problematic of uncertainty as such because they represent an area of action in which a purely adaptive behavior is excluded. The crucial issue is the construction of new combinations.

But what action theory allows understanding processes of innovation? To elucidate the systematic point of departure of this question and its reference to economic theory, as a transition to the book's last chapter we must once again examine Schumpeter and elaborate his critique of the *action theory* of orthodox economics based on the problematic of innovation. The goal is to obtain starting points for a theory of action that allows the understanding of innovative processes from Schumpeter's considerations.

It was indicated in chapter 1 that, following the tradition of Smith, Walras, Pareto, and Marshall, Schumpeter considered orthodox economic theory thoroughly adequate for the analysis of static economic processes. However, he wanted to see it supplemented by a theory that is also capable of understanding innovative processes. But such a theory, in Schumpeter's opinion, cannot be developed from orthodox economics. Instead, an understanding of the innovative dynamic requires breaking way from the action theory of *homo oeconomicus*. This general line of argumentation runs through all of Schumpeter's work and was already developed in the *Theory of Economic Development* (1961 [1911]). From the macroeconomic perspective, Schumpeter (1961:94) characterizes innovation as sudden change of economic data which, however, cannot be traced back to a change of exogenous variables (e.g., natural catastrophes). Endogenously caused change is not foreseen in neoclassical economic theory. There are no causal-analytical bridges between the previous state and the new situation that could have been anticipated by the theory. Schumpeter changes the perspective by elucidating from the perspective of *action theory* why economic theory cannot explain endogenous change. In the first edition of the *Theory of Economic Development*, Schumpeter introduced the distinction between static-hedonistic behavior and dynamic-energetic or creative action. The *manager* who follows the first type of action is distinguished by orientation to routine and a calculated action, which can be described with the rational-actor model. In contrast is the *entrepreneur* who is defined by his breaking away from this type of action. He devotes himself to the new, takes on unusual tasks, and realizes new combinations in the economy (i.e., innovations). He does this against the pressure for conformity of the social environment. For the activity of the entrepreneur, Schumpeter reserves the category of dynamic-energetic action, whose motive is outside the narrow-minded selfish action of *homo oeconomicus*. In entrepreneurial activity, "there is very little of conscious rationality, still less of *hedonism* and of individualism" (Schumpeter 1961:91), but it rather relies on intrinsic motives like a sense of obligation, joy in creation, and the will to victory.[2]

In the outline for a research project on enterprises, Schumpeter (1991) again assumes this action typological distinction in the 1940s. Now he distinguishes between *adaptive response* and *creative response* as two fundamentally different ways of reacting to changes in environmental conditions. Schumpeter explained the differences in three points. The first characteristic of the *creative response* is that it cannot be deduced ex ante by an observer. Innovative activities cannot be deduced from the data of the situation, and therefore it requires the creative achievement of an actor, which cannot be grasped in the rational-actor model of economic theory. The optimizing postulate dogmatically starts from the premise that, under given conditions, actors use optimal means for maximizing profit or utility. The second dimension refers to the radical qualitative change of the economic situation through innovations, which allows no bridges between the new and the hypothetical condition of the continuity of the old. The third dimension of the *creative response* is that this has to do "with individual decisions, actions, patterns of behavior" (412). This point refers to the indeterminacy of actions through the structure of the situation and to the significance of the acting person and his freedom of decision for the explanation of economic innovations and thus for the dynamic of economic processes. The objective possibilities are realized only through the entrepreneur, from which Schumpeter derives that economic (technological) change in capitalist societies must be investigated by studying entrepreneurial *activities*.

Two results can be seen from Schumpeter's analysis of innovative processes. First, the action theory of orthodox economics is not adequate to understand innovative processes. Second—and this is almost more fundamental—it requires an *action theoretical* approach in the study of innovative processes and the economic dynamic that emerges from it, because the origin of these processes lies in the creative reactions of actors to situational changes. Hence, such structural and systems-theoretical approaches that push the actors to the margin as epiphenomenona are not accepted. At the same time, Schumpeter's analysis should not lead to the conclusion that innovative processes in the economy are to be explained purely voluntaristically from an emphatic notion of praxis. This would be contradicted both by the results of the previous chapter, where the significance of structural rigidities for the maintenance of the capacity for action in complex environments was elaborated, and by findings of the empirical research of innovation, which indicate phenomena of path dependency and of technological trajectories (Dosi 1988). It requires the theoretical anchoring of the significance of routines, social structures, norms, and systemic rigidities that reduce complexity. At the same time, the actor as an active shaper of decisions must find sufficient systematic consideration.

Starting with these considerations, this chapter focuses on structuration theory developed by Anthony Giddens and studies an outline in sociological theory that, referring to interpretive approaches in sociology, is centered emphatically on the constitutive achievements of actors but also considers the significance of social structures for the reproduction and change of society. Since the 1960s, interpretative approaches have gained great significance in sociology, initially as a reaction to the critique of the structural-functionalist paradigm that was dominant at least in American sociology, and whose most important representative was Talcott Parsons. Interpretative approaches study the bases of society from the interactions of actors and thus have a basis in action theory. The two most significant empirically oriented schools of the interpretative approach, ethnomethodology (Garfinkel) and symbolic interactionism (Blumer), have their theoretical bases in phenomenology and in American pragmatism, particularly the work of George Herbert Mead.[3] While ethnomethodological and symbolic-interactionist studies focus on the analysis of everyday interaction situations and thus are primarily classified as microsociology, Anthony Giddens attempted to make interpretative approaches productive for a theory of society that also conceptualized macrosocial structures and their change. On the macrosocial level, structuration theory contrasts critically with functionalist theory, and on the action level with the postulate of control of action through shared values, as well as with the methodological individualism of economic theory. Starting from this line of criticism, Giddens drafts a theory that tries to understand society from the (inter)-subjectively constituted images of the world but in which the structures that actors confront are systematically taken into account. The potential significance of Giddens for the further argumentation of this book can be seen from this program.

Yet, at the same time, the debate with Giddens in the context of considerations of economic sociology is difficult because, for Giddens, unlike the authors previously discussed, economic contexts are not a major subject of study. Giddens makes only a few comments about the economy. Most of them move on a macroeconomic level and are developed in the context of the debate with historical materialism and Weber's theory of capitalism.[4] That Giddens does not discuss the functioning of markets and does not claim to conceptualize decision making in economic contexts based on structuration theory is not synonymous with underestimating the significance of economic structures for the processes of social reproduction, but simply indicates the mainly macroeconomic level considerations in the parts of the theory in which economic issues are discussed. However, another step of differentiation can be seen for the development of the relationship between economics and sociology: the explicit concern with the internal functioning of economic processes occupies only a secondary role.

This material situation does not disqualify Giddens's theory for the goal pursued here only because approaches are included in the conception that allow connecting it to the limits of economic theory elaborated here. This applies for the problem of cooperation as well as for the problem of innovation. However, the marginal position of considerations of economic sociology demands a different procedure from that of the previous chapters: the productivity of Giddens's theory for the questions of cooperation and innovation must be verified by consulting studies in economic sociology of other authors, who either refer directly to Giddens or to the interpretative approaches in sociology that are the basis of Giddens's theory.

In the following sections, I first discuss the bases of Giddens's social theory and illuminate it in relation to economic theory as well as to the sociological theories examined previously. I also examine the basis of Giddens's theory in phenomenology. In the second and third sections of the chapter, starting from the structuration theory, I consider the problems of cooperation and innovation and establish links to studies in economic sociology. In the discussion of structuration theory, it turns out that, with phenomenology, Giddens relies solely on *one* line of theory within the interpretative paradigm but ignores the second theoretical approach, symbolic interactionism and American pragmatism. This bias proves to be a limitation, especially for understanding innovative processes, precisely because conceptions of the creativity of action (Joas), which shed light on basic aspects of innovation, are included in pragmatism. Hence, in the last section, going beyond Giddens, I also examine pragmatist conceptions.

Interpretation and the Structure of Economic Action

Giddens explained the connection of his thought with motives of interpretative sociology most clearly in the volume titled *New Rules of Sociological Method* (1976). Here, Giddens treied to explain his theoretical outline based on epistemological discussions. We shall not get into a comprehensive discussion of the book here, especially since the more mature presentation of the theoretical positions can be found in the later work, *The Constitution of Society* (1984), but shall deal only with the single aspect of Gidden's adoption of interpretative sociology.

The basic starting point of Giddens's considerations is the unavoidable separation between natural and social phenomena, and the question of the resulting epistemological consequences for the social sciences. Giddens (1984:21) argues that a sociology aspiring to the positivistic ideal of science will always miss its subject matter, because in giving up the notion of understanding it disregards the ontological condition of human social life. The constitution of society take places in processes of interaction, in which actors refer meaningfully to one another and thus create, reproduce, to change social objectivity: "one *actually creates* social life through interaction with members of one's society" (23). This already shows Giddens's proximity to phenomenological sociology, whose declared program is to describe the structures of the living world through understanding the meaning connected with the actions. Thus, it is not surprising that Giddens sees two central sources for his social theory in the sociologcal phenomenology developed by Alfred Schütz and the ethnomethodology of Harold Garfinkel, which essentially influenced Schütz.

The Phenomenological Background

Before I get into Giddens's critical debate with phenomenology, I expound a few fundamental thoughts of Alfred Schütz to appreciate the potential of phenomenology for our question here. In the context of the search for the foundations of the action theory of economic sociology, the debate with phenomenological approaches may initially appear disconcerting for phenomenology is linked with socioculturally oriented studies of everyday behavior and not with the study of economic structures. In terms of the history of theory, however, this evaluation fails to see that Alfred Schütz's basis of phenomenological sociology in *Der sinnhafte Aufbau der sozialen Welt* (1993 [1932]) was intended to contribute to the solution of epistemological problems of the Austrian School of Economics founded by Carl Menger. Christopher Prendergast (1986), whose comments I refer to below, pointed out this connection and elaborated the significance of Schütz's affiliation for more than a decade with the seminar of Ludwig von Mises—Menger's "successor" as the leading representative of the Austrian School—for the development of Schütz's work.

When Schütz came upon the Mises seminar in 1922 in Vienna, the Austrian School was in an epistemological and methodological crisis, caused mainly by the controversial logical status of the asserted economic laws. Carl Menger had declared their validity a priori, which was attacked both by the representatives of the Historical School in Germany and by logical positivism which rejected synthetic judgments a priori. Such judgments were criticized either as being tautologies or as conventions. This situation provided essential motives for Schütz's work and the interest of the representatives of the Austrian School in Schütz's reconceptualization of Weber's notion of the ideal type. Moreover, however, Schütz also saw that a theory of intersubjective understanding was necessary for the subjective concept of value of the Austrian School, to give a plausible explanation of how actors understand the preferences of other actors. Such a theory was not presented, and the objective of Schütz's debate with Weber's sociology was to fill in these gaps. Hence, Schütz's early work is closely linked with virulent discussions within economic theory. *Der sinnhafte Aufbau der sozialen Welt* was not merely to produce a synthesis of Husserl and Weber but aimed mainly at solving open questions of neoclassical economics. Schütz's book can be placed alongside those of Durkheim, Weber, and Parsons, to the extent that the debate with economic questions was also central for the development of the work.[5]

However, we are less concerned here with revealing links in terms of the history of theory than with the substantial contribution of phenomenology to the discussed problems of economic action, which is inherent in the emphasis of the interpretative nature of action and in the concept of intersubjectivity. The central question for Schütz was how actors can succeed in social praxis in understanding others and their actions. For Schütz, as for Weber, action is always linked with meaning, and *verstehen* means knowing this meaning. According to Schütz, actors must succeed in shaping notions about the subjective structure of meaning, which grants every actor a reference to the meaning that other actors link with their actions. Hence, actors have to interpret their own actions and the actions of others. This conception initially appears as purely subjective. In fact, however, for the interpretative act, the actors resort to the frame of reference of the *life world*, where previous knowledge, experiences, and schemes of interpretation are found, and which provide the context of interpretation. "All interpretation of this world is based on a stock of previous experiences of it, our own or those handed down to us by parents or teachers; these experiences in the form of 'knowledge at hand' function as a scheme of reference" (Schütz 1967:7). The life world is in this sense not a private world, but a public one, which, despite different perspectives, is shared, which is a prerequisite for joint action. The rules of the life world usually cannot be verbalized by the actors, but are available only as implicit knowledge revealed in action. Schütz also supports the dimension of intersubjectivity by assuming the reciprocity of perspectives, which starts from the notion that the perspectives of the actors can be exchanged in principle—if I want to, I can see the world with the eyes of the other. The result is that, through our interpretations, we always perceive only a part of the "world horizon" (Husserl), but in principle we can also know the other aspects. Through the life world schemes of interpretation, a typification takes place that leads to the subjective circumscription of the horizon of possibility; through the use of patterns of interpretation, it allows the action of the other to be understood and to find an at least undefined familiarity in novelty. What is significant from the horizon of the life world depends on the *relevance* that is determined by the current interests of the actor, but which can be constantly changed by his *social position*. A change of the relevance system leads to a changed typification, that is, to another view of the object. Schütz understands action as a *process* shaped by outlines of the idea of a desired situation. This meaning, or the intentionality of action, can be seen in the action motives. Schütz (1967:10) stresses emphatically that the context of meaning, which makes up the world of the social, emerges from the process of human action: "All cultural objects—tools, symbols, language systems, works of art, social institutions, etc.—point back by their very origin and meaning to the activities of human subject. . . . For the same reason, I cannot understand a cultural object without referring it to the human activity from which it originates."

An important distinction especially for the cooperation problematic is made with the differentiation of social relations according to face-to-face relations, which require the physical presence of the other, and relations to *contemporaries* with whom the common ground of space and time is not shared. Schütz emphasizes the special nature of the face-to-face relation, which allows experiencing the person of the other as a unique individual, whereas relations to contemporaries are produced by means of typifications. Face-to-face relations have a higher degree of intimacy and allow the constitution of a common We in interaction, which transcends the individual meaning. Thus, the face-to face relationship is ascribed a quality in which the action goes beyond purely individual motives, which is also a central condition to explain cooperative features in those situations where individual advantages consist of pursuing a strategy of defection. The argument, therefore, is that the constitutive character of social relations and the intersubjectivity emerging from them is a central explanatory variable of cooperative relations. This idea finds support in Schütz's discussion of environmental social relationships in the early work, *Der sinnhafte Aufbau der sozialen Welt*:

> In the environmental social relation, an individual act intentionally related to the You is not isolated; instead such a relationship is constituted only in a *continuous series of such acts*, and the attitude relation in acts of attitude to strangers, the effect relation in acts of producing meaning and interpreting meaning. . . . This meshing of mutually based looking at the awareness of the You, this look as it were in one of a thousand facets of a polished mirror, from which my Self is reflected in the image, really constitutes the exceptional feature of the environmental social relation. But because the pure face-to-face relation, on which all experience of the environmental You is based, is not grasped *reflecting* in the environmental social relation, but is rather simply *experienced*, these individual mirrorings are not separate, but are brought into the view as a unity. *In a unity, the Self can look simultaneously at the phased constructing experiences of his own consciousness and at the phased sequence of events in consciousness of the You, and experience both sequences as a single one, as that of the common We.* (Schütz 1993:236ff.)

This characterization of the face-to-face relation is reminiscent of the social constitution of the self in Mead. It can be pointed out, however, that the face-to-face relation is the *only* situation in which the priority of the consciousness of individual subjects is broken through unequivocally in Schütz (Coenen 1985:96). In his debate with Schütz's work, Herman Coenen pointed out that, although it is true that concepts are found, particularly in *The Collected Papers*, that explain a social influence on individual consciousnness by socially preconstituted meaning, this does not lead to a theory of intersubjectivity in which the ultimate priority of the individual consciousness is removed. The life world, typification, and roles do refer to the significance of the social, but, according to Schütz, social knowledge exists "always only isolated, that is, as knowledge of the respective concrete subject" (Coenen 1985:93).

Giddens refers in his works not only to the phenomenology of Alfred Schütz, but especially to ethnomethodology established by Harold Garfinkel. Garfinkel builds strongly on Schütz on the background of a critique of his teacher Talcott Parsons. If Parsons assumes that social relations "succeed," because the actions of the actors can be coordinated by the general system of values, Garfinkel points to the "incompleteness" of norms and values that cannot induce concrete actions automatically. Instead, it requires the constant reproduction of a normality acknowledged by the interaction partners through reinterpretations of the situation. The crucial question for Garfinkel is how actors actually manage the normality of interaction in daily life. What is primarily important here are not scientific standards of rationality or a general system of values, but rather the willingness of the actors to maintain "normal" communications, even in the absences of a (normative) consensus, through acts of interpretation of the action of the other actors. The detailed analysis of everyday sequences of interaction reveals the many silent, never explicitly compatible assumptions, which must be maintained by the participants for successful interaction. Garfinkel's famous breaking experiments serve to discover the means with which actors maintain at least the impression of intersubjectivity and thus prevent the breakdown of communication. The task of normalization insists on a willingness for ad hoc negotiation and innovation in the situation.

Bases of the Structuration Theory

The phenomenological approach shows a changed concept of action that differs from the action theories of Durkheim and Parsons. It is based less on integrating action by norms than emphasizing the *process character of action*. In the act itself, the structure of expectation is formed, which is objectified as life world, but without getting away from the subjective performance of action. Shaping expectations is also a cognitive process, for which classifications, rules, typifications, and normalizations are as important as identification and internalization. On an epistemological

level, Giddens's social theory connects with phenomenological approaches by emphasizing the inescapable significance of the interpretation
of action situations by "laymen" for understanding the objective structure
of the social. Social theory cannot come up with any scientific standards
of rationality in the interactions of the actors but must get involved with
the interpretations found there. This leads to the emphatic inclusion of
the actors as creators of social structures. At the same time, Giddens dissociates himself from the phenomenological approaches discussed with two
arguments: on the one hand, he accuses the phenomenology of Alfred
Schütz of not really working its way to a notion of intersubjectivity;
Schütz "retains the umbilical tie to the subjectivity of the ego which distinguishes [Husserl's] elaboration of transcendental phenomenology" (Giddens 1976:31). On the other hand, he accuses the interpretative approaches of neglecting the significance of social power and structural
rigidities in their analysis of everyday interaction situations (64). As already noted, the first point of criticism in the interpretation of Schütz's
work is often mentioned (Bernstein 1976; Coenen 1985). Of course, there
is in Schütz a special sensibility for the problem of intersubjectivity because the missing concept of intersubjectivity in marginalist economics
was one of the two central motives for his work in the 1930s. But Schütz
ultimately cannot get far enough away from the centrality of the subject
in Husserl to achieve a concept of intersubjectivity that does not have its
ontological starting point in individual consciousness.

But if this is so and is also seen this way by Giddens, then it is incomprehensible that he turns to the philosophies of language of Austin and Witt-
genstein but not to the concepts of intersubjectivity in the tradition of
American pragmatism. This is significant from a sociological perspective
because symbolic interactionism brings in another interpretative research
program, which goes back to the concepts of George Herbert Mead and
pragmatism, in which the problem of intersubjectivity is handled by a
theory of the social constitution of the individual. It is also incomprehensible because Giddens is concerned with emphasizing the creative nature of
human action (Giddens 1984:23). For understanding creativity the action
theory of pragmatism is especially significant, and so at the end of the
chapter, in the context of discussing innovations, I elaborate more precisely on pragmatist conceptions.

Giddens's second point of criticism of the interpretative approaches
discussed by him is their neglect of the dimension of social power. Structuration theory (Giddens 1984) can be read as an attempt to connect
motifs of interpretative sociology with the examination of the significance
of power and history (social change). For this, the field of tension between
the intentionality of action and structures is discussed, which the actors
produce unintentionally through their actions and which they encounter

again as conditions of action. It is this interaction between actor and structure, safeguarded in the premises of the theory, that Giddens's theory protects against both poles of reducing action to structures and neglecting structural limitations in social theories based only on praxis or voluntarism. Indeed, Giddens has been repeatedly reproached with overestimating the significance of actors for the course of social development (Callinicos 1985; Clegg 1989; Collins 1992), but the dualistic construct of the theory refers to the nonreducibility of structural rigidities, so that a one-sided emphasis of one of the two sides does not result inherently from the theoretical construct. Insofar as interpretative approaches speak of the construction of social reality in action, structuration theory is also interested in the significance of purposeful human action for the reproduction of social order but connects this notion of praxis with the acknowledgment of the significance for understanding the options of actors.

The central concept of structuration theory, which expresses this interaction, is that of the "duality of structure." With it, Giddens tries to overcome a dichotomous confrontation of subject and object, action and system, and process and structure, and to express the systematic linking of the respective poles. Structures are the result of action, and at the same time, action is formed by existing structures, which have both a limiting and an enabling effect. In the systematic connection of structure and action, structures lose any ontological independence because they acquire significance only in actions as remembered codes of behavior or as resources.[6] "Human social activities, like some self-reproducing items in nature, are recursive. That is to say, they are not brought into being by social actors but continually recreated by them via the very means whereby they express themselves *as* actors" (Giddens 1984:2).

A discussion of Giddens's notion of action and structure and their connection is necessary to understand the basic concept of structuration theory. In structuration theory, action is understood as a possibility "to make a difference"; the actor could have acted differently in a given situation.[7] Ability to act in this sense implies interventions that influence or transform social events. For this, with the notion of resources, focus shifts to an element of social practice, which refers to how social influence can be exercised. Giddens distinguishes between authoritative resources, which denote the possibility of exercising influence over other persons, and allocative resources, the power to use natural resources. Access to resources is a prerequisite for action. The significance of social *power* in historical processes and the structuring significance of economic power result from the notion of resources. Yet, historically, how resources are distributed between actors remains an open question. The emphasis on allocative resources for social practices and the structuring processes that emerge from it leads Giddens to an understanding of the economy, which links it to social practices. Because social relations can be dominated by the use of material resources, so the actor can influence them in his own interest, they play a significant role. But then the economy is not a delimited social area that can be defined substantively but is rather an aspect of social practices. This "embedding" of the economy categorically excludes understanding social processes of change solely as economically determined. Instead, rules and various resources, mediated through the action, are to be examined for the recursive emergence of systemic rigidities.

In this notion of action, the actor is granted a constitutive role in the social process of reproduction. The determination of action through structures (rules and resources) is excluded, and thus a voluntary factor is systematically established. Structuration theory, in agreement with ethnomethodology, thus contrasts with the idea that action can be understood as a simple carrying out of preconceived intentions or internalized models of values (cf. Joas 1993:172ff.). Another result is that the notion of action in Giddens is not constructed from the notion of action goals and is thus dissociated from the teleological action model of economics. Instead, the unity of action is constituted in the recursive process between action and structure.

The voluntaristic element of the theory is counterbalanced, first, by granting routines a prominent significance to explain sequences of action and, second, by emphasizing the role played by unintentional results of action in the structuration process.[8] Repetition has the unintended consequence of reproducing standardized social practices and thus assumes an important function: "Routine is integral both to the continuity of the personality of the agent, as he or she moves along the paths of daily activities, and to the institutions of society, which *are* such only through their continued reproduction" (Giddens 1984:60). Thus, Giddens assumes a dominant structural element of stability in social order (which was already present in Durkheim) but also in phenomenology and in ethnomethodology. Durkheim saw habit as a prerequisite for shaping a moral order that allows the rise of reciprocal expectations of action. But Giddens does not explain routines from their function of stabilizing social relations and does not see the motive for routinized action in complying with norms but rather in an ontological need for security, which is derived from the developmental psychology of Erik Erikson.[9] For Giddens, the need for continuity in social interaction is *one* explanatory element of relations of trust.

The recognition of unintended consequences of action, which is, of course, not new for sociology, acquires significance in the relationship between action and structure: in their actions, actors produce and reproduce those structures they encounter as conditions of action without being able to control intentionally their concrete content. Unintended consequences of action exclude a control of the social by the actors. Unlike the use of the concept of unintended consequences of action in functionalist theory (Merton 1936), however, Giddens (1984:63) claims no latent functional rationality that allows actors to become simple bearers of mechanisms for social reproduction that are not transparent to them. It is instead simply undecided whether unintentionally reproduced structures contribute to filling a function or not. Finally, effects that not only are not wished for by any of the actors involved but also fill no function also result.

The critical debate with functionalism does not end in the economic theory of action for Giddens. Giddens (1982:527ff.; 1984:213) does agree with the critique of functionalist theory by representatives of methodological individualism, yet he objects to reducing society to individuals.[10] Instead, a sociological action theory, as Giddens (1982:534) elaborates in reference to Charles Taylor, must take account of the general, intersubjective meaning of action and therefore cannot start from isolated actors. In this sense, the notion of structure introduced by Giddens is also to be understood as referring to the socially shared action references, expressed in the notion of rules.

But Giddens's action theory is also different from economic individualism insofar as no action typological definitions are found in the notion of action. Precisely here an important opening can be seen, which does not commit the actors to purposive-rational action, through the premises of the theory. The notions of reflexive monitoring and practical consciousness introduced by Giddens into the description of action dissolve the separation of goal setting and action that characterizes the economic model of action into a recursive process. In this process, actors can use their knowledge about the mechanisms of system reproduction reflexively to influence and modify systemic processes. The distinction between unconscious motives of action, practical consciousness, and discursive consciousness indicates a much more complex theory of action than that of methodological individualism; reifying the control of action through fixed ends is thus rejected. The notion of "mutual knowledge," introduced with reference to the phenomenological tradition, refers to a knowledge about how interaction processes can be continued that is used implicitly by actors in sequences of action. Actors are often not aware of motives for actions and they appear in rationalized form on the discursive level. Actions are often not even guided by motives but rather play out as unreflected routines. "The *durée* of human action does presuppose intentionality, but for the most part this operates on the level of 'practical consciousness'—which is not a matter of deliberated processes of decision-making, but rather a routine 'monitoring' of the grounds of conduct in the everyday enactment of social life" (Giddens 1982:535ff.).

Giddens's notion of structure is different both from the functional and from the structural traditions of sociological theory.[11] In functional approaches, structures appear external to acts, which bring order into social action and allow for stable social relations. In structuralist thought, on the other hand, structures are interpreted as firm systems of relations that can be known by means of action manifestations. Giddens objects to both uses of the notion of structure, arguing that the praxis aspect of the ordering task of structures is insufficiently considered. Accordingly, he defines structures as reproduced social practices that influence sequences of actions over time and space as rules and resources.

> To say that structure is a "virtual order" of transformative relations means that social systems, as reproduced social practices, do not have "structures" but rather exhibit "structural properties," and that structure exists, as time-space presence, only in its instantiations in such practices and as memory traces orienting the conduct of knowledgeable human agents. (Giddens:1984:17)

In this action-centered understanding of structures, institutions are only practices that have a large space-time distantiation and thus are at the end of a continuum, whose other extreme is found in rules emerging spontaneously in interaction. This notion of structure thought from action practices once again reveals how close structuration theory is to phenomenological approaches in sociology, which refer to the emergence of "ad hoc" rules in social relations and thus to the subjectivity and reflexivity of structures (Garfinkel 1967). For Giddens (1984:77ff.), structures are not external to actors but exist only in the memory of the actors and through their realization in action. In this respect, they are an "internal" component of action. At the same time, emphasis on the significance of rules for action removes theory from the the idea of unrestricted individual utility maximization.

The Structuration of Economic Action

But what is the significance of structuration theory for the problems raised here of a sociological conceptualization of economic action? Analogous to the previous chapters, the obvious procedure would be to trace Giddens's concern with questions of economic sociology and thus attain a position to assess Giddens's contribution. In the introduction, I already indicated that, unlike the three sociologists previously examined, Giddens deals with the economy mainly from a macrosociological perspective, and does not try to develop a sociological outline of the analysis of market structures and the problems of action theory contained in them. Support for the assertion that there are conceptual elements in Giddens's structuration theory that can serve as bases for economic sociology requires applying general theoretical conceptions to questions of economic sociology. But, first, I elaborate on the few debates with economic issues in Gidden's own works.

Examining the changes of economic institutions in the capitalistic process of modernization and the formation of nation-states is the main concern in these works. In *The Nation State and Violence* (1987a), resorting to the works of Max Weber and Karl Marx, Giddens emphasizes the significance of the rise of labor markets, the concentration of production in hierarchically structured organizations, cost calculation, and financial accounting for capitalist development. The significance of a legal system in the framework of the nation-state, covered by a force of sanction, which protects property rights and introduces regulative interventions into market transactions (Giddens 1987a:148ff.), is also emphasized. Special significance is granted to the monetary system to explain the link between capitalistic development and the rise of the modern nation-state: a monetary system is historically possible only after the rise of a government machinery that has a monopoly on the internal order of the state. Giddens sees the social significance of the spread of money transactions essentially in allowing for time-space distantiation: market transactions are taken out of local contexts and the present as the time horizon.[12] Money is thus a mechanism for "disembedding" social relations in modern societies. However, Giddens is interested in studying the effect of money mainly with regard to the macrosociological explanation of capitalist development and its relation to shaping the nation-state. Monetarizing the exchange of goods results in changed possibilities of taxation, which function to reinforce centrist structures; the imposition of local taxes by the landed aristocracy (often in kind) is increasingly replaced by centralized and monetarized taxation, which both expresses the weakened position of the aristocracy and actively accelerates it (Giddens 1987a:158).

I do not pursue these development processes of economic institutions here—not because they are not interesting but because they do not concern the level of the systematic problem pursued here. What is studied are not the institutional prerequisites of the evolution of modern capitalist structures but rather specified action problems of actors in economic contexts. Only the essay "Social Theory and Problems of Macroeconomics" (1987b), where Giddens studies the relation between the theory of rational expectations and structuration theory, while explaining the relationship of action and structure in the field of economics, is significant for this question. The central thesis of the essay consists of the assertion of a parallel development of social theory and economic theory: the prevailing consensus in both disciplines until the 1960s (functionalism in sociology, Keynesianism in economics) collapsed at about the same time, and since the 1970s a theoretical development has opened in both fields, which presents methodological correspondences. This assertion is especially surprising because, on the part of economics, Giddens cites the theory of rational expectations as the key witness for this development; by radicalizing the economic assumptions of rationality and emphasizing market-clearing equlibria, this theory must be considered in many respects as another distancing of economic theory from sociological conceptualizations of the economy. For Giddens, then, the parallels apply not on the level of assumed action rationality and expected macroeconomic results but rather in the relation between the economic concepts developed in both social sciences and the social problems analyzed by them. With the notion of double hermeneutic, Giddens refers to a unique epistemological feature of the social sciences, as distinct from the natural sciences—that is, the existence of feedback effects between knowledge of the subject and the behavior of the scientific objects. The student of the social world is himself not separated from it but instead changes the social world itself by the influence of the knowledge of social processes. "The point is that reflection on social processes (theories, and observations about them) continually enter into, become disentangled with and re-enter the universe of events that they describe" (Giddens 1984:xxxiii).[13]

Giddens applies this idea, which is central for structuration theory, to the theory of rational expectations. The conclusions of the theory of rational expectations for economic policy, starting from the works of John Muth (1961) in the 1960s, and developed further by Robert Lucas (1972), claim an influence of the knowledge of economic actors on the effect of Keynsian instruments of economic policy. The background for this is the assumption that actors find themselves in a constant learning process in which they can optimize their expectations. In consequence they make no mistakes in forecasting economic events. Under the assumption that actors can correctly forecast the consequences of fiscal and monetary measures of the government, monetary policy can be counteracted by the actions of the actors and thus have no influence on economic events. The conclusion consists of rejecting Keynesian interventions because they must necessarily be based on the unconvincing assumption that, in pursuing its fiscal and monetary policy, the government has information that is not available to the other actors. The theory of rational expectations also functions as a self-fulfilling prophecy that first provides actors with the theoretical knowledge necessary to neutralize monetary and fiscal policy effectively. The not trivial conclusion is: "Keynesianism can only be effective in circumstances in which the majority of the population, or certain key sets of business actors, do not know what Keynesianism is" (Giddens 1987b:201). Giddens is not interested in defending the heroic assumptions of rationality in the theory of rational expectations, which he criticizes, but only in the principle of the effects of knowledge about economic correlations to these correlations themselves.[14] "In common with social theory, economic theory can no longer proceed without incorporating and understanding of the modes in which its own conceptions shape the environment it seeks to describe" (200).

This representation of a "double hermeneutics" in the economy indeed refers only to what Giddens sees as a central epistemological element of the social sciences, which must be taken into account to conceptualize action in economic contexts based on structuration theory. This still says nothing about the substantive elaboration of such a conceptualization because Giddens rejects the claim of rationality of the theory of rational expectations and substitutes the much weaker notion of "knowledgeability."[15] Thus, all forecasting possibilities of the theory of rational expectations, based on the strong information assumptions of the economic model, disappear. Giddens does not show what macroeconomic results are to be expected in light of a theory that starts from much weaker assumptions of rationality. Does a Keynesian fiscal and monetary policy function because the information necessary to neutralize it is not available to the actors? Are economic incidents much stronger accidental events in which unintended outcomes have incalculable consequences? How do actors in such an extremely uncertain field make decisions? These questions follow from the essay, but Giddens himself does not work on them. In any case, the emphasis on unintended outcomes of action stemming from the rejection of the strong assumptions of rationality and the indication of a side of Keynes neglected in neoclassical economics—that is, the emphasis of the significance of uncertainty and irrational action—can presage the direction a conceptualization of economic processes guided by structuration theory could take.

The missing formulation of Giddens's theory for economic issues does not in principle reflect a blind spot that would lead to the conclusion that such a conceptualization is not possible. On the contrary, we shall demonstrate that insights beyond the sociological theories previously discussed, which are interesting for understanding cooperation and innovation, can be developed from structuration theory. The next two sections are intended to carry out this task. I first discuss the problem of cooperation, then that of innovation in conjunction with it. The problematic of uncertainty will not be raised again separately, but it appears in connection with innovations.

Cooperation and Reflexivity

The cooperation problem studied in chapter 1 based on game theory is that rational actors in noncooperative games like the prisoners' dilemma do not always achieve optimal equilibria. Aside from the possibility of supergames, Pareto-inferior equilibria can be prevented only when actors are led to act "irrationally" as defined by the theory of rational choice. The introduction of social norms has a central significance both in discussions of the rational-choice literature and in sociological analyses of the cooperation problem.[16] Social norms defect from the pursuit of individually rational strategies, which are pursued in the absence of such norms. Explanations for the effect of social norms, which start from the theory of rational choice, see sanctions as the basis for norm-oriented action and try to reconstruct compliance with norms as rational individual action strategy: in the choice of their action strategy, actors calculate the costs of sanctions. On the other hand, the notion of norms elaborated in the chapters on the economic sociology of Durkheim and Parsons sees actors as incorporated into a moral order and oriented to its normative imperatives, independent of calculations of utility. For Parsons, sanctions also play a significant role, but compliance comes from the internalization of patterns of values in the socialization process, which transcends individual considerations of selfish utility maximization. Both notions of norms were criticized: a purely instrumental attitude toward norms would not lead to the desired results of action because, especially in large groups, sanctions could not be optimally imposed because of incomplete possibilities of mutual observation of the action of every other actor, and in addition the second-order free-rider problem arises. The sociological notion of norms, on the other hand, relies too much on the structuring effect of morality for social action. In Durkheim, the strong systematic reference to moral integration in premodern societies (making guilds and professional groups analogous) leads to an overestimation of the regulating force of socially obligatory norms for modern societies. In Parsons, too, the general system of values achieves predominance on the basis of the strong assumption of action-shaping internalization processes, which underemphasizes the significance of selfish individual motives. Economic contexts of modern societies are conveyed by instrumental action orientations, and externalized costs must be expected to lead to the erosion of the willingness for cooperative advance concessions of other actors (see Mansbridge 1990b:136).

Can structuration theory help us get closer to the assumptions of cooperative relations in the economic contexts of modern societies? Giddens examines cooperation in the discussion of trust. The relationship of the

two ideas is obvious: one-sided advances by Ego, either in exchange relations or in cooperation characterized by the division of labor, can be expected only when Ego starts with the assumption that the advance is not
exploited by Alter through defection. It is precisely this expectation that
can be described as trust. It is significant if we assume neither that sanctions guarantee cooperative action nor that value orientations direct action always at cooperation. Undoubtedly, we can observe trust in modern
societies; without trust economic relations would be crippled because of
prohibitively high transaction costs.[17] But how can structuration theory
help explain this existence of trust?

According to Giddens, economic relations in premodern societies are
distinguished by a minimal need to trust. There is not much division of
labor and only inchoate exchange relations. At the same time, social structures are suitable for solving the cooperation problem. In *The Consequences of Modernity*, Giddens (1990:100ff.) refers to four ways to organize the integration of action available in premodern societies which can
also be applied to economic contexts. The first means of organization is
kinship. Among relatives, one can usually be sure that the parties involved
adhere to the accepted obligations, independent of considerations of individual advantages. Second is the integration of action by the narrowly
circumscribed geographic context of action favored by the local community. The relatively low mobility contributes, in Giddens's terminology, to
the ontological security of the actors.[18] Third, religious cosmologies supply
moral and practical interpretations of personal and social life as well as
of the natural environment (Giddens 1990:103). The options of all actors
are regulated by religious stipulations, which allow every individual actor
to anticipate reactions to his actions very reliably.[19] Fourth, Giddens (104)
cites tradition as a means of structuring the future by extrapolating from
the patterns of action proved in the past. Tradition is closely connected
with routine and habit, and thus also a means of reducing the options of
Alter, whose acts can thus be foreseen by Ego. Giddens develops these
four means of stabilizing social relations in premodern societies against
the background of the general question of how environments of trust are
created in this type of society. Their applicability to the question of stabilizing relations of economic cooperation is limited by the fact that these
contexts of trust of premodern societies also contribute essentially to *preventing* the spread of the division of labor and consequently cooperation
and exchange relations emerging from it. When property rights are connected with religious cosmologies, economic action is oriented to traditions, and family relations regulate possible cooperation and exchange
relations, then economic development is restricted. Overcoming these par-
ticularities was seen in sociological theory—in both Weber and Luhmann—as a prerequisite for the rise of modern economic structures. How-

ever, the organizational means of integrating action in premodern societies are not "constructed" with regard to the rise of more efficient markets and thus do not have to prove themselves in relation to this criterion.

The development of modern capitalist societies goes in tandem with at least the tendency to destroy the contexts of trust that could assume the central function for solving the cooperation problem. But because this concurrence is not contingent itself but only reflects two connected sides of the process of modernization, the unavoidable problem of market exchange and cooperation in modern societies consists of allowing cooperation without being able to rely on the trust mechanisms of premodern societies. Repressing tradition is also a serious prerequisite for the rise of economic structures characterized by the division of labor because it releases the actors from particularistic bonds.

Conceptualization of cooperative relations in economic sociology must do justice to this ineluctably ambivalent background of increasing contingency of action expectations and a growing need to shape stable contexts of trust. Giddens's theory reflects this changed situation, by appealing to the significance of a reflexive form of social relations for shaping environments of trust in modern societies, along with the aspect of stabilized structures of expectation firmly rooted in the notion of ontological security. Giddens emphasizes the need of reflexive or recursive anchoring of reciprocal expectations of action in interaction processes, which results from the *disembedding* of institutions and social practices from local contexts determined by traditions. The contingency of cooperative relations demands their stabilization through active obligations from the actors. Trust must be constantly renewed in communications processes. It is not enough for actors to rely on the structuring influence of tradition, custom, and religious cosmologies, and there is no direct equivalent for that. Instead, relations of trust must be deliberately produced and reproduced. Giddens expresses this crucial idea in the notion of "active trust" (Giddens 1994b:186), with which he emphasizes the increasing dependence of modern societies on a discursive and dialogic commitment of potentially conflicting actors. The functioning of social integration changes because solidarity has to be produced and cannot be extrapolated from the past.

> Trust has to be won and actively sustained; and this now ordinarily presumes a process of mutual narratives and emotional disclosure. An "opening out" to the other is a condition of the development of a stable tie—save where traditional patterns are for one reason or another reimposed, or where emotional dependencies or compulsions exist. (Giddens 1994b:187)

The basic trust formed in childhood development is very important for the ability of the actors to enter into relations of trust at all, but only in connection with communicative processes does this foundation lead to forming contexts of trust. Active trust is central for cooperation in view of the time-space distantiation and the loss of guidance of action through tradition; but it is only to be achieved in communicative processes.

This connection of trust and personal relations also applies to trust in abstract expert systems. The shift of trust in persons to trust in abstract systems is a characteristic of modernity, which is distinguished by time-space distantiations. In the terminology of economic theory, it concerns relations with asymmetrical distribution of information, which can be the causes of the principal-agent problems cited in chapter 1, as well as moral hazard and adverse selection. The systems function only when sufficient trust is shown for them; even a minor doubt in trustworthiness, as shown by the example of banks, can have disastrous consequences. Referring to the work of Erving Goffman, Giddens deals with the social mechanisms through which systems reproduce the necessary trust. Here a link with the levels of system and person takes place because trust in abstract systems can be maintained only in the presence of social relations and, therefore, always requires a personal commitment. Expert systems, on the one hand, have institutional mechanisms that lead to the depersonalization of trust. These include the clear separation between performances "on stage" and the implementation of activity "backstage" (Goffman 1959), which prevent negative repercussions on trust from the revelation of insufficient professional mastery and human error. But we must also include the mechanisms of trust that relate to the internal events in expert systems by regulating activity through stipulations or an institutionalized professional morality. On the other hand, it must be possible to meet representatives of the abstract system in person. The representatives signal trustworthiness at entrance points by their performances. These include especially conveying an "attitude of business-as-usual" (Giddens 1990:85), which soothes users of the expert systems with regard to the reliability and security of the system.

Thus, trust in abstract expert systems must always be produced continuously again in communicative processes; it cannot be taken for granted. The organizational means of stabilizing social relations in premodern societies, like kinship, tradition, and religious cosmology, confront the actors as always given. They exercised a structuring influence on actions but did not become conscious as *contingent* rigidities. However, the trust granted expert systems by actors can always be revoked, and the actors are aware of this revocability. The "guardians" of tradition in premodern societies had a special access to the sacred, whereas experts in modern societies possess a technical competence, which laymen can also acquire in principle and which, moreover, is always controversial because of divergent expert opinion. Experts do not possess esoteric knowledge or privileged access to the "sacred," and so the competence awarded them and the trust placed in them are contingent. The uncertainty arising from this contingency is counteracted by institutionalized signals, but this again refers to the contingency of trust in the expert system. "Given the divided and contested character of expertise, the creation of stable abstract systems is a fraught endeavor" (Giddens 1994a:90).

The contingency of trust in abstract systems is not only established on individual levels but is also conveyed socially because the relation to the abstract systems depends on life-styles that can themselves change. The questioning of trust in technology, through social movements, can lead to negative influences on the economic system, so that the contingency of life-styles can produce tensions in overall processes of social reproduction.[20] Only through the constant *communicative reproduction of trust* can the possible insecurity growing out of the contingency of the situation be absorbed and thus prevent the implosion of the social situation.

In Giddens's argumentation, two categories of trust elements are thus considered for relations of cooperation. As an integration mechanism, the need for the active generation of trust in deliberative processes functions along with routine and habit, which have a fundamental significance for achieving the individual's ontological security.[21] But as Giddens's crucial step with regard to the previously discussed theories, I would emphasize the stress on the deliberative commitments of the actors for the production and maintenance of relations of cooperation.[22]

Giddens develops this linking of trust and discursive processes independent of economic questions,[23] but the link can be produced by enlisting studies in economic sociology. To show this, I discuss four empirical studies that refer to Giddens's structuration theory as well as to the phenomenological tradition and thus elaborate the relevance of the dimension of active trust for economic cooperation.

1. In the field of business management, Günther Ortmann (1995) applied Giddens's concept of the recursivity of structure and action to problems of cooperation in enterprises. Ortmann uses the concept of lean management to show how enterprises that are increasingly dependent on cooperative relations with subcontractors because of the limitation to core competencies can generate the capacity for cooperation. A basis for cooperation between a producer and a subcontractor, as Ortmann explains, referring to the MIT study by Womak et al. (1990), is a so-called basic contract that establishes the intention of a long-term cooperation and sets ground rules to determine prices, quality standards, provision of materials, profit margins, and the like. According to Ortmann, the basic contract concerns establishing the rules of the game, which allows the development of a cooperation game between producer and subcontractor. But only in the practical engagement of the actors involved on the basis of the agreed rules of the game does cooperation emerge, which is then a starting point

for new determinations of rules in the next round of cooperation. A circular feedback is developed in the recursivity of actions and structures of the enterprise involved, which stabilizes the cooperative relations (Ortmann 1995:311). But, with other rules of the game as a basis (traditional mass production), a competitive game between producer and subcontractor can also develop, in which a relationship of suspicion can develop and stabilize in recursive feedback loops over several rounds of activity.

In his use of concepts from structuration theory, Ortmann emphasizes structures (rules of the game) that are crucial to enable cooperation. This is also clear in Ortmann's (1995:328ff.) discussion of mutual capital linkages in networks of enterprises as the structural instrument for guaranteeing reciprocal willingness to cooperate. By mutually exchanging capital, enterprises prevent certain moves, like "hostage taking," even though they are in the interest of one of the participants of the network. Like Odysseus, who had himself chained while passing by the Sirens, it is rational for actors to give up options, if this can guarantee the cooperative action of the other enterprises involved. In Ortmann's conceptualization, however, structures assume a much stronger position than Giddens expresses in the concept of the duality of structures. Recursivity confirms the structures negotiated *before* as rules of the game without making their creation clear in the action process. At least in the examination of enterprise networks in which cooperation partners are involved with comparable potential for sanction, hence in which the conditions of cooperation cannot be dictated one-sidedly, the process of negotiating the rules of the game itself becomes the focus. How can a basic contract be made that includes the elements of trust even though this trust has not been established recursively in previous rounds of action?

2. The second example refers to an article by Karl Sandner and Renate Meyer (1994), which distinguishes between two mechanisms of order in organizations: routines and negotiations. By routines, they mean, like Giddens, waiving reflection by habitualized courses of action, which contribute essentially to reproducing the organization and to the emotional stability of the members of the organization. Through dialogue, organizations must constantly determine definitions of the situation in negotiations. The need for that results from the inadequate situation specificity of organizational structures for the distribution of tasks among the members. The labor contract cannot determine the actions of the members of the organization precisely despite the commitments in it, first because a definition of the situation of the actors that must establish the appropriateness of the respective demands is required (Sandner and Meyer 1994:190). Negotiations as processes of social interaction have the function of the social construction of reality that allow for a social order to emerge. Routines and negotiations refer mutually to one another: routines

relieve from reflection and thus reproduce ontological security. In negotiations the definitions of the situation are established, which are the most essential part of the social order in organizations.

Cooperation between actors in economic contexts, therefore, depends crucially on discursive processes of the definition of the situation, which *define the expectations*. The relation toward the cooperation partner plays a major role in that. Unlike the assumptions of economic theory, the starting point is not that actors in complex economic environments have access to clearly defined action strategies independent of the actual interaction structure, but rather that strategies are defined first in a social process. The constitutive nature of the situation offers actors the possibility of drafting strategies on the background of an awareness of the interdependent nature of the situation in which this awareness must be understood as a result of deliberative processes. To explain the possible emergence of a willingness to cooperate, we can start from a *perspective-generating force of discursive processes*, which links action strategies reflexively to the perception of the social situation.[24]

The idea of negotiation is linked with Giddens's insight of the need for active trust in modern societies. Cooperative relations are not simply given but rather have to be produced in reflexive processes, from which a recursive stabilization can then result. If we understand cooperation as an act that has no current motivation, but that one wants to have done in anticipated hindsight, then the thesis is that communication processes make it possible to transcend the pursuit of short-term individual interests, if the result of action can be defined in the collective processes of negotiation as being in one's own interest.[25] Yet the perception of the advantage of cooperative strategies is no guarantee that they will be realized. Instead this is precisely the starting point in game theory for the outcomes of noncooperative games. The connection of the link of discourse and cooperation thus requires an additional assumption, which is that the discursive process, supported by the institutional structure, produces at least so much binding force that actors in the first round of activity act as if they would trust one another.[26] For all subsequent rounds of activity, those preceding experiences of cooperation contribute to the cooperation strategy, so that recursive processes—as defined by Giddens—emerge, in the course of which rules can be consolidated as structure, and routinizing effects can occur. Actors can certainly switch from cooperation to defection at any time, but moral obligations, routinization, and the utility known from the preceding cooperation can be the three crucial factors of influence for the decision to pursue cooperative strategies in the next rounds of activity. The recursive processes convince actors that trust can substitute for an actual control of the action situation. The perception of the situation confirmed by experience and the strategies derived from it increasingly assume the nature of a condition that generates self-commitment.[27]

The two other examples of empirical studies by Charles Sabel (1993) and AnnaLee Saxenian (1989) do not refer directly to structuration theory. But they do emphasize the procedural nature of intersubjective construction of reality in which the idea of the possibility of reflexive stabilization of cooperation can again be explained in terms of economic sociology.

3. Charles Sabel challenges the validity of the assumption of economic theory that actors would exploit one-sided advances in cooperation and therefore cooperation based on trust could not materialize. Sabel (1993: 112ff.) introduces a notion of action that always perceives the individual actor in his social constitution; actors possess a reflexive self that allows them to recognize themselves as a person among other persons and to put themselves in the position of the other. The social mediation of individual definitions of interest always makes it possible in principle for actors to transcend individual calculations of utility and to coordinate their actions reflexively with other actors. This does not say anything yet about the actual emergence of cooperation, but merely presents a theoretical position that admits the possibility of the deliberative creation of cooperation. This position is clearly close to Giddens's notion of active trust but does not rely on it. For the emergence of relations of trust between actors who pursue at least partially antagonistic interests, the reinterpretation of economic conditions and the history of the relation of the actors are especially relevant. In the notion of reinterpretation, the significance of the common definitions of the situation reappears as a prerequisite for cooperative relations. Sabel explains the process of defining the situation with empirical examples of stagnant industries in Pennsylvania. Cooperative relations could be initiated between industrial enterprises that had been in a ruinous competition for years. What triggered the radical change in strategy was the government sponsorship of a discourse of enterprises on the situation of the industry, its structure, and the possibilities of cooperation. "The industry groups were invited, or invited themselves, to connive in a form of self-distraction that would allow them to catch sight of new possibilities" (Sabel 1993:130). Sabel calls this form of generating cooperation "studied trust," which is based on the possibility of redefining the collective identity of the industry and, building on that, changing the way one views one's own interest.

> The consensus is drifting from the view that individual actors know their interests, and the government's role is to remove obstacles to realizing them, to the view that it is only by recognizing their mutual dependence, that the actors can define their distinct interests, and that government's role is to encourage the recognition of a collectivity and the definition of particularity. (Sabel 1993:121)

4. AnnaLee Saxenian (1989) studied the formation of associations of enterprises and their political strategies in the high-tech areas of Silicon Valley in California and along Route 128 in Massachusetts. She was interested in the completely different relationship of the entrepreneurs to local and state political bodies as well as to the social needs of their respective regions, which is surprising because of the structural similarities of the problems of the industry. I am not interested here in Saxenian's explanation of the clear divergencies in the political commitment of the entrepreneurs, but only in the process of identity formation in one of the groups she describes. The Santa Clara County Manufacturing Group (SCCMG), founded in 1977, a merger of top managers initially from twenty-six high-tech concerns of the region, was formed in reaction to the signs of crisis in the computer industry of Silicon Valley. The entrepreneurs were motivated to establish the association by the increasing pressure of Japanese competition but also by limits on growth imposed by a housing shortage, a lack of infrastructure, and environmental pollution. From the beginning, the SCCMG sought solidarity with the political bodies of the region. A central impulse for political reforms started from a survey among industrial enterprises in the region, initiated by the group to investigate their growth plans. This unusual step of mutual revelation of strategic plans recalls the process described by Sabel of the incipient consciousness of structural solidarity of industries in Pennsylvania and the strategy formation derived from it. The result of the study (growth prognoses for new jobs of 50 percent in five years), which clearly showed the future problems of the region to the actors, motivated common regional planning activities, in which enterprises and political bodies discussed and implemented solutions to problems based on recognizing their mutual dependence. In Saxenian's account, this experience of successful cooperation became a model for the later cooperation of enterprises and politics in the region, in which the positive experiences of cooperation led recursively to the reinforcement of cooperative aspirations:

> Through these early political experiences, a shared identity was formed among Silicon Valley's industrialists. This group of engineers-turned-entrepreneurs was beginning to articulate a common understanding of the region's problems and the desired solutions. As they played an increasingly active role in the local planning process, members of the business community increasingly voiced their commitment to active promotion of the conditions for growth at the local level and to the need for business government cooperation in these efforts. With this emerging vision the SCCMG was on its way to becoming the most powerful political actor in the county. (Saxenian 1989:37)

Both examples of the deliberative emergence of cooperative relations refer to the significance of discursive processes between actors for the perception of mutual dependence and the recognition of advantages from cooperative strategies. Locating the individual situation within the structure of an industry or a region seems to have a significant influence on the action of individual actors, as a perspective of a "generalized other" (Mead 1974). Both examples show how action strategies (cooperation) are linked with the perception of one's own situation in the context of other players. A sociological alternative to the economic perspective of the problematic of cooperation emerges here: the behavior of actors in situations in which cooperation allows superior results is initially contingent. But becoming aware of mutual dependence *can* lead to processes of identity formation that allow "communities of interest" (Sabel 1993) to emerge and orient individual acts to strategies of cooperation. The success of cooperative acts can lead to their recursive stabilization. Even if this argumentation does not absolutely rule out strategies of defection, a possibility of the stabilization of cooperative acts in economic contexts is conceptualized, which explains cooperation without moving away from the idea of maximizing goals of the actors. In a *social process of the definition of interest*, however, the possibility of individual pursuit of interest must be perceived as dependent on a larger social context. The constitution of the identity of the self by experiences with others is emphasized.

If these considerations are referred to processes of change in organizational structure, especially the emergence of network structures, they represent an ambivalent background for the possibility of developing cooperation relations. On the one hand, they increase the possibilities of exploiting cooperative relations, and the awareness of this danger can lead actors not to take risks through cooperative moves in which potential gains from cooperation would not be realized. Flat hierarchies entail a more open flow of information, and network structures open possibilities of opportunistic action. On the other hand, structures decentralized by the dismantling of hierarchies are at the same time much more open for the articulation of "voice" (Hirschman 1970) and can thus structurally enable the discursive contexts that support cooperative action. For Michael Piore (1995:134), the success of network structures depends precisely on their ability "to move away from rational decision making to a more hermeneutic process."

Innovation and Creativity

The discussion of cooperation based on concepts borrowed from structuration theory shows that the strong inclusion of the actor's reflexivity allows new insights into the possibilities of overcoming inefficient equilibria. The process of perception and interpretation of the social context has constitutive significance for the choices of the actors, which can also contribute recursively to stabilize the willingness to cooperate. Thus this breaks through the alternative between the individualized actors provided only with self-interest considered by economic theory, and those sociological models that consider the actors as provided with a system of values that steers actions.

This section focuses on the aspect of innovation. In examining innovation, we must distinguish analytically between two questions. The first is, How do rational acting actors decide on the allocation of resources for the purpose of innovative activities? For the answer, we confront two kinds of difficulties: those discussed under the rubric of uncertainty and those resulting from the features of innovations as goods with positive external effects. An answer could come from the neoclassical model of utility maximization, if it succeeded in introducing investments in innovative activities into a cost-utility analysis and thus setting the groundwork for maximizing decisions. But this would presume that the success of innovative activities could be forecast under market aspects. Such an idea is obviously paradoxical because it assumes the knowledge of what is yet to be produced for the decision of the use of resources for activities, which alone can provide this knowledge. Even if investments in innovations are considered as a risky decision, a theory of optimal risk would be necessary for maximizing decisions. These considerations once again refer to the static nature of economic theory, which is interested in what we can best do with what we *already know*.

The second question, which is discussed in this section, is, How can we understand what actors do when they act innovatively? The (neoclassical) theory of economics has never dealt with innovations as *a process of creating* something new. The reason for this is inherent in the theoretical premises of the theory. A theory starting from the postulate of optimization had to treat the creation of the new as a problem of allocation and would thus miss the *process of emergence* of altered combinations. The new always does lead to altered allocation equilibria because certain resources are in greater demand and others less, but this refers only to the consequences of innovations, without illuminating the process itself in any way.

But, Parsons and Smelser, who, *pace* Schumpeter, deal with the *motives* for innovative activities,[28] cannot open the black box either. They had referred to a disequilibrium in the personality system produced by inefficient allocation of resources, which motivates innovative activities. The personality system is oriented to efficient use of resources on the basis of internalized values, so that, as in neoclassical economics, an action automatism independent of the constitutive performances of the actors is assumed, which is, however, firmly established in the normative bases of society and thus does not start solely from the individual. Neither neoclassical theory nor Parsons and Smelser, who dealt with innovations discussed in great detail by previous social theoreticians, give an answer to the problem. For the interest in economic efficiency, an understanding of what innovative action really means and what its bases are is important because inferences can be drawn for the *organization* of innovative activities that are a premise for an efficient investment of means.

How are innovative processes understood based on the concepts of structuration theory? Does Giddens's social theory offer a basis in action theory for understanding innovative activity? To approach this question, I would first like to consider Giddens's model of macrosocial change, from which some important basic thoughts can be inferred.

Social change, particularly in the formation of modern nation-states, play a central role in structuration theory. Unlike neoclassical theory with its static nature, in an examination guided by structuration theory, the dynamic of economic processes must thus be given preferential treatment. Giddens (1981:121ff.) understands the dramatic increase of the rate of technological innovations and the dynamic of economic processes developed from it as possible only in the context of the *capitalist* organization of production, thus the control of economic processes by expectations of profit. Giddens rejects both teleological and evolutionist models of history and emphasizes the contingency of historical processes. No general direction of development of historical courses can be postulated in terms of the philosophy of history; future stages cannot be forecast with the help of the social sciences. Emphasizing the contingency of historical events follows from the concept of the duality of structure, which consistently rejects the idea of a systemic self-logic. Thus Giddens's social theory is conceptually open for an examination of the genesis of new social structures that considers decisions of actors as constitutive for breaking out of existing routines.

With the notion of a recursive linkage of structure and action, it can be referred to the empirical studies of economic processes of change discussed in chapter 1. They showed that technological change cannot be understood as optimizing activity—innovations in the economy are not defined by a "one best way"—yet, they also refer to the limiting significance of structures by emphasizing path dependence and lock-in phenomena. The reflexivity of action is opposed to unilinear explanations of the dynamic of economic development along a strict path of evolution, yet it is not synonymous with refraining from evolutionary learning processes. Instead, innovations always take place against the background of existing structures.

Four fundamental aspects for analyzing innovations can be taken from Giddens's thoughts on processes of social change. (1) Processes of innovation must in principle be conceived as open; initially, the result cannot be fully anticipated or completely controlled. The shape of the new is not yet visible at first, or it emerges different from the intended product. (2) As a result, innovative activities are not to be understood as an allocation of resources for something that is already finished in cognition, but rather the innovation processes are to be described as an *attempt* in which goal setting and direction are constitutively linked with the *process* of innovation itself.[29] The intentionality of innovative action is based in the imagination of the new, which becomes concrete only in the process of construction and is thus also revised. (3) The linkage of structure and action refers to the significance of "the existing" as a background and premise for innovative processes, as well as understanding for their direction. (4) The phenomenological tradition produces the systematic establishment of a *process of acknowledgment* as a premise for the emergence of the new.[30] An objective existence of technology and technological development independent of the interpretation of the actors is challenged. Only when innovations are perceived and acknowledged as such by the actors can they attain influence as economic structures.

Despite these important aspects, we can enlist Giddens's comments about processes of social change from the 1980s only in a limited way as a theoretical model for understanding innovative processes in the economy. This is also because of the starting point of the considerations in the search for an explanation of processes of macrosocial development, which leads to an inadequate consideration of the study of the processes of action on the microsocial level, but which make innovative acts and their conditions comprehensible. It is not enough to point to the contingency of actions and unintended results of action in principle, which play a role in recursive processes. In Giddens's work in the 1980s, action theory seems to have been introduced essentially only to be able to explain the contingency of macrosocial development but without attempting in the theory to understand social change from the perspective of the actors. If this assessment is correct, the achievement of structuration theory for analyzing processes of social change consists mainly of establishing a systematic space for actors who can act, against functionalist and structuralist theories, without being able to fill this sufficiently from the perspective of the actor. But what premises are necessary on the side of the actors to produce innovations, and thus act creatively?

In his work of the 1990s, which is oriented more strongly to microsociology, in one place Giddens discusses the notion of creativity. In *Modernity and Self-Identity* (1991), in the context of a discussion of the significance of ontological security, Giddens argues that ontological security does not materialize by clinging to habitual action and blind trust in routines, but only by filling a potentially open space of action, thus through the creative use of rules of action. Creativity, which Giddens defines as "capability to act or think innovatively in relation to pre-established modes of activity" (Giddens 1991:41), is itself an essential premise for developing ontological security, because only this way are reactions adequate to the situation possible, because situations are never completely identical. In this context, creativity characterizes a cognitive aspiration motivated by the fear of the loss of security, which is undertaken with the goal of maintaining routines. This notion of creativity has its roots in Harold Garfinkel's (1967) ethnomethodology. Even routine situations always require the reflexive achievement of the actors for completion, which is to be called creative insofar as established ways of acting cannot be applied mechanically, but interaction situations demand an *adequate* way of behavior which assumes situation-dependent interpretations.[31]

This understanding of creative action introduced by Giddens and strongly shaped by Garfinkel goes beyond both the neoclassical and the Parsonian concept of technological change, but it remains focused too peripherally and too strongly on the problem of continuing situations to be able to distill a far-reaching concept of the problem of innovation. Hence, I draw considerations beyond Giddens that are in the tradition of phenomenological theory, yet go back to American pragmatism and thus to that tradition of the interpretative paradigm, which Giddens does not examine further. With this expansion, I try to elaborate more clearly the aspects of understanding innovations, which Giddens touches on but does not explain fully.

From a phenomenological perspective, Bernhard Waldenfels (1990) has dealt with the genesis of the new and thus studies the relation between continuity and break in innovations. As a philosopher, Waldenfels does not refer primarily to the sociological phenomenology of Alfred Schütz but rather to the works of Edmund Husserl, Maurice Merleau-Ponty, Martin Heidegger, and Hannah Arendt. Waldenfels also emphasizes that innovations cannot be understood as something completely new, which presents no reference to what exists. Such an understanding of action as pure creativity would either dispel or violate reality (92). Yet innovations cannot be limited to reproducing the existing order but obtain their significance precisely in the variation and transformation of the existing order. To explain, Walderfels (1990:95) distinguishes between reproductive and productive action: "By *reproductive* act, I mean an act that moves within an order, repeats shapes and structures, deals with standards, applies rules. *Productive* act, on the other hand, is an act that changes orders, reshapes and restructures shapes and structures, revises standards and rules."

Reproductive action corresponds quite precisely with Giddens's notion of creativity because Waldenfels also sees that rules for reproducing order in various contexts have to be applied differently and must be redefined.

With the notion of productive action, however, Waldenfels goes beyond it by studying the change of the basic order itself.[32] The subversive and conflictual nature of innovations appears more clearly than in Giddens.

Waldenfels's discussion of innovations appears against the background of a critique of teleological, normative, and causal theories of action that lack the latitude that distinguishes human action: action is a necessarily unfinished search for an order in an open and unfinished world (Husserl). The fundamental difference with the teleological model of action arises from the paradox of innovations cited earlier, that the actor does not know what will be at the end of the action process. What helps is "not re-remembering, but only the act itself, a seeking act, that literally *has* no goal" (Waldenfels 1990:97, emphasis in original). It becomes clear that the openness of innovation processes, which Giddens also emphasizes, clearly demands a basis in action theory that does not understand action as a completion of established goal projections. Nor is it enough to understand innovations from motives like a psychologically caused striving for security, the fulfillment of normative demands, or even more reduced, as a mechanical application of the rules of maximization; innovations have to be understood much more radically from the ontological condition of action itself. If the world is open and uncontrollable, then there is for the act no other alternative to innovative reactions on changed structures: "A logos that does not have control over a comprehensive and lasting domain, but allows limited and changing fields to emerge by responding to challenges, such a responding logos shows a special kind of productivity" (101).

An understanding of innovations must then be built on the multipremised interrelation between actors and action situations: actors must have the capacity to be able to vary and transform existing structures; at the same time, structures need not be completely controlled to keep producing the pressure of the problem which must be reacted to with recurrent innovation. If we agree with Giddens that this is a recursive process, it is the innovations themselves that also create new problem pressure by solving challenges and thus demand new innovations.[33]

These thoughts find little support in the field of economics. Gerhard Wegner (1995) has shown how the works of George Shackle can be used for a theory of innovation in the economy, which takes into account the openness of innovations. For Shackle, all decisions bear an element of creativity since they avoid repetition because of the complexity of the world.[34] The creative achievement consists of creating images of future events that become guides for decisions. The ontological condition of action, as for Waldenfels, is that the economic cosmos is created by man, but this cannot determine it. The future can be imagined but not known. A background for the imagination of future situations, which forms the intentionality of action, is the action context and its individual perception, which is dependent on the subject.

In *Beyond Individualism* (1995), the American economist Michael Piore, referring to Martin Heidegger and Hannah Arendt, also tries to develop a theoretical basis for understanding innovative processes in the economy, building on a hermeneutic, interpretative approach. According to Piore, the action theory of economics, distinguishing strictly between ends and means, structure and process, and cause and effect, cannot sufficiently explain the openness of processes of technological change and their incorporation into social contexts. The economic action theory assumes in its premises the knowledge of the means-ends relationship, without explaining where the necessary knowledge comes from and how it changes (Piore 1995:100). But the ambiguity of the action situation can only be overcome in an interpretative process in which actors first agree about the nature of the situation. The process of innovation depends on the social interpretation of the situation by the actors involved. Interpretations of the situation generate strategies of action, which are understood as adequate and thus can guide action. What is valid especially in networks of organizations, but also in industrial regions like Silicon Valley, is that innovative processes progress without a clearly defined direction, and this is crystallized only in the process of innovation itself (133). With Heidegger, Piore understands action as a constant process, progressing in time, in which the prestructure, future projections, and conditions of action of the present enter contingently.[35] Technological change and innovation are bound irrevocably with the interpretative context of action sequences. The success of enterprises that operate in rapidly changing markets with short product life cycles depend on their interpretative competence; the decision process rigidly formalized in the sequence of ends and means is invalidated.

It is now clearer how the interpretative paradigm contains a theoretical foundation for conceptualizing innovative processes in the economy, which poses an alternative to the neoclassical model of action. The thoughts of Waldenfels, Shackle, and Piore do not contradict Giddens's structuration theory, but complement it. This is no accident, because all authors refer to motifs of the phenomenological tradition, which are also central for Giddens. Although it can be seen in works of economic sociology and business management that phenomenological approaches acquire increasing validity for understanding innovative processes,[36] the second theoretical tradition of the interpretative paradigm, that is, American pragmatism, has thus far received very little attention in works dealing with processes of innovation in the economy. But the recent work of Charles Sabel (1995) and a study by Donald Schön (1983) deal with new forms of organization of innovative processes and design processes, referring explicitly to pragmatism. The insignificant attention to pragmatist concepts in economic sociology—especially in understanding innovative processes—is surprising, because the relevance of pragmatism for a theory of the creativity of action was elaborated in sociology (Joas 1996; 1993), based chiefly on the work of John Dewey. Aspects introduced for understanding innovations can be continued on this basis.

Without going into the varied discussions on the relationship of phenomenology and pragmatism, I am concerned only with showing how considerations from the tradition of pragmatism can be productively applied to understanding innovations. My guide for that is Hans Joas's (1996) action theory, which is developed essentially on the background of pragmatism and is centered on the creative dimension of action. Thus I go beyond Giddens's discussion, but at the same time remain within the horizon of the interpretative paradigm of sociology. The attachment to pragmatism is not an arbitrary expansion but exhausts the paradigm further than is represented in the work by Giddens.

With the notion of the creativity of action, Joas (1996:157) objects to the "teleological interpretation of the intentionality of action" pursued in the rational-actor model, which separates the processes of goal determination of action from action implementation. Joas opposes to it a self-reflexive understanding of intentionality which constitutively includes the situational context and the materiality of action. The action situation is thus moved to a central position in understanding action. "The concept of 'situation' is a suitable replacement for the means-ends schema as the primary basic category of a theory of action" (160). In this concept of action, the implementation of action, the ends of action, and the means used are closely linked. The goals of action and the means of action stand in a reciprocal relationship, in which goals are relatively undefined at first and are specified only by the decision about the means to be used (154). Setting ends is established in the situation in which the actors initially find themselves with rather undefined expectations. Joas's considerations follow from the pragmatist philosophy of John Dewey, which centers on the conviction of the possibility of deliberately shaping social life worlds in communicative processes. The undetermined future, this is the basic idea, is shaped on the basis of ideas, plans, theories, and normative thoughts and is thus always grasped in an unfinished process of becoming.

The action theory developed by Joas categorically avoids the difficulties for understanding innovative processes that result from the rational-actor model. The idea that actors sought optimal strategies for action goals previously determined is rejected on this theoretical background; instead, strategies and goals must be shaped in the implementation of action and thus in the social context. The open character of action situations is emphasized and thus the necessary creativity of the actor. At the same time, the emphasis on the procedural nature of all situations focuses on the tension between the new and the routines that exist in concrete action situations. New ways of acting, hence innovations, arise in the treatment of *concrete* action problems, which actors confront in a situation. It is not the abstract wish to be creative, to create something new, but rather the situation itself that demands creativity. The creativity of the actors is thus not established in the consciousness of the subject, but rather in the debate with problems of actual action situations. The theory juxtaposes the perception of the world in unreflected routines, which are stabilized as habits, and the creative achievement of actors, which is necessary because habits can encounter resistances in the objective world that destroy the unreflected expectations. The reconstruction of the interrupted action context is viewed as a creative achievement of the actor. The new ways of acting developed in the solution of the problem become the habit of action until new problems of action make the reconstruction process necessary again. According to this notion of "situational creativity" (Joas), actors are not restricted in advance to an action alternative; instead approaches to solving the action problem emerge only in the interaction of situation and cognition. The solution of a problem depends on available resources as well as the action orientations that are defined neither by a given order of values nor by goal maximization and always demand an interpretation of the situational conditions by the actors. The maximizing assumption of the rational-actor model is replaced by the procedural and situational view of innovations, which is much easier to reconcile with the empirical findings of processes of innovation.

> According to the pragmatists, every situation contains a horizon of possibilities which in a crisis of action has to be rediscovered. Hypotheses are put forward: suppositions about new ways of creating bridges between impulses to action and the given circumstances of a situation. Not all such bridges are viable. However, when the actor succeeds in building a new bridge, this serves quite concretely to enhance his capacity for action. In fact, it even changes the goals he sets himself. (Joas 1996:133)

The shape of the future space, which is open, is understood here in its procedural character, which develops as a debate between actors and the action situation. A conceptualization of innovative processes in the economy modeled on that seems adequate because it expresses the constitutive nature of the entrepreneurial action in Schumpeter's sense. This significance of the actor disappears in the teleological action model of economic theory, which relies on the ability to differentiate clearly between ends and means in action and the independence of action goals from the action situation, but this cannot explain the *process of the emergence* of the new or its integration.

The action model advocated by Joas can, however, be linked with Giddens's concept of the duality of structure. Joas himself calls attention to the close connection of this theoretical outline with "constitution theories" in sociology, which also includes Giddens's structuration theory.[37] On a general level, the agreement is that both approaches try to understand social configurations in reference to social action. More specifically, it concerns the indeterminate and contingent understanding of processes of social development, which refers to the creativity of action (see Joas 1996:234ff.). For Giddens, new structures emerge in a social process of acknowledgment and not as adaptation to a putatively given optimum. For Giddens, the duality of structure means the emergence and reproduction of structures in the implementation of action, and thus it keeps its eye on the achievements of the actors. However, in Joas's outline—going beyond Giddens—an action theory is elaborated in which the interrelation of action goal and choice of means, as well as that of situation and process, is actually developed. And the conditions under which innovative changes and not the mere reproduction of routines must be expected is also much easier to derive. This was one of Margaret Archer's (1982) central criticisms of Giddens's concept of the duality of structure. Innovations in economic contexts can be understood with Joas and with recourse to pragmatism as a breakthrough of routines that is necessary because actors are confronted with a discrepancy between perception of the problem in the situation and the solution of the problem through established ways of action. The pressure for innovation arises from the action situation, and innovations arise in intersubjective processes of action.

If we examine modern market economies, the assumption is plausible that market changes always undermine routinized ways of action and thus keep forcing reconstructions of situations and the creative closure of the action situation. Falling sales figures for a product are a market signal that indicates that the product in its present form is not a solution anymore to the problem of generating profits. Reflection sets in as to how to change the product, its production, or its marketing until a solution has been found from which the company expects success. The explanation for rapid technological change in capitalist societies then resides in the pressure conveyed through the market. This pressure must always be relieved by actors through innovations and is at the same time reproduced recursively through productivity increases, which, in a competitive economy, recreate the need for further innovations. The action of the actors is thus always already contextualized by existing technologies, economic resources, and cognitive models of perception. Even if we start from the notion that actors in economic contexts orient their creative handling of problems toward their individual utility, the openness of the action situation implies that optimal solutions cannot be deduced, but rather that "knowledgeable actors" act contingently on the background of their perception of the situation. Interest remains focused on the actor—this forms the continuity with economic theory—but the open nature of innovation in principle is considered theoretically, and innovative action is linked constitutively with the action context.

So far, the action model of pragmatism has hardly attracted any attention in economic sociology.[38] Only Charles Sabel (1995) has elaborated the significance of this concept of action for understanding innovations in decentralized forms of organizations and Donald Schön (1983) has used it for conceptualizing design processes.[39] In conclusion, I would like to discuss this use of the pragmatist theory.

The basic form of the newly emerging organization structures described by Sabel comprises teams or work groups that are entrusted with the responsibility and provided with the means to reach a goal, whose concrete form results only in the process of work itself:

> Coordination of these groups is by means of iterated goal setting: General projects such as, for example, the design of a new car, are initially determined by evaluation of best practice and prospects of competing developmental alternatives. These general goals are in turn successively decomposed, again by reference to leading example and comparison of possibilities, into tasks for teams or work groups. Then the goals are modified as groups gain experience in prosecuting the tasks as originally defined. Through these revisions, modifications in the parts lead to modifications in the conception of the whole, and vice versa. The same procedure of monitoring decentralized learning, moreover, allows each part to observe the performance of the other collaborator accurately enough to determine whether continued reliance on them, and dedication of resources to the joint projects, are warranted. Because of this connection between joint exploration of collaborative possibilities and mutual evaluation I call these systems learning by monitoring. (Sabel 1995:5)

The connection of this project-oriented and flexible organizational form of innovation processes to the pragmatist model of action is obvious and is also established explicitly by Sabel. Bench marking, simultaneous engineering, and best practice as core components of the management of organizational processes correspond with the expression in pragmatism of procedural determination of action ends and the means deployed. The ends are sharpened and are revised in the development process itself and thus conform flexibly to the knowledge newly emerged only in action. "The method of disciplined comparison that defines the core of the new firm can thus be seen as an institutionalization of practical reason: a pragmatic method of economic coordination" (27). The organization of innovation processes in flexible teams has the economic background so that, through the mutual observation in constant comparison, new possibilities discovered only in the innovation process itself can be systematically included, which at the start of the process could not have gone into the determination of ends and means. At the same time, the work groups must keep analyzing their internal organization and their relation to other groups on the background of achieving flexible project goals. The organization of processes characterized by the distribution of labor is determined by the groups themselves, but this autonomy also demands that, in light of the changing situation, the processes are always being examined critically and must be newly reconstructed (30ff.). One prerequisite for this is the exchange of information between teams or organizations within the network. Sabel's example shows how conclusions about the organization of innovative activities in enterprises can be drawn from the pragmatist understanding of creativity. The organization of innovations depends on the creation of organizational structural conditions in which "experimental action" is possible.

The second author who has used pragmatist concepts for understanding innovations is Donald Schön. Schön (1983:47) has remarked that understanding innovation as an optimizing problem would presuppose that the task of innovation could be articulated as a well-formed instrumental problem. But this is impossible, because at the beginning of a design process, ends are unspecified and unclear. Empirical studies indicate that ends are developed in the process of invention and become entirely clear only when the innovation process has been completed. As Schön (1983:68) has argued: the designer "does not keep means and ends separate but defines them interactively as he frames the problematic situation. He does not separate thinking from doing, rationating his way to the decision which he must later convert to action." This finding coincides with John Dewey's concept of "ends-in-view," which maintains that ends are loosely defined action plans that structure current action on the basis of the perception of the situation (Joas 1996:155). Ends-in-view are formed and revised in the action process itself and become more precise with the better understanding of the problem and the means for its solution. Ideas, plans, and theories are continuously revised with the new experiences that are gathered in the innovation process. Schön describes the formation and clarification of goals in innovation as a dialogue (Schön 1983) between the designer and the situation in which problems and solutions that were only vaguely understood at first become clearer until a solution has been reached.

Especially for experienced engineers, the design activity itself becomes a largely routinized process in which intuition, everyday knowledge, routines, and experience play a crucial role. This knowing-in-action (Schön 1983) is rooted in implicit understandings of the situation that form the basis of intentionality of the designer's action. It contributes to the constitution of a specific course of action upon which the actor usually does not reflect. "As long as his [the designer's] practice is stable, in the sense that it brings him the same types of cases, he becomes less and less subject to surprise. His knowing-in-practice tends to become increasingly tacit, spontaneous, and automatic, thereby conferring on him and his clients the benefits of specialization" (Schön 1983:60). This prereflective understanding of design problems also explains the empirical finding that designers often verbalize their activities very poorly. Moreover, the narrative the designers give frequently takes the form of a *post actum* rationalization that has relatively little correspondence to the actual proceedings in the innovation process itself (Davies and Castell 1992). The importance of unreflected routines demonstrates that the contingency of innovations is not reduced by the telos of action but by the meaning the situation achieves for the actor. This does not imply that actors do not pursue goals, but that envisioned solutions to problems cannot be understood independently from the prereflected context in which actors act.

It would be misleading, however, to think of design processes as entirely routinized. The reactions of new artifacts or newly discovered objects are either not or only partly known. Moreover, to be stuck in routines inhibits the creativity of innovators (Schön 1983:60f.). The discrepancy between the perception of a problem in a situation and those solutions offered by routines blocks the unreflected continuation of action. The routinized action flow will be interrupted, and designers are forced into what Donald Schön (1983) has termed "reflection-in-action," a reflective mode that corresponds to John Dewey's notion of reconstruction. This reflective mode leads actors into an experimental "conversation" with the indicated physical objects ("the situation") until the inquiry has led to a new line of action—a solution to the problem. If one understands innovations as taking place in complex situations and under conditions of uncertainty, the process of reflection-in-action cannot be depicted as a rational deliberation about means based on known ends. Instead, the "conversation" with the situation is based on the meaning given objects in interpretations.

PART THREE
CONCLUSIONS

SIX

PERSPECTIVES FOR ECONOMIC SOCIOLOGY

T HE critique discussed in chapter 1 referred to the limits of the rational-actor model as a basis for understanding action in economic contexts. It is not the assumption of behavior aiming at utility maximization that is problematic in itself but rather the assumption generally considered valid that actors could make maximizing decisions and would thus achieve optimal allocation. This critique was intended to show the significance of the complexity inherent in the situation, novelty, and the cooperation dilemma as areas of investigation that cannot be understood fully from the perspective of the rational-actor model. The result of this critique is that an economic theory that wants to address these problems comprehensively requires a different basis of action theory in its core.

Sociological theory is a suitable source for seeking such a foundation. As sociologists, Durkheim, Parsons, Luhmann, and Giddens agree that, even in economic contexts, we cannot understand action on the basis of an a priori introduced, individualized, utility-maximizing actor. This does not necessarily mean that actors do not act intentionally oriented to their perceived interests. But actions or decisions are constitutively linked with the social nature of action situations. Only by getting away from optimization as an empirical assumption does the difference between action intention and action results become a possible subject for study. By avoiding the a priori commitment to optimizing decisions, sociological theories systematically open ways to understanding the three discussed action situations of cooperation, uncertainty, and innovation.

The discussion of the four sociological theories showed what significance is attached to structural and institutional rigidity for action in situations with uncertainty. In addition, it sharpened our view of the assumptions under which actors engage in cooperation. Moreover, we elaborated how we can understand innovations in their constitutive link with the action process. None of the theories discussed offers a complete basis of a desirable action theory. In a certain sense, however, Giddens's structuration theory, which connects central elements, comes close. This theory is valid not only for the systematic link of structure and action in a relation of mutual constitution but also, for emphasizing the processual nature of action. Giddens acknowledges the significance of structural rigidities, but also maintains the perspective of action theory. Thus the central significance of reducing complexity in situations that evade optimizing decisions because of genuine uncertainty is accepted. For the cooperation problem Giddens refers to defining strategies in a process of social negotiation, which can explain why the individually rational strategies must not also dominate empirically. Structuration theory, however, does admittedly have its shortcomings with regard to those aims because of its insufficient examination of economic processes and structures.

Detailed discussions of individual aspects of the questions pursued can thus be inferred much more easily from the three other theory outlines. Luhmann's central motif resides in the debate with the problem of double contingency in economic decisions, which can only be managed if social rigidities allow Alter's action to be expected by Ego. Luhmann's economic sociology consistently rejects the possibility of a coordination of action on the basis of optimizing decisions and, because of this starting point, is especially interesting for the problem of action in situations characterized by uncertainty. For Luhmann, the overcomplexity of market information represents the limit of rational decision making for controlling economic processes. If we want to understand how decisions are made by actors deliberately oriented toward their utility, but who cannot know the optimizing alternatives ex ante, then the complexity-reducing structurings are a central subject for study. However, what is problematic, especially in understanding innovations, turns out to be the systems-theoretical perspective, as it neglects the point that action is always tied to the intentionality of actors. The interest in innovation is not exhausted by observing the change in subsequent action from an external perspective, but rather we want to know how actors come to deviate from routines and deliberately introduce novelty. This, however, also requires an action-theoretical approach. In the model of a mutual constitutional relationship of structure and action, as Giddens formulates it in his structuration theory, innovations can be understood much easier as the result of intentional changes, in which action motives (expectation of profit, technical curiosity, etc.) are connected contingently *and* constitutively with existing technical and social rigidities.

The focus of Durkheim's and Parsons's economic sociology is the problem of cooperation. For Durkheim, the analysis of action in economic contexts is linked with normative questions of social justice. The critique of economic theory also refers essentially to the liberal economic policy of exclusively market-controlled economic processes. For Durkheim, economic functions must also be incorporated into the sui generis existing normative framework of society and are dominated by it. The expected restraint of selfish action reduces the danger to society through economic crises and their repercussions in all areas of society. For Durkheim, the limits of the market consist of the threatening disorganization of a society that assigns the market the dominant role as a controlling instrument of economic and social relations. Only the limitation of the market enables social order. Important elements for understanding the action situation of cooperation can be drawn from Durkheim's considerations. Durkheim refers to the significance of moral obligations and the norms derived from them in economic relations. These norms and values penetrate the action of the actors as cultural frameworks but can also emerge in interaction itself. By turning to social norms to solve the cooperation dilemma, especially in the understanding of modern societies one is, however, confronted with the problem that actors also contravene action norms in the interest of short-term advantages. Durkheim does not sufficiently pose the consequences resulting from that. But Durkheim's emphasis of the significance of habit and institutionalized communication structures in the occupational groups does show a productive approach that refers to the only limited questioning of norms in action and the stabilization of norms in interaction processes.

To a certain extent Parsons's works in the field of economic sociology are in the tradition of Durkheim, in that economic structures and economic acts are analyzed against the background of a horizon of values shared by members of society. Unlike Durkheim, however, Parsons is no longer interested in the question of the institutional foundations of a *just* social order but rather in the prerequisites of economic productivity in modern societies. Here the systematic scheme of boundary interchanges between subsystems shows the necessary incorporation of the economy in the social system. Not only is economically rational action itself seen as a cultural product, but the social embeddedness of economic institutions forces their connection with social structures. Consumer goods not only have an economic significance that profits can be made with their production and sale, but they also contribute to shaping life-styles in society. The role of dependent gainful employment is socially tolerable only as long as the generated income guarantees the culturally adequate reproduction of the gainfully employed and their families. An independence of economic structure, in any case, would be conceivable only at the cost of anomie and would even prevent the fulfillment of economic functions. In Parsons's remarks, strong theoretical arguments can be found for the explanation of the embeddedness of economic structures even in modern societies, along with a concept that can be made productive for systematizing this incorporation. It is necessary to view the boundary processes between the economy and other areas of society. Moreover, the notion of interpenetration gives Parsons a concept significant for the question of stabilizing relations of cooperation in economic contexts. Parsons assumes that actors, as integrated personality systems, transfer values from one area of action to another. If that is so, then the various roles that actors must assume in different contexts of action exclude action oriented only to individual considerations of advantage even in the economic area. Value orientations of solidarity and cooperation, which shape family contexts, are introduced by the actors into economic action contexts and influence them. Parsons sees the limit of the market in the cultural assumptions of the market organization of economic activity. This makes the connection of economic activity and social values a prerequisite for the functioning of the market itself. The reification of the market would impair its own bases.

The strong emphasis of norms and internalized value systems in Durkheim and Parsons, however, hides the danger of a normative determinism, a reproach that was directed especially against Talcott Parsons. The (functionalist) assumption of the validity of norms is problematic not only because modern societies are distinguished by questioning the validity of rules that are taken for granted, but also because it can be assumed that the reflection of the standard of values can also contribute to their emergence and stabilization. This possibility is hinted in Durkheim's discussion of occupational groups, which are distinguished by the fact that antagonistic interests are transferred between the actors in cooperative activity on the basis of contact and conversation.[1] However, this idea is fully developed only in the phenomenological and ethnomethodological concepts, which are the background for Giddens's structuration theory. Giddens avoids the danger of a normative determinism in economic sociology by including the reflexivity of actors but without excluding norms and values as important structural elements of action. The emphasis of the social and procedural nature of negotiating the validity of modes of action, which are found especially in the tradition of American pragmatism too, is an essential starting point to explain the actual obligatory nature of action norms in modern contexts.

From these considerations represented in detail in Part II, we deduce the contribution of sociological theory for the two central questions of this book: how do actors manage to act cooperatively, and on what basis do they make decisions in situations in which they can know only ex post if they have acted advantageously? The market is not a sufficient coordination mechanism for these systematic problems. For economic cooperation, it is not enough if individualized actors, indifferent to one another, coordinate their actions through prices in the market, while striving at the same time to optimize their utility. The cooperation dilemma cannot be overcome on the basis of market coordination alone. This also applies to innovations. Various economic theories show that innovative activity stimulated only by market incentives lead to suboptimal allocation of means for innovation purposes. The uncertainty of the economic success of research activities and the possibly cost-free takeover of the results of research by competition causes this underinvestment.

To put the argumentation more precisely, I have studied the limits of orthodox economic theory at its strongest point, that is, in its understanding as a normative theory. This can be a central starting point for economic sociology from which competing models to orthodox economic theory can be developed, which are *not* understood as a moral critique of the model of *homo oeconomicus*. This does not mean that the significance of value rationality in economic contexts is negated, but in this approach the *intentional* deviation from maximizing goals is rejected as a vantage point. Considered from this point of view, norms and values essentially play a role in economic relations of modern economies because, as substitute rationalities, they contribute to enabling economic transactions by forming reciprocal expectations in situations of double contingency.

But the demand for an action theory that goes beyond the notion of maximizing applies not only for the two questions in the foreground here, but also for the two other possible starting points of economic sociology that result from the observation of "irrational" behavior with and without regret: *unintentional* deviations from maximizing decisions in economic transactions represent a productive field for empirical work in economic sociology, which can document what penetrating influence social structures and values, but also ignorance and cognitive limitations, have on decisions, even when actors act with the intention of maximizing utility. These deviations, which considerably revise the image of the functioning of modern market economies suggested by economic theory, cannot be explained on the basis of the rational-actor model but only in a framework of action theory that studies the social, cultural, and cognitive structures.

For *intentional* deviations from maximizing decisions (i.e., altruistic choices), the demand for an expanded framework of action theory also applies, which seems obvious from a sociological perspective: Weber analyzed the instrumentally-rational type of action as only one of several possible action orientations and developed an action typology in which value-rational motives are also taken into account. From the attempt to integrate altruistic action into the rational-actor model, no comprehensive and convincing theory of the operation of norms emerges because social norms and values cannot be reduced to individual calculations of utility.

What perspective for economic sociology results from the conducted studies? Unlike orthodox economic theory, the explanation of economic action in the sociological conception developed here does not start with the assumption of individual utility maximizing but rather studies the embeddedness of decisions on the basis of the assumption of intentional rationality of the actors. The focus of analytic attention shifts to the social rules on which actors base their decisions. Thus, sociological and economic approaches are distinguished not primarily in the dimension of action goals—that is, on the axis of rational versus irrational action.[2] Instead the distinctions of the approaches in the conceptualization of the relation of means to ends are in the foreground. Complexity and novelty of economic decision situations of modern economies prevent actors from understanding means-ends relationships comprehensively. The problem for actors is not so much that they have to balance their action goals between selfish interests and other norms and values, but to understand which means to use—that is, which strategies to follow—in order to make optimal use of existing resources under given constraints. Complexity leaves the relevance of parameters and their interlockings partly unknown to the actor so that decision makers cannot completely understand the consequences of strategic options. If we think of innovation, a further feature is added: for logical reasons the means-ends relations of an innovation cannot or can only very vaguely be described at the beginning of the innovative process. Here it is by definition impossible for actors to choose means rationally because the basis for rational calculation is missing: how shall we apply means rationally if we do not know the means-ends relations in any concrete sense? This uncertainty of decision situations opens up the sociological question how actors reach decisions if they cannot have complete or probabilistic knowledge of the causal consequences.

In the suggested sociological approach, thinking about economic rationality does not focus on the identification and realization of an optimal strategy but, instead, on the construction of the meaning of intentionally rational economic action. If an optimal strategy cannot be deduced mathematically from existing preferences and conditions, decisions depend on actors' definition of the situation. Such definitions constitute the intelligibility of the complex environment and are reached through contingent interpretations that are based on judgments about material conditions, causal relations, the future actions of relevant others, and assumptions about changes in technology or markets. In this process means and ends are intertwined and formed in the situation itself; they become more pronounced and undergo continuous revision as action proceeds, and as actors learn new things through further experiences, disappointments, and encouragements. The definition of the situation is seen as the result of contingent reflections of actors in a social process. This emphasizes that any situation has several readings which can be judged as adequate responses by the actor.

Yet, the definition of the situation is based on at least in part intersubjectively shared interpretations. This calls attention to the necessity of mutual correspondence among actors in the interpretation of objects or social situations as a precondition for the operation of markets. Interpretation is a social process in the sense that judgments on the relevant parameters of the situation are based on generalized expectancies that are, at least in part, intersubjectively shared.

The unmistakable sociological contribution of economic sociology can be seen in the analysis of the structures of expectation to which actors refer in decision processes, but which also emerge in their action as social rigidities. On the basis of the sociological theories discussed, such structures of expectation can be systematized in a heuristic of four comprehensive categories, which altogether characterize the social embeddedness of actors and on that basis the significance of culture, power, institutions, social structures, and cognitive processes for modern market economies can be understood.

1. *Norms and institutions.* Norms and institutions create mutual expectations for interactions and limit the choice set of actors. The sanction potential involved with norms reduces the risk that actors will not comply with obligations entered into from strategic considerations. Norms and institutions maintain their stability in the context of modern market economies, not only out of the moral convictions of the actors but also out of their significance in reducing contingency in action situations. By building choice on institutional structures, they are incorporated into the social context (Hodgson 1988). During the past twenty years, the significance of institutions has also gained increasing attention in economics (North 1990; Vanberg 1994; Williamson 1985). Unlike most economic approaches, however, sociology studies institutions and their dynamics not as defined by demands of efficiency. Instead, institutions must be legitimated within a given social order and are thus integrated into a specific social, political, and cultural context. This limits the possibilities for an institutional design impelled only by considerations of efficiency.

2. *Tradition, custom, and routine.* The notion of habitual action can be examined as a significant concept for explaining cooperation and action in complex situations. Its significance is seen both in classical sociological theory (Camic 1986) as well as in economic discussions of action under uncertainty (Knight 1985; Keynes 1973b), and is also central in contemporary discussions of economic sociology (Zukin and DiMaggio 1990). By acting on the basis of habits and routines, actors avoid costs of calculation and make it possible for a third party to form expectations with regard to their action. Routines stabilize interaction by giving up the possibility of reflection. Durkheim (1984) already referred to it in his discussion of the anomic division of labor—that rapid social change produced anomie during the process of industrialization because traditional forms of social interaction were destroyed without allowing time for the emergence of new habits. Weber saw the relations between economic units determined by habit, and his definition of traditional action implies that this action type is determined "by settled habit" (Weber 1978:12), in which an approach to explaining cooperative action is made. Giddens (1984) makes the human need for "ontological security" respon-

sible for the dominance of routinized patterns of action that reproduce social structures.

3. *Structural predispositions of decisions: social networks, organizational structures, and path dependency.* Structural approaches to explaining market behavior show how the activities of firms and individual economic actors can be understood from their specific position within a network of market participants (Burt 1992; Granovetter 1973; White 1981). Studies of network structures within industries and regions verify their significance for allocation decisions, which breaks through the atomized perspective of neoclassical theory. Social networks might be more important for explaining economic outcomes than individual preferences. Organizational structures reduce options of action by prescribing modes of action. But if we follow Parsons's thoughts, roles are also always regulated normatively by the demands of the social values, through which the interpenetration of the economy and society constitutively affects the structures of economic organizations. Path dependency refers to the significance of past decisions, which circumscribe future possibilities of choice because of switching costs, learning-curve effects, and not ignored sunk costs (David 1986). History becomes a relevant dimension of present decisions, which is relatively independent of preferences.

4. *Power.* Finally, power, which is excluded from the general equilibrium theory, structures social relations in the economy. Among the classical sociologists, Weber especially emphasized the significance of government power, power relations in organizations, and market power as central for understanding economic processes. The concept of power also allows the problem of incomplete information to be linked with political economy (Bowles 1985). The power of Ego over Alter reduces possible reactions of Alter and makes Alter's actions predictable for Ego's strategic considerations. The threat of force reduces Alter's possibilities of choice to submission or resistance. Economic transactions are imbued with the unequally distributed power of economic actors, and government power also affects decisions of production and allocation. The significance of power for the efficiency of markets is ambivalent: by forming cartels and monopolies, an efficient allocation of resources is prevented; but power can also be a premise for cooperative relations, the emergence of new industries, or competitive cost structures.

Norms, institutions, habit, social structures, and power can be understood as forms of embeddedness in economic contexts that are used in economic sociology as variables to explain economic processes and structures. Orthodox economic theory models do reflect these social mechanisms only partially and conceive of actors as undersocialized utility maximizers, removed from social relations (Granovetter 1985).

In this critique and in the significance of the concept of embeddedness, the debates with economic and sociological theory developed here are closely connected with the new economic sociology. Yet, at the same time, two significant differences result. (1) In comparison with the approach of new economic sociology that pays special attention to social network structures (Granovetter 1985; 1992), a broader approach results from the critique of orthodox economic theory here. The strong emphasis on networks of social relations is countered by making all four types of different structures of expectation appear as forms of social embeddedness with equal rights in research in economic sociology.[3] The significance of cultural rigidities and social power for transaction processes is thus systematically considered more strongly. (2) The second essential difference consists of identifying *action situations* in economic contexts that are elaborated as limits in economic theory and indicate subject areas for economic sociology, in which studies of economic processes and structure can be undertaken. Thus, the focus is also on the social embeddedness of actors in economic contexts, but the subject areas of cooperation, uncertainty, and innovation are the suggested structuring starting point of research in economic sociology. Thus, for example, starting from the sketch developed here, social network structures—which represent *one* important dimension of embeddedness of economic action—are analyzed in terms of their contribution to providing a basis for decisions in situations characterized by uncertainty. The persistence of national cultural peculiarities in the organization and institutionalization of economic processes, to cite another example, can be analyzed as contingent in the concrete form but indispensable in their function. They enable capacity for action and cooperation.[4]

By proceeding from empirical action situations, economic sociology examines the embeddedness of economic action as a derived variable; the significance of the structures of expectation is caused by the nature of the identified action situation. This leads to a systematization in which the relationship to economic theory can be formulated precisely and the embeddedness of action itself explained theoretically. Identifying the three action situations allows an explanation of *why* economic action is both determined by the market and guided by rules, without having to assume that actors would intentionally deviate from the goal of utility maximization in economic contexts. The reason lies in the structure of the situation and the incomplete processing of information of the actors. This prevents optimizing decisions and explains the insufficiency of the market as an allocation mechanism to achieve economic efficieny. On *theoretical* grounds, the claim of modernization theory that economic processes are increasingly removed from their social embeddedness with the development of market economies can be rejected. The cultural deregulation of exchange relations and the constant changes of market structures through innovative processes in modern market economies produce the uncertainty for actors, which recreates the need for orientation to the cited social mechanisms in order to maintain the ability to act. Cooperation relies on normative structures and social networks. Paradoxically, it is the embeddedness of the market that is an essential prerequisite for the efficiency of market organized economies. Thus, the difference between the mode of functioning of modern and traditional economies consists not in the dimension of embeddedness but rather in *how* the contingent structures of expectation emerge and are reproduced. Unlike traditional economies, actors in modern economic structures must also keep ascertaining the validity of the social rules discursively. The cultural background is questioned, unlike traditional societies, where the actors widely presuppose its validity. Thus contingency threatens institutionalized ways of action and cooperative relations; it forces actors to create the obligatory background in reflexive processes, whereby failure always remains as a possibility. Thus the bases of efficiency are constituted in the action process itself. The limitation of the market as a presumption of economic processes is a contingent result of social action.

Embeddedness is then not a passive concept (Whittington 1992) but rather refers to the processes of the active construction of social preconditions of markets. The embeddedness of economic action, which is the premise of economic processes, relies on increasingly more reflexively gained self-civilization. This is especially valid because of the globalization of economic processes and the decentralization of organizational structures, which tend to repress cultural presumptions and hierarchies as coordination mechanisms of economic processes. We can imagine a dialectical process in which the market and social rigidities are understood as antagonistic mechanisms of social order, which mutually reinforce and negate one another, but nevertheless remain dependent on one another. The danger of sociological considerations of the economy, not to take sufficient account of the dynamics of economic processes because they emphasize conformity and not change (DiMaggio 1988), could thus be counterbalanced. If we assume that actors remain confronted with uncertainty, which is always being reproduced in actions, that cooperation is also the contingent result of processes of negotiation that have to be deliberately reproduced, and that innovations are shaped in a field of tension between expectations of profit and socially formed rigidities, we can understand economic processes as open and changing. For this, we must also include the conflictual nature of the various institutions, structures, norms, and routines that make choice and reflection fundamentally integral components of economic action.

A theoretically guided economic sociology can make important contributions to understanding economic processes and structures that are concealed from economic theories built on the rational-actor model. Thus, economic sociology can join institutionalist approaches in economics and studies of business management that have long since moved away from the idea of an actor acting as a universal optimizer. However, keep in mind that deserting the action model of *homo oeconomicus* also leads to the far-reaching abandonment of the possibilities of formalization that result from the equilibrium view of economic theory.[5] Sociological analysis of economic action is not oriented to the model of the natural sciences. Sociological theory does not have any formalized decision theory with general predictions for economic processes. It is not understood in a way that can be formalized how habit, culture, power, social structures and institutional expectations influence economic activity. Research in economic sociology uses institutional, cultural, and structural variables in comparative studies but without obtaining results that give general and lawlike explanations of economic phenomena. As long as the relationship of intentional rationality and social structures of expectation cannot be explained in a general causal theory, the maximizing paradigm of economic theory will not be abandoned. But theoretical concepts can be developed based on including sociological parameters whose empirical use produces valuable explanations of economic structures and processes. Developments in economics itself indicate that norms, institutions, power, cognitive limitations, and social structures have a fundamental significance for understanding economic processes. It is up to sociology to make insights that originate in sociological thought more productive for understanding economic processes through the systematic development of economic sociology.

NOTES

CHAPTER ONE
THE LIMITS OF THE RATIONAL-ACTOR MODEL AS A
MICROFOUNDATION OF ECONOMIC EFFICIENCY

1. This is not to deny that, in his moral philosophy, Adam Smith considered motives other than selfish interest relevant for the maintenance of social order. This discussion deals with the development of an analytical model.

2. In *The Passions and the Interests*, Albert Hirschman (1977) discusses contemporary opinions in the eighteenth century that expected the pacification of society from an orientation to interest (acquisition of money).

3. Cf. Albert (1972); Brockway (1993); Etzioni (1988); Gorz (1989); Hollis and Nell (1975); Kahneman, Knetsch, and Thaler (1986); Polanyi: (1944); Sen (1977); Simon (1945).

4. The term "orthodox economics" is not firmly defined and can easily lead to misunderstanding because it suggests that there is a homogeneous school of theory in economics. In this book, orthodox economics means approaches to economic theory that start from the assumption of maximizing action *and* the development of Pareto-optimal equilibrium through market processes.

5. Even though economists have made this point, it has remained insignificant for economic research. A telling example of this is an article by Kenneth Arrow (1983 [1969]), in which he indicates the significance of social norms for the achievement of efficient economic results: "Norms of social action, including ethical and moral codes . . . are reactions of society to compensate for market failures. It is useful for individuals to have some trust in each other's word. In the absence of trust it would become very costly to arrange for alternative sanctions and guarantees, and many opportunities for mutually beneficial cooperation would have to be foregone" (Arrow 1983:151). Arrow's article, which criticizes the assumptions of the general equilibrium theory and refers to transaction costs and asymmetrical distribution of information as reasons for market failure, has had a marked influence on economics since the 1970s, but Arrow's emphasis on the significance of social norms for the coordination of economic activities and the achievement of efficient results has been mostly ignored.

6. The difference between risk and uncertainty is explained in the second section of the chapter.

7. Weber's position (1988) can be understood thus.

8. See Joas's first chapter (1996).

9. That economic efficiency is obviously a legitimate basis for economic action was formulated impressively by Milton Friedman (1970): "The social responsibility of business is to increase its profits."

10. It makes a decisive difference for assessing the action if the tip is given in a favorite pub that is often visited or in a restaurant one will probably never return to. In the favorite pub, the tip can be interpreted as a long-term investment in anticipated service. The example of the returned wallet is similar: if the wallet belongs to a friend whom I can assume might know that I found the wallet, the

return can be interpreted as rational action: I can guarantee that my friend will not retaliate against me.

11. See the essays in the volume edited by Jane Mansbridge (1990a).

12. Hence, replacing self-interest with a concept of rationality demanding only consistency is incompatible with the central theorem of the welfare theory. Competition equilibria fulfill the condition of Pareto optimality only if the actors maximize their expressed self-interest in the utility function at the beginning of the action. The link between Pareto optimality and efficient competition equilibria emerges because Pareto optimality is defined through the maximization of individual utility in a social situation. The postulate of action oriented toward self-interest has great strategic significance for welfare theory in that respect and cannot simply be replaced by the weaker assumption of consistency. See Sen (1987).

13. However, there are interesting counterexamples in Meyer and Zucker (1988).

14. Therefore, from the perspective of economic theory, it can be stated normatively that altruistically acting entrepreneurs who *deliberately* disregard the consistent considerations of economic theory are to be criticized for their action because they contribute to the development of socially inefficient equilibria.

15. Max Weber, too: "It is of course true that economic action which is oriented on purely ideological grounds to the interests of others does not exist. But it is even more certain that the mass of men do not act in this way, and it is an induction from experience that they cannot do so and never will" (Weber 1978: 203).

16. This does not mean having to agree with the naturalized understanding of utility-maximizing of economic theory. The rational action orientation of actors is itself but one institutionalized form of action that is dependent on a definite social structure. Yet for now this does not change anything on the empirical level, as long as we are talking about social formations where instrumental action orientations in economic contexts dominate.

17. Precisely, this should be: *at least* two actors. However, the bilateral exchange is the simplest model to start with here.

18. For this argumentation, see especially the work of Williamson (1975; 1985).

19. For a survey, see Stiglitz (1994) and Schumann (1992:416ff.). The concept is explained later in this chapter.

20. The pioneer work of game theory is the book by von Neumann and Morgenstern (1944). A German survey of the cooperation problem in game theory is given by *Ökonomie und Gesellschaft, Jahrbuch* 12, *Soziale Kooperation*, 1995.

21. Examples of this are in Etzioni (1988) and Frank (1992).

22. With several examples, Jon Elster (1989, ch. 5) has shown that cooperation can lead to inefficient equilibria (e.g., in oligopolistic market structures and cartels) or that only the cooperation of a few actors, but not all of them, leads to an efficient result. The negative influences of cartels and oligolopolies are naturally also subjects of economic literature.

23. Another external solution for an n-person prisoner's dilemma is seen in the property rights approach in the creation of private property rights.

24. A Nash equilibrium consists of a noncooperative game when none of the players involved can achieve a higher utility through a different strategy as long

as the other players adhere to their strategy. A Nash equilibrium refers to a self-stabilizing agreement of the players because no rationally acting participant has an interest in deviating from the strategy.

25. Because no single author of the theorem is known.

26. See Elster (1989:4ff.). However, the problem of backward induction can be solved theoretically with slight modifications. See Kreps (1990:104).

27. A classical and still interesting study for the significance of trust in business relations is Macaulay (1963).

28. For the information presumptions in repeated games, see Aumann (1985).

29. See Macaulay (1963), Granovetter (1985), and Sabel (1993). A major difference between sociological and economic considerations of trust in long-term relations is that willingness for cooperation in sociology is attributed to past experiences; in economics, on the other hand, it is ascribed to expectations of the future action of a third party.

30. Coleman (1990b:45) notes that in the two-person prisoners' dilemma, a cooperative result can be achieved by conceiving of the situation as a bilateral exchange. If it is possible for both actors to communicate with each other, they can agree to yield their own behavioral options to one another. This exchange is conceivable because the allocative results for both actors are improved. However, this solution can be conceived only for the two-person prisoner's dilemma and presumes mutual trust of the actors for the exchange.

31. This is also confirmed by Hechter (1990b:15): "Hence, these institutions can persist only by precluding free riders, or by assuring would-be cooperators that they are not liable to be exploited by defectors."

32. Such a concept of norms in sociological theory is naturally linked especially to the work of Talcott Parsons.

33. This behavior is also considered by Jon Elster (1983b) in the metaphor of "sour grapes."

34. This was one of the main criticisms expressed in reviews of Coleman's *Foundations of Social Theory*. See Baron and Hannan (1994:1115).

35. Elster (1989:196) points to a cognate form of behavioral motivation, which he aptly characterizes as magical thinking. It is based on the confusion of causal and diagnostic reality or on the belief that one can change the cause by acting on the basis of the symptoms. The actor's consideration can be formulated as: "If I cooperate, there is a good chance that the other will cooperate too. Being like me, he will act like me. Let me, therefore, cooperate to bring it about that he does too" (197). It could be shown in experiments in cognitive psychology that actors do in fact act as if they think like this.

36. I shall not go into the argument presented by Ullmann-Margalit (1977), because, despite the title, *The Emergence of Norms*, I don't think this says anything about the genesis of norms. Norms appear instead as a deus ex machina in a functionalist argumentation: the essential proposal says "that generalized PD-structured situations (PD = Prisoners' Dilemma) constitute a type of contexts which are prone to generate norms. Unfolding this contention somewhat, the idea is the following: A situation of the generalized PD variety poses a problem to the participants involved. The problem is that of protecting an unstable yet jointly beneficial state of affairs from deteriorating, so to speak, into a stable yet jointly

destructive one. My contention concerning such a situation is that a norm, backed by appropriate sanctions, could solve this problem. In this sense it can be said that such situations 'call for' norms. It can further be said that a norm solving the problem inherent in a situation of this type is *generated* by it" (Ullmann-Margalit 1977:22).

37. See especially the discussion on functionalism and rational-choice theories in *The Journal of Theory and Society* (1982).

38. Jane Mansbridge (1990b) argues that relations of trust are eroded by exploitation. Only by reducing the costs of unselfish behavior can these be stabilized. See Offe (1989).

39. See Jon Elster (1989:139ff.). Elster also presents some examples that illustrate this argument.

40. For a consideration of uncertainty as a subject of German economic theory of the nineteenth and early twentieth centuries, see Priddat (1993). Wubben (1994) has a broader scope. Both books show that economics has recently paid more attention to the problem of uncertainty, mainly in connection with the works of the first half of this century.

41. This explanation of profits is no longer advocated in economics today. The explanation of profits developed by Chamberlain (1933) at about the same time, which derives them from product differentiation, is more influential.

42. For secondary literature dealing with Keynes's notion of uncertainty, see Hodgson (1988), Lawson (1985), and Shackle (1972; 1974).

43. Keynes (1973a:34). In his article of 1937 responding to criticism of the major work of 1936, Keynes defined his concept of uncertainty:

By "uncertain" knowledge, let me explain, I do not mean merely to distinguish what is known for certain from what is only probable. The game of roulette is not subject, in this sense, to uncertainty; nor is the prospect of a Victory bond being drawn. Or, again, the expectation of life is only moderately uncertain. Even the weather is only moderately uncertain. The sense in which I am using the term is that in which the prospect for a European war is uncertain, or the price of copper and the rate of interest in twenty years hence, or the obsolescence of a new invention, or the position of private wealth owners in 1970. About these matters there is no scientific basis on which to form any calculable probability whatever. We simply do not know. Nevertheless, the necessity for action and for decision compels us as practical men to do our best to overlook the awkward fact and behave exactly as we should if we had behind us a good Benthamite calculation of a series of prospective advantages and disadvantages, each multiplied by its appropriate probability, waiting to be summed. (Keynes 1973b:114)

44. For a summary of the argumentation of the general equilibrium theory, see Hahn (1980) and Weintraub (1974).

45. See Arrow (1984); Harsanyi (1986); Hammond (1987); Hirshleifer and Riley (1992); Postlewaite (1987).

46. One of the most important ideas that indicates a way out of market failure on the basis of an asymmetrical distribution of information is the concept of signaling developed by Michael Spence (1973). The sellers of high-quality merchan-

dise can impart that through signals, like extended warrantees or the establishment of trademarks. However, the theory of signaling is based on the fact that it is cheaper for the supplier of high-quality merchandise to send these signals than for the supplier of worse merchandise.

47. This distinction was introduced by Arrow (1985c).

48. See the work of Coase (1990) and Williamson (1975; 1985).

49. This observation was formulated aptly by Dosi and Orsenigo (1988:14ff.): "Schumpeter stressed the dichotomous role of markets and tried to reconcile them in an uneasy compromise between, first statics and equilibrium—to which Walrasian processes were supposed to apply—and second, dynamics—with the domain of entrepreneurship, disequilibrium and qualitative change of the economic system."

50. Schumpeter (1934:125) also emphasized uncertainty as an important situation characteristic of innovative behavior.

51. The first such classification refers to Hicks (1932), whose concept of neutrality analyzes technical progress, given a constant factor input ratio between capital and labor, as having no influence on the distribution of income. Technical progress that saves labor or capital has effects on the distribution of the social product between the factors of labor and capital and is therefore not neutral. In the Hicks-neutral progress, production elasticities remain constant and the marginal rate of factor substitution is not changed by technical progress. This connection is represented geometrically by a parallel shift of the isoquant to the origin. Empirically, however, it must be assumed that technical progress changes the marginal rate of factor substitution and thus saves either capital or labor. But such progress would conflict with the equilibrium assumptions of the neoclassical theory if it disturbed the dynamic equilibrium of an economy. A growth equilibrium demands the constancy of the coefficient of capital, which indirectly also demands the constancy of interest. Another concept of neutrality of technical progress refers to Harrod, which shows that, despite factor substitution, the distribution ratios can be maintained in the economy. The Harrod classification shows that technical progress and factor substitution can be equilibrated so that capital coefficient, interest, and income distribution remain constant. "These implications assign a paramount significance to the Harrod-neutral progress in the theory of equilibrated growth" (Walter 1977:572). A third concept of neutrality results from the inversion of the Harrod-neutral progress. If we do not start from a constant capital coefficient but rather from a constant wage and labor coefficient, the result is a concept known as a Solow-neutral progress. Such a capital saving progress does not emphasize organizational changes of more efficient labor insertions but changes of material capital, in which the shift of the production function is linked exclusively with a reduction of capital insertion and so leads to an isocost curve in which the factor ratio is changed in favor of a higher share of labor. In the Solow-neutral progress, too, the distribution of income between capital and labor remains unaffected.

52. For a summary, see Dosi (1988).

53. Thus Nordhaus and Tobin (1972) wrote: "The [neoclassical] theory conceals, either in aggregation or in the abstract generality of multisectoral models, all of the drama of events—the rise and fall of products, technologies, and industries, and the accompanying transformation of the spatial and occupational distri-

butions of the population. Many economists agree with the broad outlines of Schumpeter's vision of capitalist development, which is a far cry from growth models made nowadays in either Cambridge, Massachusetts or Cambridge, England. But visions of that kind have yet to be transformed into a theory that can be applied to everyday analytic and empirical work" (quoted by Nelson and Winter 1982:204). However, Nelson and Winter's works attempt to fill in these holes.

54. For consideration of an evolutionary theory of technological change, see especially Nelson and Winter (1982) and Nelson (1994).

55. It is estimated that the social yields of research and development are double those of private yields. See Mansfield et al. (1977).

56. For the nature of innovations as partially public goods, Arrow refers to a paradox of information as an economic good, which makes its availability in a competitive market difficult. The paradox is that the value of information for the purchaser "is not known until he has the information, but then he has in effect acquired it without costs" (Arrow 1985a:111).

57. This is the case, for example, when techniques are imitated. The success of the Japanese economy in the 1960s can be attributed especially to the appropriation of knowledge of goods manufactured in other nations.

58. If we consider the illegal area, the limitation of property rights by espionage is also to be cited. What is special about espionage—distinct from theft—is that the person harmed is not missing anything and may never discover the crime or may discover it only much later.

59. This strategy can be observed, for example, in the production of food. The composition of Coca Cola or certain herb-flavored liqueurs are kept secret.

60. See Elster (1983a:109).

61. The element of creative behavior in Schumpeter's theory of the entrepreneur has been emphasized especially by Harry Dahms (1995). Dahms also refers to the changes made by Schumpeter in the second edition of *Theory of Economic Development*. Thus Schumpeter dropped the distinction between static-hedonistic and dynamic-energetic behavior.

62. Since the work of Max Weber has been studied comprehensively, we shall forego a monographic chapter on this classic of sociological thought. See especially Swedberg (1993). However, aspects of Weber's thought appear in other chapters and in an appendix to chapter 20.

63. Among the exceptions, Herbert Spencer's sociology is the most important.

CHAPTER TWO
ÉMILE DURKHEIM: THE ECONOMY AS MORAL ORDER

1. In Germany, this interpretation is especially connected with the work of René König (1978). In the more recent Durkheim interpretation, the connection between awareness of social crisis and Durkheim's sociology was selected by Hans-Peter Müller (1983) as a starting point for studying Durkheim's work.

2. See Müller (1983:15). George Weisz (1983:90) refers to the significance ascribed to the universities, even politically, for overcoming the crises of French society: leading politicians of the Third Republic like Jules Ferry, Paul Bert, and Léon Bourgeois "believed that higher education, properly directed, could promote

consensus in a society divided by bitter social, political, and religious conflicts. They hoped that professors would apply scientific procedures to the study of social problems in order to elaborate the theories and ideas which in turn would promote political moderation and social integration."

3. This shows Durkheim's political involvement. In the French political spectrum, Durkheim affiliated with the republican forces whose program for overcoming the crisis of France was aimed neither at revolutionary abolition nor at restoration, but rather at a social stabilization of the Third Republic on the basis of the program of the values of the French Revolution. Through social reform, the goal of a "just social order" was to be achieved (Müller 1983:20).

4. See chapters 7 and 8 in Durkheim (1958).

5. The term utilitarianism is used here as introduced into sociology particularly by Talcott Parsons. Camic (1979) has shown that Parsons did not use it to convey the actual breadth of utilitarian thinking.

6. See the chapter on anomic suicide in Durkheim (1951) and in book 3 of *The Division of Labor in Society* (1984).

7. For the distinction between normal and pathological, see Durkheim (1966).

8. So far, the economic sociology of the Durkheim School has not received much attention. For a general classification, the work of John Craig (1983) is helpful; Craig cites the most important writings of Simiand and Halbwachs. In Germany, Hansjürgen Daheim (1981) has dealt with the works of Simiand.

9. Durkheim introduces the term institution in the preface to the second edition of *The Rules of Sociological Methods* but does not separate it systematically from social facts (see Müller 1983:75). As institutions, Durkheim characterized "all the beliefs and all the modes of conduct instituted by the collectivity" (Durkheim 1966:lvi). Like social facts, institutions are therefore characterized by their behavior-regulating influence.

10. According to Durkheim (1966:122), contract theories see society as "a work of art, a machine constructed entirely by hand of man, which, like all products of this kind, is only what it is because men have willed it so." Durkheim also criticizes the resulting discontinuity of the individual and society: the individual, initially independent of all sociality, is coerced by an external restraint to a social compact behavior, but this restraint does not appear as something natural. "Man is thus naturally refractory to the common life; he can only resign himself to it when forced" (121).

11. See Durkheim (1978a:46). For the analogy to Walras, I rely on Steiner (1992).

12. Social facts are not universal rules but are always valid in a concrete historical situation. Durkheim (1966:113) talks of the "internal constitution of the social group," in which he includes "the products of previous social activity . . . law, established customs, literary and artistic works." This is important because Durkheim's frequent analogies to the natural sciences can convey the impression that he is interested in laws in society whose validity is independent of time and place. Although Durkheim programmatically represents the natural sciences as a model for the methodology of sociology, an ambivalence about this model can be discerned in respect to the constraint of the milieu.

13. The irony of this critique is that marginal utility theory, whose program was also outlined in deliberate analogy with the natural sciences (Mirowski 1989), comes closer to the model than Durkheim, who considered social laws as related to milieu. In *Principles of Economics* (1871), Menger had already asserted the a priori validity of economic laws. Even allowing Durkheim this limitation of positivism in his concept of sociology, his assertion of the existence of social laws, as this term is used in the natural sciences, is called into question. Thus, the critique of economic theory can also be critically turned against Durkheim's own conception that there are social laws in the sense of the natural sciences, as stated in his early works.

14. In this vein, Durkheim (1978b:81) granted political economy a hybrid status "between art and science."

15. See also Durkheim (1960a:340; 1978a:64; 1966:34ff.).

16. A later programmatic article says that economic facts are "integrated with the collective functions; they become inexplicable when they are violently removed from that context" (Durkheim 1978a:81).

17. For a critique of the contrast between normal and pathological in Durkheim, see Lukes (1985:28ff.).

18. Note that Durkheim practically does not deal with the institution of money. This is especially amazing since Durkheim (1900) knew Simmel's epoch-making work, *The Philosophy of Money*, which appeared in 1900, and discussed it in *L'Année Sociologique*. Not surprisingly, Durkheim's very negative criticism challenged Simmel's central thesis that money exercised an essentially moral influence on society and can attain structural significance for social relations. Neither before nor after the criticism of Simmel's book is there any proof that Durkheim engaged in a systematic debate with the role of money. But in the *Rules*, money is cited as an example of a social fact. See Durkheim (1966:2).

19. For Durkheim, division of labor means especially the functional differentiation of professional fields. See Joas (1996); Rüschemeyer (1985); Schmid (1989).

20. That in *The Division of Labor in Society*, Durkheim relied solely on the solidarity effect of functional differentiation is also unlikely, as Hans Joas (1996:59) explains, on the background of his criticism of economic theory: "He had had to resort to a position he had himself previously criticized: the belief in the benevolent moral consequences of the modern economy, which he regarded as an illusion of political economy."

21. See Holton (1992:189).

22. It can be assumed that Durkheim recognized that the contract as an institution cannot exercise social constraints on the exchange partners sufficiently to connect them back to the idea of a just social order, and that, in his later writings, he shifted his consideration to other institutions to regulate the economy. In the later writings, especially in *Suicide* and the second foreword to *The Division of Labor in Society*, Durkheim relies more strongly than in *The Division of Labor in Society* on the establishment of professional groups as the institution to transcend the antagonism of exchange relations. Contract law regulates the elaboration of contracts only within a very wide margin, because the legislature's main task is to protect freedom of contract. This can also be seen as an interesting

reason for Durkheim's more sober approach to the state as a power of economic regulation. See inter alia Durkheim (1984:297).

23. Durkheim (1992) discusses this in detail in Lectures 15 through 18 of the book on *Professional Ethics*.

24. The problem of value in Durkheim is the subject of the next section.

25. In another place, Durkheim (1984:162) says: "Summing up, therefore, the contract is not sufficient by itself, but is only possible because of the regulation of contracts, which is of social origin."

26. Correspondingly, Durkheim also challenges the assumption that social development reaches a one-sided extension of private contracts and thus an atrophying of socially regulated social relations. As proof of this, Durkheim cites the historical origin of marriage and adoption contracts, showing that the relations regulated in them initially had a private character and gradually became stronger subjects of social regulation. See Durkheim (1984:154ff.). Therefore, Durkheim sees the scenario of an increasing desiccation of morally regulated relations and their conversion to purely private contract relations as a one-sidedly curtailed representation of the modernization process, which lacks a central element. An interesting parallel to this argumentation can be seen in Habermas's argumentation of the simultaneous development of system *and* life world in the process of modernization. See Habermas (1984).

27. Durkheim sees inheritances especially as a cause of the unequal power of the parties to the contract. See Durkheim (1992:263ff.).

28. Durkheim's price theory is the subject of the next section.

29. Aside from the improbability that actors in modern society will subject themselves to such a moral bond, that still leaves the problem that an essential advantage of the market vis-à-vis other economic control mechanisms consists precisely of its lack of moral assumptions. See Heilbroner (1986) and Hirshman (1977).

30. This also modifies the break often assumed in the literature on Durkheim between Durkheim's optimistic perspective in *The Division of Labor in Society* and the pessimism concerning the anomie of economic relations in the later works. See inter alia, Schmid (1989:633). Even in *The Division of Labor in Society*, Durkheim starts from the need for a strict moral regulation of private economic exchange relations.

31. With the exception of the discussion of anomic division of labor in book 3 of *The Division of Labor in Society*. As is shown later, the concept of overcoming anomie expresses a theory of order that understands moral integration as emerging from the interactions of the actors.

32. Joas (1996:60–61) also criticizes Durkheim's *Division of Labor in Society* for not distinguishing "between the antagonistic division of labor by the marketplace and the non-antagonistic division of labor by organized cooperation." Durkheim could assume the emergence of a new morality from the division of labor only because he thought of the division of labor as the reflexive insight into the demands of cooperation. It would be interesting to study the reverse hypothesis of how far solidary relations can emerge from the market. Market relations are not only antagonistic, but are also characterized by the feature of "antagonistic cooperation" (Kliemt 1986). In a hypothetical construction in *Economy and Soci-*

ety, Weber describes how new legal regulations develop "from habituation to an action" (Weber 1978:754). "The parties to the new arrangements are frequently unconcerned about the fact that their respective positions are insecure in the sense of being legally unenforceable. They regard legal enforceability by the state as either unnecessary or as self-evident; even more frequently do they simply rely upon the self-interest or the loyalty of their partners combined with the weight of convention" (756).

33. Only agency theory considers organizations as consisting of contract relations.

34. In any case, it can be claimed that Durkheim did not sufficiently separate between various forms of division of labor. But this may be understood if we examine the problem he was primarily interested in: neither market relations nor internal cooperation can be understood perfectly—as was shown in chapter 1— starting from the rational-actor model. The problem of defection exists in both forms of division of labor, and it can be argued for both forms that the moral integration of the actors is imperative. If Durkheim wanted to show this as opposed to Spencer's individualistic social theory, he did not need to distinguish between various forms of the division of labor.

35. See Durkheim (1951:364): "When one chooses progress and improvement, that also goes hand in hand with a certain level of anomie."

36. What counters this interpretation of *The Division of Labor in Society* is that Durkheim cited increasing competition (!) because of the density of interactions as one of the causes of the division of labor.

37. Simon Clarke (1991:179) grasps the ambivalent relation of Durkheim and classical sociology between individualism and collectivism: "In rejecting political economy, these critics were not rejecting liberalism. Thus they were not prepared to fall into the arms of the conservatives in subordinating the individual to supra-individual principles. The result is that in all of these theories we find a constant dualistic tendency with the individual, on the one hand, and the state or society, on the other, appearing as complementary ends without any rigorous theory of the relations between the two."

38. This view was rejected by the economists who participated in the discussion. Yves Guyot answered Durhkeim: "Value is determined by two objective elements: the price of production costs and the purchasing power" (quoted in Durkheim 1908:116).

39. It is not clear whether Durkheim was aware of the economic discussion of the relationship of value and price in his argument against the classical labor theory of value. Durkheim gives no references to economic literature on this problem. For the significance of this discussion for the development of economics, see Clarke (1991).

40. See the introduction to this chapter, as well as the work of König (1978) and Müller (1983).

41. See also Durkheim (1951:249; 1978b:81).

42. Yet this does not mean that Durkheim would systematically delineate the labor market because of the specific characteristics of the commodity traded there. Durkheim (1984:310ff.) sees the distinctions in the social power of the actors as problematic and refers to the limited mobility of the worker. But what is lacking,

for example, is the reference that workers cannot strategically regulate their offer on the market or that the concentration of resources in collective action is subject to specific restrictions. See Offe and Wiesental (1980); Purdy (1988).

43. In *Professional Ethics and Civic Morals* (1992:209), Durkheim describes the components of the value of a good as "a sense of true usefulness of things and services, of the labor they have cost, of the relative ease or difficulty in procuring them, traditions and prejudices of every kind, and so on."

44. By linking prices to social notions of justice, Durkheim is in the tradition of the medieval theory of the just price. This tradition referred to moral standards for price setting and rejected the individual pursuit of profit. Individual use of economic chances was to be prevented. Historically, however, the price regulation aimed at by the theory of the just price foundered in the late Middle Ages with the expansion of long-distance commerce and the developing capitalistic economy; market-oriented price theories of classical economics developed with the consolidation of market structures. This context of intellectual history is interesting because it refers again to the unsolved ambiguity in Durkheim's economic sociology between moral order and the expansion of economic freedom. The introduction of a just price would demand the abolition of the antagonism between actors that characterizes the market. A just price for determining the actual exchange relations does not exist not only because of the contemporary anomie observed by Durkheim but also because it would be incompatible in principle with a market order.

45. I refer here to Reuter's (1994) description.

46. Another difference between the two theories of value is that Durkheim always sees price as an expression of public opinion, and a discrepancy of both must be regarded as anomie, a deviation from a supposed normality. The price mechanism of the market thus has only a place in the theory as a model of explanation for a pathological condition of economic relations. Veblen, on the other hand, has no trouble acknowledging the reality of the market price determination. His criticism of economic reality operates in the field of tension between social optimality and the reality behind it—see Veblen (1979[1899]). It is not the significance of the market for the determination of the price that is challenged, but merely the claim of neoclassical economics that the market produces a socially desirable allocation of goods.

47. For a critique of Veblen's technocratic model, see Bell (1980).

48. See book 3 of *The Division of Labor in Society.*

49. See Durkheim (1992:292ff.; 1984:303). In both places, however, Durkheim's clear distance from government measures of social reform can be seen. He did seem to welcome these, but did not estimate that they would have great significance for the task of the moral reintegration of the economy. Durkheim's skepticism about the government for the task of social regulation can also be seen in the third section of chapter 7 in book 1 of *The Division of Labor in Society.*

50. See Durkheim (1992:214). Durkheim obviously took the emphasis of the centrality of a reform of property law for the development of a "just" social order oriented toward meritocratic principles from Saint-Simon. See Durkheim (1958).

51. This critique is also made by Lockwood (1992:81). Durkheim "is not at all concerned with the structure and dynamics of the economic system which produces inequalities of power and wealth."

52. This applies in competitive markets and complete information of the market participants.

53. This was also argued by Karl Polanyi (1944), who views the attempt at a pure market coordination of economic exchange in the nineteenth century as historically unique and analyzes it as the cause of the social and political instability that led to World War I. For Polanyi, economic relations have to be embedded socioculturally in relations of reciprocity or redistribution in order not to be socially destabilizing.

54. See, for example, Weber (1978:24f., 635ff.). A description of the significance of the concept of habit in classical sociological theory was presented by Charles Camic (1986).

55. See Giddens (1984) and the last chapter of this book.

56. For the significance of habits and routines in the contexts of economic decision, see also Granovetter (1985) and Nelson and Winter (1982).

57. The most detailed argument with Durkheim's concept of the professional group is the study by Kurt Meier (1984), who tried to make the concept productive for the debate on neocorporatism.

58. In the foreword, Durkheim also notes that he had intended to write a special study on professional groups, but "other plans" had prevented that. See Durkheim (1984:xxxi).

59. See Durkheim (1984:xxxiv). See also Camic (1986:1053).

60. See Durkheim (1992:276ff.). In the foreword to the second edition of *The Division of Labor in Society*, Durkheim objected drastically to the growth of importance of the state in society: "A society made up of an extremely large mass of unorganised individuals, which an overgrown state attempts to limit and restrain, constitutes a veritable sociological monstrosity" (Durkheim 1984:liv).

61. The connection between economics and physics was studied in detail by Philip Mirowski (1989).

62. Like Marshall (1961) and Pareto (1980).

63. An important exception is the economic theory of Adolph Löwe. For a discussion, see Ganssmann (1996).

64. For Durkheim's positivistic formulation of sociology in *The Rules of Sociological Method*, however, it is not the debate with economics that is decisive, but rather the reference to Comte and the tradition of the French Enlightenment.

65. This does not mean that there had been no attempt to integrate economics back into an overall concept of social science. Stölting (1986:78ff.) gives a good review of such "conciliation attempts" between sociology and economics in the German-language context, which lasted until the 1930s.

66. See the citations in chapter 1 of Joas (1996).

67. While this interpretation of the differentiation of economics and the subsequent formation of sociology with the acknowledgment of economics as a reconstruction of the history of development seems valid, note too that it thus concerns a historically contingent development. It can at least be imagined that sociology developed as an encyclopedic social science. Support for a reintegration of the two fields, which lasted until the 1930s, indicates the problematic nature of the process of differentiation between them.

68. On the other hand, Hennis (1987) objected to this interpretation, which emphasizes differences between Weber and the Historical School. Hennis tries to show how strongly all of Weber's work is in the tradition of the understanding of the economy shaped by the Historical School (especially Knies). On a substantial level, this is not to be challenged. Weber's use of the economic model of action as an "ideal type" and the admonition that economic action in modern contexts also includes other aspects of action than instrumental ones show this on a theoretical level. At any rate, Hennis's claim of a methodological continuity (see Hennis 1987:162ff.) between Weber's position in the essay on objectivity of 1949 and the position of the Historical School does not seem correct to me. In any case, Hennis's position is formulated as a weak hypothesis when he writes that the "past masters" of the Historical School had "also paved the way 'methodologically'" (166).

69. See the citations in the chapter 1 of Joas (1996).

CHAPTER THREE
TALCOTT PARSONS: THE ECONOMY AS A SUBSYSTEM OF SOCIETY

1. See Camic's (1991) biographical references.

2. Most of these articles are reprinted in Camic (1991). For the explanation of the development of his work, see the autobiographical remarks in Parsons (1977).

3. Arguments with Parsons's understanding of economics are in Alexander (1984); Gould (1991); Holton (1986); Rocher (1975); Saurwein (1988); Swedberg (1986). For Parsons's early work, see Burger (1977); Camic (1991); Perman (1995); Wearne (1989); Wenzel (1990).

4. Utilitarianism here is always used in the sense of Parsons's understanding of this term. For a critical reflection of Parsons's interpretation of the utilitarian tradition, see the work of Charles Camic (1979).

5. See, inter alia, Alexander (1984; 1987); Joas (1996); Münch (1990); Wenzel (1990).

6. For that, we refer to the works of Alexander (1987), Camic (1991), Wearne (1989), and in the German context, especially to the outstanding study by Wenzel (1990).

7. Ralph Schimmer (1997) especially has systematically worked out the significance of populism for the development of Veblen's work.

8. In articles of the 1930s, Parsons kept repeating that he was a sociologist: "The reader is asked to bear in mind that the present writer is a sociologist, not an economist" (Parsons 1991a:153).

9. In his autobiographical writings, Parsons (1977:24) notes: "It gradually became clear to me that economic theory should be conceived as standing within some sort of theoretical matrix in which sociological theory also was included."

10. As in the article, "Some Reflections": "It will be necessary to consider the place of economics in the whole system of the sciences of action" (Parsons 1991a:162).

11. The justification for developing the system of action indicated in the article "Some Reflections on the 'Nature and Significance of Economics'" shows that it crystallized in the debate with the question of a sociological conceptualization of

economics. Harald Wenzel (1990) in particular referred to the significance of the epistemological positions of the historian of science Lawrence Henderson and the philosopher Alfred North Whitehead for Parsons's methodological conception of "analytic realism."

12. Parsons also uses the accusation of behaviorism to reject Veblen's institutionalist economics. Parsons sees Veblen's appeal to customs to explain action in economic contexts as a behavioristic version of the concept of institution, which he sees as a clear regression vis-à-vis the action theory of orthodox economics. See Parsons (1934–35:440ff.).

13. This distinction between technology and economics also refers back to Robbins (1969:35).

14. Interestingly, Parsons sees this view of sociology as an analytically differentiated scientific discipline developed furthest in Georg Simmel. See Parsons (1991a:167; 1949a:772ff.). However, the chapter on Simmel written originally for *Structure* is not included in the published version. For the relationship of Simmel to Parsons see the work of Donald Levine (1991).

15. For such an attempt, see Gould (1991).

16. See Keynes (1964), Loasby (1976), and Hodgson (1988), especially the explanations of that in chapter 1.

17. The most precise German discussion of Parsons's scientific theoretical position is the study by Wenzel (1990), which especially elaborates the significance of Alfred North Whitehead's analytical realism.

18. In the context of this study, the differences between an analytical basis of sociology and Weber's methodological concepts cannot be discussed in detail. But in this context, the reader is referred to the work of Alfred Schütz (1993), the correspondence between Schütz and Parsons in the 1940s (Schütz and Parsons 1977), and the articles by Holton (1989), Prendergast (1986) and Zaret (1980).

19. Sauerwein (1988) showed in this context that Parsons also qualifies the juxtaposition of sociology and economics. From the integrative angle of sociological theory, economic rationality cannot be regarded "from outside" as a decisive principle but can "only be reconstructed in the logic of its cultural and normative meaning" (Saurwein 1988:23).

20. This was *General Economic History*, published in 1927.

21. For details about Frank Knight and his relation to Parsons, I refer to Perman (1995).

22. Perman (1995:12). Camic (1991) especially indicated that Parsons's intellectual attempt to define a sociological discipline was also motivated by the effort to establish the discipline firmly within the American university system. Yet it must be added that the strong economic orientation in determining the analytical subject matter of Parsons's sociology naturally also left him vulnerable in terms of sociology. This is especially valid because sociology in the United States in the mid-1930s was already institutionalized in the university. Indeed, this did not apply to Harvard.

23. This hypothesis already appeared in *The Social System* (1951), even if it was not yet elaborated: "Here we find the point of departure of economic theory as a special branch of the theory of social systems" (Parsons 1951:124). In the *Marshall Lectures*, Parsons expresses his own surprise at this discovery which he

became aware of while working out the lectures because the theory of social systems had not been developed based on the economy or economic theory (Parsons 1986:20).

24. I cannot agree with Gould's (1991) assessment that Parsons's position changed in this regard between *The Structure of Social Action* and the works relating to economics of the 1950s. *The Structure of Social Action* was constructed as a "devastating critique of utilitarian theory" (Gould 1991:91), but orthodox economics was to be able to keep its place in the action frame of reference.

25. See the critique of Pearsons (1957). For economic reviews, see Bumoln (1957); Hutchinson (1957); Worswick (1957). The skepticism of the economists is also expressed by the fact that, after Parsons delivered the first *Marshall Lecture*, many did not appear for any of the other lectures. See Smelser (1981:146) and Swedberg (1986:V).

26. Parsons connects the subsystem with the function of goal achievement (G) with the polity. The connection of concrete social fields with functional imperatives is clearly weaker in the other two subsystems. Thus, the integrative subsystem is identified with the cultural patterns of value of society and the pattern maintenance system is made congruent with the stable institutionalized aspects of culture.

27. For Parsons's concept of utility, see my subsequent discussion.

28. One of the early critiques of viewing the economy as a social system consists of the reproach that Parsons and Smelser assume no unequivocal position with regard to the action typological significance of their allocation of the economy. Harry W. Pearsons's criticism (1957) is that the adaptive function can also mean the specific action type of purposive rationality. This objection, formulated against the background of Polanyi's critique of neoclassical economic theory, implied that the use of Parsons's theoretical framework was limited to modern market economies. See Pearsons (1957:314). This critique is especially relevant with respect to the boundary interchanges conceptualized by Parsons and Smelser between the subsystems of society (and within the economic system), which are applied as performance sanction mechanisms analogous to market processes. But the critique does not apply because Parsons and Smelser do not delineate the economy on the basis of a typology of action, but rather under functional criteria of the systems demands for the reproduction of society. The AGIL scheme is outlined against the background of a functionally differentiated society. In traditional societies, however, the same function requirements must be fulfilled, with the difference that no differentiated organizations develop for it and the economic action orientation is institutionalized only to a small extent.

29. See Arrow. For a brief explanation of Arrow's impossibility theorem, see Backhouse (1985:307ff.).

30. The second area, along with boundary interchanges, in which Parsons and Smelser produce a correspondence with economic theories on a fundamental level is the allocation of production factors to the functional demands of the economic subsystem. The production factor of capital is allocated to the adaptive subsystem; land, to the pattern maintenance system; organization or entrepreneurship, to the integrative system; and labor, to the goal-attainment system.

31. Assigning the family to the pattern maintenance system is not developed in *Economy and Society* but prior to that in the *Working Papers* (Parsons et al.:1953).

32. An example of that would be Marxist social theories based on the distinction of use value and exchange value, which emphasize the notion of reification. Marcuse (1964) among others, used this theoretical distinction to quarrel with the alienating character of mass consumption.

33. Parsons and Smelser's argumentation naturally does not show the historical genesis of money, but only considers the functional need of the use of money for differentiation in the economy as a social subsystem.

34. While theoretical views of money play only a subordinate role in *Economy and Society*, in the 1960s Parsons (especially Parsons 1963) develops an innovative view of money that interprets it as a symbolically generalized medium. The analysis of money as a medium of communication, which the economy uses to regulate its boundary processes with other subsystems, becomes the model for Parsons's theory of media, which conceptualizes symbolically generalized media for all subsystems. Parsons describes money with reference to economic theories of money as an exchange medium, whose function consists of measuring value (Parsons 1963:236). Thus, money is symbolic "in that, though measuring and thus 'standing for' economic value or utility, it does not itself possess utility in the primary consumption sense—it has no 'value in use' but only 'in exchange,' i.e. for possession of things having utility" (236). Offers for the purchase or sale of goods or services can be communicated with the medium of money. Parsons pursues the development of money historically from its metallic form, in which it still possesses value itself. In differentiated economies structured on money, this link is completely dissolved, so that money becomes worthless from the point of view of its use value. Parsons explains the theoretical problem arising from the worthlessness of money, that is, why an individual in an exchange process should be willing to deliver a good in exchange for worthless money, by the degree of freedom the actor achieves through the medium of money: the buyer can give money for any good, he can buy from any supplier, he can freely determine the time of the acquisition, and he is free to accept or reject the conditions of the purchase. The disadvantage of the worthlessness of money is compensated for by the gain of options and motivates acceptance of the medium in exchange. Yet there is still the risk that money is not accepted by a third party or becomes worthless through inflation. This danger exists when money is not linked in some form to a good that possesses use value itself. But, for Parsons, separating money from the historical origin in precious metals is a prerequisite for its efficient functioning as a medium of exchange, which is why this risk is structurally contained in differentiated economies. The confidence of the economic actors in the stability and acceptance of the symbolic medium is based on its institutionalization. "There must be an element of bindingness in the institutionalization of the medium itself—e.g. the fact that the money of a society is a 'legal tender' which must be accepted in the settlement of debts which have the status of contractual obligations under the law" (240). Thus Parsons explains the willingness to accept money not as a rational decision of the actors, but rather as a reference to an external, normatively legitimated force of sanction. A prerequisite for the development of the money

economy is the separation of economic exchange processes from the embedding in culturally sanctioned expectations of reciprocity. Only under this condition are the degrees of freedom acquired through the acquisition of money relevant; otherwise they cannot be exercised on the basis of institutionalized obligations. Yet Parsons does not deal with the question of whether the use of money is an expression of diminishing bonds of reciprocity in society or whether money plays an active role in dissolving cultural traditions. With the concept of symbolically generalized media, Parsons does not shed any light on the structural influence of money; see Ganssmann (1986). If money is considered at all, it is in its egalitarian effect, as expressed aptly by Parsons in the sentence, "all dollars are created free and equal" (Parsons 1963:242). In exchange processes regulated by money, the social status of buyer or seller is unimportant; only the price is decisive for the acquisition. But Parsons considers it possible nonetheless that extraeconomic issues in connection with the status of the buyer also enter into exchanges regulated by money (ibid.).

35. This does not apply to the efficiency wage model presented by Akerlof (1984), in which the orientation of the agents' actions to the interests of the principals is achieved by complying with standards of fairness.

36. See the interesting work of Johannes Berger (1992; 1995), which deals with the principal-agent approaches from a sociological perspective. Samuel Bowles and Herbert Gintis (1990), who introduced the term "contested exchange," have attempted to establish a bond between Marx and principal-agent approaches.

37. "Boundary roles" means that "boundary processes are both roles in the system, and in at least one other with which it interpenetrates" (Parsons 1986:27). Interpenetration means that "the same concrete unit, the role of an individual or a collectivity, is a unit in more than one system at the same time" (26). In terms of definition, the term "boundary role" contains the process of interpenetration.

38. By emphasizing prestige, Parsons also refers to Durkheim's concept of the institution. In the preface to the second edition of *The Rules of Sociological Method* (1966:lvi), Durkheim used the social constraint resulting from institutions, among other things, to explain that this receives a prestige which exercises a binding effect on action.

39. See Parsons and Smelser (1956:143). Compared with his position in *Economy and Society*, Parsons's position in the *Marshall Lectures* is more skeptical vis-à-vis the integrative capacity of the institutionalization of the occupation roles (Parsons 1986:50ff.). In the *Marshall Lectures*, Parsons considers the extraeconomic incorporation of the role bearer even within the organization as influencing behavior, because the conflict cannot be completely transcended.

40. Here, Parsons probably used the introduction of the five-dollar day in Henry Ford's factory as an empirical basis. In another text, Ford is explicitly mentioned in the same relevant connection. See Parsons (1960:137).

41. Like many other places in *Economy and Society*, this also shows the close connection between Parsons's general theoretical thoughts and the concrete social structure of the 1950s. The same also applies to the reference to Keynes's theory.

42. See Parsons and Smelser (1956:156). What is meant by a connection with economics is not clarified methodologically in Parsons and Smelser's explanations. The course of the labor supply function in the neoclassical labor market

theory does not absolutely depict its empirical course, but it does allow the labor market model to be formulated mathematically. On the basis of the standards of theory in economics, a sociological *connection* to labor market economics had to be general and able to be formulated mathematically. But such a project is neither announced nor carried out in *Economy and Society*.

43. Here too, there is a clear parallel with Durkheim, who considered unjust contracts as a central cause of socioeconomic crises.

44. Parsons's analogy to credit allocation shows how tautly economic concepts are strained in the framework of the theory. Concurring with economic theory, credit can indeed be designated as general purchasing power, but credit allocation is oriented primarily to economic goals (particularly interest and investment security) and not to social goals. In any case, the latter can be usefully claimed for government allocation of credit.

45. Technological know-how itself progresses on two more stages, of general scientific knowledge, and as a most general stage of "cognitive raw material" (Parsons and Smelser 1956:132). Neither stage has any relationship to the economic system.

46. The "investment contract" is seen as an institutional equivalent of the labor contract, and the role of ownership is equivalent to the occupational role. The institution of the investment contract includes first the interest-oriented dimension of a mutually advantageous exchange, that is, the time-limited surrender of capital in exchange for the payment of interest. But, according to Parsons's basic notion of institution, the contract cannot be exhausted in this instrumental dimension. Instead, the investment contract also includes an integrative aspect and is thus established firmly in the general system of values. On the integrative level, the common expectation consists of the productive investment of capital, which ensures deposits and creates an altogether stabilizing confidence in the economy. Moreover, investments are incorporated into the common convictions of a public responsibility for the productive use of capital (Parsons and Smelser 1956:129). The multidimensionality of the institutional relation between organization and investor stabilizes this relation and also refers beyond the individual economic interest.

47. However, an empirical program that studies the values common to the polity and the economy can be added to Parsons's thory. See Holton (1986:74).

48. In an early critique of *Economy and Society*, Terence Hopkins (1957) argues that the use of Parsons and Smelser's theory was limited to modern societies. Yet this mistakenly inferred from the empirical reference point for the elaboration of *Economy and Society*, which was explicitly set in modern societies to the applicability of the theoretical concepts. These have at least the claim of universal validity. However, for Parsons, orthodox economic theory, whose applicability depends on the empirical existence of a rational-action orientation, is limited to modern societies.

49. See Parsons (1951:125). However, this argumentation can be interpreted as a salvage attempt intended to defend the universal applicability of the outlined theoretical scheme, which relies on the premise of the possibility of incorporating economic theory.

CHAPTER FOUR
NIKLAS LUHMANN: THE ECONOMY AS AN AUTOPOIETIC SYSTEM

1. For a discussion of the problems of causality and probability in Weber, see Coser (1977:224ff.).

2. Luhmann's social theory is both closely related and fundamentally counter to that of Talcott Parsons. Both theoretical approaches share a common systematic starting point. Society is understood as a social system, which is subdivided into subsystems, which form environments for one another. Correspondingly, Luhmann analyzes the economy as a social system. The two theoretical approaches also share a common metatheoretical frame of reference, from which social structures are examined. At the same time, Luhmann's theory deviates from Parsons's in five fundamental premises: (1) the division of society into subsystems each with specific communications media is not introduced analytically by Luhmann but as a factual description of the functioning and delimitation of subsystems; (2) systems are not conceptualized in an interchange relationship to the social systems around them according to the input-output model but rather as self-referentially closed; (3) the economy is not dependent on a normative system of values for its reproduction but only on the possibility of continuing meaningful communication; (4) the system rationality of the economy is not thought to depend on the institutionalization of a specific type of action; (5) for Parsons systems are action systems, whereas for Luhmann social systems consist only of communication, and actors are located in the environment of the system. Parsons was interested in exposing the institutional preconditions for the realization of purposive rational behavior in the economy. Luhmmann's critique of the utilitarian theory is more radical because he disregards completely the possibility of an inference of a subsystem by classifying a type of action.

3. See the work of Baecker (1988; 1991; 1993).

4. See Berger (1987); Gomez and Probst (1985); Kasper (1991); Kirsch and zu Knyphausen (1991); Wimmer (1989). For critical debates with Luhmann's economic sociology, I would emphasize Beckenbach (1989); Berger (1987); Ganssmann (1986); and Münch (1990; 1994).

5. The theory of autopoietic systems was essentially developed by the Chilean biologists Maturana and Varela. The concept, as it is used today in the social sciences, refers mainly to the works of Niklas Luhmann. Kirsch and zu Knyphausen (1991) indicate that the theory of autopoietic systems was introduced into the social sciences from biology on two levels: by understanding individuals as autopoietic systems, which constitute the realm of the social by their specific type of interaction; and, the variant dealt with here, by constituting the theory, on the level of general systems theory, which then includes social systems as special cases.

6. The environment of the system means everything that is not in the system itself. For a functionally differentiated social system (economy, politics, etc.), all other subsystems are the environment, like the natural environment and psychological systems (processes of consciousness). For the concept of the psychological system, see Luhmann (1995a:255ff.).

7. In modern economies, this essentially means stocks of money: "Money helps the ability to wait" (Luhmann 1981:395). Or, as Shackle (1958:195) expresses it: "Money is dope, a tranquilizer against the effect of not knowing what to do."

8. This can also be challenged. The economists John R. Presley and John G. Sessions (1994) argued in a debate with the principles of the Islamic economy that the ban on interest can lead to a more efficient allocation of capital because more information flows to the lender.

9. The general social system means society, which is subdivided into functionally differentiated subsystems. The characteristic of social systems is to be seen in that these consist of meaningful communications as their elements. According to Luhmann, society is "the most encompassing system of meaningful communications" (Luhmann 1989:28). Accordingly, society exists only as long as communication takes place and would cease to exist the moment communication stops. This notion of society excludes both consciousness (mental systems) and all events of the natural environment. Thus, in society understood as a social system, the complexity in events occurring in the world is reduced so much that only those events that are communication occur. Communication is linked essentially to speech but also includes gestures, body language, and the like (Kasper 1991:12). Accordingly, the subject of society is everything that can be communicated, and Luhmann characterizes society as "uncommonly rich in frequencies" (Luhmann 1989:16). Communication is initially simply structurally limited by the always momentary and partial view of the world, because "everything cannot be said all at once" (ibid.).

10. Luhmann defines the economic system as "all those operations transacted through the payment of money" (Luhmann 1989:51). This definition results from the premises of self-referentiality, the reduction of complexity, and autopoiesis. By reducing the economic system to payments, Luhmann constricts the scope of his statements on social formations that regulate exchange relations monetarily. The social function of providing for material needs is indeed universal but is to be found as a problem for differentiating a specialized subsystem only in those societies that institutionalize money. The economy as a partial social system can be differentiated only by duplicating scarcity in the medium of money. The theory does not expand to the explanation of pre-modern societies that do not have a differentiated medium of money. The limited scope of Luhmann's concept of the economy represents an important objection to the outline. See Mader (1985).

11. For a critical discussion of the concept of symbolically generalized media of communication, see Ganssmann (1996), Gould (1976), and Habermas (1980).

12. Luhmann (1988a:191). For Weber (1978), too, along with the private and government ownership in production means, the *money economy* was the most important prerequisite of modern bureaucracy and market economies.

13. Codes denote the final consistency of the system and cannot be replaced without destroying the autopoiesis of the system. In terms of evolutionary theory, codes are, in a way, the predecessor of the differentiation of social subsystems; they contribute to forming the subsystem. The differentiation of the economic system is based historically on the institution of property, which first enables a distinction between owning and not owning, and thus the orientation of the scarcity problematic to this semantics. Similarly, the distinction between just and un-

just is a prerequisite for the differentiation of the legal system, and the difference between true and untrue a prerequisite for the emergence of the scientific system (Luhmann 1989:41–42). In referring to the economic system, payments are made, which presuppose the ability to pay and also create the ability to pay. The operations of the economic system are depleted in making decisions about payments and observing the payments of others.

14. Moreover, money is to make access to scarce goods acceptable for the third party who is excluded from access to goods because access is paid for. Thus, money is assigned a socially pacifying role; it "averts violence for the area it can order" (Luhmann 1988a:253). This reasoning is unsatisfactory insofar as it presents no advance vis-à-vis barter, in which the purchaser of one item has to turn over another item. In any case, Luhmann can refer to the abstraction from the concrete item, which allows attention to be focused solely on the value dimension of the transfer of property. But this assumes a perfect abstraction of the material dimension of the goods which cannot easily be assumed. Drawing analogies from the scarcity of money and goods overlooks the differences between the two: "While limiting the supply of money is dictated solely by the functional demands of the monetary system, limiting the supply of goods is determined by conditions of production or nature" (Beckenbach 1989:893).

15. If systems observe their own observations or the observations of other systems, this is considered second-order observations.

16. Descriptions are observations articulated in words, hence not gestures, body language, and the like.

17. Everything that is produced as difference or can be presented in this form (see Willke 1987a:100), in which difference must also make sense for the system, can be observed. Thus, for the economic system the difference of good and evil (the leading difference of religious systems) is meaningless, while the difference of owning and not owning guides behavior.

18. The stimulation of a system by its environment is called resonance, which sets the system in motion, in which the system can react only according to its own structures (possibilities of processing information). See Luhmann (1989:25).

19. Thus, in the observation and description of itself and its environment, the system constructs its own identity, which emerges from the constant internal system processing of the difference of the nonidentical. Applied to society, the consequence of this view implies that there is no longer any guiding center as in stratified societies; instead, the functional realms form environments for each other, which cannot mutually substitute for one another. The economic system structurally negates all general responsibility for the direction of development of society and is indifferent to the consequences of its own action, as long as these do not reappear in the code appropriate to the system.

20. Ganssmann (1986) notes that this can be seen as a critical perspective of Luhmann's economic sociology.

21. For the economic discussion of the information content of prices, see Allen (1981) and Grossmann and Stiglitz (1976; 1980).

22. Although the selection criterion, at least for enterprises, is also legally established, that is in the bankruptcy law.

23. This is not to claim that Münch did not see the difference between code and program. On the contrary, he elaborated this distinction clearly (Münch 1994:398ff.). This makes it even more surprising that he decided on a fundamental renunciation of Luhmann's concept.

24. For a critical debate with the problem of permanence in systems theory, see Habermas (1971).

25. Here, once again, the difference between Luhmann's concept of the economy as a system and the general equilibrium theory is seen. The criterion for Luhmann is the reproduction of the capacity to pay. The problem of efficient resource allocation and striving for equilibrium of markets, the centerpiece of the general equilibrium theory, does not interest Luhmann. In a certain sense, the theory is emptied further by Luhmann. At the same time, the contingency of economic action opens the possibility of moving away from market determinism.

26. The concept is formulated especially succinctly in the following sentence: "Thus the system functions only, if in reference to the willingness for payment, at a certain price, both a true and a false assumptions are made; moreover, it requires that in the course of the observation of observation true assumptions are made regarding false assumptions and false assumptions regarding true assumptions" (Luhmann 1988a:119).

27. See Luhmann (1981) and Kirsch and zu Knyphausen (1991:86). The centrality of decisions for organizations was already emphasized by Cyert and March (1963), who talked about organizations as decision systems.

28. This also confirms the remarks in the preceding section, which explained the significance of the external control of the economic system by programs.

29. Luhmann's view is conveyed in this statement. In more recent discussions of the theory of organization, phenomena are studied that contradict it. Thus, Meyer and Zucker (1988) analyze "permanently failing organizations," which nevertheless reproduce themselves because of their institutional incorporation into social traditions.

30. For the concept of organizational latitude, see Sydow (1985).

31. Unlike Knight (1985), Luhmann (1988a:121) does not distinguish risk from the notion of uncertainty by the possibility of calculating probabilities.

32. The definition of the contexts of decisions in complex organizations determines their *redundancy*. In the theory of autopoietic systems, redundancy is a gradual term with the complement *variety*. The redundancy of a system is thus high when the diversity of decisions is small. Therefore, the maximum value of redundancy is achieved in a system when only one decision is constantly reproduced. With the increase of its redundancy, a system also reduces its own complexity and as a result, changes the complexity difference vis-à-vis the environment. On the other hand, the variety of the system increases when the range of decisions made is expanded, allowing the system more varied decisions (Luhmann 1988b:174). "Organizations can constantly oscillate between inclusion or rejection of noise and between loss and reproduction of redundancy . . . which maintains the autopoiesis . . . in various ways and can increase the structural complexity of the system or can decrease it toward constant variety and higher redundancy" (Luhmann 1988b:175).

33. But this does not mean that there is no longer any latitude for decisions. Only if redundancy reaches its maximum value would this be the case.

34. In approaches of strategic management, tables used to depict the range of possible reactions of companies in case of conflict (resistance, cooperation, adaptation, avoidance) start initially from the normative idea of a fluent equilibrium between enterprises and relevant environments. See Achleitner (1985:142ff.). The strategy of resistance, on the other hand, tries only to adapt the environment to the enterprise. It would be interesting to ask if the assumptions of Luhmann's systems theory can be proved empirically by means of the four possible types of strategies. Luhmann starts with the assumption that enterprises can receive impulses from the environment only if these result in new market opportunities or if emerging costs can be passed on. The thesis had to state that the strategy of adaptation can be used when at least one of the two conditions is fulfilled. Resistance occurs when the position relating to its own ability to pay is worsened (when the specific time horizon of the business had to be taken into account) by adaptation to the environment.

35. As explained earlier, this applies only for cognitive expectations. Normative expectations are held onto despite disappointment (Luhmann 1969). Management literature is full of examples of organizational rigidity that demonstrate holding onto expectations despite their known inefficiency. See, among others, Argyris and Schön (1978).

36. With this view of the management process, the theory of autopoietic systems can be connected to several concepts of organization studies. Some of these concepts are to be discussed briefly. Gomez and Probst (1985) indicate that the selective perception of the environment made possible by programs creates invariances that are necessary for the survival of the enterprise in a complex environment. They relate to the concept of the organizational culture. Through values, norms, and convictions prevailing in the organization, the enterprise insures itself "a certain degree of autonomy," which enables it not to react to all the demands made on it from the environment, which would make it "very quickly loose control over its fate" (25). Gomez and Probst use IBM as an example of the function of enterprise culture. The dictum, "IBM means service" operates invariably as a doctrine of the enterprise "while everything else in it changes" (26). Dierkes and Hähner (1991:107) talk of the filtering function of the organization culture: "On the basis of traditional notions and ideals and against the background of common expectations, notions of value are shaped within an organization, which are shared by all members of the organization and act as a filter in the perception of the environment of the enterprise. . . . The culture of the organization as the determining factor in the perception of the environment also assumes an intense influence on what problems enterprises are sensitive to and which are not perceived." Even though both Gomez and Probst and Dierkes and Hähner cite only one program for reducing complexity, the remarks do explain the basic assumption of the the relation of enterprise and environment represented here: the program of culture predisposes decisions by constructing expectations and thus selecting the perception of the environment. But as a program, culture is also contingent: IBM could have focused on other notions of values and norms. This does not mean that culture produces the environmental resonance in the enterprise

that also guarantees its autopoiesis. Instead, the enabled resonance can also produce dysfunctional results for the enterprise. Organization cultures can work as blinders that keep enterprises from reacting effectively to events in the environment. Kirsch and zu Knyphausen (1991:90ff.) expand the model of selection mechanisms cited by Gomez and Probst. They describe as semantics the self-description in enterprises a whole series of programs for the selection of environmental events. These include narratives, planning handbooks, models, and enterprise doctrines that are understood as *models of meaning* of the organization. As a supplement, Schreyögg (1991:283) cites the organization structure as an instrument of selection. Organization rules can be understood, according to Schreyögg, as "anticipatory decisions" that order "the action field" and select "the desired options from the immense wealth of possibilities." In this sense, concepts of leadership can also be understood as selection programs.

37. Thus Beckenbach (1989:899): "Consequently, nothing excludes expanding the horizon of economic communication beyond the inclusion of prices."

38. Yet a simple error must be noted: the plurality of expectations manifested in structures of the organization, self-descriptions of enterprises, and styles of leadership that were indicated earlier, can thoroughly contradict one another. Thus, actual internal organizational expectations on which decisions are oriented need to be distinguished from merely declamatory statements. Establishing environmental protection goals in enterprise guidelines does not imply anything about whether environmental protection is in fact a relevant difference scheme for decisions of the enterprise. It can also simply serve to reduce the noise of the environment without actually changing the allocation of payments. *Official goals* and *operative goals* can be distinguished here, as Charles Perrow (1961) puts it. Official goals indicate externally acknowledged action guidelines for organization members; operative goals, on the other hand, indicate the action guidelines actually followed by the members. The distinction made by Argyris and Schön (1978) between *espoused theories* and *theories in use*, as well as the ceremonial nature of formal structures in organizations studied by Meyer and Rowen (1977) are also analogous here.

39. With this skeptical assessment of the results of resonance inherent in theory as a constant possibility, Luhmann contradicts Schreyögg's (1991:282) assessment. The controlling process "oriented to plans or goals turns out to be . . . dangerously wrong." Schreyögg argues that systems must satisfy latent contradictory functional demands, which they can do only when their planning and organization shows a high variance and they "allow for a relatively lot of latitude for their subsystems, in order to be able to absorb environmental complexity to the required degree" (283). Staehle (1990:571) formulates it somewhat more carefully: "The question is whether under such conditions [of turbulent environments] there can still be meaningful (strategic) planning or whether it is better to give it up completely and try instead to achieve the enterprises's permanent willingness to learn and change through *organizational* (flexible, organic teams) or *personnel* (shaping and reshaping, the selection of more creative workers) measures."

40. Schreyögg (1991:277) does see the contrast between Luhmann's systems theory and the postulate of the internal portrayal of environmental complexity (Ashby 1952: "Only variety can match variety"), but he also demands the most

extensive flexibility of organization and planning structures. In the language of systems theory, a flexible reaction to various environmental demands can mean nothing other than the increase of internal variance, and thus the tendency to level the complexity difference between system and environment; hence its demand ultimately goes toward incorporating the environment into the system. This underestimates the significance of boundaries for the ability of enterprises to operate.

41. This does not apply to the early work, where Luhmann deals with the cooperation problem in *Trust and Power* (1979).

42. See especially Habermas's critique (1987).

43. The declared incommensurabilty of self-referential systems has turned out to be one of the central problems in the discussion of Luhmann's theory of autopoietic systems. This problem has also been emphasized by Bendel (1993) and Willke (1987b). Luhmann (1992) reacted to that with the concept of structural coupling.

44. The assumption that morality in the economy can prevent its differentiation and thus possible welfare benefits can be made. But it is merely asserted that a horizon of meaning shared by the actors *can* make a central contribution to the cooperation problem.

45. This is clearly seen by Pierre Bourdieu in the discussion of social capital: "The profits produced by belonging to a group are also bases for the solidarity which enable these profits" (Bourdieu 1983:192).

46. This is also a central point of Habermas's (1985:440) critique: "This social dimension of meaning is not realized through a convergence of horizons of understanding that assemble around identical significances and intersubjective claims of validity and *merge* in the consensus of something thought or said."

47. See Luhmann (1968b). In a later article (Luhmann 1988c), Luhmann returns to this subject, interestingly, without any reference to the notions of autopoiesis and self-referentiality.

48. The remarks of Esser (1993:493ff.) and the article by Heidenescher (1992) refer especially to Luhmann's notion of action.

49. Quoted in Esser (1993:507).

50. It is quite revealing that, in Luhmann's numerous works on the economy, innovations are not discussed. Thus only related concepts like social change (Luhmann 1995a) and novelty (Luhmann 1995b) can help.

CHAPTER FIVE
ANTHONY GIDDENS: ACTOR AND STRUCTURE IN ECONOMIC ACTION

1. See also Emirbayer and Goodwin (1994).

2. See Schumpeter (1961:138). This is also confirmed by current research on technology. Rammert (1992:16) shows that, especially in basic research in technology, what applies is no longer "the strict criteria of economic guidance and control, but rather the profession oriented and disciplinary standards of science"; empirical studies show that "the market and profit prospects of technical products have not even been seen in their early phases by economic actors."

3. In relation to Luhmann, it must be indicated in terms of the history of theory, that the debate with phenomenology was also central to him. Along with the

works of Weber, Gehlen, and Parsons, Husserl's phenomenology plays a central role for Luhmann's work. Mathias Heidenscher (1992), especially, has indicated Luhmann's relation to the phenomenological tradition by explaining the agreement in central concepts like meaning, standardizing, world horizon, and relevance. This congruence is not to be disputed if, at the same time, as here, it is indicated that, by analyzing society as systems, Luhmann nevertheless abandons the bases of phenomenology—and the sociology of *verstehen* in general. The focus of this tradition was always on the question of the actor and his intentionality but not the self-referentiality of systemic structures. The transference of important central concepts from phenomenology is not identical with a connection to this theoretical tradition.

4. An exception is the essay, "Social Theory and Problems of Macroeconomics." See Giddens (1987b).

5. The agreement also relates to the attempt to develop a uniform basis for the social sciences in general on the basis of an epistemological program.

6. Margaret Archer (1982:459) has accurately objected to the concept of duality of structure that it remains "fundamentally non-propositional." This means that Giddens does not mention the conditions under which action simply reproduces existing structures and those under which processes of social change are initiated.

7. This notion of action that emphasizes contingency seems to be compatible with Luhmann's notion of contingency in system events. The crucial difference is that Luhmann's notion of event renounces consideration of the actor and ascribes code allocation to the system, not to acting subjects.

8. For the significance of routines in Giddens's theory, see also Sandner and Meyer (1994).

9. The notion of ontological security refers to the significance of the development of a belief "in the reliability and nurturance of human individuals" (Giddens 1990:97), which develops in childhood experiences. Referring to the work of Erik Erikson, Giddens (1984:51ff.) emphasizes the significance of basic trust established in early childhood development for the possibility of normal human communication. Ontological security refers to an emotional phenomenon, namely "to the confidence that most human beings have in the continuity of their self-identity and in the constancy of the surrounding social and material environment of action" (92). The notion of ontological security is closely linked with routinized and habitualized action, because routines reinforce the feeling of emotional security (Giddens 1994a:101).

10. Thus: "The methodological individualists are wrong in so far as they claim that social categories can be reduced to descriptions in terms of individual predicates. But they are right to suspect that 'structural sociology' blots out, or at least radically underestimates, the knowledgeability of human agents, and they are right to insist that 'social forces' are always nothing more and nothing less than mixes of intended and unintended consequences of action undertaken in specifiable contexts" (Giddens 1984:220).

11. Giddens's notion of structure is to be distinguished from his notion of system, which corresponds to the meaning of structure in the functionalist tradition. As a system, Giddens indicates the network of actions produced and reproduced

in space and time. By talking of "degrees of systemness," Giddens makes it an empirical question of what intensity of systemic determination of actions is to be expected in a social configuration to be studied.

12. Here, Giddens refers to the monetary theory of Keynes and to Simmel's *Philosophy of Money* (1900). In Keynes, the link of money and time plays a central role. Simmel sees the money economy as the prerequisite for the extension of means-ends chains that allow for an increasingly more abstract time-space integration. See Giddens (1990:21ff.). For a discussion of Giddens's understanding of money, see Dodd (1994).

13. The other side of this process, naturally, is that the studied subject also influences and changes the process of research. "The theories and findings of the social sciences cannot be kept wholly separate from the universe of meaning and action which they are about. But, for their part, lay actors are social theorists, whose theories help to constitute the activities and institutions that are the object of study of specialized social observers or social scientists" (Giddens 1984:xxxii–xxxiii).

14. The conceptualization of such recursive processes in economics can be pursued with reference to other theory developments. One example is technical stock market analysis (chart analysis) in which the further development of financial markets is predicted from past performance. But this occurs only when investors, based on the analysis of the expected performance, orient their action to the prognoses.

15. By "knowledgeability," Giddens means "everything which actors know (believe) about the circumstances of their action and that of others, drawn upon in the production and reproduction of that action, including tacit as well as discursively available knowledge" (Giddens 1984:375).

16. See the remarks in chapter 1.

17. This can be seen directly with the use of money, which assumes that actors trust sufficiently that they can obtain "valuable" goods for "worthless" money at a later point in time. The spread of monetary systems is a feature of modern economies, which have to have the necessary "reserves of trust." This does not mean that trust *always* brings advantages of economic efficiency.

18. This element of stable structures of social relations accords with Durkheim's conviction that economic anomie is evoked by rapid processes of change that do not allow forming reciprocal-action expectations. But the significance of narrowly circumscribed social networks of relations in local communities can also connect with considerations of the theory of rational choice: faced with the lack of alternative possibilities of cooperation and exchange, actors expect repeated games that can last over long periods of time. Moreover, the transparency of individual actions for the other members of the community is high, so that actions can be reciprocally observed and defection sanctioned.

19. Here, too, links to Durkheim's explanations can be shown. Durkheim's explanation of the genesis of private property understands making the land sacred as a protection of the right of property. The fear of divine (social) fury, evoked by the forbidden entrance on land that is taboo, reduces the action options of the actors.

20. As an example, Giddens (1994a:90) cites the possibility of a broad turning away from the consumer orientation in the population, which would make the existing economic institutions fall into depression because of the drop in demand.

21. However, the status of unreflected, habitual action changes through the disintegration of traditions. These lose their authenticity and now become relics that are simply signs for life-styles or have a neurotic character as compulsions.

22. Here a development in Giddens's argumentation can be seen. In the early 1990s, when *The Consequences of Modernity* appeared, Giddens stressed the mainly passive nature of trust in abstract systems through processes of routinization (see Giddens 1990:115ff.). The notion of active trust is now more developed in *Reflexive Modernization* (1994b), with Ulrich Beck and Scott Lash.

23. However, in the example of the change of organization structures by leveling hierarchies, Giddens (1994b:187) does mention the effects of institutional reflexivity on economic structures.

24. This formulation is intended to evoke the discourse ethic of Habermas, who emphasizes the binding force of language for practical reason. Even if discourse in Habermas is much more significant than in Giddens, both authors refer to the discursive process, which proves that constitution theories in sociology have essential correspondences. An interesting reference to Habermas's theory in the question of the emergence of procedures of self-control has been presented by Claus Offe (1989), who talks of relations of association. Offe (1989:756) also goes into the question of institutional rules that support cooperative acts by contributing to the minimization of the risk of exploitation: in the "favorable case, the institutional and procedural conditions of the context can be created so that they make 'responsible' bargaining both obvious and reasonable."

25. James Coleman (1990c:108) also refers to the link of communication and trust: "The more extensive the communication between the trustor and the other actors from whom the trustee can expect to receive placements of trust in the future, the more trustworthy the trustee will be."

26. Common markers like matching group membership (religious, political, ethnic, gender, age, etc.) can have a supporting effect here. See Offe (1996:17ff.).

27. Thus an argumentation is pursued that is contrary to game theory. In game theory, it is the expectation of *future* gain from cooperation that generates cooperation; in the approach proposed here, trust derives from the present and the past. In economics, on the other hand, it is "bygones are bygones."

28. See chapter 3.

29. A good example of this is the Internet, whose further development cannot be predicted by anyone. Only in the process of the further development itself do the contours emerge that determine the next steps.

30. Emphasizing these aspects of the *social constitution of the new* naturally contradicts the neoclassical idea of perfect knowledge of optimal factor combinations in the production process. The subject dependency of the new, which also results from the problem of the perception of the new as new, is also emphasized by Wegner (1995:185).

31. Here the difference with Parsons and Smelser can be easily seen; they saw the motive for innovative action in striving for conformity to norms. Giddens's interpretation of the motivation of actors is psychological.

32. This does not mean that innovations emerge in structureless space of action, as it were; instead, "it breaks with the past by continuing it, and continues it by interrupting the course of things" (Waldenfels 1990:96). The latitude for innovations emerges from the conceivable plethora of possible solutions that are also marked out by existing structures.

33. In the context of economics, the market immediately occurs here naturally as an uncontrolled structure, whose uncontrollability is constantly reproduced by innovations.

34. See especially Shackle (1972; 1974). Wegner (1995:198), however, correctly criticizes Shackle's notion of decision for not sufficiently considering the possibility of routine behavior.

35. Thus Hannah Arendt: "Only action has the capacity to do what natural scientific 'research' now does every day, that is, institute procedures whose end is uncertain and unpredictable" (Arendt 1981:226).

36. See also the works of Ortmann (1995) and Sydow et al. (1994), which are not discussed here.

37. By constitution theories, Joas (1996:231) includes "all those sociological theories which set out to make social processes intelligible in terms of the actions of the members of a society without assuming there to be some underlying transhistorical development trend and without borrowing—except for merely pragmatic reasons—from models that are foreign to the social sciences."

38. One further exception to this is the work of Neil Fligstein (2001).

39. Design, which includes not only the activities of industrial engineers but also of product designers and architects, among others, is broadly defined as "changing existing situations into preferred ones" (Simon 1981).

CHAPTER SIX
PERSPECTIVES FOR ECONOMIC SOCIOLOGY

1. See also Joas's (2000) comments for the emphasis of the significance of communication for the emergence of values.

2. As an example for this proposal of the difference of sociology and economics, see Pareto (1980) and Samuelson (1947).

3. For such a broad understanding of embeddedness, see also Zukin and DiMaggio (1990).

4. Which does not rule out the possibility that forms of cultural embeddedness exist that also have dysfunctional results.

5. This has only a limited application for the analysis of social network structures, for whose formal analysis a well-formulated methodological apparatus is available (see Burt 1992; Emirbayer and Goodwin 1994).

BIBLIOGRAPHY

Abramovitz, Moses (1956). "Resource and Output Trends in the United States since 1870." *American Economic Review*, P+P, 46:5–23.

Achleitner, Paul M. (1985). *Sozio-politsche Strategien multinationaler Unternehmungen*. Berlin and Stuttgart.

Aimard, Guy (1962). *Durkheim et la science économique*. Paris.

Akerlof, Georg A. (1970). "The Market for 'Lemons': Quality Uncertainty and the Market Mechanism." *Quarterly Journal of Economics* 84:488–500.

———. (1984). "Gift Exchange and Efficiency-Wage Theory." *American Economic Review*, P+P, 74:79–83.

Albert, Hans (1972). "Modell-Platonismus. Der neoklassische Stil des ökonomischen Denkens in kritischer Beleuchtung." In Ernst Topitsch, ed., *Logik der Sozialwissenschaften*, pp. 406–34. Cologne.

Alexander, Jeffrey (1982). *The Antinomies of Classical Thought: Marx and Durkheim*, Theoretical Logic in Sociology, vol. 2. Berkeley and Los Angeles.

———. (1984). *The Modern Reconstruction of Classical Thought: Talcott Parsons*. Berkeley and Los Angeles.

———. (1987). *Twenty Lectures: Sociological Theory since World War II*. New York.

Allen, Beth (1981). "Generic Existence of Completely Revealing Equilibria for Economies with Uncertainty When Prices Convey Information." *Econometrica* 49:1173–99.

Archer, Margaret (1982). "Morphogenesis versus Structuration: On Combining Structure and Action." *British Journal of Sociology* 33:455–83.

Arendt, Hannah (1981). *Vita Activa oder vom tätigen Leben*. Munich and Zurich.

Argyris, Chris, and Donald Schön (1978). *Organizational Learning*. Reading, Mass.

Arrow, Kenneth J. (1951). *Social Choice and Individual Values*. New Haven and London.

———. (1971). "Political and Economic Evaluation of Social Effects and Externalities." In M. Intriligator, ed., *Frontiers of Quantitative Economics*, pp. 3–35. Amsterdam.

———. (1983) [1969]. "The Organization of Economic Activity: Issues Pertinent to the Choice of Market versus Nonmarket Allocation." In *General Equilibrium: Collected Papers of Kenneth J. Arrow*, 2:133–55. Cambridge.

———. (1984) [1971]. "Exposition of the Theory of Choice under Uncertainty." In *Individual Choice under Certainty and Uncertainty: Collected Papers of Kenneth J. Arrow*, 3:172–208. Cambridge.

———. (1985a) [1962]. "Economic Welfare and the Allocation of Resources for Invention." In *Production and Capital: Collected Papers of Kenneth J. Arrow*, 5:104–19. Cambridge.

———. (1985b) [1962]. "The Economic Implications of Learning by Doing." In *Production and Capital: Collected Papers of Kenneth J. Arrow*, 5:157–80. Cambridge.

Arrow, Kenneth J. (1985c). "The Economics of Agency." In John W. Pratt and Richard J. Zeckhauser, eds., *Principals and Agents: The Structure of Business*, pp. 37–51. Boston.

Arrow, Kenneth J., et al. (1961). "Capital-Labor Substitution and Economic Efficiency." *Review of Economics and Statistics* 43:225–50.

Arrow, Kenneth J., and Gerald Debreu (1954). "Existence of an Equilibrium for a Competitive Economy." *Econometrica* 22:265–90.

Ashby, W. Ross (1952). *A Design for a Brain*. London.

———. (1958). "Requisite Variety and Its Implications for the Control of Complex Organizations." *Cybernetica* 1:83–96.

Aumann, Robert J. (1985). "Repeated Games." In George R. Feiwel, ed., *Issues in Contemporary Macroeconomics*, pp. 209–42. London.

Axelrod, Robert (1984). *The Evolution of Cooperation*. New York.

———. (1986). "An Evolutionary Approach to Norms." *American Political Science Review* 80:1095–1111.

Backhouse, Roger (1985). *A History of Modern Economic Analysis*. Oxford.

Baecker, Dirk (1987). "Das Gedächtnis der Wirtschaft." *Theorie als Passion*, pp. 519–46. Frankfurt.

———. (1988). *Information und Risiko in der Marktwirschaft*. Frankfurt.

———. (1991). *Womit handeln Banken?* Frankfurt.

(1993). *Die Form des Unternehmens*. Frankfurt.

Baron, James N., and Michael T. Hannan (1994). "The Impact of Economics on Contemporary Sociology." *Journal of Economic Literature* 32:1111–46.

Barry, Brian (1970). *Sociologists, Economists and Democracy*. London.

Beck, Ulrich, Anthony Giddens, and Scott Lash (1994). *Reflexive Modernization*. Stanford.

Beckenbach, Frank (1989). "Die Wirtschaft der Systemtheorie." *Das Argument*, no. 178:887–904.

Bell, Daniel (1980). "Veblen and the Technocrats." In *The Winding Passage: Essays and Sociological Journeys, 1960–1980*, pp. 69–90. Cambridge.

Bendel, Klaus (1993). "Funktionale Differenzierung und gesellschaftliche Rationalität." *Zeitschrift für Soziologie* 22, no. 4: 261–78.

Berger, Johannes (1987). "Autopoiesis." In Hans Haferkamp, and Michael Schmid, eds., *Beiträge zu Luhmanns Theorie sozialer Systeme*, pp. 129–52. Frankfurt.

———. (1990). "Entdifferenzierung als Perspective für Marktwirtschaften?" In Wolfgang Zapf ed., *Modernisierung moderner Gesellschaften. 25. Deutscher Soziologentag*, pp. 233–47. Frankfurt and New York.

———. (1992). "Der Konsensbedarf der Wirtschaft." In Hans-Joachim Giegel, ed., *Kommunikation und Konsens in modernen Gesellschaften*, pp. 151–96. Frankfurt.

———. (1995). "Warum arbeiten die Arbeiter? Neomarxistische und neodurkheimianische Erklärungen." *Zeitschrift für Soziologie* 24, no. 6:401–21.

Bernstein, Richard (1976). *The Restructuring of Social and Political Theory*. New York.

Biervert, Bernd, and Joseph Wieland (1990). "Gegenstandsbereich und Rationalitätsform der Ökonomie und der Ökonomik." *Sozialphilosophische Grundlagen Ökonomischen Handelns*, pp. 7–32. Frankfurt.

Bourdieu, Pierre (1983). "Ökonomisches Kapital, kulturelles Kapital, soziales Kapital." In Reinhard Kreckel, ed., *Soziale Ungleichheit*, pp. 183–98. Göttingen.

Bowles, Samuel (1985). "The Production Process in a Competitive Economy: Walrasian, Neo-Hobbesian, and Marxian Models." *American Economic Review* 75:16–36.

Bowles, Samuel, and Herbert Gintis, (1990). "Contested Exchange: New Microfoundations for the Political Economy of Capitalism." *Politics and Society*, 18: 165–222.

Braverman, Harry (1974). *Labor and Monopoly Capitalism: The Degradation of Work in the Twentieth Century*. New York.

Brockway, George (1993). *The End of Economic Man*. New York and London.

Bryant, Christopher, and David Jary, eds. (1991). *Giddens' Theory of Structuration: A Critical Appreciation*. London and New York.

Buchanan, James (1989). *Explorations into Constitutional Economics*. Houston.

Bumoln, Thomas (1957). Review of *Economy and Society*, by Talcott Parsons and Neil Smelser. *American Economic Review*, 47:686–89.

Burger, Thomas (1977). "Talcott Parsons, the Problem of Order in Society, and the Program of an Analytical Sociology." *American Journal of Sociology* 83:320–34.

Burt, Ronald (1982). *Toward a Structural Theory of Action*. New York.

———. (1992). *Structural Holes*. Cambridge, Mass.

Callinicos, Alex (1985). "A. Giddens: A Contemporary Critique." *Theory and Society* 14:133–66.

Camic, Charles (1979). "The Utilitarians Revisited." *American Journal of Sociology* 85:516–50.

———. (1986). "The Matter of Habit." *American Journal of Sociology* 91:1039–87.

———. (1987). "The Making of a Method: A Historical Reinterpretation of the Early Parsons." *American Sociological Review* 52:421–39.

———. (1991). Introduction to *Talcott Parsons: The Early Essays*, edited by Charles Camic, pp. IX–LXIX. Chicago.

Campbell, David (1995). "The Relational Constitution of Contract and the Limits of 'Economics.' Kenneth Arrow and the Social Background of Markets." Sheffield. Unpublished Manuscript.

Cezanne, Wolfgang (1994). *Allgemeine Volkswirtschaftslehre*. 2 ed. Munich.

Chamberlain, Edward H. (1933). *Theory of Monopolistic Competition*. Cambridge, Mass.

Chazel, François (1989). "Théorie économique et sociologie: adversaires ou complices? La réflexion d'un 'classique': Talcott Parsons." *Sociologie et sociétés* 11:39–53.

Child, John (1972). "Organizational Structure, Environment and Performance: The Role of Strategic Choice." *Sociology* 6:1–22.

Clarke, Simon (1991). *Marx, Marginalism and Modern Sociology: From Adam Smith to Max Weber.* 2 ed. London.

Clegg, Stewart (1989). *Frameworks of Power.* London.

Coase, Ronald (1990). *The Firm, the Market and the Law.* Chicago and London.

Coenen, Herman (1985). *Dieseits von subjektivem Sinn und kollektivem Zwang.* Munich.

Coleman, James (1988). "Social Capital in the Creation of Human Capital." *American Journal of Sociology* 94:95–121.

———. (1990a). "Norm-Generating Structures." In Karen Schweers Cook and Margaret Levi, eds., *The Limits of Rationality*, pp. 250–73. Chicago and London.

———. (1990b). "The Emergence of Norms." In Michael Hechter, Karl-Dieter Opp, and Reinhard Wippler, eds., *Social Institutions: Their Emergence, Maintenance and Effects*, 35–59. Berlin and New York.

———. (1990c). *Foundations of Social Theory.* Cambridge, Mass.

Collins, Randall (1988). "The Durkheimian Tradition in Conflict Sociology." In Jeffrey Alexander, ed., *Durkheimian Sociology*, pp. 107–28. Cambridge.

———. (1992). "The Romanticism of Agency/Structure versus the Analysis of Micro/Macro." *Current Sociology* 40:77–97.

Coricelli, Fabrizio, and Giovanni Dosi (1988). "Coordination and Order in Economic Change and the Interpretative Power of Economic Theory." In Giovanni Dosi et al. eds., *Technical Change and Economic Theory*, pp. 124–47. London and New York.

Corning, Peter A. (1982). "Durkheim and Spencer." *British Journal of Sociology* 33:359–82.

Coser, Lewis (1977). *Masters of Sociological Thought.* 2 ed. New York.

Craig, John E. (1983). "Sociology and Related Disciplines between the Wars: Maurice Halbwachs and the Imperialism of the Durkheimians." In Philippe Besnard, ed., *The Sociological Domain: The Durkheimians and the Founding of French Sociology*, pp. 263–89. Cambridge.

Cyert, Richard, and James G. March (1963). *A Behavioral Theory of the Firm.* Englewood Cliffs, N.J.

Daheim, Hansjürgen (1981). "François Simiand. Ein empirisch-theoretischer Ansatz in der Wirtschaftssoziologie." In Heine von Alemann and Hans Peter Thurn, eds., *Soziologie in weltbürgerliche Absicht. Festschrift für René König zum 75. Geburtstag*, pp. 175–99. Opladen.

Dahms, Harry F. (1995). "From Creative Action to the Social Rationalization of the Economy: Joseph A. Schumpeter's Social Theory." *Sociological Theory* 13:1–13.

Dasgupta, Partha, and Joseph Stiglitz (1980a). "Industrial Structure and the Nature of Innovative Activity." *Economic Journal* 90:266–93.

———. (1980b). "Uncertainty, Industrial Structure, and the Speed of R&D." *Bell Journal of Economics* 11:1–28.

David, Paul A. (1975). *Technical Choice Innovation and Economic Growth.* Cambridge.

———. (1986). "Understanding the Economics of OWERTY: The Necessity of History." In W. N. Parker, ed., *Economic History and the Modern Economist*, pp. 30–49. Oxford.

Davies, Simon P., and Aldrian M. Castell (1992). "Contextualizing Design: Narratives and Rationalization in Empirical Studies of Software Design." *Design Studies* 13:379–92.

De Vries, Michael (1997). "Die Paradoxie der Innovation." In Frank Heideloff and Tobias Radel, eds., *Organisation und Innovation*, 75–87. Munich.

Dierkes, Meinolf, and Katrin Hähner (1991). "Sozioökonomischer Wandel und Unternehmensleitbilder. Ein Beitrag zur Untersuchung der Wahrnehmunsprozesse und Reaktionsweisen von Unternehmen auf Umfeldanforderungen." *WZB Papers* FS II 91–108. Berlin.

DiMaggio, Paul (1988). "Interest and Agency in Institutional Theory." In Lynne Zucker, ed., *Institutional Patterns and Organizations*, Cambridge, Mass.

DiMaggio, Paul, and Walter Powel (1983). "The Iron Cage Revisited: Institutional Isolorphism and Collective Rationality in Organizational Fields." *American Sociological Review* 48:147–60.

Dodd, Nigel (1994). *The Sociology of Money: Economics Reason and Contemporary Society*. Cambridge.

Dosi, Giovanni (1988). "Sources, Procedures, and Microeconomic Effects of Innovation." *Journal of Economic Literature*. 26:1120–71.

Dosi, Giovanni, and Luigi Orsengio (1988). "Coordination and Transformation: An Overview of Structures, Behaviors and Change in Evolutionary Environments." In Giovanni Dosi et al., eds., *Technical Change and Economic Theory*. Pp. 13–37. London and New York.

Duesenberry, James (1960). Comment on "An Economic Analysis of Fertility." In Universities National Bureau Committee for Economic Research, ed., *Demographic and Economic Change in Developed Countries*, ed., Princeton.

Durkheim, Émile (1885). Review of *Bau und Leben des sozialen Körpers*, Bd. 1, by A. Schaeffle. *Revue Philosophique* 19:84–101.

———. (1900). "Besprechung von George Simmel, *Philosophie des Geldes.*" *L'Année Sociologique* 5:140–45.

———. (1908). "De la position de l'économie politique dans l'ensemble des sciences sociales." *Journal des Économistes* 18:113–15, 117–20.

———. (1951) [1897]. *Suicide: A Study in Sociology*. Translated by John A. Spaulding and George Simpson. Glencoe, Ill.

———. (1958). *Socialism and Saint-Simon*. Translated by C. Sattler. Yellow Springs, Ohio.

———. (1960a). Prefaces to *L'Année Sociologique*, vols. 1 and 2. In *Émile Durkheim, 1858–1917: A Collection of Essays, with Translations and a Bibliography*, edited by Kurt Wolff, pp. 341–53. Translated by Charles Blend. Columbus, Ohio.

———. (1960b). "Sociology and Its Scientific Field." In *Émile Durkheim, 1858–1917: A Collection of Essays, with Translations and a Bibliography*, edited by Kurt Wolff. pp. 354–75. Translated by Charles Blend. Columbus, Ohio.

———. (1965) [1912]. *The Elementary Forms of Religious Life*. New York.

———. (1966) [1895]. *The Rules of Sociological Method.* Translated by Sarah A. Solovay and John Mueller. New York.

———. (1971). *Le Socialisme.* Paris.

Durkheim, Émile. (1975) [1887]. "La science positive de la morale en Allemagne." In *Emile Durkheim, Textes,* edited by Victor Krady, 1:267–343.

———. (1978a) [1887]. Opening Lecture. In *Émile Durkheim on Institutional Analysis,* pp. 43–70. Translated by Mark Traugott. Chicago.

———. (1978b). "Sociology and the Social Sciences." In *Émile Durkheim on Institutional Analysis,* pp. 71–87. Translated by Mark Traugott. Chicago.

———. (1979). Review of *Philosophie des Geldes,* by George Simmel. *Social Research,* pp. 321–28.

———. 1984 [1893]. *The Division of Labor in Society.* Translated by W. D. Halls. New York.

———. (1992) [1896–1900]. *Professional Ethics and Civic Morals.* London.

Durkheim, Emile, and Paul Fauconnet (1903). "Sociologie et sciences sociales." *Revue Philosophique* 55:465–97.

Edgeworth, Francis Ysidro (1881). *Mathematical Physics: An Essay on the Application of Mathematics to the Moral Sciences.* London.

Elster, Jon (1983a). *Explaining Technical Change.* Cambridge.

———. (1983b). *Sour Grapes.* Cambridge.

———. (1986). Introduction to *Rational Choice,* pp. 1–33. New York.

———. (1989). *The Cement of Society: A Study of Social Order.* Cambridge.

———. (1990). "When Rationality Fails." In Karen Schweers Cook and Margaret Levi, eds., *The Limits of Rationality,* pp. 19–51. Chicago and London.

Emirbayer, Mustafa, and Jeff Goodwin (1994). "Network Analysis, Culture and the Problem of Agency." *American Journal of Sociology* 99:1411–53.

Esser, Hartmut (1993). *Soziologie. Allgemeine Grundlagen.* Frankfurt and New York.

Etzioni, Amitai (1988). *The Moral Dimension: Towards a New Economics.* New York.

Filloux, Jean-Claude (1977). *Durkheim et le socialisme.* Geneva.

Fligstein, Neil (2001). *The Architecture of Markets,* Princeton.

Frank, Robert (1990). "Rethinking Rational Choice." In Roger Friedland and A. F. Robertson, eds., *Beyond the Marketplace: Rethinking Economy and Society,* pp. 53–87. New York.

———. (1992). *Strategie der Emotionen.* Munich.

Freeman, Christopher (1987). "Innovation." *New Palgrave,* 2:858–60.

Friedman, Milton (1970). "The Social Responsibility of Business Is to Increase Its Profits." *New York Times Magazine,* September 13, pp. 122–26.

Gambetta, Diego (1988). "Can We Trust Trust?" In *Trust: Making and Breaking Cooperative Relations,* pp. 213–37. Oxford.

Ganssmann, Heiner (1986). "Geld—ein symbolishch generalisiertes Medium der Kommunikation? Zur Geldlehre in der neueren Soziologie." *Prokla,* no. 63:6–22.

———. (1996). *Geld und Arbeit.* Frankfurt and New York.

Garfinkel, Harold (1963). "A Conception of Experiments with 'Trust' as a Condition of Stable Concerted Actions." In O. J. Harvey, ed., *Motivation and Social Interaction*, pp. 187–238. New York.

———. (1967). *Studies in Ethnomethodology*. Englewood Cliffs, N.J.

Geertz, Clifford (1992). "The Bazaar Economy: Information and Search in Peasant Marketing." In Mark Granovetter and Richard Swedberg, eds., *The Sociology of Economic Life*, pp. 225–32. Boulder.

Giddens, Anthony (1971). *Capitalism and Modern Social Theory: An Analysis of the Writings of Marx, Durkheim, and Weber*. Cambridge.

———. (1976). *New Rules of Sociological Method*. New York.

———. (1978). *Durkheim*. Glasgow.

———. (1981). *A Contemporary Critique of Historical Materialism*. London.

———. (1982). "Commentary on the Debate." *Theory and Society* 11: 527–39.

———. (1984). *The Constitution of Society*. Berkeley and Los Angeles.

———. (1986). Introduction to *Emile Durkheim: Durkheim on Politics and the State*, pp. 1–31. Oxford.

———. (1987a). *The Nation State and Violence*. Berkeley and Los Angeles.

———. (1987b). "Social Theory and Problems of Macroeconomics." In *Social Theory and Modern Sociology*, pp. 183–202. Cambridge.

———. (1990). *The Consequences of Modernity*. Cambridge.

———. (1991). *Modernity and Self-Identity: Self and Society in the Late Modern Age*. Stanford.

———. (1994a). "Living in a Post Traditional Society." In Ulrich Beck, Anthony Giddens, and Scott Lash, *Reflexive Modernization*, pp. 56–109. Stafford.

———. (1994b). "Risk, Trust, Reflexivitiy." Ulrich Beck, Anthony Giddens, and Scott Lash, *Reflexive Modernization*, pp. 184–97. Stanford.

Gilbert, Michael (1978). "Neo-Durkheimian Analyses of Economic Life and Strife: From Durkheim to the Social Contract." *Sociological Review* 26:729–54.

Gintis, Herbert (1975). "Welfare Economics and Individual Development: A Reply to Talcott Parsons." *Quarterly Journal of Economics* 89:291–302.

Goffman, Erving (1959). *The Presentation of Self in Everyday Life*. Harmondsworth.

Gomez, Peter, and Gilbert Probst (1985). "Organisationelle Geschlossenheit im Management sozialer Institutionen—ein komplementäres Konzept zu den Kontingenz-Ansätzen." *Delfin* 5:22–28.

Gorz, André (1989). *Kritik der ökonomischen Vernunft*. Berlin.

Gould, Mark (1976). "Systems Analysis, Macrosociology, and the Generalized Media of Social Action." In Jan J. Loubser, et al., eds., *Explorations in General Theory in Social Science*, pp. 470–506. New York.

———. (1988). "Parsons against Marx: 'An Earnest Warning . . .'" *Sociological Inquiry* 51:197–218.

———. (1989). "The Problem of Order in Hobbesian and Lockean Theory." Paper presented at the 1989 meeting of the American Sociological Association, San Francisco.

———. (1991). "Parsons' Economic Sociology: A Failure of Will." *Sociological Inquiry* 61:89–101.

Granovetter, Mark (1973). "The Strength of Weak Ties." *American Journal of Sociology* 78:1360–80.

———. (1985). "Economic Action and Social Structure: The Problem of Embeddedness." *American Journal of Sociology* 91:481–510.

Granovetter, Mark. (1990). "The Old and the New Economic Sociology: A History and an Agenda." In Roger Friedland and A. F. Robertson, eds., *Beyond the Market*, pp. 89–112. New York.

———. (1992). "Economic Institutions as Social Constructions: A Framework for Analysis." *Acta Sociologica* 35:3–11.

Granovetter, Mark, and Richard Swedberg, eds. (1992). *The Sociology of Economic Life*. Boulder.

Gravelle, Hugh, and Ray Rees (1992). *Microeconomics*. 2 ed. London and New York.

Grossman, Sanford J., and Joseph E. Stiglitz (1976). "Information and Competitive Price System." *American Economic Review*, P+P, 66:246–53.

———. (1980). "On the Impossibility of Informationally Efficient Markets." *American Economic Review* 70:393–408.

Gul, Faruk (1991). "On the Bayesian View in Game Theory and Economics." Research Paper no. 1991. Stanford University.

Gülich, Christian (1989). " 'Organisation' der Wirtschaft. Von Durkheims Berufsgruppen zu Bouglés Solidarismus." *Zeitschrift für Soziologie*. 18:220–29.

Gurwitsch, Aron (1971). Introduction to *Alfred Schütz, Gesammelte Aufsätze*, 1:XV–XXXVIII. The Hague.

Gutenberg, Erich (1958). *Einführung in die Betriebswirtschaftslehre*. Wiesbaden.

Habermas, Jürgen (1971). "Theorie der Gesellschaft oder Sozialtechnologie? Eine Auseinandersetzung mit Niklas Luhmann." In Jürgen Habermas, *Niklas Luhmann: Theorie der Gesellschaft oder Sozialtechnologie*, 142–290. Frankfurt.

———. (1980). "Handlung und System—Bemerkungen zu Parsons' Medientheorie." In Wolfgang Schluchter, ed., *Verhalten, Handeln und System. Talcott Parsons' Beitrag zur Entwicklung der Sozialwissenschaften*, pp. 68–105. Frankfurt.

———. (1984). *Theory of Communicative Action*. Translated by Thomas McCarthy. Boston.

———. (1987). *The Philosophical Discourse of Modernity*. Translated by Frederick Lawrence. Cambridge, Mass.

Habermas, Jürgen, and Nikas Luhmann (1971). *Theorie der Gesellschaft oder Sozialtechnologie*. Frankfurt.

Hahn, Frank (1970). "Some Adjustment Problems." *Econometrica* 38:1–17.

———. (1980). "General Equilibrium Theory." *Public Interest*, special issue, pp. 123–38.

Hammond, Peter (1987). "Uncertainty." *New Palgrave* 4:728–33.

Hannen, Michael, and John Freeman (1977). "The Population Ecology of Organizations. *American Journal of Sociology* 82: 929–64.

Harsanyi, John C. (1977). *Rational Behaviour and Bargaining Equilibrium in Games and Social Situations*. Cambridge.

———. (1978). "Bayesian Decision Theory and Utilitarian Ethics." *American Economic Review*, P+P, 68:223–28.

———. (1986). "Advances in Understanding Rational Behavior." In Jon Elster, ed., *Rational Choice*, pp. 82–107. New York.

Hayek, Friedrich A. (1948). *Individualism and Economic Order.* Chicago.

Hechter, Michael (1990a). "On the Inadequacy of Game Theory for the Solution of Real-World Collective Action Problems." In Karen Schweers and Margaret Levi, eds., *The Limits of Rationality*, pp. 240–49. Chicago and London.

———. (1990b). "The Emergence of Cooperative Social Institutions." In Michael Hechter, Karl-Dieter Opp, and Reinhard Wippler, eds., *Social Institutions: Their Emergence, Maintenance and Effects*, pp. 13–33. Berlin and New York.

Hegselmann, Rainer (1992). "Moralität im iterierten Gefangenendilemma." In Martin Hollis and Wilhelm Vossenkuhl, eds., *Moralische Entscheidung und rationale Wahl*, pp. 183–90. Munich.

Heidenescher, Mathias (1992). "Zurechnung als soziologische Kategorie. Zu Luhmanns Verständnis von Handlung als Systemleistung." *Zeitschrift für Soziologie* 21:440–55.

Heilbron, Johan (1990). "The Tripartite Division of French Social Science: A Long-Term Perspective." In Peter Wagner, Björn Wittrock, and Richard Whitley, eds., *Discourses on Society: The Shaping of the Social Science Disciplines, Sociology of the Sciences Yearbook, 1991*, pp. 73–92. Dordrecht, Boston, and London.

Heilbroner, Robert (1986). *The Worldly Philosophers.* New York.

Heiner, Ronald (1983). "The Origin of Predictable Behavior." *American Economic Review* 73:560–95.

Hennis, Wilhelm (1987). *Max Webers Fragestellung.* Tübingen.

Hicks, John Richard (1932). *The Theory of Wages.* London.

Hirschman, Albert O. (1970). *Exit, Voice, and Loyalty.* Cambridge, Mass.

———. (1977). *The Passions and the Interests: Political Arguments for Capitalism before Its Triumph.* Princeton.

———. (1986). *Rival Views of Market Society.* New York.

Hirshleifer, Jack, and John G. Riley (1992). *The Analytics of Uncertainty and Information.* Cambridge.

Hodgson, Geoffrey (1988). *Economics and Institutions.* Oxford.

Hollis, Martin (1991). *Rationalität und soziales Verstehen.* Frankfurt.

———. (1992). "Honour among Thieves." In Martin Hollis and Wilhelm Vossenkuhl, eds., *Moralische Entscheidung und rationale Wahl*, pp. 115–30. Munich.

Hollis, Martin, and Edward Nell (1975). *Rational Economic Man: A Philosophical Critique of Neo-Classical Economics.* Cambridge.

Holton, Robert J. (1986). "Talcott Parsons and the Theory of Economy and Society." In Robert J. Holton and Bryan S. Turner, *Talcott Parsons on Economy and Society*, pp. 27–105. New York.

———. (1989). "Max Weber, Austrian Economics, and the New Right." In Robert J. Holton and Bryan S. Turner, *Max Weber on Economy and Society*, pp. 30–67. London and New York.

———. (1992). *Economy and Society.* London.

Hopkins, Terence K. (1957). "Sociology and the Substantive View of the Economy." In Karl Polanyi, Conrad M. Arensberg, and Harry W. Pearson, eds., *Trade and Market in the Early Empires*, pp. 270–306. Glencoe, Ill.

Hrebiniak, Lawrence G., and William F. Joyce (1985). "Organizational Adaptation: Strategic Choice and Environmental Determinism." *Administrative Science Quarterly* 30:336–49.

Hummell, H. J. (1988). "Moralische Institutionen und die Ordnung des Handelns in der Gesellschaft. Die 'utilitaristische' Theorietradition und die Durkheimsche Herausforderung." In K. Ebert, ed., *Alltagswelt und Ethik*, pp. 245–71. Wuppertal.

Hutchinson, T. W. (1957). Review of *Economy and Society*, by Talcott Parsons and Neil Smelser. *Economica*, pp. 376–77.

Joas, Hans (1986). "Giddens' Theorie der Strukturbildung." *Zeitschrift für Soziologie.* 15:237–45.

———. (1993). *Pragmatism and Social Theory.* Chicago.

———. (1996). *The Creativity of Action.* Translated by Jeremy Gaines and Paul Keast. Cambridge.

———. (2000). *The Genesis of Values.* Translated by Gregory Moore. Cambridge.

Johnson, Harry M. (1973). "The Generalized Symbolic Media in Parsons' Theory." *Sociology and Social Research* 57:208–21.

Kahneman, Daniel, Jack L. Knetsch, and Richard Thaler (1986). "Fairness as a Constraint on Profit Seeking: Entitlements in the Market." *American Economic Review* 76:728–41.

Kaldor, Nicholas, and James A. Mirlees (1962). "A New Model of Economic Growth." *Review of Economic Studies* 29:174–92.

Kant, Immanuel (1996). *The Metaphysics of Morals.* Translated by Mary Gregor. Cambridge and New York.

Kasper, Helmut (1991). "Neuerungen durch selbstorganisierende Prozesse." In Wolfgang Staehle and Jörg Sydow, eds., *Managementforschung*, 1:1–74.

Kennedy, Charles (1964). "Induced Bias in Innovation and the Theory of Distribution." *Economic Journal* 74:541–47.

Kern, Horst, and Michael Schumann (1984). *Das Ende der Arbeitsteilung. Rationalisierung in der industriellen Produktion.* Munich.

Keynes, John Maynard (1964) [1936]. *The General Theory of Employment, Interest, and Money.* New York.

———. (1973a) [1921]. *Treatise on Probability.* London.

———. (1973b)[1937]. "The General Theory of Employment." In *The Collected Writings of J.M. Keynes*, pp. 21:109–23. London.

Kirsch, Werner, and Dodo zu Knyphausen (1991). "Unternehmungen as 'autopoietische' Systeme?" In Wolfgang Staehle and Jörg Sydow eds., *Managementforschung*, 1:75–101.

Kirzner, Israel M. (1985). *Discovery and the Capitalist Process.* Chicago and London.

Kliemt, Hartmut (1986). *Antagonistische Kooperation.* Freiburg and Munich.

Knight, Frank H. (1921). *Risk, Uncertainty, and Profit.* Chicago.

König, René (1978). *Emile Durkheim zur Diskussion.* Munich and Vienna.

Kotowitz, Y. (1987). "Moral Hazard." *New Palgrave* 3:549–51.

Kreps, David (1990). *Game Theory and Economic Modeling.* Oxford.

———. (1991). "Corporate Culture and Economic Theory." In James E. Alt and Kenneth A. Shepsle, eds., *Perspectives on Positive Political Economy*, pp. 90–143. Cambridge.

Kuttner, Robert (1985). "The Poverty of Economics." *Atlantic Monthly*, February, pp. 74–84.

Latsis, Spiro (1972). "Situational Determinism in Economics." *British Journal of Philosophy of Science* 23:207–45.

Lawson, Tony (1985). "Uncertainty and Economic Analysis." *Economic Journal* 95:909–27.

Leifer, Eric M., and Harrison C. White (1986). "A Structural Approach to Markets." In Mark Mizruchi and Michael Schwartz, eds., *Intercorporate Relations*, pp. 85–108. Cambridge.

Levine, Donald (1991). "Simmel and Parsons Reconsidered." In Roland Robertson and Bryan S. Turner, eds., *Talcott Parsons: Theorist of Modernity*, pp. 187–204. London.

Loasby, Brian (1976). *Choice, Complexity and Ignorance: An Enquiry into Economic Theory and Practice of Decision Making*. Cambridge.

Lockwood, David (1992). *Solidarity and Schism: The Problem of Disorder in Durkheimian and Marxist Sociology*. Oxford.

Löwe, Adolph (1935). *Economics and Sociology*. London.

Lucas, R. E. (1972). "Expectations and the Neutrality of Money." *Journal of Economic Theory* 4:103–24.

Luhmann, Niklas (1968a). *Zweckbegriff und Systemrationalität*. Frankfurt am Main.

———. (1968b). *Vertrauen. Ein Mechanismus zur Reduktion sozialer Komplexität*. Stuttgart.

———. (1969). "Normen in soziologischer Perspective." *Soziale Welt* 20:28–48.

———. (1970). "Wirtschaft als soziales System." *Soziologische Aufklärung*, 1:204–231. Opladen.

———. (1979). *Trust and Power*. New York.

———. (1981). "Organisationen im Wirtschaftssystem." *Soziologische Aufklärung*, 3:390–415. Opladen.

———. (1983). "Das sind Preise." *Soziale Welt* 34:153–70.

———. (1985). Reply to H. Mader. *Zeitschrift für Soziologie* 14:333–34.

———. (1988a). *Die Wirtschaft der Gesellschaft*. Frankfurt.

———. (1988b). "Organisation." In Willi Küpper and Günther Ortmann, eds., *Mikropolitik. Rationalität. Macht und Spiele in Organisationen*, pp. 165–85. Opladen.

———. (1988c). "Familiarity, Confidence, Trust: Problems and Alternatives." In Diego Gambetta, ed., *Trust: Making and Breaking of Corporate Relations*, pp. 94–107. Oxford.

———. (1989). *Ecological Communication*. Translated by John Bednarz Jr. Chicago.

———. (1991). "Risiken im Wirtschaftssystem." *Soziologie des Risikos*, pp. 187–200. Berlin and New York.

———. (1992). "Operational Closure and Structural Coupling: The Differentiation of the Legal System." *Cardozo Law Review* 13:1419–41.

————. (1995a). *Social Systems*. Translated by John Bednarz Jr. with Dirk Baecker. Stanford.

Luhmann, Niklas. (1995b). "Die Soziologie und der Mensch." *Soziologische Aufklärung*, Opladen.

————. (2000). *Art as a Social System*. Translated by Eva M. Knodt. Stanford.

Lukács, Georg (1971). *History and Class Consciousness*. Cambridge, Mass.

Lukes, Steven (1985). *Emile Durkheim: His Life and Work. A Historical and Critical Study*. Stanford.

Macauley, Stewart (1963). "Non-Contractual Relations in Business: A Preliminary Study." *American Sociological Review* 28:55–67.

Mader, Helmut (1985). "Zu Luhmanns Aufsatz: 'Die Wirtschaft der Gesellschaft als autopoietisches System,' in *ZfS* 4, 1984." *Zeitschrift für Soziologie* 14:330–32.

Mansbridge, Jane J., ed. (1990a). *Beyond Self-Interest*. Chicago.

————. (1990b). "On the Relation of Altruism and Self-Interest." In *Beyond Self-Interest*, pp. 133–43. Chicago.

Mansfield, Edwin, et al. (1977). "Social and Private Rates of Return from Industrial Innovation." *Quarterly Journal of Economics* 91:221–40.

March, James (1986). "Bounded Rationality, Ambiguity, and the Engineering of Choice." In Jon Elster, ed., *Rational Choice*, pp. 142–70. New York.

Marcuse, Herbert (1964). *One Dimensional Man*. Boston.

Marshall, Alfred (1961) [1890]. *Principles of Economics*. London.

Marwell, Gerald and Ruth Ames (1981). "Economists Free Ride: Does Anyone Else?" *Journal of Public Economics* 13:295–310.

Marx, Karl (1967). *Capital*. New York.

Maturana, Humberto, ed. (1982). *Erkennen: Die Organisation und Verkörperung von Wirklichkeit*. Braunschweig and Wiesbaden.

Mead, George Herbert (1974) [1934]. *Mind, Self, and Society*. Chicago.

Meier, Kurt (1984). *Emile Durkheims Konzeption der Berufsgruppen. Eine Rekonstruktion und Diskussion ihrer Bedeutung für die Neokorporatismus-Debatte*. Berlin.

Menger, Carl (1883). *Untersuchungen über die Methode der Sozialwissenschaften*. Vienna.

————. (1884). *Die Irrthümer des Historismus in der deutschen Nationalökonomie*. Vienna.

————. (1981) [1871]. *Principles of Economics*. Translated by James Dingwall and Bert F. Hoselitz. New York.

Mertens, Jean-François (1989). "Supergames." In *New Palgrave: Game Theory*, pp. 238–41. London.

Merton, Robert K. (1936). "The Unanticipated Consequences of Purposive Social Action." *American Sociological Review* 1:894–904.

Metcalfe, S. (1987). "Technical Change." *New Palgrave* 4:617–20.

Meyer, John W., and Brian Rowen (1977). "Institutionalized Organizations: Formal Structure as Myth and Ceremony." *American Journal of Sociology* 83:340–63.

Meyer, Marshall W., and Lynne G. Zucker (1988). *Permanently Failing Organizations*. Newbury Park, Calif.

Mirman, Leonard J. (1989). "Perfect Information." *New Palgrave: Game Theory*, pp. 194–98. London.

Mirowski, Philip (1989). *More Heat than Light: Economics as Social Physics*. Cambridge.

Müller, Hans-Peter (1983). *Wertkrise und Gesellschaftsreform. Emile Durkheims Schriften zur Politik*. Stuttgart.

———. (1986). "Gesellschaft, Moral und Individualismus. Émile Durkheims Moraltheorie." In Hans Bertram, ed., *Gesellschaftlicher Zwang und moralische Autonomie*, 71–105. Franfurt.

Müller, Hans Peter, and Michael Schmid (1988). "Arbeitsteilung, Solidarität und Moral. Eine werkgeschichtliche und systematische Einführung in die 'Arbeitsteilung' von Emile Durkheim." In Émile Durkheim, *Über soziale Arbeitsteilung*, 481–532. Frankfurt.

Münch, Richard (1987). *Theory of Action: Towards a New Synthesis Going beyond Parsons*. London and New York.

———. (1990). "Die Wirtschaft der Gesellschaft—ein autopoietisches System?" *Soziologische Revue* 15:381–88.

———. (1994). "Zahlung und Achtung. Die Interpenetration von Ökonomie und Moral." *Zeitschrift für Soziologie* 23:388–411.

Muth, John F. (1961). "Rational Expectations and the Theory of Price Movements." *Econometrica* 29:315–35.

Nelson, Richard R. (1994). "Evolutionary Theorizing about Economic Change." In Neil Smelser and Richard Swedberg, eds., *Handbook of Economic Sociology*, pp. 108–36. Princeton.

Nelson, Richard R., and Sidney G. Winter (1982). *An Evolutinary Theory of Economic Change*. Cambridge, Mass.

Neumann, John von, and Oskar Morgenstern (1944). *The Theory of Games and Economic Behavior*. New York.

Nordhaus, William, and James Tobin (1972). *Economic Research: Retrospect and Prospect: Economic Growth*. New York.

North, Douglass (1990). *Institutions, Institutional Change, and Economic Performance*. Cambridge.

Oberschall, Anthony, and Eric M. Leifer (1986). "Efficiency and Social Institutions: Uses and Misuses of Economic Reasoning in Sociology." *Annual Review of Sociology* 12:233–53.

Odiorne, George (1967). *Management by Objectives*. Upper Saddle River, N.J.

O'Driscoll, Gerald, and Mario Rizzo (1985). *The Economics of Time and Ignorance*. Oxford.

Offe, Claus (1989). "Bindung, Fessel, Bremse. Die Unübersichtlichkeit von Selbstbeschränkungsformeln." In Honneth et al., eds. *Zwischenbetrachtungen im Prozess der Aufklärung*, pp. 739–74. Frankfurt.

———. (1990). "Die Wirtschaft der Gesellschaft." *Soziologische Revue* 15:389–93.

———. (1996). "Trust and Knowledge: Rules and Decisions." Berlin. Unpublished manuscript.

Offe, Claus, and Helmut Wiesental [1980]. "Two Logics of Collective Action," Reprinted in Claus Offe, *Diorganized Capitalism* (Cambridge, Mass., 1985) pp. 170–220.

Ökonomie und Gesellschaft. (1995). Yearbook 12: *Soziale Kooperation.* Frankfurt.

Oliver, Christine (1991). "Strategic Business Responses to Institutional Processes." *Academy of Management Review* 16:145–79.

Olson, Mancur (1965). *The Logic of Collective Action.* Cambridge, Mass.

Ortmann, Günther (1995). *Formen der Produktion. Organisation und Rekursivität.* Opladen.

Ouichi, William G. (1980). "Markets, Bureaucracies and Clans." *Administrative Science Quarterly* 25:129–41.

Pareto, Vilfredo (1980). *Compendium of General Sociology.* Minneapolis.

Parsons, Talcott (1932). "Economics and Sociology: Marshall in Relation to the Thought of His Time." *Quarterly Journal of Economics* 46:316–47.

———. (1934–35). "Sociological Elements in Economic Thought." *Quarterly Journal of Economics* 49, nos. 3–4:414–53, 645–67.

———. (1948). Introduction to *Max Weber: The Theory of Social and Economic Organization.* pp. 3–86. Glencoe, Ill.

———. (1949a) [1937]. *The Structure of Social Action.* Glencoe, Ill.

———. (1949b). "The Rise and Fall of Economic Man." *Journal for General Education* 4:46–53.

———. (1951). *The Social System.* Glencoe, Ill.

———. (1954a) [1939]. "The Professions and Social Structure." *Essays in Sociological Theory,* pp. 34–49. Glencoe, Ill.

———. (1954b) [1940]. "The Motivation of Economic Activities." *Essays in Sociological Theory,* pp. 50–68. Glencoe, Ill.

———. (1960). *Structure and Process in Modern Societies.* New York.

———. (1963). "On the Concept of Political Power." *Proceedings of the American Philosophical Society* 107:232–62.

———. (1971). *System of Modern Societies.* Englewood, N. J.

———. (1975). "Commentary on Herbert Gintis 'A Radical Analysis of Welfare Economics and Individual Development.'" *Quarterly Journal of Economics* 89:280–90.

———. (1977). "On Building Social System Theory: A Personal History." In *Social Systems and the Evolution of Action Theory,* pp. 22–76. New York.

———. (1978). *Action Theory and the Human Condition.* New York.

———. (1982). *On Institutions and Social Evolution.* Edited by Leon H. Mayhew. Chicago and London.

———. (1986) [1953]. *The Marshall Lectures.* Research Reports from the Department of Sociology Uppsala University, no. 4. Uppsala.

———. (1991a) [1935]. "Some Reflections on 'The Nature and Significance of Economics.'" In *The Early Essays,* edited by Charles Camic, pp. 153–80. Chicago.

———. (1991b) [1935]. "The Place of Ultimate Values in Sociological Theory." In *The Early Essays,* edited by Charles Camic, pp. 231–57. Chicago.

Parsons, Talcott, Robert F. Bales, and Edward A. Shils (1953). *Working Papers in the Theory of Action*. Glencoe, Ill.

Parsons, Talcott, and Edward A. Shils, eds. (1951). *Toward a General Theory of Action*. Cambridge, Mass.

Parsons, Talcott, and Neil Smelser (1956). *Economy and Society*. London.

Pearsons, Harry W. (1957). "Parsons and Smelser on the Economy." In Karl Polanyi, Conrad M. Arensberg, and Harry W. Pearson eds., *Trade and Market in Early Empires*. Glencoe, Ill.

Perman, David (1995). *Dangerous Liaisons: Parsons and Orthodox Economics*. Unpublished manuscript.

Perrow, Charles (1961). "The Analysis of Goals in Complex Organizations." *American Sociological Review*, pp. 854–66.

Peters, Thomas J., and Robert H. Waterman (1982). *In Search of Excellence*. New York.

Piore, Michael J. (1995). *Beyond Individualism: How Social Demands of the New Identity Groups Challenge American Political and Economic Life*. Cambridge, Mass., and London.

Piore, Michael J., and Charles F. Sabel (1989). *Das Ende der Massenproduktion*. Frankfurt.

Polanyi, Karl (1944). *The Great Transformation*. Boston.

Porter, Michael (1985). *Competitive Advantage*. New York and London.

Portes, Alejandro, and Julia Sensenbrenner (1993). "Embeddedness and Immigration: Notes on the Determinants of Economic Action." *American Journal of Sociology* 98:1320–50.

Postlewaite, A. (1987). "Asymmetric Information." *New Palgrave* 1:133–35.

Powell, Walter (1991). "Expanding the Scope of Institutional Analysis." In Walter Powell and Paul DiMaggio, eds., *The New Institutionalism in Organizational Analysis*, pp. 183–203. Chicago and London.

Prendergast, Christopher (1986). "Alfred Schütz and the Austrian School of Economics." *American Journal of Sociology* 92:1–26.

Presley, John R., and John G. Sessions (1994). "Islamic Economics. The Emergence of a New Paradigm." *Economic Journal* 104:584–96.

Priddat, Birger P. (1993). *Zufall, Schicksal, Irrtum. Über Unsicherheit und Risiko in der deutschen ökonomischen Theorie vom 18. bis ins frühe 20. Jahrhundert*, vol. 1. Marburg.

Probst, Gilbert J. B. (1984). *Self-Organization and Management of Social Systems: Insights, Promises, Doubts, and Questions*. Berlin.

Purdy, David (1988). *Social Power and the Labour Market: A Radical Approach to Labour Economics*. Basingstoke.

Putnam, Robert D. (1993). "The Prosperous Community: Social Capital and Public Life." *American Prospect*, pp. 35–42.

Radner, Roy (1968). "Competitive Equilibrium under Uncertainty." *Econometrica* 34:31–58.

Rammert, Werner (1992). "Wer oder was steuert technischen Fortschritt? Technischer Wandel zwischen Steuerung und Evolution." *Soziale Welt* 43:7–25.

Rapoport, Anatol (1989). "Prisoners' Dilemma." *New Palgrave: Game Theory*, pp. 199–204. London.

Reuter, Norbert (1994). *Der Institutionalismus. Geschichte und Theorie der evolutionären Ökonomie.* Marburg.

Riker, William, and Peter C. Ordeshoor (1973). *An Introduction to Positive Political Theory.* Englewood Cliffs, N.J.

Robbins, Lionel (1969) [1932]. *An Essay on the Nature and Significance of Economics as a Science.* London.

Rocher, Guy (1975). *Talcott Parsons and American Sociology.* New York.

Romer, Paul M. (1986). "Increasing Returns and Long-Run Growth." *Journal of Political Economy* 94:1002–37.

———. (1990). "Endogenous Technical Change." *Journal of Political Economy* 98:71–102.

Rosen, S. (1985). "Implicit Contracts: A Survey." *Journal of Economic Literature* 23:1144–75.

Rosenberg, Nathan (1976). *Perspectives on Technology.* Cambridge.

Ross, Dorothy (1991). *The Origins of American Social Science.* Cambridge.

Rüeschemeyer, Dietrich (1982). "On Durkheim's Explanation of the Division of Labor." *American Journal of Sociology* 88:579–89.

———. (1985). "Spencer und Durkheim über Arbeitsteilung und Differenzierung: Kontinuität oder Bruch?" In Niklas Luhmann ed., *Soziale Differenzierung—zur Geschichte einer Idee,* pp. 163–80. Opladen.

Ryan, Alan (1987). "Property." *New Palgrave* 3:1029–31.

Sabel, Charles F. (1993). "Studied Trust: Building New Forms of Cooperation in a Volatile Economy." In Richard Swedberg, ed., *Explorations in Economic Sociology,* pp. 104–44. New York.

———. (1995). "Design, Deliberation, and Democracy: On the New Pragmatism of Firms and Public Institutions." Unpublished manuscript.

Salter, W.E.G. (1960). *Productivity and Technical Change.* Cambridge.

Samuelson, Paul (1947). *Foundations of Economic Analysis.* Cambridge, Mass.

———. (1965). "A Theory of Induced Innovation along Kennedy-Weizsäcker Lines." *Review of Economics and Statistics* 47:343–56.

Sandner, Karl, and Renate Meyer (1994). "Verhandlung und Struktur: Zur Entstehung organisierten Handelns in Unternehmen." In Georg Schreyögg, and Peter Conrad, eds., *Managementforschung,* 4:185–218. Berlin and New York.

Saurwein, Karl-Heinz (1988). *Ökonomie und soziologische Theoriekonstruktion. Zur Bedeutung ökonomischer Theorieelemente in der Sozialtheorie Talcott Parsons'.* Opladen.

Saxenian, AnnaLee (1989). "In Search of Power: the Organization of Business Interests in Silicon Valley and Route 128." *Economy and Society* 18:25–70.

Schimank, Uwe (1985). "Der mangelnde Akteurbezug systemtheoretischer Erklärungen gesellschaftlicher Differenzierung—Ein Diskussionsvorschlag." *Zeitschrift für Soziologie,* 14:421–34.

Schimmer, Ralf (1997). *Populismus und Sozialwissenschaften im Amerika der Jahrhundertwende.* Frankfurt and New York.

Schluchter, Wolfgang, ed. (1979). *Verhalten, Handeln und System. Talcott Parsons' Beitrag zur Entwicklung der Sozialwissenschaften.* Frankfurt.

———. (1981). *The Rise of Western Rationalism.* Translated by Guenther Roth. Berkeley.

Schmid, Michael (1989). "Arbeitsteilung und Solidarität. Eine Untersuchung zu Emile Durkheims Theorie der sozialen Arbeitsteilung." *Kölner Zeitschrift für Soziologie und Sozialpsychologie* 41:619–43.

———. (1993). "Emile Durkheims *De la division du travail social* (1893) und deren Rezeption in der deutschen Soziologie." *Berliner Journal für Soziologie* 4:487–507.

Schmoller, Gustav (1883). "Zur Methodologie der Staats- und Sozial-Wissenschaften." *Schmollers Jahrbuch* 2:975–94.

Schön, Donald (1983). *The Reflective Practitioner: How Professionals Think in Action.* New York.

Schreyögg, Georg (1991). "Der Managementprozess—neu gesehen." In Wolfgang Staehle and Jörg Sydow eds., *Managementforschung* 1:255–89.

Schumann, Jochen (1992). *Grundzüge der mikroökonischen Theorie.* 6th ed. Berlin.

Schumpeter, Joseph (1950). *Capitalism, Socialism and Democracy.* New York.

———. (1961) [1911]. *Theory of Economic Development.* Translated by Redvers Opie. Cambridge, Mass.

———. (1991) [1946]. "Comments on a Plan for the Study of Entrepreneurship." In Richard Swedberg, ed., *The Economics of Capitalism,* pp. 406–28. Princeton.

Schütz, Alfred (1967). *Collected Papers.* Vol. 1. The Hague.

———. (1970). *On Phenomenology and Social Relations.* Chicago and London.

———. (1993) [1932]. *Der sinnhafte Aufbau der sozialen Welt.* Frankfurt.

Schütz, Alfred, and Talcott Parsons (1977). *Zur Theorie sozialen Handelns. Ein Briefwechsel.* Frankfurt.

Scott, Richard (1991). "Unpacking Institutional Arguments." In Walter Powell, and Paul DiMaggio, eds., *The New Institutionalism in Organizational Analysis,* pp. 164–82. Chicago and London.

———. (1994). "Institutions and Organizations: Toward a Theoretical Synthesis." In Richard Scott and John W. Meyer, eds., *Institutional Environments and Organizations,* pp. 55–80. Thousand Oaks, Calif.

Selten, Reinhard (1978). "The Chain-Store Paradox." *Theory and Decision* 9:127–59.

Sen, Amartya K. (1977). "Rational Fools: A Critique of the Behavioral Foundations of Economic Theory." *Philosophy and Public Affairs* 6:317–44.

———. (1987). "Rational Behavior." *New Palgrave* 4:68–76.

Shackle, G.L.S. (1958). "The Economist's Model of Man." *Occupational Psychology* 32:195–213.

———. (1972). *Epistemics and Economics.* Cambridge.

———. (1974). *Keynesian Kaleidics.* Edinburgh.

Simmel, Georg (1990) [1900]. *The Philosophy of Money.* Translated by Tom Bottomore and David Frisby. London and New York.

Simon, Herbert (1945). *Administrative Behavior.* New York.

———. (1957). *Models of Man.* New York.

———. (1981). *The Sciences of the Artificial.* Cambridge, Mass.

———. (1992). *Economics, Bounded Rationality and the Cognitive Revolution.* Brookfield, Vt.

Smelser, Neil J. (1981). "On Collaborating with Talcott Parsons: Some Intellectual and Personal Notes." *Sociological Inquiry* 51:143–54.

Smith, Adam (1976). *The Wealth of Nations*. Chicago.

Solow, Robert M. (1957). "Technical Change and the Aggregate Production Function." *Review of Economics and Statistics* 39:312–20.

Spence, Michael (1973). "Job Market Signaling." *Quarterly Journal of Economics* 87:355–74.

Staehle, Wolfgang (1983). *Funktionen des Managements*. Bern and Stuttgart.

———. (1990). *Management*. 5th ed. Munich.

Steele. G. R. (1993). *The Economics of Friedrich Hayek*. London and New York.

Steiner, Philippe (1992). "Le fait social économique chez Durkheim." *Revue française de sociologie* 33:641–61.

Stiglitz, Joseph E. (1994). "The Role of the State in Financial Markets." *Proceedings of the World Bank: Annual Conference on Development Economics*, pp. 19–52.

Stölting, Erhard (1986). "Soziologie und Nationalökonomie. Die Wirkung des institutionellen Faktors." In Sven Papcke, ed., *Ordnung und Theorie. Beiträge zur Geschicthe der Soziologie in Deutschland*, pp. 69–92. Darmstadt.

Swedberg, Richard (1986). Introduction to *The Marshall Lectures*, by Talcott Parsons, I–XXXIV. Research Papers from the Department of Sociology Uppsala University, no. 4. Uppsala.

———. (1987). "Economic Sociology: Past and Present." *Current Sociology* 35:1–221.

———. (1991). *Joseph A. Schumpeter: His Life and Work*. Cambridge and Oxford.

———, ed. (1993). *Explorations in Economic Sociology*. New York.

Sydow, Jörg (1985). *Organisationsspielraum and Büroautomation*. Berlin and New York.

Sydow, Jörg, et al. (1994). *Organisation von Netzwerken. Strukturationstheoretische Analysen der Vermittlungspraxis in Versicherungsnetzwerken*. Opladen.

Taylor, Michael (1990). "Cooperation and Rationality: Notes on the Collective Action Problem and Its Solutions." In Karen Schweers Cook and Margaret Levi, eds., *The Limits of Rationality*, pp. 222–40. Chicago and London.

Turner, Bryan S. (1992). Preface to *Emile Durkheim: Professional Ethics and Civic Morals*, pp. XIII–XLI. 2d ed., London.

Ullmann-Margalit, Edna (1977). *The Emergence of Norms*. Oxford.

Vanberg, Viktor J. (1994). *Rules and Choice in Economics*. London and New York.

Veblen, Thorstein (1921). *The Engineers and the Price System*. New York.

———. (1979) [1899]. *The Theory of the Leisure Class*. New York.

———. (1990) [1898]. "Why Is Economics Not an Evolutionary Science." In *The Place of Science in Modern Civilization and Other Essays*, pp. 56–81. New York.

von Foerster, Heinz (1985). "Über das Konstruieren von Wirklichkeiten." In *Sicht und Einsicht*, pp. 25–41. Braunschweig and Wiesbaden.

Voss, Thomas (1982). "Rational Actors and Social Institutions: The Case of the Organic Emergence of Norms." In Werner Raub, ed., *Theoretical Models and Empirical Analyses*, pp. 76–100. Utrecht.

Wagner, Peter (1990a). "Science of Society Lost: On the Failure to Establish Sociology in Europe during the 'Classical Period.'" Reprinted in Peter Wagner, Björn Wittrock, and Richard Whitley, eds., *Discourses on Society: The Shaping of the Social Science Disciplines, Sociology of the Sciences Yearbook* (Dordrecht, Boston, and London, 1991), pp. 219–45.

——. (1990b). *Sozialwissenschaften und Staat. Frankreich, Italien, Deutschland 1870–1980*. Frankfurt and New York.

Waldenfels, Bernhard (1990). *Der Stachel des Fremden*. Frankfurt.

Walras, Léon (1896). *Études d'economie politique appliquée*. Paris.

——. (1898). *Études d'economie sociale*. Paris.

——. (1954) [1874] *Elements of Pure Economics, or the Theory of Social Wealth*. Translated by William Jaffe. Homewood, Ill.

Walter, Helmut (1977). "Technischer Fortschritt." *Handbuch der Wirtschaftswissenschaften*, 7:569–83. Stuttgart.

Wearne, Bruce (1989). *The Theory and Scholarship of Talcott Parsons to 1951*. Cambridge.

Weber, Max (1892). *Die Verhältnisse der Landarbeiter im ostelbischen Deutschland*. Leipzig.

——. (1927). *General Economic History*. Translated by Frank Knight. London.

——. (1949). "Objectivity in Social Science and Social Policy." In Edward A. Shils and Henry A. Finch, eds., *Methodology of the Social Sciences*, Glencoe.

——. (1958). *The Protestant Ethic and the Spirit of Capitalism*. Translated by Talcott Parsons. New York.

——. (1978). *Economy and Society*. Berkeley.

——. (1988) [1894]. "Die Börse." In *Gesammelte Aufsätze zur Soziologie und Sozialpolitik*, pp. 256–322. Tübingen.

——. (1992) [1895]. "Der Nationalstaat und die Volkswirtschaftspolitik" Freiburg Inaugural Lecture. In *Gesamtausgabe*, 4:544–74. Tübingen.

Weede, Erich (1992). *Mensch und Gesellschaft. Soziologie aus der Perspektive des methodologischen Individualismus*. Tübingen.

Wegner, Gerhard (1995). "Innovation, Komplexität und Erfolg. Zu einer ökonomischen Handlungstheorie des Neuen." In Eberhard K. Seifert and Birger P. Priddat, eds., *Neuorientierungen in der ökonomischen Theorie*, pp. 181–204. Marburg.

Weintraub, E. Roy (1974). *General Equilibrium Theory*. London.

Weisz, George (1983). "The Republican Ideology and the Social Sciences; the Durkheimians and the History of Social Economy at the Sorbonne." In Philippe Besnard, ed., *The Sociological Domain: The Durkheimians and the Founding of French Sociology*, pp. 90–119. Cambridge.

Weizsäcker, Carl Christian v. (1966). *Zur ökonomischen Theorie des technischen Fortschritts*. Göttingen.

Wenzel, Harald (1990). *Die Ordnung des Handelns. Talcott Parsons' Theorie des allgemeinen Handlungssystems*. Frankfurt.

White, Harrison C. (1981). "Where Do Markets Come From?" *American Journal of Sociology* 87:517–47.

Whitehead, Alfred (1925). *Science and the Modern World*. New York.

Whittington, Richard (1992). "Putting Giddens into Action: Social Systems and Managerial Agency." *Journal of Management Studies* 29:693–712.

Williamson, Oliver (1975). *Markets and Hierarchies*. New York.

Williamson, Oliver. (1985). *The Economic Institutions of Capitalism*. New York.

———. (1991). "Comparative Economic Organization: The Analysis of Discrete Structural Alternatives." *Administrative Science Quarterly* 36:269–96.

Willke, Helmut (1987a). "Systembeobachtung, Systemdiagnose, Systemintervention—weisse Löcher in schwarzen Kästen?" In Günter Schiepek, ed., *Systeme erkennen Systeme*, pp. 94–114. Munich and Weinheim.

———. (1987b). "Strategien der Intervention in autonome Systeme." In Dirk Baecker, et al., eds., *Theorie als Passion*, pp. 333–61. Frankfurt.

Wimmer, Rudolf (1989). "Die Steuerung komplexer Organisationen. Ein Reformulierungsversuch der Führungproblematik aus systemischer Sicht." In Karl Sander, ed., *Politische Prozesse in Unternehmen*, pp. 131–56. Berlin.

Womack, James P., Daniel T. Jones, and Daniel Roos (1990). *The Machine That Changed the World: Based on the Massachusetts Institute of Technology 5-Million Dollar 5-Year Study of the Future of the Automobile*. New York.

Worswick, G. (1957). Review of *Economy and Society*, by Talcott Parsons and Neil Smelser. *Economic Journal* 67:700–702.

Wrong, Dennis (1961). "The Oversocialized Conception of Man in Modern Sociology." *American Sociological Review* 26:83–93.

Wubben, Emil (1994). *Markets, Uncertainty and Decision-Making: A History of the Introduction of Uncertainty into Economics*. Tinbergen Institute Research Series, no. 55. Tinbergen.

Zaret, David (1980). "From Weber to Parsons to Schutz: The Eclipse of History in Modern Social Theory." *American Journal of Sociology* 85:1180–1201.

Zelizer, Viviana (1979). "Human Values and the Market: The Case for Life Insurance and Death in 19th Century America." *American Journal of Sociology* 84:591–610.

Zukin, Sharon, and Paul DiMaggio (1990). Introduction to *Structures of Capital: The Social Organization of the Economy*, pp. 1–36. Cambridge.

INDEX

of, 134–135; on rational-actor model, 11–12
patent systems, 63
path dependency, 245, 292
pattern-maintenance system, 192–193, 197, 311n.30, 312n.31; boundary processes between economy and, 162–192; institutions of, 163, 164
payment: calculation of, 223; as code, 214–215; connecting, 218; in economic system survival, 216; programs for, 224–227; scarcity and motives for, 226–227
payment decisions: ability to pay and, 220–221; in complexity reduction, 230; economic organizations and, 227–233; expectations and, 227–228; intervening semantics in, 234; reasons for, 206–207
Pearson, Harry W., 311n.28
perfect information, 25
perfect market, deviations from, 184
permanence problem, 222–223, 318n.24
permanently failing organizations, 318n.29
Perrow, Charles, 320n.38
personality, occupational role and, 170
personality system, 195; disequilibrium of, 270
phenomenology, 246, 288, 321–322n.3; in Giddens's economic action theory, 247–253; pragmatism and, 275; sociological, 272–273; transcendental, 252
Piaget, Jean, 94
Piore, Michael, 269, 275
Plato, 108
Polanyi, Karl, 8, 308n.53, 311n.28
political conflict, 69
political instability, 69–70
polity, 180, 183, 311n.26; in control of economic functions, 182; interest in economy, 185
population ecology approach, 216
populist movement, 137
positivism, 13, 203–204; limitation of, 304n.13
positivistic sociology theory, 308n.64
Postlewaite, A., 48
Powell, Walter, 242
power, 295; structural inequality of, 103–104; unequal distribution of in contracts, 89–90
power relations, 292
practical reason, institutionalization of, 280

pragmatism: phenomenology and, 275; in understanding innovations, 275–277
pragmatist action model, 279
praxis, 245, 256
prebourgeois society, 118
premodern societies, 235, 261, 262–263
Prendergast, Christopher, 248
Presley, John R., 316n.8
price, 125; in communication processes, 215; in coordination of decentralized economic decisions, 38; cultural values in setting, 175; determined by market versus just social order, 93–94; economic analysis of, 77; information on, 226; language of, 221; neoclassical theory of, 99–100, 101; normative theory of, 98–107, 159; public opinion in, 307n.46; religious influence on, 99; social justice and, 307n.44; as sociological data, 77–78; unjust, 92–93, 103–104, 106; versus value, 102–103
price theory, 83
principal-agent problem, 1, 19, 207; labor market inefficiency and, 48
principal-agent theory, 166–167, 313n.36
prisoner's dilemma, 20–21, 260, 298n.23, 299–300n.36; external solutions of, 28–33; functionalist solution of, 33–36; internal solution of, 22–28; several-person, 25–26; solution for, 22; two-person, 299n.30
private interests, pursuit of, 2
private property: appropriation of, 126; genesis of, 323n.19; legitimization of, 112; rights of in innovation, 62–63
private property rights: as appropriation of collective property, 109–110; historical development of, 111–112; in innovation, 62–63; limitation of, 302n.58; moral foundation of, 108–109
private rights, 91
probability, uncertainty and, 39–40
Probst, Gilbert, 319–320n.36
product design, 325n.39
product innovations, 188–189
production, 18, 19; capitalist organization of, 271; division of labor in, 19, 20, 21; process of, 324n.30; technology of, 112–114
production decisions, 165
production factors: allocation of, 311n.30; suboptimal allocation of, 107

situational complexity, 233–234
situational creativity, 277
situational determinism, 145, 226
Smelser, Neil, 135, 152–155, 158, 159, 161, 162–163, 165, 166, 167–170, 172–174, 177–188, 189–196, 198–200, 270, 311n.28, 312n.33, 313–314n.42, 313n.39, 314n.48, 324n.31
Smith, Adam, 7, 20, 51, 84, 125–126, 136, 244, 297n.1; moral feeling of, 139–140
social action: in economic contexts, 81; regulation of, 74–75; structure of, 136–138
social background, 236
social bond, necessity of, 86–87
social capital, 321n.45
social change: creativity in, 271–281; innovation in, 238–239; social structures in, 245–246; structures in, 322n.6
social cohesion, 69; economic institutions in, 71–72; strong, 94–95
social conflicts, antagonistic interests in, 199–200
social constitution of the new, 324n.30
social constraints, 75, 76, 313n.38; negative sanctions and positive attraction in, 93–94
social controls: failure of, 187–188; ineffective, 173
social development: normal, 93; pathological, 92–93
social embeddedness, 9–10, 291–293; of economic relations, 124–125; of exchange relations, 90–91
social factors, 139
social facts, 74, 76, 106, 202, 303n.12; economic institutions as, 81–114; heterogeneity of, 112–113
social forces, 322n.10
social formations, classification of, 193
social functions, 79–80; disturbed, 118
social goals, 180
social integration: conflict-free, 199–200; contract in, 84–98; crisis of, 133
social interpretation, 275
social justice, 286; prices and, 307n.44
social laws, 78, 304n.13; naturalness of, 77
social networks, 292, 293, 323n.18, 325n.5; in cooperation, 294
social norms: in cooperation, 287; in efficient economic results, 297n.5; emergence of, 123–124; influencing expectations, 28–29; internalization of, 31–32
social obligations, 86–87; within clan, 88
social order: actions that stabilize, 145–146; coordinated with ultimate ends, 144–145; emergence of, 210; just, 199; moral individualism in, 95; motives in, 297n.1; overcoming uncertainty for, 204–205; solutions of problem of, 135–136; stability of, 201; theory of, 71
social phenomena, 78
social positions, 249; based on meritocratic principles, 118
social power, 145, 252, 253, 306–307n.43; in economics, 140; personal wealth and, 103–104
social praxis, actors in, 249
social process theories, 325n.37
social reform, 70; government measures of, 307n.49
social regulation, 81–82
social relations, 29–30, 249; contingent shaping of, 75; organizational stabilization of, 261–263; pacification of, 69; regulation of, 305n.26; stabilization of, 86–87, 116–117; stable structures of, 323n.18; trust in, 261–262
social reproduction: equilibrium conditions of, 159–160; functional needs of, 160–161
social responsibility, 297n.9
social rules, 75
social semantics, 211–212
social structures, 295; actors in creating, 251–255; in cooperative relationships, 27; in social change, 245–246
social subsystems: codes in, 214–215; differentiation of, 316–317n.13; general, 316n.9; integrative functioning of, 189–190; normative integration of, 144–146
The Social System (Parsons), 163, 193–196
social theories, 315n.2; holistic concept of, 127–128
social values, 99; determining, 100–101; economy and, 287–288; guiding economic relations, 122–123; internalized, 205; in motivational structures, 189–190
social wealth, distribution of, 186
socialization, 164, 200; internalized social values in, 205; mechanisms of, 195–196;